Male Homosexuality

RICHARD C. FRIEDMAN, M.D.
With a foreword by Roger A. MacKinnon, M.D.

Male Homosexuality

A CONTEMPORARY PSYCHOANALYTIC PERSPECTIVE

Yale University Press
New Haven and London

Published with assistance from the foundation established in memory of Amasa Stone
Mather of the Class of 1907, Yale College.

Note on confidentiality: All biographical material in this book has been carefully
disguised to protect confidentiality. All names of patients and subjects are fictitious. No
person may be identified from material presented herein.

Set in Galliard type by The Composing Room of Michigan. Printed in the United
States of America by Vail-Ballou Press, Binghamton, N.Y.

Library of Congress Cataloging-in-Publication Data

Friedman, Richard C., 1941–
    Male homosexuality.

    Bibliography: p. 275
    Includes index.
    1. Homosexuality, Male.   2. Identity (Psychology)   3. Psychosexual
development.   I. Title.   [DNLM: 1. Homosexuality.   2. Men—psychology.   3.
Psychosexual Development.   WM 615 F911m]
HQ76.F774   1988   616.85'834   87–27931
ISBN 0–300–03963–8 (alk. paper)

The paper in this book meets the guidelines for permanence and durability of the
Committee on Production Guidelines for Book Longevity of the Council on Library
Resources.

10   9   8   7   6   5   4   3   2   1

To the memory of my father,
William Friedman,
and my father-in-law,
Mervyn Matorin

Contents

Foreword

Male Homosexuality: A Contemporary Psychoanalytic Perspective is a book of exceptional breadth and comprehensiveness. This comes as no surprise to me because I have known Dr. Friedman since the beginning of his residency and I have followed his career in academic psychiatry with considerable enthusiasm.

His interest in human sexual behavior antedates his psychiatric training and provides the foundation for his multidisciplinary approach to this timely topic. In addition to his training in neurobiology and research he is an accomplished psychoanalyst and psychiatrist. His work on the Advisory Committee on Psychosexual Disorders for *DSM-III* was an enriching experience both for him and for the other members of that committee.

Dr. Friedman's tone is scientific and nonjudgmental. His scientific views, as implied above, are eclectic and clearly presented. He never hesitates to state the issues that he does not understand, as well as the traditional psychoanalytic viewpoints that he feels are unsupported by data or that are in contradiction to available data.

This book is written for a mixed audience of serious scholars and it will be useful to anyone with a major interest in the topic. It is not designed for beginners unfamiliar with psychoanalytic concepts, although he has included a reasonable amount of psychoanalytic theory to help those readers lacking formal psychoanalytic training.

The book itself is divided into four sections. In part 1, Dr. Friedman carefully reviews the literature of biological research concerning the role of testosterone, estrogen, and other hormones during and after the prenatal period. He particularly focuses on Dorner's work on prenatal androgenization of the central nervous system. Dr. Friedman then reviews the role of genetic factors in male homosexuality as revealed by twin studies. This research shows a high degree of concordance for monozygotic twins and a higher than expected incidence in first-degree relatives.

Friedman then reviews the work of several investigators revealing the fact that childhood gender identity and gender role disturbances are associated with the later emergence of predominant or exclusive homosexuality. The author concludes this section with a summary of the development of Freud's ideas on homosexuality in the context of the limited knowledge of neuroendocrine mechanisms available at that time. He also reviews and critiques the various psychodynamic family studies.

In part 2 the author considers psychopathology and its interrelationship with male sexual orientation. Here, it becomes clear that the author uses the concept of homosexuality as an adjective to describe sexual behavior rather than as a noun to refer to a type of person. He discusses homosexuality in the context of the individual's overall ego and superego organization and in relation to his total mental health or illness. Dr. Friedman skillfully uses case material to make his points that higher-level character disorders have a higher level of sexual functioning and vice versa regardless of whether the individual is heterosexual or homosexual.

Part 3 provides an excellent review of the concepts of core gender identity and gender role/identity as well as crystallization of sexual orientation and the onset of erotic life. When the childhood fantasies are of a homosexual nature there are usually adverse consequences for the individual's self-esteem.

The author differentiates childhood unmasculinity from childhood effeminacy, in that the former is manifested later and no studies similar to those on childhood effeminacy (which usually leads to adult homosexuality) have been done. In both parts 2 and 3, Friedman draws extensively on his broad clinical experience. The cases are reported in detail and carry a ring of clinical truth.

In his fourth part, Friedman considers theoretical issues. It is in this part of the book that the author allows himself to become more speculative, as he synthesizes a modern holistic approach. It is also here that the author's views become most controversial. But unless there are new ideas there can be no cause for controversy.

Using the work of Stoller, Money and Erhardt, Diamond and others, Friedman weaves a new fabric of childhood development into basic Freudian theory. For example, "gender theory . . . supports Freud's idea that sexual orientation is usually not determined at birth. Freud suggested, however, that there is a normative homosexual developmental phase which provides a nidus for fixation." Friedman states, "In Freud's view, therefore, the potential to develop conscious homosexual or heterosexual fantasies is universally present. The heterosexual developmental track is only a conscious one, and unconscious homosexual potential remains. But modern concepts indicate that gender experience precedes and organizes erotic experience, not the reverse, as

Freud thought." Friedman does not directly address the issues of the infant's capacity to respond with sexual arousal to a variety of stimuli as postulated by Freud and supported by unpublished studies by R. Spitz.

The core of the author's theory is revealed in the following statement: "The constructs of unconscious homosexuality and unconscious heterosexuality proposed here are radically different from those proposed by previous theoreticians. The primary difference is in the idea that the workings of the unconscious mind are bounded initially by gender differentiation and later by sexual fantasy differentiation. The same process of differentiation applies to homosexual and heterosexual boys. The content differs but the process does not. I hypothesize that following differentiation, most heterosexual men are not prone to unconscious homosexuality. There is no such construct in their unconscious minds. Similarly, following differentiation, most exclusively homosexual men are not prone to unconscious heterosexuality." To put this dramatic statement into perspective, the author conceptualizes a limited bisexual male population in which either the homosexual or the heterosexual portion of fantasies has been repressed.

In anticipation of the obvious criticism of his theory, the author states, "Analytic thinking has tended to equate passive-feminine with homosexual behavior. This unfortunate tendency ignores the distinction between gender-related and erotic experience and behavior. Keeping this distinction in mind, one notes that some men whose erotic fantasy is exclusively heterosexual represent the self in feminine or unmasculine gender-valued imagery. Clinically, this phenomenon is usually episodic and is associated with profound shame and loss of masculine self regard. These episodes often occur in response to various types of psychosexual stress, such as competitive defeat by a powerful male or failure to perform sexually. One patient, for example, was shamed by a powerful boss. 'I felt like he whipped my ass,' he said, 'and I left our meeting with my tail between my legs.' That night, the patient dreamed that he was gang-raped by hoodlums. He was further shamed by this dream because he had never experienced erotic arousal associated with homosexual imagery in waking life or in remembered dreams, and he had negative feelings about homosexuals."

"Homoerotic imagery was chosen to symbolize damage to the male (sexual-gender) self. This wound to the gender-valued self-representation was associated with damage to masculine self-esteem."

While Friedman's viewpoint initially challenges our time-honored beliefs as psychoanalysts, his position deserves serious consideration. He makes the important statement in his conclusion that many aspects of the mechanism by which fantasized imagery is joined with lustful affect still remain obscure.

In the final chapter the author reflects on psychoanalysis, science, and homosexuality. His final statement captures the tone of the entire book. "A historical perspective . . . suggests that the next phase of the growth of psychoanalysis must involve enthusiastic movement toward empiricism and integration of psychoanalytic views with those from other fields. This movement should enhance understanding of all areas of human behavior, including that of sexual orientation."

We are indebted to Dr. Friedman for this serious and comprehensive work. I have enjoyed reading it and will undoubtedly read it again.

Roger A. MacKinnon, M.D.
Professor of Clinical Psychiatry
Columbia University, College of Physicians and Surgeons

Acknowledgments

The inspiration for this book came from educational experiences earlier in my career.

At the University of Rochester School of Medicine and Dentistry I was fortunate to spend a year in the laboratory of Dr. Seymour Reichlin. Dr. Reichlin's brilliance, patience, kindness, sense of humor, and warmth were appreciated beyond measure. Dr. George Engel's lectures on psychological development in health and disease were also remarkably enlightening.

Dr. Lawrence Kolb created a superb educational environment in the Department of Psychiatry, Columbia Presbyterian Medical Center, during the years of my residency. Dr. Kolb's commitment to patients and his unique ability to teach young physicians to become psychiatrists made a lasting impression. Dr. Roger MacKinnon's seminar on interviewing technique was of the highest excellence. Dr. MacKinnon set standards for the functioning of clinicians which few of his students could ever achieve but which charted the way for continual self-improvement during the course of a professional lifetime.

My training analyst and my supervisors at the Center for Psychoanalytic Studies, Columbia University, provided wonderful learning experiences in clinical psychoanalysis. I am most grateful to Drs. George Goldman, Aaron Karush, Willard Gaylin, and Robert Liebert.

I owe my interest in sex research and sex education primarily to the late Drs. Raymond VanDeWiele and Gilbert Vossburgh of the Department of Obstetrics and Gynecology, Columbia Presbyterian Medical School; and I hope that something of their spirit lives on in this volume. To the Commonwealth Fund goes my special gratitude for financial support between 1975 and 1977. The ideas put forth in this book were in large part formulated during those years, during which I taught human sexuality at Columbia Medical School and carried out research at the International Institute of Human Reproduction. I also wish to express my thanks to the Sears Foundation and the National Merit Scholarship Corporation for financial aid which made it possible for me to attend Bard College, where my education began.

I am grateful to Dr. Roy Schafer for directing my attention to the importance of Hartmann's ideas about autonomous ego functions for my own theories about homosexuality.

The manuscript for *Male Homosexuality* went through many revisions in response to feedback from colleagues. Dr. Charles Winkelstein reviewed chapters 1–4. Even more important than his helpful observations was his warm encouragement at the beginning of the project. Drs. Zira DeFries and Michael Aronof, Mr. David Kellner, and Ruth Corn, M.S.W., put forth perspicacious commentary. Drs. Michael Stone and Heino F. L. Meyer-Bahlburg were kind enough to provide detailed criticism of the entire manuscript. I learned a great deal from their thoughtful reviews. During an unforgettable evening, Drs. Eric Marcus and Eslee Samberg discussed *Male Homosexuality* with erudition and surgical precision. As a result of their observations, chapters 13–19 were entirely rewritten. After I (naively) thought that the book was finished at last, Dr. Susan Coates contributed insightful criticism on each chapter. This led to yet another revision of *Male Homosexuality*.

Special thanks are due to Luis Minaya of the New York State Psychiatric Institute for assistance with library work.

Ms. Camille Castro typed all versions of the manuscript. It has been an unmitigated pleasure to collaborate with such an energetic and diligent colleague.

Gladys Topkis, my editor, has been most helpful and greatly appreciated. I also wish to acknowledge Stephanie Jones for her sensitive and meticulous editorial work with the manuscript.

Thanks are also due the students I have worked with over the years. Although a great deal changes with time, the irreverent questioning of good students fortunately does not.

My two oldest children, Heidi and Carla, were grown and pursuing their own careers during the gestation of this book. This was not the case with my son, Jeremiah Simon Friedman (JS). The first chapters of *Male Homosexuality* were written with JS on my knee. By the time I had reached chapter 19, two and a half years later, JS was my officemate. His desk was next to mine, and many were the days on which each of us worked on his own manuscript. My somewhat unanticipated colleague was not unappreciated. Writing is often a lonely undertaking; JS's companionship made it less so.

No words can express the degree to which my wife, Sue, has been of assistance. Her love and support nourished this book and sustained me. She was available for countless discussions at all hours. Although fully engaged in her own career, she managed to function both as an editor and critic of *Male Homosexuality* and as the kind of enthusiast every writer needs.

Introduction

In this book, I have tried to develop a model of homosexuality that combines psychoanalytic clinical theory with extra-analytic research findings. Freud (a neuropsychiatrist), Kinsey (an entomologist), and Masters (a gynecologist), to name only a few important scholars, have given us a collage of knowledge, attitudes, and experience with regard to homosexuality. Since its inception psychoanalysis has recognized the necessity of making use of knowledge from biological psychiatry, developmental psychology, neuropsychology, anthropology, sociology, and other fields. Recently, however, there has been explosive growth in numerous areas that have contributed to understanding human sexual behavior. The diversity of disciplines from which contributions have come has led to startling advances and fragmentation and dissension.

I am appreciative of the contributions of many psychoanalysts who have worked at the border between psychoanalytic psychology and other fields. Three such scholars whose writings have particularly influenced my viewpoint are Morton Reiser, Robert Stoller, and George Engel. Engel's biopsychosocial model is used throughout this book. The model allows new developments in biological and social knowledge to be integrated into psychology without the threat that study of the intrapsychic levels of influence on behavior will become obsolete. The biopsychosocial model also places responsibility on those involved in biological or social-clinical work to be conversant with intrapsychic phenomena.

In this book I take a different approach to the theoretical and clinical problems of male sexual orientation than that offered in previous psychoanalytic treatments of the subject. I treat homosexuality as a window opening onto the larger vistas of psychoanalytic theory, much of which is in need of critical reevaluation and revision. Two aspects of psychoanalytic psychology in particular need of change are those involving psychic determinism and sex differences in behavior. Models of psychic determinism, once invoked as an explanation for many psychopathological syndromes, are outdated, and an essential problem facing psychoanalysis today is the task of adapting theories to the fact that psychic determinism is inadequate to explain most dimensions of psychological functioning. Another problem involves the fact that sex differences in behavior have been found to be more profound and far-reaching than had been realized. For this reason this book is explicitly about the psychology of men and boys, not about sexual orientation in both genders. Theories about normal development and psychopathology in one gender should not be assumed to apply to the other unless explictly specified.

The organization of this book is in keeping with recognition of the importance of integrating extra-psychoanalytic research observations with psychoanalytic-therapeutic clinical findings and theory. Part 1 is largely devoted to extra-psychoanalytic research (although relevant psychoanalytic investigation is also reviewed). Part 2 reflects my experience as a member of the Advisory Committee on Psychosexual Disorders for the third edition of the American Psychiatric Association's *Diagnostic and Statistical Manual* (*DSM-III*). The revision marked the transition in American psychiatry from a predominately psychodynamic point of view to a biodescriptive point of view. One can hardly question the generally positive effects of *DSM-III*. But the move away from a psychodynamic frame of reference did not completely solve basic problems about psychopathology in the area of sexual orientation, and these are discussed in part 2. Relationships between gender identity, erotic fantasy and activity, and psychodynamics are considered in light of recent developments in the theory of character pathology. Concepts about homosexuality in successive editions of *DSM* are placed in historical perspective. Following a section focusing on development (part 3), I review theoretical issues and make a number of suggestions for revision of psychoanalytic concepts (part 4). The book closes with emphasis on the need for ongoing research on male sexual orientation. Much attention has been devoted to the idea that homosexuality is not a single entity. The same observation may be made about psychoanalysis itself: no one person or group embodies the ideas and ideals of psychoanalysis. The richness of Freud's legacy is available to all. The scientific-clinical dimension of his work now mandates a scientific response. As this response becomes more common, Freud's valid insights will be preserved and his incorrect speculations will fade away. I hope this book will facilitate this type of change.

PART ONE

Biopsychosocial
Research and
Male Homosexuality

1

Introductory Concepts

No definition of the term *homosexuality* has been universally accepted by clinicians and behavioral scientists (Panel 1986). Articles or books about homosexuality usually refer to some combination of four behavioral components: erotic fantasies, sexual activity with others, perceived sense of identity, and social role. In this book the words *homosexuality* and *heterosexuality* are not explicitly defined: their meaning depends on the context in which they are used. The terms *sexual fantasies* and *erotic fantasies* are used interchangeably to refer to consciously perceived fantasies associated with feelings that are specifically sexual. Sexual feelings, in turn, are assumed to be associated with the physiological changes of the sexual response cycle as described by Masters and Johnson (1966) and with changes in the central nervous system that are only partially understood to date. An individual's social role as homosexual/gay, heterosexual/straight, or bisexual is determined as a result of his or her public declaration that he or she belongs to one of these groups. In contrast, the private belief that one belongs to such a group involves one's sense of inner identity. Erotic fantasies, sexual activity with others, sense of identity, and social role may be congruent or incongruent in a given individual.

For instance, a man may fantasize about sex with men, engage exclusively in homoerotic acts, feel that his inner identity is homosexual, and publicly live a homosexual role. Alternatively, an individual may have sexual fantasies predominately about males but engage in erotic activity to orgasm with both sexes. He may feel that his inner identity is homosexual but may live publicly (either single or married) as a heterosexual (Friedman, Green & Spitzer 1976). Adoption of a heterosexual social role even if one has predominately homosexual erotic fantasies and a sense of homosexual identity is understandably common in homophobic social settings.

There is no universally accepted definition of sexual orientation just as there is none of homosexuality. The term *sexual orientation* has been used to describe both human and animal behavior. When used in this book with reference to human beings, the term connotes one's subjective sense of being homosexual (gay), heterosexual (straight), or bisexual. The concept of identity as it relates to sexual orientation is quite complex. Self-labeling is the product of social, cognitive, and psychodynamic factors interacting in diverse ways. Erik Erikson (1959) put forth the following views about identity:

> It is this identity of something in the individual's core with an essential aspect of a group's inner coherence which is under consideration here; for the young individual must learn to be most himself where he means most to others—those others to be sure who have come to mean most to him. The term identity expresses such a mutual relation in that it connotes both a persistent sameness within oneself (self-sameness) and a persistent sharing of some kind of essential character with others. . . .
>
> At one time then it will appear to refer to a conscious sense of individual identity; at another to an unconscious striving for a continuity of personal character; at a third, as a criterion for the silent doings of ego synthesis; and finally as a maintenance of an intersolidarity with a group's ideals and identity.

Erikson's description of ego identity will be taken as the basis for the concept of identity as gay/homosexual, straight/heterosexual or bisexual (this concept is different from gender identity, discussed in chapter 3). Since homosexual identity / social role is often synonymous in general usage with gay identity / social role, a comment about the history of the word *gay* is in order. According to John Boswell (1980):

> The Provençal word "gai" was used in the thirteenth and fourteenth centuries in reference to courtly love and its literature and persists in Catalan, Provençal's closest living relative, as a designation for the "art of poesy" ("gai saber"), for a "lover" ("gaiol"), and for an openly homosexual person. It is by no means clear that the last-named use is not borrowed from English, but such contamination would not constitute proof that "gai" had not meant "homosexual" at some earlier point. The cult of courtly love was most popular in the south of France, an area noted for gay sexuality, and some troubadour poetry was explicitly homosexual. Moreover, both troubadour poetry and courtly love were closely associated with southern French heretical movements, especially the Albigensians, who were internationally suspected of favoring homosexuality. Possibly "gai" also acquired homosexual connotations outside areas familiar with the full range of troubadour eroticism. . . . Numerous European languages used "gay" or its cognates, however, in reference to sexual looseness. Grimm, *Deutsches Wörterbuch* (Leipzig, 1878), s.v. "gahe" (4), gives "irrational," or "ill-considered," reminiscent of the medieval application of . . . ("irrational") to gay people; but more obviously relevant parallels are to be found in the Castilian "gaya" and older

English "gay," both used in reference to female prostitutes or the life-style of the men who resort to them (for English usage, see *OED,* s.v. "gay," A.2.a, b). Although the popular association of prostitution with homosexuality is apparently unfounded . . . it is ancient and pervasive. One may in any event easily imagine a transference of the idea of the sexual looseness of prostitution to the immorality attributed to homosexual persons in hostile environments. In the early twentieth century "gay" was common in the English homosexual subculture as a sort of password or code. Its first public use in the United States outside of pornographic fiction appears to have been in the 1939 movie *Bringing Up Baby,* when Cary Grant, wearing a dress, exclaimed that he had gone gay. (p. 43)

Subsequently the meaning of *gay* continued to evolve until it came to refer to a self-perception of one's identity and/or social role as homosexual. The word does not refer to a gender role/identity disorder (cross-dressing, for example), nor does it mean happy or frivolous. The word *gay,* meaning "happy," and the word *gay* meaning "homosexual" are homonyms and the use of one may in some people summon up conscious or unconscious associations to the other. It is important to keep these two meanings of *gay* clearly distinct. The personal and social meanings of homosexual identity are as serious as the meaning of other aspects of identity.

KINSEY, SEX, AND IDENTITY

The term *homosexual* has been used in the scientific and popular literature alike as both an adjective and a noun. Kinsey and his co-workers (Kinsey, Pomeroy & Martin 1948), whose influence on recent ideas about sexuality can hardly be overestimated, objected to the latter usage. They stressed that a person should not be described as being "a homosexual" or a "heterosexual," writing, "We have objected to the use of the terms heterosexual and homosexual when used as nouns which stand for individuals" (p. 657). Kinsey and colleagues suggested the model of a continuum for describing subjective homosexual–heterosexual experience and activity with others. The Kinsey study found that a large group of individuals was exclusively heterosexual in interest and/or activity, a small group was exclusively homosexual, and a large group was mixed in varying degrees. The seven-point scale (0–6) used by Kinsey and colleagues to indicate degrees of homosexuality–heterosexuality has been reproduced in countless articles, books, and slides (fig. 1.1):

0. Individuals are rated as 0's if they make no physical contacts which result in erotic arousal or orgasm, and make no psychic responses to individuals of their own sex. Their socio-sexual contacts and responses are exclusively with individuals of the opposite sex.
1. Individuals are rated as 1's if they have only incidental homosexual contacts which have involved physical or psychic response, or incidental psychic responses without

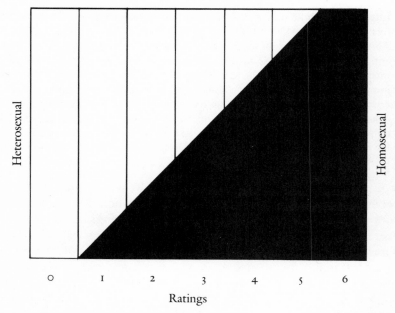

Ratings

Fig. 1.1 Heterosexual–homosexual rating scale.
Based on both psychologic reactions and overt experience, individuals rate as follows:
0. Exclusively heterosexual with no homosexual
1. Predominantly heterosexual, only incidentally homosexual
2. Predominantly heterosexual, only more than incidentally homosexual
3. Equally heterosexual and homosexual
4. Predominantly homosexual, but more than incidentally heterosexual
5. Predominantly homosexual, but incidentally heterosexual
6. Exclusively homosexual
Source: Kinsey, Pomeroy, & Martin, 1948, p. 638.

physical contact. The great preponderance of their sociosexual experience and reactions is directed toward individuals of the opposite sex. Such homosexual experiences as these individuals have may occur only a single time or two, or at least infrequently in comparison to the amount of their heterosexual experience. Their homosexual experiences never involve as specific psychic reactions as they make to heterosexual stimuli. Sometimes the homosexual activities in which they engage may be inspired by curiosity, or may be more or less forced upon them by other individuals, perhaps when they are asleep or when they are drunk, or under some other peculiar circumstance.

2. Individuals are rated as 2's if they have more than incidental homosexual experience, and/or if they respond rather definitely to homosexual stimuli. Their heterosexual experiences and/or reactions still surpass their homosexual experiences and/or reactions. These individuals may have only a small amount of homosexual experience or

they may have a considerable amount of it, but in every case it is surpassed by the amount of heterosexual experience that they have within the same period of time. They usually recognize their quite specific arousal by homosexual stimuli, but their responses to the opposite sex are still stronger. A few of these individuals may even have all of their overt experience in the homosexual, but their psychic reactions to persons of the opposite sex indicate that they are still predominantly heterosexual. This latter situation is most often found among younger males who have not yet ventured to have actual intercourse with girls, while their orientation is definitely heterosexual. On the other hand, there are some males who should be rated as 2's because of their strong reactions to individuals of their own sex, even though they have never had overt relations with them.

3. Individuals who are rated 3's stand midway on the heterosexual–homosexual scale. They are about equally homosexual and heterosexual in their overt experience and/or their psychic reactions. In general, they accept and equally enjoy both types of contacts, and have no strong preferences for one or the other. Some persons are rated 3's, even though they may have a larger amount of experience of one sort, because they respond psychically to partners of both sexes, and it is only a matter of circumstance that brings them into more frequent contact with one of the sexes. Such a situation is not unusual among single males, for male contacts are often more available to them than female contacts. Married males, on the other hand, find it simpler to secure a sexual outlet through intercourse with their wives, even though some of them may be as interested in males as they are in females.

4. Individuals are rated as 4's if they have more overt activity and/or psychic reactions in the homosexual, while still maintaining a fair amount of heterosexual activity and/or responding rather definitely to heterosexual stimuli.

5. Individuals are rated 5's if they are almost entirely homosexual in their overt activities and/or reactions. They do have incidental experience with the opposite sex and sometimes react psychically to individuals of the opposite sex.

6. Individuals are rated as 6's if they are exclusively homosexual, both in regard to their overt experience and in regard to their psychic reactions.

It will be observed that this is a seven-point scale, with 0 and 6 as the extreme points, and with 3 as the midpoint in the classification. On opposite sides of the midpoint the following relations hold:

0 is the opposite of 6
1 is the opposite of 5
2 is the opposite of 4

(Kinsey, Pomeroy & Martin 1948, pp. 638–41)

The importance of continuity as a concept applicable to sexual behavior was much emphasized by the Kinsey investigators:

> Males do not represent two populations, heterosexual and homosexual. The world is not to be divided into sheep and goats. Not all things are black nor all things white. It is a fundamental of taxonomy that nature rarely deals with discrete categories. Only the human mind invents categories and tries to force facts into separated pigeon-holes. The living world is a continuum in each and every one of its aspects. The sooner we learn this concerning human sexual

behavior, the sooner we shall reach a sound understanding of the realities of sex. (p. 639)

On the one hand the continuum model for sexual experience and activity must be regarded as a conceptual advance. Not only did it provide a clear convention for describing sexual history but also it may have served to counter social prejudice against homosexuals. Irrational prejudice, the norm in Kinsey's time and unfortunately common enough in our own, is characterized by stimatization and scapegoating (Goffman 1963). Stigmatization and scapegoating involve labeling some individuals as members of an outcast group; they therefore thrive on discrete categories, not on continua. Kinsey's report that an enormous number of people experienced some degree of homosexual arousal and/or activity probably also served to counter social forces that encourage the stigmatization and scapegoating of people labeled homosexual. On the other hand, human sexuality involves the sense of identity. Kinsey's exclusive emphasis on erotic experience and activity only addresses one aspect of the issue.

In our culture, the sense of identity appears frequently to be influenced by homosexual–heterosexual considerations. In general, it is safe to say that heterosexual identity is assumed as the cultural norm. This fact is dramatically illustrated simply by asking people what features about themselves contribute to their sense of identity. Lifelong heterosexuals (lifelong 0's on the Kinsey scale) do not usually list heterosexuality along with gender, race, age, religion, nationality, familial status, vocation, and so on when asked to describe themselves in this way. Heterosexuality is simply assumed to be present. For example, a colleague of mine responded as follows:

Q. What aspects of yourself make up your identity?
A. Let me put it in terms of identifying information, as if I were writing a case report about myself. I am a forty-five-year-old white Catholic American psychiatrist, father of two.
Q. Anything else?
A. Committed, loving husband, also an involved son and son-in-law. Northeasterner, Ivy Leaguer. My college is important to my identity.
Q. Anything else?
A. Jogging! Unless I jog twenty-five miles a week I get crazy. In the past ten years being a jogger has become an integral part of my identity.
Q. Are you heterosexual?
A. Of course.
Q. Is heterosexuality an important part of your identity?
A. Obviously.
Q. Would you have mentioned it if I hadn't asked you?
A. Probably not, I take it for granted.

Among people who have experienced homosexual arousal and/or activity, on the other hand, questions of identity deriving from sexual experience are common. As a therapist, I have seen innumerable individuals who seek consultation because they have homosexual feelings and wish to know if therefore they are gay. The request for consultation focuses on the person's sense of identity as a consequence of his sexual experience. When it comes to their sense of identity, people think categorically: "I am a man, an engineer, an American," and so on. Categorical models are by definition discontinuous. In the famous remark about sheep and goats, quoted above, the investigators may have used descriptive narrative to represent prescriptive sentiments. It may well be that people should not sort others into discrete categories on the basis of sexual fantasies or activity. However, from the descriptive point of view, people often do feel as if they were, in Kinsey's terms, sheep or goats. When Kinsey wrote "only the human mind invents categories," he was describing a universal attribute of cognitive functioning through which people organize their sexual experience. This feature of human functioning has no adequate behavioral model among nonhuman species.

Individuals who label themselves on the basis of sexual orientation (gay/homosexual, heterosexual, bisexual) have extremely variable sexual histories. Many people who consider themselves heterosexual have had homosexual experience, either subjectively in fantasies or with others. Many people who view themselves as gay or homosexual in identity have had heterosexual experience. In individuals who think of themselves as bisexual, the perceived sense of identity probably matches sexual experience more frequently. I suspect, however, that, for reasons that go beyond the scope of this chapter, most men who are bisexual in terms of their sexual experience probably perceive themselves as being straight or gay.

In clinical practice one often finds similar sexual histories among people who perceive themselves to be homosexual and among those who perceive themselves to be heterosexual. Two examples illustrate this point.

> A college student who had never had sexual experience with males or females was sexually attracted to and had sexual fantasies about both. Because his fantasies about males were more frequent, intense, and pleasurable than those about females, he could be placed at 4 on the Kinsey scale. He saw himself as gay, was active in a homosexual organization, and experienced the sense of being gay as an essential and enduring feature of his identity.
>
> Another college student was sexually attracted to both genders and had experienced sex with both males and females. He felt that sex with males was as pleasurable as that with females. His sexual fantasies sometimes involved males, sometimes females. Although this young man's fantasy life and experience were rated 3 on the Kinsey scale, he considered himself heterosexual. Raised in a sexually permissive setting, he believed that homosexual fantasy and activity did not threaten his heterosexual stance. His attitude toward current sexual partners was casual and recreational, but he aspired to fatherhood and family life in the future, when he "settled down."

Neither of these individuals perceived sexual fantasies and activity, or their sense of identity, as a source of distress for which therapeutic relief was sought. Of course, this is not always the case. Therapists must have models of the mind complex enough to be relevant to all the extremely different individuals who require assistance from them. For example, a typical patient may say something like this:

> "At this point in my life, having been married and divorced, having fathered two children, feeling overwhelmed with homosexual feelings but also in love with a woman who excites me sexually, believing homosexuality to be normal but experiencing irrational guilt because of my religious childhood, I think I should tell my woman lover that I am gay and abandon plans for marriage. *Should* I do this? *Am* I gay?"

Complex clinical problems such as these are discussed later in the book. Chapters 2, 3, and 5 focus on men who are predominately homosexual in fantasy and activity and who usually see themselves as gay. There I emphasize recent developments in the field of psychoneuroendocrinology, gender role/identity, and familial influences on psychosexual development. These developments are relevant for a modern psychoanalytic view of sexual orientation.

2

Psychobiological Considerations

During the past fifty years there has been recurrent interest in the idea that diminished masculinity, hypothetically associated with homosexuality, might also be associated with, and perhaps caused by, some type of endocrine abnormality. A number of studies in the 1940s supported this hypothesis (e.g., Glass, Devel & Wright 1940; Myerson, Neustadt & Rak 1941). This research was far from definitive, however, and the opposing view, that homosexuality is a purely psychological phenomenon, also had articulate advocates (e.g., Perloff 1949). The latter idea seemed to be supported by the findings that administration of androgen influences the intensity of sexual desire but not sexual orientation and that homosexuality is not produced by castration. It could be argued that testosterone, a physical substance, can best be understood as a concrete representation of the psychological concept of masculinity. One would not expect testosterone to be diminished among homosexual individuals since *ideas* about masculinity (or anything else) cannot be detected by measuring physical substances in the body. Some theoreticians felt that testosterone's hypothetical role in sexual orientation attracted interest because of an unfortunately widespread tendency toward biological determinism.

The initial surge and subsequent decline of scientific interest in psychohormonal correlational studies in adult males seemed compatible with this skeptical attitude. However, new research, particularly that focused on prenatal neuroendocrine influences on sexual orientation, indicates the importance of a model based on interactions between nature, nurture, and sexual orientation rather than one stressing all-or-nothing alternatives. The theme of multifactorial etiologies of homosexuality is a recurrent one, and the need for interdisciplinary collaborative research is repeatedly emphasized in the literature.

11

For example, Loraine and colleagues (1970) found abnormally low urinary testosterone in two exclusively homosexual men. Their report was particularly interesting because a third man, who was bisexual, was found to have no such abnormality, and higher than normal levels of testosterone were found in four female homosexuals. To their credit, the authors did not suggest a simple explanation for their observations. Instead, their report emphasized interactionism:

> The present paper has attempted to emphasize the highly complex nature of the clinical condition of homosexuality in the human. Kenyon . . . has stressed that the aetiology of homosexuality is essentially multifactorial, and with this concept we are in complete agreement. Psychological factors are undoubtedly of great importance in relation to pathogenesis, while the studies reported here suggest that abnormalities of endocrine function may also be peculiarly suited to a collaborative approach between psychiatrists and endocrinologists, and it is to be hoped that, in the future, interdisciplinary studies of this type will become increasingly prevalent. (p. 448)

PLASMA HORMONE LEVELS

Because plasma testosterone–homosexuality correlational studies in adult males have attracted considerable recent attention, I discuss them here despite the fact that this line of research ultimately proved unrewarding. The possibility of a correlation between plasma hormone levels and male sexual orientation was greeted with enthusiasm, widely tested, then dispassionately discarded. But a review of the plasma testosterone approach will direct the reader's attention to the processes by which change occurs in psychobiological and psychoanalytic theories of behavior—an important subtext of this book.

The research conducted by Loraine and colleagues stimulated a more ambitious investigation by Kolodny, Masters, Hendryx, and Toro (1971). The dramatic results of this investigation, published in the prestigious *New England Journal of Medicine*, sparked widespread interest in psychohormonal correlation and led to numerous additional studies. Kolodny and colleagues found that men who were predominately or exclusively homosexual had significantly depressed plasma testosterone levels in comparison to those of heterosexual men. The 30 homosexual men studied were distributed across the spectrum of the Kinsey scale. Plasma testosterone levels seemed to be negatively correlated with the subjects' ratings on the scale, so that a linear stepwise descent of group mean levels occurred from K–2 (predominately heterosexual) to K–6 (exclusively homosexual). The Kolodny team's findings not only were dramatic in themselves but had additional power because they replicated the previous study by Loraine and his colleagues.

The surge of research that followed Kolodny's report yielded initially inconsistent results, some positive (Starka, Sipova & Huni 1975), some negative (Birk et al. 1973; Brodie et al. 1974). The inconsistent findings may have been due to variations in the design of the studies. The problems of design are considerable in research on hormone levels. For example, psychological stress may influence plasma testosterone levels, as was demonstrated in an elegant longitudinal study of young men at officer candidate school (Kreuz, Rose & Jennings 1972). In these young men, plasma testosterone levels were depressed during an early, stressful phase of training but returned to normal later, during a less stressful phase. This research raised questions about studies involving homosexual subjects, many of whom live in environments which include a great deal of irrational prejudice against homosexual individuals. In a homophobic culture, can it be assumed that homosexual and heterosexual subjects experience and/or cope with stress similarly? Psychological stress may have an impact on the low plasma testosterone levels originally assumed to be a biological marker of homosexuality. Furthermore, plasma testosterone levels may be depressed by alcohol and other drugs (Mendelson & Mello 1974; Mendelson, Mendelson & Patchu 1975). Some studies on hormone–behavior relationships controlled for confounding variables such as these, but others did not. This qualification notwithstanding, enough data have been accumulated by now to indicate the emergence of a negative theme.

It does not appear at present that hormone levels or hormone production in postpubescent males are associated etiologically with homosexuality. Meyer-Bahlburg (1984), in a summary of 27 studies of blood testosterone levels in homosexual males, noted that most of the research found no differences between homosexual and heterosexual men. The investigations that were the most meticulously designed, using careful techniques for selecting subjects and taking measurements on multiple occasions, revealed that plasma testosterone levels were not depressed in homosexual men. One such study (Brodie et al. 1974) actually found homosexual subjects' plasma testosterone levels to be elevated!

Negative findings were also obtained with regard to correlation of homosexuality with increased plasma estrogens or decreased testosterone/estrogen ratios. Studies of gonadotrophin levels, other aspects of the functioning of the hypothalamic-pituitary-testicular axis, and other types of hormones (i.e., prolactin, androstenedione) have yielded similar results (Meyer-Bahlburg 1984). Correlation between blood levels of hormones and sexual orientation in adult males does not seem to be a promising area for future investigation. Study of the influence of prenatal neuroendocrine influences on sexual behavior, however, yields more interesting results.

NEUROENDOCRINE INFLUENCE ON SEXUAL ORIENTATION

Preliminary Evidence

In extensive experiments with rats, Dörner established that if males were exposed to a temporary deficiency of androgen during a critical prenatal period of brain differentiation, then when they were mature, under the influence of normal levels of androgen, they would manifest female-like sexual behavior. Dörner also reported that a positive estrogen feedback effect on luteinizing hormone (LH) occurred in rats deprived of androgen during the prenatal brain differentiation phase. This effect was similar to that found in normal females, but it did not occur in females androgenized during the brain differentiation phase or in males castrated after the brain differentiation phase had occurred. Dörner's observation of a positive estrogen feedback effect on LH in homosexual men, but not in heterosexual or bisexual men, was compatible with the hypothesis that sexual orientation in the human appears to be under central nervous system influence, as in the rat (Dörner, Gotz & Rohde 1975; Dörner 1976; Dörner et al. 1980).

Dörner speculated that inadequate prenatal androgenization of the central nervous system leads to a partially female differentiated brain. The female differentiation effect influences the central nervous stem but not the genitalia; it theoretically occurs during a critical phase of brain organization. According to Dörner's theory, androgen levels at puberty can be normal in such an individual, since puberty is an activational phase, not an organizational one.

Gladue, Green, and Hellman studied neuroendocrine response to estrogen administration in homosexual men, heterosexual men, and women (1984). The rationale for this investigation was as follows: in women, ovulation is triggered by an LH surge from the pituitary gland. This sudden increase in LH is a response to rising estrogen levels during the follicular phase of the menstrual cycle. This positive feedback effect can also be elicited with exogenously administered estrogens. In men, estrogens usually suppress LH, thereby producing a negative feedback effect. Dörner observed that in homosexual men, intravenous injection of estrogen produced an initial decrease in serum LH level, followed by a significant, delayed increase above the initial level. In heterosexual men, however, injection of estrogen produced a decrease in serum LH which was not followed by an increase above the initial value. Gladue's research was well controlled for stress and use of drugs, and all the women were tested during the early (follicular) phase of the menstrual cycle. There was a clear sex difference in LH response to the infused estrogen (premarin), and the differences in LH response between homosexual and heterosexual men were significant. These differences did not appear until 72 hours after the estrogen challenge, at which time the homosexual men showed pronounced positive feedback response. The data revealed that the homosexual males fell between heterosexual males and females. The investigators concluded, "This invites the idea that there may be physiological developmental components in some homosexual men" (Gladue 1984, p. 1496). They noted that they intentionally selected for study only lifelong homosexual men and that the homosexual and heterosexual men they studied were at opposite poles of the Kinsey spectrum. But most males who experience homosexual fantasies or engage in homosexual activity are not lifelong and exclusive homosexuals (Kinsey, Pomeroy & Martin 1948).

This investigation certainly warrants psychoanalytic attention, but a cautious approach is needed toward all potentially exciting findings. Gooren's (1986) attempt to replicate Gladue's study was unsuccessful. Baum and colleagues (1985) pointed out that the Gladue team's findings may be due to differences in testicular functioning, not brain organization, between homosexual and heterosexual men.

Dörner not only theorized that androgen deficit during a critical prenatal phase led to homosexuality in men but that androgen excess at such a phase produced homosexuality in women. Observations of women who were exposed to excess androgen in utero support the latter hypothesis. Money, Schwartz, and Lewis (1984) reported increased incidence of bisexuality or homosexuality among women with a history of treated adrenogenital syndrome. (This is a condition in which the adrenal cortex produces excessive amounts of masculinizing hormone [androgens] and decreased amounts of other hormones [cortisol and aldosterone]. The abnormality in function of the adrenal gland begins during fetal life. When the adrenogenital syndrome occurs in females, it produces virilization.) These patients received cortisol therapy during childhood, correcting the androgen excess. Their sexual orientation, therefore, may have been influenced by prenatal androgenization of the brain. Ehrhardt and colleagues (1985) also found increased bisexuality and homosexuality among women who were exposed prenatally to diethylstilbestrol (DES), which has masculinizing/defeminizing effects on brain organization.

Money and Lewis (1982) reported an increased incidence of homosexuality among a group of boys with idiopathic adolescent gynecomastia (IAG, development of excessive breast tissue). Although only ten cases were studied, the three homosexual individuals had childhood histories of gender role / gender identity disorders that well preceded the onset of gynecomastia. Money and Lewis hypothesized that a prenatal factor might have influenced both sexual orientation and breast development in these youngsters. But since 70 percent of the group was heterosexual, the investigators posited that this prenatal factor would represent a "threshold disposition susceptibility or vulnerability" to homosexuality rather than a necessary and sufficient cause.

Despite the suggestive findings outlined above, the evidence to date argues only for possible neuroendocrine influence on homosexuality in some subgroups, rather than suggesting that neuroendocrine factors cause homosexuality in the general population. Because the data are limited, the need for additional research is generally acknowledged.

Aggression and Rough-and-Tumble Play

Neuroendocrine factors may influence sexual orientation indirectly rather than immediately and directly. For example, many psychoanalysts believe that adaptation to aggression both in oneself and others during childhood is associated with the ultimate shaping of sexual orientation. Prenatal hormonal effects on brain differentiation probably influence sex differences in aggression during childhood and adulthood. Here I discuss the significance of sex differences in aggression and in rough-and-tumble play with regard to possible neuroendocrine influences on male sexual orientation.

The term *aggression* lends itself particularly well to imprecise usage in clinical discussions. One has only to look at the index of Stepansky's monograph *A History of Aggression in Freud* (1977) to appreciate the complexity of the subject under discussion. I present only a few headings:

> Aggression: As cruelty impulse, and death instinct, as masculine instinctual strain, as mastery impulse, and primary destructiveness: see also aggressive instinct; sadism.

Ideas connoting destructiveness, mastery, assertion, and masculinity are suggested by the index, and indeed they are somehow involved in most psychoanalytic discussions of the topic. Scholars have emphasized the umbrella nature and multiple meanings of the term aggression. Maccoby and Jacklin (1974) stated, "the word 'aggression' refers to a loose cluster of actions and motives that are not necessarily related to one another" (p. 226). Moyer (1974) noted that aggressive behavior can be categorized according to the type of eliciting stimulus, the nature of the aggressive response, and the physiological basis for the aggressive activity. He proposed categories of aggressive behavior as follows: "predatory, intermale, fear-induced, irritable, maternal, sex-related, and instrumental" (p. 336). Sex differences in aggression are among the more pronounced characteristics of human behavior. In Moyer's words:

> In all mammalian species from mouse to man, the male is the more aggressive sex. In man, the male is the primary perpetrator of violent crimes. . . . It has been suggested that the trait that has the greatest statistical difference in differentiating criminals from noncriminals is that of sex. . . . since history has been recorded males have committed more crimes of violence than have females in all nations and all communities within those nations. (p. 335)

Maccoby and Jacklin (1974) put it this way:

> In the history of humankind, group efforts to seize territory, possessions or governments by force have been the province of men; so have efforts to resist the incursions of others. Societies are rare indeed that have placed women in the front ranks of their armies. Forceful person-to-person power struggles (duels, jousting, boxing) whether for blood or "sport" have also been exclusively male endeavors. Why should this be so? (p. 228)

Males, in a variety of cultures, at all ages, and regardless of the definition of aggression or the type of measure used in studies, are consistently found to be more aggressive than females. Of particular interest here are the facts that this sex difference is found in prepubertal children as well as adults and that it includes rough-and-tumble play. Such play in young children does not usually involve the intention to harm. This type of activity involves body contact, throwing the body through space, vigorous exercise of the muscular-skeletal system, pushing, running, jumping. Aspects of rough-and-tumble play (e.g., wrestling, tackling) may seem aggressive and such behavior may indeed be involved in power-dominance relationships. Rough-and-tumble behavior does not, however, seem to be primarily motivated by a need to be assaultive, at least in young children; it is, in fact, a type of play. The significance of sex differences in aggression and rough-and-tumble play for the psychology of male sexual orientation is discussed below.

In searching for the reason such dramatic sex differences in aggression exist in humans, Maccoby and Jacklin (1974) considered the possibility that they were entirely due to learning and socialization. After meticulous critical evaluation of the available data, they discarded this hypothesis. Although learning effects are apparent, the accumulated behavioral information strongly suggests that underlying biological differences influence the behavioral differences in aggressiveness between the sexes, prepubertally as well as postpubertally.

Maccoby and Jacklin were influenced in their conclusion not only by the psychological literature but also by the psychoneuroendocrine research initiated by Young, Guy, and Phoenix (1965). These investigators (working with rodents) noted that the organizing effect of fetal androgens might involve nonsexual as well as sexual behavior. In a now classic investigation of female primates, they induced pseudohermaphroditism in fetuses by injecting the mothers with testosterone (propionate) during pregnancy. They then analyzed naturalistically occurring social interactions between the offspring, pseudohermaphroditic females and normal females. They found that "a number of social behaviors known to be sexually dimorphic, and without any immediate instrumentality relative to mating, appear to have been influenced in the masculine directions by our prenatal treatments with androgen" (p. 186). This was true not only of aggressive behaviors, such as display of facial threat (e.g., baring of teeth), but also of rough-and-tumble play. Prenatal androgen appeared to affect these behaviors, which occur early in life, at a time when there are no sex differences in peripheral levels of androgens. These findings in primates were basically compatible with Ehrhardt's well-known studies of humans. Fetally androgenized genetic females with early corrected adrenogenital syndrome or with progestin-induced hermaphroditism (with early surgical intervention if needed) were found to be energetically athletic during childhood. More like boys than like the girls in the control group, they enjoyed throwing their bodies through space and tumbling about (Ehrhardt 1968a, b; Money & Ehrhardt 1972).

The research thus suggests that childhood behavioral dimorphism involving rough-and-tumble activities reflects the influence of prenatal androgenization. It is noteworthy that when the childhood backgrounds of homosexual men are investigated, one of the most common findings in both patients (Bieber et al. 1962) and nonpatient subjects (Saghir & Robins 1973) is avoidance of rough-and-tumble activities. This avoidance is usually associated with fear of injury, fear of fighting, and a sense of being clumsy and fragile. The aversion to rough-and-tumble activities may or may not coexist with overt feminine behavior during childhood. Many homosexual men who do not report cross-dressing, having feminine mannerisms, or preferring feminine activities in childhood nonetheless say they avoided rough-and-tumble play (Friedman & Stern 1980b). This may be the most common childhood trait of prehomosexual boys.

In trying to make sense of this phenomenon, it is important to stress that aversion to rough-and-tumble play among prehomosexual males can best be understood as phase-specific: in this day and age it hardly needs to be empha-sized that homosexual men are not unaggressive or unassertive and that they engage in all kinds of activities, including strenuous and dangerous ones. Maccoby and Jacklin (1974) astutely point out, however, that in early child-hood dominance and leadership among boys may depend heavily on aggres-sion and skill at rough-and-tumble activities. As children mature, dominance and leadership come to depend on a greater variety of other complex social skills. The time phase during which the rough-and-tumble constellation ap-pears to be of greatest importance is probably prolonged from preoedipal to prepubertal years. Of course, the rough-and-tumble constellation does not cease altogether to be important after puberty: high school football heroes, for example, may have great peer group status. But during adolescence the sense of masculine competency is probably influenced by a wider variety of factors than during early childhood years.

It is interesting that the very constellation of activities apparently influenced by prenatal androgens should be so commonly abnormal in prehomosexual youngsters. It seems possible to read the data about rough-and-tumble play as indirect evidence supporting the hypothesis of partial female brain differentia-tion in such individuals. Childhood aversion to rough-and-tumble play almost certainly does not directly cause homosexuality. However, the trait may pre-dispose a boy to psychosocial interactions leading in that direction. Since male aversion to such activities may be expressed over a lengthy period of child-hood, it may have an impact on and be influenced by gender identity differ-entiation, the formation of psychic structure (particularly specific aspects of the ego ideal), and the quality of object relations.

Some of the complex interactions involving rough-and-tumble play, boy-hood aggression, peer status, and masculine self-esteem are illustrated in clinical research I carried out with masculine, psychologically well-adjusted nonpatients (Friedman & Stern 1980b). One group consisted of seventeen lifelong, exclusively homosexual men. The other consisted of seventeen life-long exclusively heterosexual men. Thirteen of the seventeen homosexual sub-jects (76 percent) reported chronic, persistent terror of fighting with other boys during boyhood and early adolescence. The intensity of this fear approximated a panic reaction. These men never recalled responding to challenge from a boyhood peer with counterchallenge, threat, or attack. This pervasive dread of peer aggression was a powerful organizing force in their minds. Anticipatory anxiety resulted in phobic responses to social activities; the fantasy that fighting might occur led these boys to avoid a wide variety of social interactions, especially rough-and-tumble activities (defined in our investigation as body-contact sports such as football and soccer).

These subjects reported that painful loss of self-esteem and loneliness resulted from their extreme aversion as boys to aggressive peer interactions. All but one (twelve of thirteen) felt chronically hungry for closeness with other boys. Unable to overcome their dread of potential aggression in order to win respect and acceptance, these boys were labeled sissies by their peers. They grew up in environments characterized by well-stratified male peer groups in which status was based on athletic ability, particularly rough-and-tumble and/or aggressive activities. These twelve subjects recalled that they had the lowest possible peer status during juvenile and early adolescent years. Alternately ostracized and scapegoated, they were exposed to continual humiliation.

All of these men denied that they were effeminate as boys. Only three formed compensatory close relationships with girls and enjoyed such activities as doll play and hopscotch. The rest simply remained chronically isolated and fantasized friendships with other boys. One prehomosexual boy who dreaded male peer aggression enlisted the aid of an older and stronger protector who fended off potential aggressors. He was therefore able to avoid having to pay a high social price for his intense fear. He did not avoid social interactions with other boys, was not scapegoated by peers, and was not labeled a sissy.

All thirteen men reported that as youngsters they had had markedly negative feelings about their bodies. Ten of the subjects described themselves as soft and flabby. All identified their boyhood physiques (in six cases, to their consternation) as "like a girl's." Two others (one with bilateral deafness) felt themselves to be too thin and equated thinness with frailty and fragility. Another man reported that as a boy he had had poor vision and, as a result, had "hated his body." In all cases, the body was perceived as being easily damaged. All subjects expressed a strong fear of physical injury were they to engage in contact sports.

Only two of the heterosexual boys (12 percent) reported fear of real or fantasized boyhood aggression similar in quality, chronicity, and consequence to that of the prehomosexual males. Like the thirteen prehomosexual boys, they dreaded fighting and avoided certain social situations as a result. They were assigned the lowest peer status and labeled sissies. Both perceived their bodies to be soft and fragile, and both were lonely during childhood years. One of these boys engaged in doll play and hopscoch.

No prehomosexual youngster among the seventeen had any degree of experience with fighting or rough-and-tumble activities during juvenile years. None engaged in even the modest juvenile sex-typed interactions described by the least aggressive preheterosexual youngster (e.g., actively pushing another boy in anger).

Thirteen heterosexual subjects related that they engaged in some peer aggression during boyhood and adolescence. All of them occasionally initiated attack, all responded to challenge with counterchallenge, to threat with counterthreat, and to attack with counterattack at least some of the time. Four of the thirteen reported having initiated such aggression more frequently than not; they also reported being peer group leaders. Those who engaged in fighting did not always find it enjoyable; they were frequently anxious, but nonparticipation was viewed as incompatible with their value systems. It should be emphasized that none of these preheterosexual youngsters was unusually belligerent. None ever actually harmed another child, had trouble with police because of assaultive behavior, or experienced difficulties in school. They did not, however, phobically avoid fighting. Despite varying degrees of timidity, all engaged in some aggression and made no extreme efforts to avoid it. Mastery of the anxiety resulting from fear of defeat and injury was an important source of self-esteem during their juvenile years.

The research described above shows, first of all, that aversion to rough-and-tumble activities is integrally associated with object-relationship development. Furthermore, although subjects avoided specific rough-and-tumble and aggressive activities during boyhood and adolescence (e.g., fighting, contact sports), there is no evidence that this avoidance led to permanent global impairment in assertiveness. Indeed, the lives of these men suggested just the opposite: many became leaders, some in activities that required a high degree of physical courage. Most of the boys in this study grew up in environments in which acceptance by other males was conditional upon some degree of competency at rough-and-tumble activities. This was not only true of peers but appeared to be the case with fathers and father figures as well. The message transmitted by other males to these boys was clear and consistent: "You are not like us! You are not adequately masculine!" It is important to consider these cases not as evidence of the constitutional defect of vulnerable children but rather from the point of view of "fit" between children and the peer groups that circumstances required them to adapt to. In these cases, the fit was poor because the available male peer groups were rigid and harshly judgmental about sex-role behavior, and in addition because the excluded or scapegoated children seemed unable to behave in ways that would have secured them entry and acceptance.

One cannot help but wonder how these individuals would have developed if the males they idealized had had a more flexible and abstract concept of masculine competency. They were not able to assimilate this view from females. In many cases, mothers, sisters, and female friends attempted to persuade these youngsters that they were indeed adequate males. This proved ineffective during the juvenile phase of development. When these men were boys of ages eight, nine, and ten they needed to be respected and valued by other males. As one put it, "it didn't matter that my mom taught me that strong men are gentle, or that a pianist is as much a man as John Wayne. When I told that to other boys on my street they laughed at me. That made me seem more a mama's boy than ever."

This study illustrates that an apparently simple activity such as rough-and-tumble play may affect highly complex interactions between social, cognitive, and psychodynamic levels of organization. These interactions may powerfully influence the structure of the mental apparatus during certain phases, such as the prepubertal juvenile phase.

The findings about prehomosexual boys' aversion to rough-and-tumble activities lend indirect support to the prenatal androgen deficiency hypothesis for the etiology of homosexuality. It has yet to be demonstrated, however, that a subgroup of boys with marked aversion to rough-and-tumble activities actually has partial female brain differentiation. Presumably, such research will be forthcoming. I suspect that some subgroups will be found with the biological marker and some without it.

Prenatal Stress Syndrome

Thus far the possibility has been raised that impaired prenatal androgenization of the brain may influence the development of homosexuality in human males. The question of mechanism naturally arises: how might prenatal androgenization be interfered with (if indeed this does occur)? Here, the story of prenatal stress syndrome is relevant for the contemporary psychoanalyst.

In 1972, Ward observed that male rats born of mothers subjected to experimental stress during pregnancy manifested impaired male sexual behavior and increased female-like sexual behavior. The behavioral effects, which occurred when the offspring reach adulthood, were irreversible and profound. Ward's findings have been widely replicated (e.g., Rhees & Fleming 1981). The stress effect applies to male fetuses only, does not involve reproductive morphological structures, and does not occur if rats are subjected to stress after birth. In searching for the cause of the behavioral effect, Ward and her co-workers measured plasma testosterone in fetuses at the time when sexual differentiation occurs. In contrast to a control group of male fetuses, which exhibited an increase in testosterone levels on gestation day 18, prenatally stressed fetuses showed a testosterone decline on days 18 and 19. After that, there were no differences between stressed and control fetuses. Specific enzymes used by fetal cells to synthesize testosterone were measured, and one such enzyme (D^5-3^b-hydroxysteroid dehydrogenase) responded to stress in a similar way. It was suggested, therefore, that the fetus's ability to synthesize testosterone was temporarily impaired by prenatal stress. This temporary impairment seemed to influence postpubertal sexual behavior but not reproductive morphology.

In a review of this work, Ward (1984) emphasized that there are differences between primates and rodents in sexual behavior differentiation, and she observed that cross-species generalization to humans would be premature at present. Ward's research cannot be taken as an animal model of human homosexuality. It is of considerable importance, however, that an animal model exists in which environmental influence on the mother affects biochemical processes in the male fetal gonad, thus altering the structure of the brain and affecting postpubertal sexual behavior.

Dorner compared homosexual and heterosexual men's histories of stressful events and noted that a significantly greater amount of prenatal maternal stress was reported in the homosexual group (Dorner et al. 1980). The retrospective nature of this investigation, however, makes interpretation of the data difficult. Dorner also observed that, in Germany, apparently a larger proportion of men born during the war and postwar period were homosexual than previously or subsequently. Although some have taken this as evidence in favor of prenatal stress, postnatal environmental influences (e.g., father absence) could have also contributed to this type of distribution. Moreover, Dorner's database consisted only of homosexuals "registered by sexologists and venerologists." It is apparent from the scant data available to date that much additional research is needed on prenatal stress in humans. The prenatal stress syndrome, however, fits nicely with the hypothesis of neuroendocrine influence on homosexuality.

MacCulloch and Waddington (1981) proposed that autoantibodies to testosterone could be produced by pregnant women. These antibodies might cross the placenta and inhibit the activity of fetal testosterone. Other mechanisms that could deplete androgen during a critical period of brain differentiation theoretially include alcohol or drug use by the mother, toxic reactions, and acute illness. The list of mechanisms by which transient interference with the function of the fetal gonad might occur seems long.

PSYCHONEUROENDOCRINE CONSIDERATIONS IN GENDER IDENTITY

Since effeminacy is more common in the background of male homosexuals than in heterosexuals, and since a majority of effeminate boys become homosexual adults, psychoneuroendocrine influences on gender identity might overlap with such influences on male homosexuality. Some qualifications must be pointed out immediately, however. First, there is no reason to think that most homosexual men were fully effeminate as children. Many may have manifested some effeminate traits; many may have felt unmasculine but not necessarily feminine; and some may have experienced no gender identity disturbance during childhood. Second, biological influences on effeminacy may be very different from those on homosexuality. In view of behavioral associations between gender identity disturbance and homosexuality, however, it is certainly reasonable at least to consider the psychoneuroendocrinology of gender identity in a discussion of homosexuality.

Until the mid-1970s, the best available data seemed to indicate that the individual's basic enduring sense of being male or female, his or her core gender identity, resulted from postnatal psychosocial influences rather than prenatal hormonal ones. The conclusion that core gender identity differentiates as a result of learning (except in transsexuals) was reached through elaborate studies carried out primarily at Johns Hopkins University by Money and collaborators (Money & Ehrhardt 1972). The researchers studied hermaphrodites with identical biological defects who had been raised as boys in some circumstances and girls in others. Other situations were studied in which attempts had been made to change core gender identity at varying points in the life cycle. Study of individuals with rare chromosomal anomalies and other types of pathology (lack of genitalia, receptor insensitivity to androgen, precocious puberty, and many other conditions) led to the central concepts of gender identity differentiation. According to these concepts, gender identity is not determined by chromosomal or gonadal sex but differentiates according to which sex the child is reared as. Furthermore, gender identity may be changed before the age at which it differentiates and becomes part of the core self concept. The Johns Hopkins data seemed to indicate that psychosocial effects on gender identity overrode prenatal endocrine effects.

Questions were recently raised about this model, however, by the research of Imperato-McGinley and colleagues (1974, 1981). In 1974, they reported on a unique subgroup of male pseudohermaphrodites with 5ª reductase deficiency, an autosomal recessive genetic anomaly. In this condition, the prenatal and neonatal exposure of the brain to testosterone is that of the normal male, but the enzyme deficiency produces ambiguous external genitalia and many of these individuals are raised as girls. However, the children then undergo a masculinizing puberty, with voice deepening, growth of the previously clitoris-like phallus, development of a rugated, hyperpigmented scrotum, full descent of the testes, and a muscular habitus. Sexual histories were obtained from eighteen of these pseudohermaphrodites. Sixteen changed gender identity from female to male at some time following puberty. One subject developed a severe gender identity disorder, dressing as a woman but manifesting extremely masculine mannerisms and having sex with women. Only one of these individuals continued to maintain female gender identity following puberty. Imperato-McGinley noted that in most cases to date in which gender identity is concordant with rearing but discordant with chromosomal and gonadal sex, castration and sex hormone therapy were initiated. In the pseudohermaphroditic individuals she described, however, postpubertal effects of testosterone on a prenatally masculinized brain appeared to override sex of rearing. Imperato-McGinley thus challenged the hypothesis that gender identity becomes fixed by eighteen months to four years of age. She pointed out that much of the data on matched pairs discordant for sex of rearing but concordant for biological sex were derived from pseudohermaphrodites who were functionally testosterone-deficient prenatally. Meyer-Bahlburg (1984) critically reviewed Imperato-McGinley's research, pointing out unresolved methodological difficulties in interpretation. Postnatal learning effects may have occurred in these subjects: their inner world may have been constructed from early childhood around the belief that they were "different" in some sense. Despite this, the evidence for prenatal androgen effects cannot be dismissed. Imperato-McGinley's research is compatible with the hypothesis that in humans, prenatal androgens may influence a variety of dimorphic behaviors as well as gender identity. Although there is no strong evidence at present of a direct biological factor in boyhood effeminacy, this area warrants ongoing investigation.

In general it seems clear that postnatal learning exerts an extremely powerful influence on the establishment of gender identity in humans. The underlying biological factors that might influence the child's readiness to learn how to be a boy or a girl, however, have not been fully established. The complex relationships between homosexuality and gender identity / gender role are further discussed in chapter 3 and in the developmental section of the book (part 3).

PSYCHONEUROENDOCRINOLOGY AND PSYCHOANALYSIS

A number of questions are raised by the research discussed above. For example, for the sake of argument let us suppose that the theory of partial feminization of the brain in the etiology of homosexuality were on a firmer empirical foundation than it is at present. Even then, demonstration of neuroendocrine differences between men at opposite ends of the Kinsey spectrum could not be taken as proof of an immediate, direct influence of brain organization on sexual orientation. As illustrated in the discussion of rough-and-tumble play, behavior may be influenced by biological factors in a powerful but indirect way. Differences in endocrine tests or measurements between groups at opposite ends of the Kinsey scale (including the response of LH to estrogen infusion) might be related to biopsychosocial sequences of events from birth on. These hypothetical differences in neuroendocrine functioning do not necessarily prove direct, immediate brain control of sexual orientation. It is possible that the brain effect is primarily on nonerotic behaviors during childhood. Homosexual and heterosexual men therefore may be differentially predisposed toward sequences of nonerotic intrapsychic and psychosocial experience and activity. These sequences (or critically important segments) may ultimately shape sexual fantasy and the motivation to engage in homosexual or heterosexual activity. For example, the key effect may not be on sexual orientation during adulthood but on gender disturbance during childhood. Neither Dörner nor Gladue, Green, and Hellman have published psychobiographical material about their subjects. Biopsychosocial relationships between brain differ-entiation and the development of the mental apparatus thus still remain to be elucidated.

From the developmental perspective it should be pointed out that psycho-analytic and psychobiological theories of the etiology of homosexuality do not necessarily represent competing points of view. The psychoanalytic theories all share the idea that childhood traumata lead to anxieties which ultimately result in homosexuality. These theories concern behavior and events during the preoedipal and oedipal phases. (For example, one theory holds that if a boy identifies with his controlling, seductive mother rather than with his indif-ferent father, he experiences the identification and the wish to be loved by his father as his mother would be in the form of homosexual erotic imagery.) Since the time frames involved in the two types of theories are sequential, one can readily imagine children moving along a path from prenatal predisposition to preoedipal, oedipal, and postoedipal phases characterized by the psycho-dynamic and psychosocial patterns emphasized in the psychoanalytic literature about homosexuality. One might thus speculate that a son's capacity to iden-tify with his father and to disidentify from his mother (Greenson 1968; Stoller 1974) is often influenced by prenatal androgen effects. This need not always occur, however. There should be room in models of etiology for direct bio-logical disposition toward homosexuality, indirect biological effects, and predominately psychodynamic influences. This type of spectrum model is in keeping with Freud's general model for the etiology of many behaviors, in-cluding homosexuality (1905/1953).

Mention of identification and disidentification raises the broader question of whether gonadal steroids influence the structure and function of psycholog-ical defenses generally. It is possible, and in my view likely, that many defenses and mechanisms of interaction between defenses and external environment are influenced by prenatal hormones. Imperato-McGinley's observations, dis-cussed above, suggest that the possibility of such interaction is worth thinking about.

Another reason for giving this area some attention involves cognition and perception. We cannot adequately consider the notion of defense without having at hand some model of cognition and perception. The mechanisms underlying identification with specific aspects of an object are presently un-known. Psychoanalytic theory does not tell us why a person identifies with a particular facet of an object, rather than a different facet, and psychoneuroen-docrinology also sheds little light directly on this area. It is apparent, however, that androgens may influence perception and cognition: this is suggested by demonstrations of sex differences in verbal and spatial abilities (Harris 1978) and in dyslexia (Hier 1979), and by impairment of spatial ability in androgen-deficient men (Hier & Crowley 1982). Prenatal hormonal effects may act through many behavioral systems leading to final common pathways. Early in life, these hormonal effects on the brain may influence the ease with which key identifications occur, and the ease with which apparent identifications can be discarded when adaptation so requires. This possibility seems important not only because of the research discussed above but also because of the likelihood that prenatal testosterone may have wide-ranging effects not only on the embryonic development of the brain but also on the immune systems. In discussing research supporting this conclusion, Geshwind commented both on the normative integration of diverse physiological systems and on the history of ideas, observing that the fields of cerebral dominance, neuroendocrine embryology, and immunology developed independently (Geshwind & Behan 1984). Although researchers tended to think of these fields as discrete systems, Geshwind's scholarship indicated that they are interrelated. Geshwind and Behan observed that intrauterine testosterone may influence the development of both the left hemisphere of the brain and the thymus. Thus, testosterone may affect cerebral hemispheric dominance and also the susceptibility to immune disorders. Geshwind also suggested that childhood dyslexia might be influenced by prenatal testosterone, a hypothesis compatible with the proportionately greater frequency of dyslexia in boys than in girls. The far-reaching effects of prenatal sex steroid hormones are also illustrated by the phenomenon of sex differences in such abilities as mathematics (Kolata 1983). Geshwind's research did not directly focus on sexual orientation. But this line of investigation indicates that complex relationships among behavior, cerebral dominance, and the immune system may be influenced by prenatal androgen in ways not previously appreciated, and it lends support to the general hypothesis that the effect of prenatal androgen on postnatal development may be profound. Geshwind's criticism of researchers who continue to view fields of knowledge as if they were unconnected is also applicable to the relationship between psychoanalytic theory and the neural sciences. The need to bridge the gap between these two fields underlies the stance I take in this chapter (see also chapter 19).

Before leaving the topic of the influence of brain on mind, I should note that although there is no compelling evidence to date that human sexual orientation is controlled immediately and directly by the brain, there is some evidence to suggest that sexual fantasy may be influenced by the central nervous system. Heath's (1975) induction of complete sexual response cycles in human beings via chemical and electrical stimulation of the brain with depth electrodes suggests that this might be the case. Benedek and Rubenstein's (1939) research on the associations between mind and brain in the menstrual cycle also suggests that in the human being sexual fantasy may be influenced to a greater degree by biological factors than is generally appreciated.

Benedek and Rubenstein were able to predict menstrual cycle phase by blindly analyzing the content of therapy sessions of fifteen patients in psychoanalysis. The investigators described a pattern in which the first part of the cycle, prior to ovulation, was a period of increased self-esteem and desire for erotic stimulation during which the individual's self-image was active. Active and passive-receptive tendencies were optimally fused at ovulation, and the subsequent luteal phase of the cycle was characterized by passivity; as assessed from blind analysis of sexual fantasies, associations, and dreams, motivation for sexual activity during the luteal phase was heavily procreational. This research had some methodological problems, and it did not explicitly focus on homosexuality–heterosexuality (Friedman 1982). These criticisms notwith-standing, this rich prospective investigation suggested that, at least in the women studied, the quality of the sexual fantasy life of the mind was somehow linked with the control of the menstrual cycle by the brain. This raises the intriguing possibility that other links between brain and mind may directly influence and be influenced by human sexual behavior.

THE ROLE OF GENETICS

A discussion of psychobiology in relation to sexual orientation would be incomplete without some mention of genetics. Comparisons of sexual orienta-tion in monozygotic (MZ) and dizygotic (DZ) twins have provided the most interesting data. In 1953 Kallman investigated concordance for sexual orienta-tion in homosexual MZ twins compared to DZ twins. In every instance of homosexuality among forty MZ twins, homosexuality (usually of similar Kinsey scale rating) also occurred in the other twin. This dramatic 100 percent concordance rate was not found among the DZ twins, of whom only 11.5 percent were rated 3–6 on the Kinsey scale. Kallman's findings were basically compatible with those of Sanders (1934), who reported five out of six MZ twins concordant for homosexuality; and Habel (1950), who observed con-cordance for homosexuality in three out of five MZ twins and in none of five DZ twins. Following Kallman's influential article, however, a number of cases of divergent sexual orientation in MZ twins were reported (Rainer et al. 1960; Kolb et al. 1961; Klintworth 1962; Parker 1964; Zuger 1976; McConagy & Blaszczynski 1980). I had occasion to study both the psychological develop-ment and hormonal levels of one such pair (Friedman, Wollesen & Tendler 1976).

Each twin was extensively interviewed and blood hormone levels were measured on multiple occasions. The twins were twenty-five years old at eval-uation. Neither had had previous contact with mental health professionals. Sam lived in a metropolis with his male lover and worked as an executive. Howard lived in the suburbs of a neighboring city with his wife and two children and worked as a gym teacher. A physical exam was within normal limits for both twins except that Howard was moderately obese. Sam was 74½ inches tall and weighed 212 pounds. Howard was 74¾ inches tall and weighed

260 pounds. They related to me in a forthright manner, without observable evidence in either of a gender identity disorder.

Sam had been born first, weighing 6 pounds, 2 ounces; Howard had weighed 6 pounds, 8 ounces at birth. The slight difference in size persisted throughout the twins' childhood and, as a result, the boys could be told apart. Their father was a blue-collar worker, their mother a housewife. Both parents were practicing Catholics and there was no discussion of sex in the home.

Psychological development diverged from early childhood. Sam's first memories were of feeling insecure and vulnerable. He recalled that at age five, he had been envious of girls because they were taken care of by men when they grew up. Sam always felt closer to his mother than to his father, perceiving the latter as withdrawn and passive. Until his adolescent years his closest playmate was Howard; at that time, however, the twins initiated a persistent pattern of spending leisure time separately. Sam stayed home after school helping his mother with housework or playing hopscotch with neighborhood girls, while Howard remained outside with male peers. Although not effeminate, Sam was athletically awkward and temperamentally unassertive. The last to be chosen for team sports, frightened of rough-and-tumble activities, he had low status with other boys.

Sam was ashamed of his body. As early as age five, he recalled, he felt that his nipples were similar to his mother's. In later years, he felt that he had a feminine habitus even though others perceived him to be masculine. During his boyhood and early adolescence Sam was labeled a "mama's boy" and "the twin who liked to read" by casual acquaintances, peers, and extended family.

Sam clearly recalled that the first time he became romantically attracted to a young man was when he was five years old, at an uncle's wedding. His sexual life remained relatively dormant until age nine, when he found himself intensely aroused by the sight of a teenager urinating. Erotic fantasies were subsequently profuse and they exclusively involved males. Self-masturbation began with puberty at age thirteen and at the time of the interview was practiced a few times per month. Masturbatory fantasies were also exclusively homosexual, as was the manifest content of infrequent erotic dreams.

When he was ten, Sam was the passive partner in an episode of intracrural intercourse initiated by an older boy. No further homoerotic activity occurred until age fourteen, when for about a year he engaged in mutual masturbation and fellatio with neighborhood boys. As far as Sam was aware, the other boys considered this activity heterosexual, since heterosexual pornographic magazines were viewed during the experiences and fantasies about females were verbalized. Sam was indifferent to the heterosexual talk and profoundly stimulated by the homosexual activity. After the group spontaneously dissolved, Sam maintained a heterosexual image because he feared social ostracism. He had brief encounters with seven female partners, each of whom initiated sexual behavior, usually consisting of masturbation, fellatio, or anal intercourse. His fantasies during sex were homosexual; coitus rarely occurred. Sam continued to present a heterosexual facade, although he fell in love with his college roommate, a seventeen-year-old heterosexual male athlete. At age twenty-two, Sam decided to engage in sexual activity with male partners on a regular basis. Since then, he had averaged four orgasms per week and neither experienced nor desired sex with a female. Sam cross-dressed only once—at a Halloween party at the age of eight. Despite childhood envy of females, he never desired anatomical change of sex.

Howard recalled feeling secure as a young child. He perceived his father as quiet in disposition but loving, gentle, and strong. He always felt closer to his father than to his mother and actively rebelled against her control. Unlike Sam, Howard enjoyed spending leisure time with his father, engaging in activities such as woodworking or bowling.

Howard was the target of continual maternal disfavor because of his sloppiness, rowdiness, and poor performance as a student. During boyhood and adolescence, he was a peer group leader, athletically graceful, and fiercely competitive at team sports. He responded to challenge with attack and usually emerged the victor in fights with other boys. Howard viewed his body with pride and never felt unmasculine or feminine. From about age eight, he was known as "the twin who liked sports." Although he recalls feeling sexually oriented toward females at this age, his interest in sex was minimal until puberty, when sexual fantasies with exclusively heterosexual erotic imagery proliferated. During the group homosexual activity that occurred at age fourteen, Howard pretended he was having sex with a girl. He lost interest in this group a year later when he began dating girls. During the first few postpubertal years, nocturnal emissions with heterosexual dreams occurred on a weekly basis. Self-masturbation did not begin until age eighteen, however, because of feelings of shame. Since then, masturbation had been practiced with intermittent frequency and with exclusively heterosexual imagery. Howard fell in love at age fifteen and dated his girlfriend steadily until high school graduation. Mutual inhibition restricted sexual activity to petting. However, Howard usually had erections and orgasms without direct genital manipulation. At age eighteen, he first experienced coitus with a girl he married the following year. Howard stated that he and his wife enjoyed mutually satisfying sexual intercourse approximately four times per week.

The differences in gender identity / gender role behavior experienced and expressed by these twins are similar to that described for all identical male twins of divergent sexual orientation reported to date and are in keeping with the general findings on the relationship between sexual orientation and gender identity discussed in chapter 3. Despite their radically different inner psychological worlds, the twins showed no differences in mean blood testosterone levels, which were normal.

Comparisons between MZ and DZ twins are of greater scientific power if the individuals studied were adopted at birth and raised in different environments. The first such data were published recently by Eckert and colleagues (1986). These investigators identified two sets of homosexual male MZ twins who were separated at birth and raised in different families. Sexual histories were obtained during adulthood. In one pair the results were dramatic and in keeping with a hypothesis of genetic influence on sexual orientation: the two individuals had a number of behavioral traits in common, including homosexuality. Although their histories of gender disturbance were not reported, in a letter to me Dr. Heston revealed that each twin had "described feelings of femaleness before age nine." This finding is compatible with the discussion of gender identity/role in chapter 3 and with the model of psychological development presented in chapters 13–18. Results obtained from the second set of twins were not so clear-cut. Whereas one twin had been exclusively homosexual after age nineteen, the other, a married father of four, regarded himself as exclusively heterosexual. He had, however, engaged in a homosexual affair between the ages of fifteen and eighteen.

Although the histories of the concordant twin pair are compatible with the theory of genetic influence on sexual orientation, they are also compatible with prenatal endocrine influence. The model of prenatal testosterone deficit at a critical period allows for the possibility that such a deficit occurs in some subgroups as a consequence of genetic determinants. Recognition of the possibility that prenatal testosterone inhibition may occur either with or without genetic influence highlights the need to conceptualize etiological influence in terms of multiple subgroups. Finally, the mechanisms leading to homosexuality in the concordant twin pair reported on by Eckert and colleagues may not have involved prenatal testosterone deficit at all.

There is no question that twin studies provide important insights into biological research on human sexual orientation. Even a single set of MZ twins raised apart from birth and concordant for homosexuality offers meaningful data about the importance of biological influences on human sexual orientation. The fact that the twins described above developed gender identity disturbances at the same age makes the evidence for biological influence even more compelling. More research is needed to clarify the intermediate mechanisms leading to differentiated sexual orientation in identical twins separated at birth and reared apart. Also needed are studies comparing MZ and DZ twins. (Eckert and colleagues took sexual histories of DZ twins separated at birth, but none of these pairs included a homosexual subject.)

Pillard and colleagues recently provided evidence that male homosexuality may be familial (Pillard, Poumadere & Caretta 1982; Pillard & Weinrich 1986). They studied the families of predominately homosexual and heterosexual men. Of the heterosexual men, 4 percent had homosexual brothers. In contrast, 20 percent of the brothers of homosexual men were homosexual or bisexual. The investigators found no evidence for increased incidence of homosexuality among sisters of homosexual men as compared to heterosexual controls. This research will no doubt be followed up by studies of second-degree relatives in addition to siblings and by studies of individuals from different geographical locations.

A Sociobiological Perspective

Ruse (1981) recently pointed out that the possibility of genetic influence on sexual orientation is compatible with theories of the etiology of homosexuality put forth by sociobiologists. One theory suggests that homosexuality might result from balanced superior heterozygote fitness.

> Balanced superior heterozygote fitness is not merely a theoretical possibility, it does have empirical confirmation. The best known case occurs in the human species. In certain black populations, as many as 5% die in childhood from sickle-cell anemia, a genetic disease. The apparent reason for the persistence of this disease is that heterozygotes for the sickle-cell gene have a natural immunity to malaria, also widespread in these populations. Because the heterozygotes are fitter than either homozygote, the sickle-cell genes stay in the populations, and in each generation, a number of children die from anemia.
>
> . . . Suppose that homosexuality is a function of the genes and that possession of two "homosexual genes" makes a person homosexual. Let us also suppose, however, that heterozygotes, possessors of one "homosexual gene" and one "heterosexual gene," were fitter than homozygotes for "heterosexual genes," in other words, that by one means or another, heterozygotes reproduce more than heterosexual-gene homozygotes. It then follows naturally that the existence and persistence of homosexuality is a function of superior heterozygote fitness. Moreover, the theory can easily accommodate the fact that sometimes homosexual persons reproduce. All that is necessary for the theory to work is that they reproduce less than heterosexual individuals. Also note that if one chooses from among the many estimates of the incidence of homosexuality a reasonable figure or about 5% of the total population, this can be accommodated by the theory, for 5% is the approximate figure suggested for sickle-cell anemia. (Needless to say, I draw this analogy not as proof, but simply to show that we are talking about a mechanism which could, in theory, handle the phenomenon of homosexuality.)

The second model put forth by sociobiologists is that of kin selection. The idea here is that homosexuality is hypothetically associated with altruism toward relatives. Although the homosexual individual does not reproduce, the gene pool is preserved because his or her altruistic behavior results in increased reproductive fitness of others in his family unit. Another hypothesis is that the genetic influence is primarily on the parents' behavior:

> If the genes could give rise to behavior in one or both parents that would in some way and under special circumstances cause one offspring to become a nonreproducer, and this were in the parent's reproductive interests, such genes would be preserved and even multiplied by selection. Obviously, the circum-

stances would have to be rather special. Normally, if a parent would be better off with fewer potentially reproductive children, its best reproductive strategy would be not to have surplus offspring in the first place. However, another way to bring about the same situation would be for the parent's genetically caused behavior to force one offspring not merely not to compete with his siblings, but to aid the siblings in their reproductive quest. If the behavior could induce such altruism, it might well pay a parent to have an extra offspring, even though the offspring would never itself reproduce. This, then, is the essence of parental manipulation, although it must be pointed out that, despite the language, sociobiologists do not mean to imply conscious manipulative intent on the part of the parent. Indeed, the mechanism might well be more effective if both parent and child were unaware of what was going on. (Ruse 1981, p. 12)

An overview of the field of genetics suggests that in some subgroups there may be genetic influence on sexual orientation. Data indicating genetic influence are still scant, however, and the mechanisms through which such influence might operate are as yet not established. Of course, the potential influence of genetics in some subgroups by no means rules out the possibility of environmental influence. Behaviorally similar forms of homosexuality may fall along a spectrum with regard to nature/nurture influences. In some cases, the behavior may be strongly influenced by the individual's genetic makeup—this is suggested by the MZ twin set reported by Eckert and colleagues (1986). In other instances, however, the environment might play a greater role, and many forms of homosexuality may not be genetically influenced at all.

The same cautious reasoning should be applied to the broader question of biological influences on human sexual orientation. On the one hand, it seems likely that biological parameters do influence the etiology of homosexuality in subgroups of males. But these effects are probably indirect and partial, and intermediate psychobiological mechanisms remain to be fully established. There are, however, enough positive studies to command the attention of psychoanalytic theoreticians.

For this chapter I selected aspects of the psychobiological field that I felt to be of particular relevance to psychoanalytic psychology. This discipline was framed to be of interest to psychodynamically oriented psychotherapists. For more inclusive reviews of psychobiological aspects of sexual orientation and related topics, see Wilson 1975; Kirsh and Rodman 1977; Meyer-Bahlburg 1977, 1982, 1984; Ehrhardt and Meyer-Bahlburg 1981; McEwen 1983; and Rose 1985.

3

Gender Identity and Male Homosexuality

According to Stoller (1985), *gender identity* "is a term used for one's sense of masculinity and feminity; it was introduced to contrast with 'sex,' a term that summarizes the biological attributes that add up to 'male' or 'female'" (p. 1034). Money and Ehrhardt (1972) define the term as follows: "Gender identity is the sameness, unity, and persistence of one's individuality as male or female (or ambivalent) . . . especially as experienced in self-awareness and behavior. Gender identity is the private experience of gender role, and gender role is the public expression of gender identity." In this chapter I summarize evidence indicating that gender identity disturbances in childhood strongly predispose males toward predominant or exclusive homosexuality during adulthood. Before proceeding, however, it is necessary to clarify such concepts as disorder, disturbance, abnormality, behavioral pathology, and so on.

The question of when behavioral deviation from a defined norm should be considered psychopathology has been much debated. One perspective on the issue is seen in a recent study of the development of homosexual men that used a category called "gender role noncomformity" in an apparent effort to avoid value-laden medical terminology (Bell, Weinberg & Hammersmith 1981). I take a different approach. Concepts of pathology, unless otherwise stated, are in keeping with the general philosophy of psychiatric disorder expressed in the latest edition of the American Psychiatric Association *Diagnostic and Statistical Manual (DSM-III-R)*.

The distinction between nonconformists and people with psychopathology is usually clear enough during childhood. Extremely and chronically effeminate boys, for example, should be understood as falling into the latter category. As one considers later phases of the life cycle, however, one finds a wide

33

spectrum of behavior that properly exists outside the clinical domain. Concepts of masculinity, femininity, and androgyny may have personal meanings far removed from commonly accepted social norms without the implication of psychopathology. Clinical concepts are often somewhat imprecise and admittedly fail to do justice to the rich variability of human behavior. Whether a given behavior should be considered psychopathological or simply socially deviant may not be easy to determine. Having underscored these limitations, I nonetheless believe that clinical concepts are ultimately helpful. Accordingly, when I use such obviously value-laden terms as disorder, abnormality, and psychopathology, they are meant to indicate behavior that most clinicians, relying upon common sense, clinical experience, and the scientific and clinical literature, would place in the clinical domain.

Gender identity may be abnormal in a way that is concrete, gross, and easy to diagnose. The major category of gender identity disorder of childhood in the *DSM-III-R*, for example, emphasizes distress about being a boy and a concurrent intense desire to be a girl. Diagnostic criteria include preoccupation with stereotypically female activities or repudiation of male anatomical structures. The manual also allows for diagnosis of other disorders of gender identity (Gender Identity Disorder Not Otherwise Specified) but no diagnostic criteria are put forth for this.

Gender identity may be disturbed in more subtle, less concrete ways than those specified in *DSM-III-R*. For example, many boys feel *unmasculine* without necessarily wishing to be girls. Effeminacy is a well-defined syndrome that meets the *DSM-III-R* criteria for childhood gender identity disorder, but unmasculinity has not yet been well described in terms of symptom criteria.

Profound feelings of masculine inadequacy may lead to a negative self-evaluation that can remain part of the self-concept for years. A persistent sense of oneself as shamefully unmasculine should be distinguished from fleeting feelings of unmasculinity that occur throughout the life cycle. Whereas wide but relatively brief fluctuations in the state of masculine self-regard are probably the norm, a consolidated, persistent sense of masculine inadequacy should in my view be seen as a manifestation of a gender identity disorder. The development of the self in a gender-valued way (i.e., perception of oneself as "masculine enough") is discussed in chapters 13–18.

A history of gender identity pathology (including effeminacy and chronic, extreme unmasculinity) is much more common among men who are predominately or exclusively homosexual than among men who are predominately or exclusively heterosexual. This correlation between childhood gender identity disturbance and persistent, predominant homosexuality during adulthood has been noted by many investigators using diverse strategies and methods of research (e.g., Bell, Weinberg & Hammersmith 1978, 1981; Bieber et al. 1962; Green 1985, 1987; Harry 1983; Holeman & Winokur 1965; Money and Russo 1979; Saghir & Robins 1973; Whitam 1977, 1980; Whitam &

Zent 1984; Zuger 1976, 1984). The childhood finding seems to be associated with homosexuality per se, distributed both across all types of psychopathology and among men without significant psychopathology. At present, I believe this is the only correlation between psychopathology and homosexuality that may be taken as an established fact.

Among the numerous investigations that bear on this area are retrospective studies of adult patients (Bieber 1962) and nonpatients (Saghir & Robins 1973), retrospective cross-cultural studies (Whitam & Zent 1984), comparisons of identical twins of divergent sexual orientation (Friedman, Wollesen & Tendler 1976), and studies of children with gender identity disorders (Zuger 1984; Green 1987). I comment in detail on four studies of homosexuality which illustrate strikingly similar findings despite important differences in the theoretic orientation and methodological approach of the investigators.

THE BIEBER STUDY (1962)

This research, often identified by the name of the senior investigator, Dr. Irving Bieber, was important not only because of the data it produced about homosexuality but also because it showed that a large group of psychoanalytic clinicians could carry out a major research endeavor effectively.

In 1952, the Society of Medical Psychoanalysts formed a research committee. Members of the committee had 20 male homosexual patients in treatment who were utilized in a pilot study. Three copies of a questionnaire were distributed to each member of the society together with instructions to fill out the questionnaire on every male homosexual patient presently in treatment. (The members were requested to fill out additional questionnaires if they were treating more than three male homosexual patients.) Members who were treating fewer than three homosexual patients were asked to fill out the unused questionnaires for heterosexual male patients, who formed the comparison sample. No formal instruction for selection of the comparison cases was given. Seventy-seven analysts participated in the study. In 1955 a progress report was presented to the membership of the society and a supplementary questionnaire was developed, which was sent to the original participating analysts as well as to others who were treating homosexual men. The final homosexual group consisted of 106 men, 30 of whom were bisexual. There were 100 heterosexual comparison patients. Most lived in the New York City area.

The authors distinguished effeminacy from a constellation of other behaviors compatible with the concept of unmasculinity discussed above. (They did not use the rubric *unmasculinity* to indicate a behavioral category, however.) They characterized effeminacy predominately in terms of a certain type of posturing and vocal intonation that amounted to a "caricaturing of female mannerisms." Of the homosexual men studied, 34 percent had been effemi-

TABLE 3.1 Developmental Differences between Homosexual
and Heterosexual Patients

	Percent of Sample	
	Homosexual	Heterosexual
Was excessively fearful of physical injury in childhood	75	46+
Avoided physical fights	89	55+
Play activity before puberty was predominately with girls	33	10+
Was "lone wolf" in childhood	60	27+
Did not participate in competitive group games	83	37+
Did not play baseball	84	38+

Note: The difference between the groups is significant at the + .001 level.
Source: Bieber et al. 1962, p. 175.

nate at some time during their lives. Currently, 25 percent were mildly effeminate, 2 percent markedly so. In contrast, some degree of effeminacy was reported in only 5 percent of the heterosexual controls. The investigators found that nineteen homosexual men had been effeminate both as children and as adults. Seven patients had been effeminate as children but were not effeminate during adulthood. Seven others denied childhood effeminacy but were effeminate as adults. Among the heterosexual controls, only two had been effeminate since childhood. Even allowing for bias, retrospective distortion, and so on, the difference between groups with regard to effeminacy was dramatic.

A number of other developmental differences were found between the homosexual and heterosexual groups. In comparison to heterosexual controls, the homosexual patients reported that as children they had avoided fighting and competitive games and sports, had been fearful of physical injury, and had been isolated from their peers (table 3.1).

The investigation carried out by the Society of Medical Psychoanalysts attracted the criticism that a number of conclusions were reached about homosexuality per se based on assessment of a skewed sample: critics argued that a group of medical analysts, biased in favor of an illness model of homosexuality, studied "sick" patients (i.e., patients in therapy) and then made conclusions about a form of behavior (homosexuality) that occurs among people who are not sick and are not patients. Whether one agrees or disagrees with the model of homosexuality proposed by Bieber and colleagues, there is no denying the fact that a study of patients in analytic treatment in New York City must necessarily involve an unusual group. But since the processes of data collection and reporting are presented in detail in the monograph, it is possible to evaluate the data collected separately from the investigators' conclusions. On the one hand, the analytic community awaits similar investigations in other areas throughout the world. On the other hand, it is interesting how well the Bieber data about disordered gender identity and gender role behavior fit with research carried out by nonpsychoanalytic investigators who studied sexual orientation among individuals who were not patients.

BELL, WEINBERG, AND HAMMERSMITH (1981)

Bell, a psychologist, and Weinberg and Hammersmith, sociologists, carried out a large study of sexual orientation in the San Francisco Bay area in 1969–79. Their sample consisted of 979 homosexual and 477 heterosexual men and women. An attempt was made to attain even distribution by age and education among subjects, and blacks as well as whites were included in the research. The investigators also attempted to interview subjects recruited from a given source in approximate proportion to the homosexual population likely to be found there. (For example, more homosexual men are likely to be found in gay bars than in gay baths, and the sample reported on in this study reflects these differences.) Heterosexual subjects were obtained using block and stratified random sampling techniques in the Bay area. Homosexual subjects were recruited at gay bars, gay baths, on specific streets, at public parks, beaches, and restrooms. In addition, invitations to participate were sent to people on mailing lists provided by gay bookstores and homophile organizations. Advertisements of various types were used, and subjects in the study enlisted others. Almost five thousand individuals were recruited. Their case files were compartmentalized for subsequent data analysis on the basis of certain characteristics (e.g., race, age, education). Individuals to be interviewed were then chosen at random from the various research cells. The investigators did not restrict the heterosexual sample to unmarried people, reasoning that whereas age and education are comparable characteristics among homosexual and heterosexual individuals, marital status is not.

> For example, a middle-aged male who is unmarried is clearly atypical of heterosexual males in general, while one would expect to find middle-aged homosexual males to be unmarried. In addition, many homosexual adults are involved in quasi marriages in which they and their partner live together, share expenses, and enjoy the same satisfactions as married heterosexuals. (Bell, Weinberg & Hammersmith 1981, p. 38)

Despite their careful techniques, the investigators noted, "we do not claim to have a representative sample of American homosexuals, or even of those residing in the San Francisco Bay area" (p. 19).

A lengthy interview schedule was developed. Interviewers were mostly graduate students who had some additional training in the use of the instrument and in interview technique. The Kinsey scale was used to place subjects in homosexual–heterosexual comparison groups. Most homosexual subjects were exclusively so in activity and fantasy (K–5 to K–6) and most heterosexual individuals were also exclusively so (K–0).

The data on development collected in this study were analyzed by means of path analysis. A description of this statistical procedure exceeds the scope of this book, but its purpose is to determine the degree to which particular independent variables (in this case, events during development) influence a dependent variable (in this case, homosexuality). The independent variables were organized according to a life history developmental model. Questions were grouped into composite measures by means of factor analysis. The researchers suggested that inferences about causal behavioral chains made with this approach are more accurate than retrospective research usually allows.

The major psychodevelopmental difference between homosexual and heterosexual groups was in what the investigators termed "gender conformity." Whereas 70 percent of the heterosexual men had enjoyed sports activities such as baseball and football as children, only 11 percent of homosexual men had. In contrast, 68 percent of homosexual men, but only 34 percent of heterosexual men, had enjoyed such solitary activities as drawing or reading when they were children. As children, 46 percent of homosexual men and 11 percent of heterosexual men had enjoyed such stereotypically feminine activities as playing house, hopscotch, or jacks. Childhood cross-dressing occurred in 37 percent of homosexual and 10 percent of heterosexual subjects. Whereas 67 percent of heterosexual men felt they had been very masculine as children, only 18 percent of homosexual men did. Heterosexual men were more likely than homosexual men to have viewed themselves as very strong during childhood (41% vs. 25%). More homosexual men than heterosexual men felt they had been very passive (22% vs. 8%), or very submissive (20% vs. 3%) children. The authors stated:

> Our preliminary comparisons support the contentions of others that prehomosexual boys tend to be less "masculine" in their personal traits than preheterosexual boys. . . .
>
> Childhood masculinity was highly interrelated with variables pertaining to childhood play activities and thus was included in the more general composite measure called Childhood Gender Nonconformity. . . . Childhood Gender Nonconformity turned out to be more strongly connected to adult homosexuality than was any other variable in the study. (p. 80)

In this investigation, slightly less than half of the homosexual men were classified as relatively effeminate and the remainder as relatively noneffeminate. This classification was based on two highly intercorrelated measures: the extent to which the interviewers judged effeminacy to be present in the interview, and how masculine or feminine the respondent rated himself as having been while growing up. (It is interesting that, for reasons not stated, apparently no effort was made to ascertain how masculine or feminine the subject saw himself at the time of the interview.)

> Regardless of which group we are talking about, the development of male homo-sexuality is closely linked to gender nonconformity. Even among the noneffemi-nate homosexual men this Dislike of Boys' Activities is the strongest predictor of Adult Homosexuality. While their nonconformity may not have been so obvious either when they were growing up or in adulthood, it would appear that where they thought they stood on a masculine–feminine continuum when they were young was predictive of their eventual sexual orientation. (p. 200)

Bell, Weinberg, and Hammersmith concluded that their study corrobo-rated other investigations that have found prehomosexual children to perceive themselves as less masculine than preheterosexual children do. The types of behavior that they termed gender nonconformity were found to relate directly "to experiencing both homosexual activities and homosexual arousal before age 19, [to] a sense of an explicitly sexual or at least gender-related difference from other boys, and [to] a delay in feeling of sexual attraction to girls, as well as an adult homosexual preference." The authors quoted from their interviews with homosexual men to illustrate their psychobiographical conclusions:

> "I was never a real boy. I was afraid of fighting."
> "I was easily bullied and have never forgiven myself for that."
> "I was more passive and when I was hurt I would show it more."
> "I was called the sissy of the family. I had been very pointedly told I was effemi-nate." (p. 78)

In comparing the results of this investigation to the Bieber study, the radically different points of view of the research groups must be kept in mind. One would have to search diligently to find two studies whose frames of reference were so different (table 3.2). Brief quotations from each study under-score this point:

> This study provides convincing support for a fundamental contribution by Rado on the subject of male homosexuality: A homosexual adaptation is a result of "hidden but incapacitating fears of the opposite sex." (Bieber et al. 1962, p. 303)
>
> We assume that homosexuality is a pathological condition, and our data strongly support this assumption. (Ibid., p. 305)

> As for homosexuals' social and psychological adjustment, we have found that much depends upon the type of homosexual being considered. Many could very well serve as models of social comportment and psychological maturity. Most are indistinguishable from the heterosexual majority with respect to most of the nonsexual aspects of their lives. (Bell & Weinberg 1978, p. 230)
>
> Perhaps the least ambiguous findings of our investigation is that homosex-uality is not necessarily related to pathology. (Ibid., p. 231)

TABLE 3.2 Differences in Two Studies of Homosexuality

	Bieber et al. (1962)	Bell et al. (1978, 1981)
Site of study	New York area	San Francisco Bay area
Homosexual participants	Patients in psychotherapy and psychoanalysis	Nonpatients recruited from numerous places
Heterosexual participants	Patients in psychotherapy and psychoanalysis	Nonpatients randomly selected
Interviewers	Medical psychoanalysts	Mostly graduate students
Principal investigators	Medical psychoanalysts	Psychologists and sociologists
Method of data collection and documentation	Psychoanalysts collected data in the psychoanalytic and psychotherapeutic situation. Database consisted of analysts who filled out questionnaires constructed by a research committee	Interviewers used a detailed structured interview to collect data from homosexual and heterosexual subjects. Interviewers were trained and data collection was highly supervised
Theoretic orientation of investigators	Investigators believed that homosexuality is a form of psychopathology motivated by unconscious anxiety about heterosexuality	Investigators did not view homosexuality as a form of psychopathology

Homosexuals do not bypass heterosexuals' developmental phases and all remain potentially heterosexual. . . .

We are firmly convinced that psychoanalysts may well orient themselves to a heterosexual objective in treating homosexual patients rather than "adjust" even the more recalcitrant patient to a homosexual destiny. A conviction based on scientific fact that a heterosexual goal is achievable helps both patient and psychoanalyst to take in stride the inevitable setbacks during psychoanalysis. (Bieber et al. 1962, p. 319)

Exclusive homosexuality seemed to be something that was firmly established by the end of adolescence and relatively impervious to change or modification by outside influences. . . . To therapists we would suggest that exclusive homosexuality is so deeply ingrained that one should not attempt or expect to change it. (Bell, Weinberg & Hammersmith 1981, p. 211)

Bell, Weinberg and Hammersmith (1981) strongly criticized the impact of psychoanalytic theory on homosexual patients who have received psychotherapy.

> In view of our findings we question whether psychoanalytic theory can be considered very useful in understanding male homosexuality even among men in clinical samples. . . . therapists may teach their homosexual clients to see or interpret their family backgrounds in ways that are consistent with the therapists' particular theoretical perspective. (p. 210).

Given the radically different perspectives of the two sets of investigators, it is especially striking that the findings of both studies were in basic agreement with regard to childhood gender identity / gender role abnormalities in prehomosexual children.

SAGHIR AND ROBINS (1973)

These researchers were descriptive psychiatrists who interviewed nonpatient volunteers. They did not consider homosexuality to be psychopathological and had no model of etiology prior to data collection; that is, Saghir and Robins had no particular views about the relation between unconscious conflict and homosexuality, developmental fixations and homosexuality, and so on.

> In approaching systematically non-patient groups of homosexual men and women, we did not set out to prove an *a priori* hypothesis since we did not consciously take definitive stands on homosexuality. We felt neutral emotionally, believing that our task was to increase knowledge and promote scientific objectivity in an area where data were often lacking and preconceived notions frequently prejudiced and misleading. To avoid some of the trappings in previous research on homosexuality, we restricted ourselves to description and analysis within the limits of the available data. (Saghir & Robins 1973, pp. 3–4)

The homosexual subjects for their study were primarily recruited from homophile organizations in Chicago and San Francisco. Some additional subjects were referred to the study by friends or were recruited at gay bars. Of 104 males initially recruited, 15 were eliminated from the study because of past histories of psychiatric hospitalization. Heterosexual subjects were obtained from sampling within a large apartment complex in St. Louis County. The investigators attempted to match the groups for marital status, age, socioeconomic class, and religion. The criteria for inclusion in the homosexual sample were "self report of homosexual orientation and a history of repetitive overt homosexual activity continuing beyond the age of 18" (p. 6). The criteria for inclusion in the heterosexual sample were "similar to those applied to the homosexuals except that sexual psychologic preference and behavior had to be exclusively heterosexual after the age of 18. Furthermore, the subjects had to be single. If divorced, separated or widowed the duration of such a marital state must have existed for at least two years" (p. 7). Out of 40 declared heterosexual men interviewed, 35 were included in the study. Four of these men were excluded for being homosexual and one for being bisexual.

All subjects participated in a structured interview. The approach used to assess psychopathology was in keeping with the criteria-based, categorical method developed at Washington University.

> In evaluating the extent and nature of psychopathology among the homosexual men and women, we decided to limit ourselves to past and present manifest pathology. We are not interested in assessing an ideal state of mental health, but in determining the degree of symptomatic dysfunction. Consequently we geared our psychiatric assessment mostly to the evaluation of well-studied psychiatric disorders with adequate data on clinical manifestations and natural history. (p. 8)

In discussing sampling, the authors asserted that truly representative samples of homosexual people are impossible to obtain because the contemporary social climate of prejudice leads many individuals to keep their homosexuality secret. Obviously, studies must be confined to those individuals who come forward. Saghir and Robins observed, however, that their homosexual subjects were by and large highly functional and exhibited "some adjustment to their homosexuality and to the world at large." They hoped that "studying such a sample would counteract to a large extent the charges that psychiatrists in their prejudice against homosexual(s) study only the 'sick' homosexuals and subsequently generalize to the homosexual at large" (p. 16).

The investigators did not distinguish in terms of categorical assignment between childhood effeminacy and unmasculinity. They found dramatic differences between groups in what they termed "sissiness." Thus 67 percent of the homosexual men, in contrast with 3 percent of heterosexual subjects, were considered sissies during childhood and early adolescence. Most of the pre-homosexual youngsters were considered sissies because they had no male buddies, played mostly with girls, and did not participate in sports. The authors were impressed with the subjects' reports of their anguish as children who were teased mercilessly by peers; rejected by members of their family, particularly males; and chronically lonely. They quoted their subjects:

> I was always bony, and my dad used to belittle me, calling me "scrawny," as if saying, how could I be stuck with such a freak. I was the reverse of what he expected. In school I was called "needle," "pin," "pipsqueak" because of my high pitched voice. . . .

> My whole childhood was one of being teased. My older brother made life miserable for me. I was a sissy and a mama's boy. This went on through grade school and high school. I never competed with kids and I had to learn to adapt to kids in other ways. I got along with schoolmates until the time of playing ball and then I

avoided it to avoid being called sissy. I was terribly embarrassed in physical competition. (p. 20)

Of the homosexual group as a whole, although 67 percent had been considered sissies, only 27 percent had had repetitive, persistent desires to be female. In most cases, these desires started prior to age ten and disappeared prior to age twenty. However, 22 percent of those who had wished as children to be female continued to experience these wishes as adults. Of these an extremely small minority actually considered surgical change of sex. Only 3 percent of the heterosexual group reported that they had longed to be female during childhood. Of the homosexual men, 16 percent—in comparison to 3 percent of the heterosexual men—cross-dressed during childhood on several occasions.

It is reasonable to place the incidence of childhood effeminacy among homosexuals in this study as somewhere between the 16 percent who reported repetitive cross-dressing and the 27 percent who reported the desire to be female. This frequency is similar to the figure reported by the Bieber study of 25 percent incidence of childhood effeminacy in the homosexual sample. The overall incidence of sissiness found by Saghir and Robins, 67 percent, is only slightly lower than the frequency of specific gender role abnormalities reported by Bieber (see table 3.1). Saghir and Robins asked their subjects to assess themselves on a three-point scale regarding (present) masculinity/femininity. Of the subjects, 25 percent considered themselves definitely feminine. An additional 14 percent did not consider themselves adequately masculine. No heterosexual men considered themselves feminine, and only one thought of himself as neuter. The interviewers found effeminacy—judged in terms of gestures, use of makeup, voice, and walk—to be present in 16 percent of the homosexual men (all of whom described themselves as feminine) and in none of the heterosexual group. The investigators concluded that "more homosexual than heterosexual men as children and adults display cross-gender behavior. However, only a minority of them exhibit such behavior in adulthood, and the behavior of the majority is consistent with appropriate masculine conduct" (p. 107). They noted that they probably underdiagnosed present effeminacy somewhat since they judged it to exist only when it was clearly obvious. The incidence of (current) effeminacy they observed was similar to the figures obtained by Bieber. Saghir and Robins found other types of psychopathology to occur with similar frequency in both homosexual and heterosexual groups. This was true of both lifetime and present prevalence of psychiatric disorder.

The study carried out by Saghir and Robins used nonpatient groups, structured interviews, and strict criteria for making diagnoses. The investigators were not psychoanalysts and specifically renounced psychoanalytic assumptions about homosexuality. The results of this investigation are compatible with the other studies discussed with regard to the association between gender identity / gender role abnormalities and male homosexuality.

TABLE 3.3 Number of Respondents in Four Samples
of Heterosexual and Homosexual Men

	Heterosexual	Homosexual
United States	58	36
Guatemala	40	62
Brazil	16	23
Philippines	34	30

Source: Whitam & Zent 1984

WHITAM AND ZENT (1984)

Whitam and Zent are sociologists who interviewed nonclinical groups of male homosexuals in the United States, Guatemala, Brazil, and the Philippines. Childhood behavior investigated included doll play, cross-dressing, being regarded as a sissy, play preference for girls, and preference for the company of adult females. The results were dramatic: significant differences in childhood cross-gender behavior were found between homosexual and heterosexual men in all four countries for each item assessed (tables 3.3 and 3.4). The investigators noted that the countries selected for investigation differed with regard to attitudes and values about homosexuality. The United States was considered the most hostile and repressive, the Latin countries relatively tolerant, and the Philippines the most tolerant. Despite such differences, the same pattern of response occurred in each country. The authors concluded:

> The data suggest that early cross-gender patterns occur in the childhood experiences of homosexuals in each of the four societies, strongly supporting earlier findings that cross-gender behavior is associated with later sexual orientation. This relationship appears regardless of cultural context, and the specific patterns of early cross-gendering are similar in divergent societies. (Whitam & Zent 1984, p. 432)

OTHER STUDIES LINKING CHILDHOOD EFFEMINACY AND HOMOSEXUALITY

The results of the four studies discussed above are in keeping with other retrospective studies carried out by Grellert, Newcomb, and Bentler (1982), Harry (1982, 1983), Henry (1941), Holeman and Winokur (1965), and Zuger (1984), and with all investigations of identical twins of divergent sexual orientation.

These data are also in agreement with ongoing studies of effeminate boys. Recently Green and Zuger independently reported the results of long-term follow-up studies in this area. Green (1985) compared the adult sexual orientation of clinically referred effeminate boys and volunteers matched for age,

TABLE 3.4 Chi-Square Analysis of Differences between Heterosexuals and Homosexuals in Early Cross-gender Behavior

	Significant at .05	Significant at .001	Explanatory note
1. As a child were you interested in dolls, paper dolls, sewing, cooking, etc.?			
American	.05	NS	Homosexuals were interested in dolls
Guatemalan	.05	.001	Homosexuals were interested in dolls
Brazilian	.05	NS	Homosexuals were interested in dolls
Filipino	.05	.001	Homosexuals were interested in dolls
2. As a child did you like to dress in women's clothes, shoes, jewelry, purses?			
American	.05	.001	Homosexuals cross-dressed
Guatemalan	.05	.001	Homosexuals cross-dressed
Brazilian	.05	NS	Homosexuals cross-dressed
Filipino	.05	.001	Homosexuals cross-dressed
3. As a child were you regarded as a sissy?			
American	.05	.001	Homosexuals were regarded as sissies
Guatemalan	.05	.001	Homosexuals were regarded as sissies
Brazilian	.05	.001	Homosexuals were regarded as sissies
Filipino	.05	.001	Homosexuals were regarded as sissies
4. As a child did you prefer play activities with boys or girls?			
American	.05	.001	Homosexuals preferred play with girls
Guatemalan	.05	.001	Homosexuals preferred play with girls
Brazilian	.05	NS	Homosexuals preferred play with girls
Filipino	.05	.001	Homosexuals preferred play with girls
5. As a child did you prefer company of adult males or females?			
American	.05	.001	Homosexuals preferred female company
Guatemalan	.05	.001	Homosexuals preferred female company
Brazilian	.05	NS	Homosexuals preferred female company
Filipino	.05	.001	Homosexuals preferred female company
NS = Not significant			

Source: Whitam & Zent 1984

gender, sibling sequence, and a number of other variables. The mean age of the boys when first seen was seven and a half, and many were in late adolescence or early adulthood at follow-up. None of the comparison subjects was bisexually or homosexually oriented; 68 percent of the gender-disordered children were. Of the effeminate boys, 43 percent were felt to be predominately or exclusively homosexual (a Kinsey scale rating of 5–6) (see table 3.5). The association between effeminacy and homosexuality in Green's sample will probably turn out to be even stronger than initially reported, since at the time of follow-up a number of the effeminate boys were still in early adolescence, had not engaged in sexual activity with others, and apparently did not experience homosexual

TABLE 3.5 Ages at First Evaluation and Follow-up Sexual Orientation Scores of Forty-Four Males Who Manifested Extensive Cross-Gender Behavior during Boyhood

	Age (years)		Sexual Orientation Score	
Subject	First evaluation	Follow-up	Fantasy	Behavior
1	8	18	0	–
2	7	13	0	–
3	10	19	0	0
4	4	14	0	–
5	9	22	2	2
6	8	20	6	6
7	10	21	5	5
8	7	14	0	–
9	6	19	5	4
10	5	15	0	–
11	6	17	6	–
12	8	17	2	–
13	5	15	1	–
14	7	21	5	5
15	10	23	6	6
16	7	16	1	0
17	4	16	5	–
18	4	16	5	4
19	8	21	2	2
20	6	18	0	–
21	6	20	6	6
22	8	18	4	–
23	10	20	5	5
24	10	20	6	6
25	7	16	0	0
26	8	19	6	6
27	6	20	2	6
28	6	23	4	–
29	5	14	0	1
30	6	18	6	4
31	8	20	4	4
32	5	18	0	0
33	7	18	5	6
34	10	21	4	3
35	6	19	5	4
36	10	22	4	4
37	7	21	6	6
38	5	17	0	0
39	4	18	4	–
40	5	14	0	–

Table 3.5 continued

Subject	Age (years)		Sexual Orientation Score	
	First evaluation	Follow-up	Fantasy	Behavior
41	8	21	5	5
42	10	21	5	5
43	8	20	4	4
44	5	19	5	5

Note: Age range: 13–23
Source: Green 1985

fantasies. Future follow-up of these youngsters might well reveal that a sub-stantial number become predominately or exclusively homosexual. Green also observed that twelve of the effeminate boys had received extensive therapy during the course of the study. He reported, "the rates of bisexual/homosexual orientation in the treated group were comparable to that of the entire group" (p. 341).

Zuger (1984) reported on a long-term follow-up of fifty-five effeminate boys seen in private practice. Effeminacy in this sample was generally noted by families prior to age six. Most patients were seen from early childhood; seven cases were lost to follow-up. Of the remainder, 72.9 percent were homosexual, 6.3 percent heterosexual, and 20.8 percent of uncertain sexual orientation. (The uncertain cases consisted of three children too young to warrant a definite assignment to a sexual orientation category and seven others who provided sparse data.) Interestingly, Zuger too reported that many of the effeminate boys who became homosexual had had psychiatric treatment. Zuger hypoth-esized that childhood effeminacy is congenital and antedates all male homosex-uality.

Money and Russo (1979) followed five effeminate boys into adulthood. All became homosexual. Bakwin (1968) reported on ten additional cases and found homosexuality in six of them. Zuger (1984) pointed out that in this study three of the other cases depended exclusively on the mother's judgment. If these cases are considered uncertain and excluded from data analysis, six of seven, or 86 percent of this sample, turned out to be homosexual.

The combined results of numerous investigations lead to the conclusion that childhood gender identity / gender role disturbances are associated with predominant or exclusive homosexuality in adulthood. Absence of such distur-bance diminishes the likelihood that a boy will become a man who is ex-clusively or predominately homosexual. This does not mean that homosex-uality invariably results from such disturbances or that predominant or exclusive homosexuality invariably begins with them. Behavioral variability is the rule in psychobiology, particularly aspects of behavior that involve human sexuality. In the field of sex differences in behavior, for example, the differences alluded to are usually between statistical means for a specified behavior, with substantial overlap between groups. It should come as no surprise, therefore, that effeminate heterosexuality exists (although its existence does pose a problem for theoreticians). But an association as powerful from the statistical and scientific point of view as that between childhood gender identity disturbance and adult homosexuality must command the attention of clinicians and theoreticians alike. The distinction between past and present is important to emphasize in this regard. Freud was well aware of a fact that now seems obvious, namely, that a great many men who are predominately or exclusively homosexual are entirely masculine by the usual definitions. The ways the apparently contradictory data about childhood and adulthood can be interpreted will be discussed in parts 2–4, which deal with psychopathology and development.

4

Freud's *Three Essays* Revisited

Theories of biological influences on the etiology of homosexuality were common in the nineteenth century. Sulloway, in *Freud, Biologist of the Mind* (1979), notes that some of these included the idea that the male brain somehow developed in a female-like manner. Freud critically reviewed the available biological data about sexual behavior; however, after his death there was a great accretion of knowledge about the behavioral consequences of prenatal steroid hormone effects on the brain. These consequences involve both non-sexual and sexual behavior and are relevant for understanding sex differences in behavior as well as sexual orientation. Abundant knowledge about gender identity has also accumulated since Freud's death. Advances in psychobiology and in aspects of developmental psychology involving gender identity / gender role have made some of Freud's views obsolete. In this chapter I review some of Freud's ideas in light of the material presented in chapters 2–3. Concepts expressed in Freud's *Three Essays on the Theory of Sexuality* (1905/1953) will be used to illustrate a few key issues in the history of psychoanalytic thought about homosexuality.

FREUD'S VIEW OF PSYCHOENDOCRINOLOGY

Early in the *Three Essays* Freud summarized a theory of central nervous system influence on gender-related behavior. This nineteenth-century theory, in some ways similar to contemporary biological theories, was not viewed sympathetically primarily because of a paucity of data available to support it.

> The theory of bisexuality has been expressed in its crudest form by a spokesman of the male inverts: "a feminine brain in a masculine body." But we are ignorant

49

of what characterizes a feminine brain. There is neither need nor justification for replacing the psychological problem by the anatomical one.

. . . According to Krafft-Ebing . . . every individual's bisexual disposition endows him with masculine and feminine brain centres as well as with somatic organs of sex; these centres develop only at puberty, for the most part under the influence of the sex gland, which is independent of them in the original disposition.

. . . We have not even any grounds for assuming that certain areas of the brain ("centres") are set aside for the function of sex as is the case for instance with those of speech. (Freud 1905/1953, pp. 142–43)

Later in the *Three Essays,* Freud returned to a discussion of the importance of the intrauterine phase of life in sexual behavior. He quoted a source published in 1919 which suggested that in homosexual men, the male sex substance responsible for sexual maturation at puberty may have been present in smaller than usual amounts during intrauterine development. Freud cited Ferenczi's puzzlement at the finding that the first peak in "male physiological substance," which apparently occurred during early intrauterine life, did not coincide with the early efflorescence of infantile sexual life, which occurs at ages three and four. This did not disturb Freud: "There is of course no need to expect that anatomical growth and physical development must be exactly simultaneous" (1905/1953, p. 177). Freud noted the powerful effects of physiology on sex determination and sex behavior of animals and on sexual excitement in humans.

It has become experimentally possible . . . to transform a male into a female, and conversely a female into a male. In this process the psychosexual behavior of the animal alters in accordance with the somatic sexual characters and simultaneously with them. It seems, however, that this sex determining influence is not an attribute of that part of the sex-glands which gives rise to the specific sex cells (spermatozoa and ovum) but of their interstitial tissue upon which special emphasis is laid by being described in the literature as the "puberty gland." It is quite possible that further investigation will show that this puberty-gland has normally a hermaphrodite disposition. If this were so the theory of the bisexuality of the higher animals would be given anatomical foundation.

. . . It seems probable then that special chemical substances are produced in the interstitial portion of the sex glands; these are then taken up in the blood stream and cause particular parts of the central nervous system to be charged with sexual tension. (p. 215)

By the "puberty gland," Freud seems to have referred to the testes. Freud realized therefore that the feeling of sexual excitement was influenced by a chemical substance, which we know today to be testosterone. He also knew that this substance was somehow involved in determining the sex of an animal. But these quotations illustrate how far Freud was from fully appreciating modern concepts of chromosomal, gonadal, hormonal, and morphological sex and central nervous system sexual dimorphism. He was not aware of the effect of sex steroid hormone on the brain during prenatal life or of its resulting influences on erotic and nonerotic behavior in humans. Without such knowledge, Freud could not adequately conceptualize sex differences in development or psychosexual development. (The relation of these issues to the etiology of homosexuality is discussed in chapter 2.)

FREUD'S VIEW OF GENDER IDENTITY AND GENDER ROLE

In discussing "the differentiation between men and women," Freud alluded to the limitations of the gender psychology of his time: "It is essential to understand clearly that the concepts of 'masculine' and 'feminine' whose meaning seems unambiguous to ordinary people are among the most confused that occur in science" (1905/1953, p. 219). These terms, he observed, sometimes connoted "activity" and "passivity," sometimes indicated biological sex, and sometimes referred to masculine and feminine traits. The first usage was in Freud's view the most important for psychoanalytic theory.

Although apparently aware of distinctions between gender-related behavior and sexual behavior (i.e., active–passive, masculine–feminine, and heterosexual–homosexual), Freud lacked specific terminology to express the distinctions. He thus condensed gender-related behavior and sexual behavior in his writings. This condensation reflected not only a lack of terminology but a way of thinking as well (i.e., one equating passivity, femininity, and homosexuality). Many psychoanalysts have retained Freud's condensed way of thinking about sex and gender, particularly with regard to psychodynamic aspects of male homosexuality.

Freud's rudimentary understanding of gender-related behavior imposed considerable limitations on his theories. For example, immediately after outlining the libido theory he made an astonishing comment about behavioral dimorphism: "As we all know it is not until puberty that the sharp distinction is established between the masculine and feminine characters. From that time on, this contrast has a more decisive influence than any other upon the shaping of human life" (1905/1953, p. 219). This quotation illustrates Freud's fondness for the idea of masculine and feminine character, an idea which has subsequently been confused with masculine and feminine characteristics and male and female characteristics. Moreover, today we know that behavioral dimorphism begins before puberty. In addition, Freud's model that associates the "feminine character" with female sexual development has been amply criticized (e.g., Sherfey 1966; Fisher 1973). The concepts of masculinity and femininity as applied to characterology have probably influenced the erroneous view assumed by some that all homosexual individuals (however defined) have abnormal character structures.

The major limitations of Freud's views about homosexuality resulted from insufficient appreciation of prenatal psychoendocrine influences, insufficient distinction between gender-related behavior and sexual behavior, and lack of knowledge about the timing of development of sex differences in behavior. In these three areas a great expansion of knowledge occurred after Freud's death.

Freud's belief that he could make generalizations about large areas of behavior from data obtained in the psychoanalytic situation led to further problems with his theories of homosexuality. Given the state of scientific knowledge in his time it is understandable that Freud should have been enthusiastic about this application of the new psychoanalytic technique. But Freud's progressive interest in general principles of mental functioning as observed in the psychoanalytic situation caused inconsistencies in his views about homosexuality. In the *Three Essays*, much of the writing, particularly in the early editions, is scientific in tone. When he reported insights about homosexuality garnered by means of the psychoanalytic method, Freud's tone changed, and a medical-pathological model of homosexuality emerged.

Freud's scientific approach to homosexuality is clear in his discussion of "inversion." Freud defined an "invert" as a man or woman whose sexual objects were members of the same sex. Although reliable estimates were not available, such people were thought to be numerous. Freud proposed three major subdivisions of inversion: absolute or exclusive; amphigenic, or attracted to both sexes; and contingent, primarily attracted to the opposite sex but in certain situations able to derive sexual satisfaction from members of the same sex. Having put forth these basic definitions, Freud proposed a criterion, later used in *DSM-III*, for identifying so-called pathological homosexuality: he noted that inverts varied in their acceptance of their sexual desires. Some viewed inversion as compatible with their attitudes, values, and self-concepts, while others felt that they suffered from a "pathological compulsion." (Unlike *DSM-III*, however, Freud did not suggest that one group was in some way healthier than the other.) Freud observed that inversion may begin from the earliest memory or at any point thereafter; that it may be constant or variable; that traumatic interactions with the opposite sex might influence variability; and that a homosexual-heterosexual continuum seemed to exist: "though the distinctions cannot be disputed," he noted, "it is impossible to overlook the existence of numerous intermediate examples of every type so that we are driven to conclude that we are dealing with a connected series" (Freud 1905/1953, p. 138).

Freud stated as a simple matter of fact that not only were inverts frequently normal in other ways, but that they included some of the most creative contributors to society throughout history. The concept of "degeneracy" as a cause of illness, in vogue in the nineteenth century, was dismissed as a possible cause of inversion. Freud's discussion of the influence of nature and nurture in the etiology of inversion has stood up well and attests to his stubborn refusal to frame concepts in terms of simple dichotomous categories such as biological and psychological. For example, Freud presented as the major argument that inversion is acquired the fact that certain types of life experience were routinely found in the backgrounds of inverts. But his counter-argument speaks for itself:

> The apparent certainty of this conclusion is, however, completely countered by the reflection that many people are subjected to the same sexual influences (e.g., to seduction or mutual masturbation, which may occur in early youth) without becoming inverted or without remaining so permanently. We are therefore forced to a suspicion that the choice between "innate" and "acquired" is not an exclusive one or that it does not cover all the issues involved in inversion. (1905/1953, p. 140)

As Freud acquired more experience with psychoanalysis, however, he tended to justify his assertions about scientific matters not only on the basis of superior insight but also because he and his colleagues were using a method of treatment and research that no one else had access to. At times, the complex and evolving psychoanalytic method was treated as if it were an invention like the microscope or the light bulb. The "discoveries" of psychoanalytic research were reported in the form of "conclusions" based on personal observation. Many of these were formulated after the first edition of the *Three Essays* was published, and they account for contradictions about inversion in the final (and generally accepted) edition. For example, Freud stressed that inversion is not necessarily associated with impairment of character. However, the psychoanalytic method suggested that "in inverted types predominance of archaic constitutions and primitive psychical mechanisms is regularly to be found" (p. 146).

Freud dispassionately discussed the anus as a sexual organ (disavowing partisanship in his inimitable way):

> Where the anus is concerned, it becomes still clearer that it is disgust which stamps the sexual aim as perversion. I hope however I shall not be accused of partisanship when I assert that people who try to account for this disgust by saying that the organ in question serves the function of excretion and comes in contact with excrement—a thing which is disgusting in itself—are not much more to the point than hysterical girls who account for their disgust at the male genitals by saying that it serves to void urine.
>
> The playing of a sexual part by the mucous membrane of the anus is by no means limited to intercourse between men: preference for it is in no way characteristic of inverted feeling. On the contrary it seems that paedecatio with a male owes its origin to an analogy with a similar act performed with a woman: while mutual masturbation is the sexual aim most often found in intercourse between inverts. (p. 152)

Freud's psychoanalytic experience, however, suggested that among the most "essential characteristics" of primitive mental mechanisms found in inverts is "retention of the erotic significance of the anal zone" (p. 146). Psychoanalysis also allegedly discovered that unconscious fears of heterosexuality are frequently present in inverts: "Their compulsive longing for men has turned out to be determined by their ceaseless flight from women" (p. 145).

In every case of inversion examined via psychoanalysis, the same developmental pathway was found, characterized by identification with a woman and the taking of oneself as a sexual object. This narcissistic mechanism led the patient to search for a young man resembling the perceived self to be loved as the mother loved the prehomosexual child. Freud also asserted that psychoanalysis indicated that unconscious homosexual object choice is universal.

> Psychoneuroses are also very often associated with manifest inversion. In such cases the heterosexual current of feeling has undergone complete suppression. It is only fair to say that my attention was drawn to the necessary universality of the tendency to inversion in psychoneurotics by Wilhelm Fliess . . . after I had discussed its presence in individual cases. This fact, which has not been sufficiently appreciated, cannot fail to have a decisive influence on any theory of homosexuality. (p. 166)

It is clear from the material quoted above that Freud's view of homosexuality and homosexual individuals was inconsistent. On the one hand, he presented a scientific overview compatible in tone with his well-known letter to the mother of a homosexual man (1935/1981) and with his belief that homosexuality should not prevent one from becoming a psychoanalyst (1921/1980). On the other hand, he stressed homosexual patients' "primitive" mental mechanisms.

Of course, Freud also felt that women were more primitive and more prone to psychopathology than men. In the *Three Essays,* for example, he made the following comments about female sexual development and about the relationship between femininity and psychopathology:

> When at last the sexual act is permitted and the clitoris itself becomes excited it still retains a function: the task, namely, of transmitting the excitation to the adjacent female sexual parts just as—to use a simile—pine shaving can be kindled in order to set a log of harder wood on fire. . . .
>
> When erotogenic susceptibility to stimulation has been successfully transferred by a woman from the clitoris to the vaginal orifice, it implies that she has adopted a new leading zone for the purpose of her later sexual activity; a man on the other hand retains his leading zone unchanged from childhood. The fact that women change their leading erotogenic zone in this way, together with the wave of repression at puberty, which, as it were, puts aside their childish masculinity, are the chief determinants of the greater proneness of women to neurosis and especially to hysteria. These determinants therefore are intimately related to the essence of femininity. (1905/1953, p. 221)

Freud's homosexual patients may have been unusually disturbed and primitive. But it also seems possible that Freud's reaction to them was influenced by the same Victorian world view that severely limited his understanding of females. To the degree that Freud consciously and unconsciously believed that male homosexuals were like women, he may have been particularly likely to interpret their mental mechanisms as primitive.

Freud's claims about the numerous discoveries made using the psychoanalytic method exerted great influence on subsequent analysts' views of homosexuality. The psychoanalytic literature is replete with clinical vignettes confirming Freud's findings about homosexuality reported in the *Three Essays*. The fact that Freud's views were inconsistent has received less emphasis.

A COMMENT ON FREUD'S WRITING STYLE

Perhaps equally influential on psychoanalytic thought as Freud's observations about homosexuality was his writing style. At times his literary genius appeared to dominate his scientific genius, blurring the distinctions between assertion, observation, inference, and hypothesis. Given the power of Freud's style it is easy to see why so many of his opinions have been accepted as if they were facts.

I offer here a few examples of incorrect assertions in the *Three Essays*, not only to illustrate how far we have moved beyond some of Freud's notions, but also to convey a sense of the restless energy of his mind. The emphasis in these passages is mine:

> At this point we must also mention the production of sexual excitation by rhythmic mechanical agitation of the body. . . . The existence of these pleasurable sensations—and it is worth emphasizing the fact that in this connection the concepts of "sexual excitation" and "satisfaction" can to a great extent be used without distinction, a circumstance we must later endeavor to explain . . . is *confirmed by the fact* that children are so fond of games of passive movement such as swinging and being thrown up into the air, and insist on such games being incessantly repeated. Some people can remember that in swinging they felt the impact of moving air upon their genitals as an immediate sexual pleasure. (p. 201)

> *It is only* children with a sexual instinct that is excessive, or has developed prematurely, or has become vociferous owing to too much petting, who are inclined to be timid. (p. 224)

> One such factor is spontaneous sexual precocity, whose presence at least *can be demonstrated with certainty* in the aetiology of the neuroses, though, like other factors, it is not in itself a sufficient cause. (p. 240)

One wonders whether the style with which Freud expressed clinical observations and inferences exerted as great an influence on psychoanalytic thought as the clinical insights themselves.

The preceding chapters illustrate the necessity to evaluate continuously the relevance of new findings toward a theory of sexual orientation. A contemporary psychoanalytic reevaluation of models and mechanisms in male homosexuality is an important component of the need to update psychoanalytic theory generally. The state of tension between large theories and newly emergent knowledge is an integral part of the scientific process and has traditionally been found in all areas of science and medicine.

5

The Role of the Family
in the Etiology
of Homosexuality

Research described in chapters 2–3 suggests that childhood gender identity / gender role disturbances are associated with and probably predispose to predominant or exclusive homosexuality in men. The etiological importance of pathognomonic familial interactions, on the other hand, has not been definitively established. Although many studies suggest that certain types of familial interactions lead to homosexuality (Bieber et al. 1962; Van Den Aardweg 1984), other investigations have not found this to be the case (Bell, Weinberg & Hammersmith 1981; Siegelman 1981). I provide here a critical overview of the family literature with emphasis on its relevance for psychodynamically oriented clinicians. All the studies are of males unless otherwise stated.

Psychoanalytic theoreticians originally implicated mother fixation as a key mechanism in the etiology of homosexuality and observed that such fixation usually occurred as a consequence of an excessively close mother–son relationship and a distant father–son relationship (Fenichel 1945). The idea that this family pattern leads to homosexuality has acquired substantial empirical support in studies carried out since the 1930s. In 1936 Terman and Miles found this protypical family pattern in the backgrounds of 77 homosexual men. Subsequently Jonas (1944) reported similar findings in 60 homosexual surgical patients in comparison to controls, Miller in 50 effeminate homosexual prisoners (1958), and Westwood in a significant proportion of 127 homosexual volunteers from the community (1952, 1960).

In 1959 West reported an elegantly designed medical records study which tested the hypothesis that case histories of homosexual male neurotic patients, when contrasted with those of comparable heterosexual patients, would more often indicate unsatisfactory father–son and excessively intense mother–son relationships in childhood. The homosexual and control groups, matched for age and diagnosis, were neurotic inpatients at Maudsley–Bethlehem Joint Hospital. Abstracts of family histories were prepared that included no material identifying subjects as homosexual or heterosexual. The quality of the mother–son and father–son relationships were blindly rated on a four-point scale. Detailed criteria were given for assessing both relationships. Two raters independently scored the records, but their scores were highly correlated so that one score could be used for the entire sample.

A dramatic difference was found between the homosexual and control groups that supported the investigators' hypothesis. The homosexual men significantly more frequently than the heterosexual men had overintense mother–son relationships and unsatisfactory father–son relationships. West emphasized that this *combination* of parental relationships characterized the homosexual men in comparison to the heterosexual men. He mentioned the limitations of case record research but pointed out that his study was designed to exclude the effects of bias on investigators or judges. West did not advance a theory to explain the differences between homosexual and heterosexual groups, but he observed that a variety of mechanisms could lead to the familial pattern described.

West's study was followed by the ambitious and influential project carried out by Bieber and colleagues (1962; see chapter 3). The significant items in the mother–son relationship that distinguished homosexual patients from comparison patients are listed in table 5.1. A characteristic type of mother–son interaction was more commonly reported in the childhoods of homosexual men than heterosexual: the mothers of homosexual boys appeared to be more closely involved with their sons, more anxiously overcontrolling, and more discouraging of autonomy. But key items found in the family backgrounds of homosexual men were also frequently present in the heterosexual controls. The few items that were infrequent in heterosexual men's backgrounds were also present in a relatively small percentage of homosexual patients. For example, 16 percent of the mothers of heterosexual boys discouraged masculine activities and attitudes, and only 37 percent of the mothers of homosexual boys did. A *majority* of mothers of homosexual patients, therefore, apparently did *not* overtly discourage masculine activities. Whereas a small minority of mothers of heterosexual men (11%) encouraged feminine activities and attitudes, a relatively small minority of mothers of homosexual men did as well (35%). All in all, although the data about the mothers of homosexual men do appear to tell a story of anxious overinvolvement, the overlap between homosexual and heterosexual groups was considerable.

The significant items in the father–son relationship that distinguished homosexual patients from comparison patients are presented in table 5.2. Once again, the theme of a protypical negative father–son relationship in the backgrounds of the homosexual men emerges. Once again, however, overlap be-

TABLE 5.1 Significant Items Regarding Mother-Son Relationships Which Distinguish Homosexuals from Comparisons (in percent)

		Answered Yes	
	N =	H 106	C 100
1. Sibling preference: Was patient mother's favorite[a]?		66	50*
2. Did mother demand to be the prime center of the patient's attentions?		61	36†
3. Was she dominating?		81	65*
4. Was she seductive?		57	34*
5. Amount of contact (time spent between mother and patient):			
(a) Great deal		56	27†
(b) Average		20	53
(c) Little		15	11
(d) Very little		7	9
(e) Absent		2	0
6. Did mother encourage masculine activities and attitudes?		17	47†
7. Did mother discourage masculine activities and attitudes?		37	16**
8. Did mother encourage feminine activities and attitudes?		35	11†
9. Was mother considered to be puritanical?		62	48*
10. Was mother considered to be sexually frigid?		64	47**
11. Did mother try to ally with son against husband?		62	40**
12. Did mother openly prefer patient to husband?		58	38**
13. Did mother want patient to grow up to be like some particular individual?		26	27
(a) Like mother?		6	0*
(b) If male, was he a virile male?		9	21*
14. Were there families with other male siblings?		64	63
15. If yes, was mother, as compared to other siblings[b]:			
(a) More intimate with patient?		56	29*
16. Does analyst believe mother interfered with patient's heterosexual activity?		58	35**
17. Was patient the mother's confidant?		52	36*
18. Was mother the patient's confidante?		39	23*
19[c]. Was mother *unduly* concerned about protecting the patient from physical injury?		58	39*
20. Did mother's concern about health or injury cause her to interfere with or restrict his play, social or other activities?		49	26†
21. Does the patient consider his mother to have been overprotective?		61	46*

(*continued*)

Table 5.1 continued

	Answered Yes	
	H	C
N =	106	100
22. Does analyst consider patient's mother to have been overprotective?	67	43**
23. In childhood, was the patient *excessively* dependent on his mother for advice or direction in making decisions?	64	42**
24. Does patient feel his mother "babied" him?	61	41**
25. Did mother administer frequent enemas?	15	4*
26. Which parent does the patient feel he could cope with more easily? Mother?	64	48**
27. Did patient use the technique of rebellion to cope with mother?	9	23*

aBased on number of families in which patient had siblings.

bBased on number of families in which patient had male siblings.

cQuestions 19–27 were derived from equal samples of 96 homosexuals and comparisons. These questions were on the Third (Second Supplementary) Questionnaire and there was no Third Questionnaire for 10 homosexual cases (106 − 10 = 96) and 4 comparison cases (100 − 4 = 96).

*.05 level of significance

**.01 level of significance

†.001 level of significance

Source: Bieber et al. 1962

tween the two groups is marked. For example, of heterosexual comparison subjects, 24 percent were their father's least favored child; only 47 percent felt accepted by their fathers (thus, presumably 53 percent did not); 60 percent experienced father absence, and 37 percent hated their fathers. Only 51 percent of these patients remembered their fathers expressing affection for them and only 50 percent felt that they were currently respected by their fathers.

In the introduction to their monograph, Bieber and colleagues emphasized that it would be simplistic to incriminate one particular type of parent interaction (i.e., overprotective mothers or detached fathers) in the etiology of male homosexuality. The data suggested instead that a particular *constellation* of mother–father–son interactions appeared to be influential. A "triangular family system," in their view, led to homosexuality:

> The "classical" homosexual triangular pattern is one where the mother is CBI (i.e., Close Binding Intimate) and is dominant and minimizing toward a husband who is a detached father, particularly a hostile-detached one. From our statistical analysis, the chances appear to be high that any son exposed to this parental combination will become homosexual or develop homosexual problems. (p. 172)

TABLE 5.2 Items Distinguishing Fathers of Homosexual
and Control Groups (in percent)

	H	C
N =	106	100
1. Patient is father's favorite[a]	7	28†
2. Another sibling is father's favorite[a]	59	36**
3. Patient is least favored child[a]	44	24**
4. Patient felt accepted by father	23	47**
5. Time spent with patient:		
little, very little, father absent	87	60†
6. Father encouraged masculine attitudes	45	60*
7. Patient knowingly hated father	60	37†
8. Patient both hated and feared father	57	31†
9. Patient respected father	28	48**
10. Patient accepted father	20	50†
11. Father expressed affection for patient	25	51**
12. Father had less respect for patient than for other male		
siblings[b]	42	19*
13[c]. Patient sided with father in parental arguments:		
in childhood	7	23**
in adolescence	11	25*
14. Patient coped with father more easily than with mother	21	40**
15. Technique for coping with father: rebellion	8	20*
16. Patient feared his assertiveness would:		
anger father	76	55**
hurt father	7	18*
17. Patient feels father considered his needs	6	20**
18. Patient feels currently respected by father	30	50**
19. Patient regards father as admirable	16	47†
20. Patient was excessively dependent on father	7	19*

[a]Based on number of families with siblings
[b]Based on number of families with male siblings
[c]Items 13–20 based on 96 cases
*.05 level of significance
**.01 level of significance
†.001 level of significance
Source: Bieber et al. 1962

Of 206 patients in the total sample, 30 homosexuals and 11 comparisons were reported to have had the combination described above, CBI mother and detached hostile father. Of the 11 comparison patients in this group, information about "homosexual problems" was available in 9 cases, of whom 7 did indeed have such difficulties (i.e., expressions of homosexuality or conflicts about homosexuality that were not sufficient to lead to a homosexual diagnosis). The investigators observed that 76 homosexual males did not have the protypical family pattern in their backgrounds. An important finding, however—which has probably been underemphasized by subsequent researchers—was that some parenting patterns were completely absent in the backgrounds of the homosexual patients: for example, "not remarkable mothers paired with any type of father, or warmly related fathers paired with any type of mother were absent in the nuclear triads of homosexuals" (p. 144).

Bieber and colleagues formulated a developmental model to explain how the interaction between the growing child and his parents could lead to homosexuality. According to this model, there is an unsatisfactory marriage and the father retreats from intimacy with both his wife and the prehomosexual youngster. The mother devalues her husband, idealizes her son, and forms an excessively close bond with him.

> By the time the H-son has reached the preadolescent period, he had suffered a diffuse personality disorder. Maternal over-anxiety about health and injury, restriction of activities normative for the son's age and potential interference with assertive behavior, demasculinizing attitudes and interference with sexuality, interpenetrating with paternal rejection hostility and lack of support, produce an excessively fearful child. Pathologically dependent upon his mother and beset by feelings of inadequacy, impotence and self-contempt, he is reluctant to participate in boyhood activities thought to be physically injurious—usually grossly overestimated. His peer group responds with humiliating name-calling and often with physical attack which timidity tends to invite among children. His fear and shame of self made worse by the derisive reactions of other boys only drives him further away. Thus he is deprived of important empathic interactions which peer groups provide. (p. 316)

The investigation carried out by the Society of Medical Psychoanalysts is subject to criticism on several counts. Most commonly expressed has been objection to the researchers' willingness to make inferences about homosexuality per se based on data collected exclusively from patients in treatment. Churchill (1967) and others observed that the patient population studied by Bieber and colleagues was skewed in a number of ways, including toward psychopathology. In addition, the investigators believed prior to conducting their research that homosexuality was a form of psychopathology resulting from developmental traumata: "All psychoanalytic theories assume that adult homosexuality is psychopathologic and assign differing weights to constitutional and experiential determinants. All agree that the experiential determinants are in the main rooted in childhood, and are primarily related to the family" (p. 18).

The possibility of bias must be considered whenever researchers share a specific theory prior to data collection and interpretation. Furthermore, all psychoanalytic research is subject to the potentially distorting effects of transference and countertransference. Two important ways transference–countertransference phenomena could have influenced results in the Bieber investigation are immediately apparent. First, patients may have consciously or unconsciously sensed their analysts' convictions about the etiology of homosexuality. This could have led them to emphasize aspects of their past histories in keeping with their perception of analysts' expectations. Second, data were collected during psychoanalytic treatment. The psychoanalytic method of free association in a relatively unstructured setting leads to regression and activation of infantile conflicts. Practicing psychoanalysts routinely find that the way patients appear to remember their parents changes during treatment and depends on numerous influences, including recovery of lost memories, insight, and working through of unconscious conflicts. When patients are queried about their parents early in analysis their responses are often different than they might be later. This potentially distorting effect could be studied by comparing changes in responses about parents made by homosexual and heterosexual men during psychoanalysis. This was not done in the Bieber investigation (nor has it been done subsequently). In this research, the effects of retrospective distortion (universally present in retrospective behavioral research) might have been amplified by the effects of transference regression.

Another limitation of retrospective methods is the difficulty of distinguishing cause from effect. This problem is illustrated in the histories of the identical twins divergent for homosexuality and heterosexuality discussed in chapter 2. Both men believed that they had been treated similarly by their father. The heterosexual twin, however, remembered his father as reserved but quietly loving, while the homosexual twin remembered him as withdrawn and coldly detached. Both men recalled many incidents involving their father in which they agreed about the overt behavior but recalled the emotional context differently. For example, their father often came home late, ate dinner quickly, and silently retired to his woodworking shop in the basement. The heterosexual twin approved of this behavior: after he established a home of his own, he too discouraged "idle chatter" at the dinner table and had a woodworking shop in his basement. The homosexual twin disliked his father's activity. As an adult he became a gourmet who relished conversation during leisurely dinners, and he had an aversion to woodworking tools. Both twins recalled that their father encouraged them to join him on occasion. The preheterosexual boy often did so, but the prehomosexual twin rarely did. Later in life he resented the fact that his father appeared unwilling or unable to develop interests closer to his own.

In looking backward at behavioral sequences, one is faced with the proverbial chicken–egg problem. In the case of the twins, it seems impossible to determine who initiated the cycle of mutual rejection and progressive distancing between the homosexual man and his father. The dynamic described by Bieber and colleagues may have been present in this family. But the data are also compatible with the hypothesis that a loving (if somewhat quiet and constricted) father was rejected by one of his sons. That son, later to become a homosexual man, may have had special, even rigid needs that his father, no matter how well intentioned, could not meet because of his own rigidities.

In 1963, Brown reported on 40 airmen who were seen in consultation because of predominant or exclusive homosexuality. Their relationships with their fathers during childhood were universally poor. Furthermore, 30 had the father–son / mother–son family pattern described by Bieber and colleagues. Brown concluded that the triangular family pattern described by Bieber and colleagues was "beyond doubt" related to the development of male homosexuality.

Evans, aware of the problems posed by the Bieber findings, carried out a thoughtfully designed investigation in 1969. Noting that Bieber's data were based on analysts' reconstruction of patients' early development, Evans obtained data directly from subjects. To expand the database beyond patients in psychotherapy, Evans questioned 43 homosexual and 142 heterosexual males who had never sought psychotherapy. The subjects, all from the Los Angeles area, were volunteers in a study of cardiovascular disease. They were similar to those studied by Bieber and colleagues with regard to age, education, occupation, and sibling status. Each subject completed a 27-item questionnaire adapted from the Bieber study. The results were very similar to those obtained by Bieber:

> The homosexuals more often described themselves as frail or clumsy as children and less often as athletic. More of them were fearful of physical injury, avoided physical fights, played with girls and were loners who seldom played baseball and other competitive games. Their mothers more often were considered puritanical, cold toward men, insisted on being the center of the son's attention, made him her confidant, were "seductive" toward him, allied with him against the father, openly preferred him to the father, interfered with his heterosexual activities during adolescence, discouraged masculine attitudes and encouraged feminine ones. The fathers of the homosexuals were retrospectively considered as less likely to encourage masculine attitudes and activities and they spent little time with their fathers, were more often aware of hating him and afraid he might physically harm them, less often were the father's favorite, felt less accepted by him and in turn, less frequently accepted or respected the father. (Evans 1969, p. 130)

Despite the similarity in results, Evans's conclusions about the etiology of homosexuality were much more cautious and ambiguous than those expressed by Bieber and colleagues. Although the scores for several sets of questions were significantly different between groups, there was a good deal of overlap. For example, although the father–son relationships of homosexual men were protypically negative in comparison to heterosexual men's, some homosexual subjects reported good relationships with their fathers and some heterosexual men reported very bad relationships with theirs. The same type of overlap existed with regard to mother–son relationships. In keeping with the findings discussed in chapter 3, Evans found relatively little overlap on questions directed at uncovering childhood gender identity / role difficulties. In discussing his results, Evans stressed the possibility that in some instances "the child's innate characteristics at least partially determined parental reactions and attitudes toward him" (p. 135). Evans claimed that Bieber underemphasized the effect of constitutionally determined traits in children on family interactions. He concluded, "the results of the present study agreed closely, with those obtained by Bieber et al., but they neither supported nor refuted the Bieber conclusions as to causal relationships. The complicated problem of the etiology of homosexuality probably could be more productively investigated with a prospective study" (p. 135).

Apperson and McAdoo followed up on Bieber's (1962) and West's (1959) observations in 1968. In an effort to diminish the confounding effects of global psychopathology, Apperson and McAdoo selected groups who were functioning in the community. Unlike Bieber and colleagues, who studied outpatients, and West, who reported on inpatients, Apperson and McAdoo's subjects were socially adjusted men "maintaining reasonably normal lives." Twenty-two homosexual men were compared to the same number of controls. A scale was used to measure "perception of parent behavior." Marked differences were obtained in perception of the father: the homosexual men perceived their fathers as having been more critical, impatient, and rejecting. Differences between groups regarding the mothers were less striking. The homosexual men reported that their mothers were less restrictive. The data concerning the fathers therefore replicated the Bieber findings, whereas the data about the mothers did not. The authors speculated that the latter difference may have reflected the different populations studied by the two research teams.

Another source of support for the Bieber study's findings came from an investigation reported by Snortum and colleagues in 1969. The researchers converted key questions from the Bieber interview into a form suitable for a self-administered test. The subjects were 46 males being evaluated for possible separation from military service because of homosexuality. They were compared to two control groups of nonpatients: enlisted men in basic training and civilian college students. The results were similar to those described by Bieber with regard to mother–son and father–son relationships (the preadolescent unmasculine self-concept was also found significantly more frequently in the homosexual men's reports). The authors suggested that the "pathological interplay between a close-binding, controlling mother and a rejecting and detached father is not unique to the subculture of sophisticated upper-middle class families who engage psychoanalysts" (p. 763) but is also present in a broader group of homosexual subjects. Despite statistically significant differences on questionnaire items between homosexual and heterosexual groups, there was overlap between groups, as in the Bieber sample.

O'Connor (1964) compared 50 homosexual men in the Royal Air Force to

50 neurotic outpatients. He found that during childhood homosexual men were statistically more likely to have had poor relationships with their fathers and to have turned to their mothers as protypes. Braatan and Darling (1965) reported that, in comparison to heterosexual control subjects, homosexual college students more often described their mothers as having been excessively close and their fathers detached or indifferent. Bene (1965) compared 83 well-adjusted homosexual men to 84 married men recruited from the medical and technical staff of a hospital. The subjects were given a test and a questionnaire designed to assess family relations history. The results were dramatic with regard to the father–son relationship: "far fewer homosexual than married men thought that their fathers had been cheerful, helpful, reliable, kind or understanding while far more felt that their fathers had no time for them, had not loved them and had made them feel unhappy" (p. 805). The results on mothers did not reveal impressive differences. There was a tendency for homosexual men to remember their mothers as nagging and hostile more often than heterosexual subjects. The authors interpreted their findings to mean that homosexual men might be closer to their mothers than to their fathers, *not* because of the intensity of the tie to the mothers but in reaction to a poor relationship with the father. Bene suggested that a pattern including both maternal overindulgence-overprotection and paternal negligence might lead to a type of homosexuality skewed toward the psychopathological side of a hypothetical spectrum.

Thompson and colleagues (1973) compared 127 well-educated white male homosexuals to 123 heterosexual matched controls. Most of the subjects lived in the Atlanta area. A questionnaire derived from Bieber (1962) and Evans (1969) was administered. Aspects of psychological functioning were also assessed. The results regarding family interactions were strikingly similar to those reported by Bieber and colleagues, both for patterns of parent–child interaction and for childhood unmasculinity.

Stephan (1973) carried out a study of antecedents of homosexuality in political activists. The sample consisted of 88 male members of a homophile organization in Minnesota and 105 heterosexual controls, psychology students. Stephan stressed the differences between his sample and Bieber's: for example, whereas 64 percent of the homosexual men in Bieber's sample would have prefered to be heterosexual and 90 percent feared exposure of their homosexuality, only 21 percent of Stephan's sample would have preferred to be heterosexual and 36 percent feared exposure. The results indicated marked differences between heterosexual and homosexual groups compatible with the observations of West (1959) and Bieber (1962). The differences were greater with regard to the father–son relationship than the mother–son relationship. The former was overtly negative for homosexual men in ways described by Bieber. Stephan reported, "on no variable did the homosexuals evaluate their fathers favorably" (p. 509). The mother–son relationship, although problematic for many homosexual men, showed more overlap with heterosexual men. As reported in the Bieber study, during childhood most of the homosexual men were loners and sissies who had predominantly female friends and avoided competitive sports. Stephan concluded that the similarity of his findings to Bieber's suggests that patients' retrospective biases did not influence the Bieber data, since gay activists' biases about homosexuality are opposed to those of psychotherapy patients. "The fact that the results were so similar implied that within the general limitations of the retrospective method the basic structures of the family background and early social experiences of homosexuals may be considered to be fairly well established" (p. 512).

Saghir and Robins (1973) found that the early home environment of the homosexual men in their study was characterized by more discord between the parents and more general stress than was found among heterosexual subjects. The father–son relationship was markedly defective among homosexual in comparison to heterosexual men. Of homosexual men 84 percent (in comparison to 18 percent of controls) reported that their fathers were detached, indifferent, and uninvolved.

> This lack of involvement and interest was not an isolated behavior for the fathers of the homosexual men. It was rather part of a pattern of relative disengagement from the affairs of the family.
>
> . . . The majority of the fathers of heterosexuals (71%) made the decisions at home, and took an active role in its welfare, while only 40% of the fathers of homosexuals played the dominant role at home in terms of making decisions, executing discipline and handling major financial responsibility. (p. 144)

Saghir and Robins suggested that poor athleticism among prehomosexual children might have contributed heavily to the poor father–son relationships in this group: Homosexual men "recalled that their fathers rarely played with them, rarely shared any activities with them, and were often harsh, calling them names that were derogatory to their self-image and self-esteem. The father often noticed their lack of interest in sports and lack of participation in boys' activities" (p. 144). The homosexual men overwhelmingly rejected their fathers as suitable role models during childhood; the heterosexual men in general did not.

Unlike Bieber's study, Saghir and Robins's sample did not on the whole describe mothers as being seductive and close binding. Rather, they were described as involved, interested, and consciously supportive. The mothers did, however, tend to regard rough-and-tumble play negatively and to engage in feminine activities with their sons. The prehomosexual boys far more frequently than the preheterosexual boys viewed their mothers as suitable role models. Although impressed with the importance of familial interactions in the etiology of homosexuality, Saghir and Robins emphasized the need for caution when considering the causes of such a complex form of human behavior:

About one-fifth of [homosexual men] report a positive relationship with their fathers and one-third of the heterosexuals report a primary identification with their mother. . . . Whereas Bieber suggests a parental diad in the etiology of homosexuality and Evans adds the son in a triad relationship, we believe that the association of a poor parental relationship and male homosexuality is not necessarily a causative association although it may be an important contributing factor. (p. 152)

Bell, Weinberg, and Hammersmith (1981) recently carried out an investigation involving a method of data interpretation called path analysis. Patterns of familial interaction in homosexual and heterosexual groups were compared, and path analysis was used to estimate the degree to which certain types of interaction actually influenced the etiology of homosexuality. The investigators reported that in childhood and adolescence, the relationships of homosexual men with their fathers were negative in comparison to those of heterosexual men. The homosexual men perceived their fathers as being more hostile, more detached, and less close to them than did the heterosexual men. Fewer homosexual subjects remembered liking or respecting their fathers. There were differences between groups with regard to mothers as well. More homosexual than heterosexual men felt close to their mothers when they were growing up. Homosexual men could talk more easily to their mothers and felt that they had been maternally overprotected. There was no evidence for maternal seduction in either group, and the two groups reported similar memories of their mothers being hostile, rejecting, controlling, unfair, or detached. Homosexual men more frequently remembered their mothers as stronger than their fathers. More of the mothers of homosexual men made most of the decisions about the children. Although there were no differences between groups with regard to overall quality of parental relationships (e.g., marital discord, stress in the home), more of the homosexual men felt that the mother was the dominant parent.

The investigators found the protypical family pattern to be present in the backgrounds of some homosexual men (especially with regard to father–son interaction), but their analysis suggested that it was but a minor influence on the emergence of homosexuality. The interpretations of psychohistorical information by Bell, Weinberg, and Hammersmith have been criticized most recently by Van Den Aardweg (1984). Bell, Weinberg, and Hammersmith alleged that, unlike other retrospective approaches, path analysis allowed them to discriminate among influences on homosexuality and to give each a particular weight at a particular time of childhood development. This claim seems unlikely. No approach to data interpretation can convert retrospective methods to prospective methods: one is limited by the data one has to analyze. In addition, the meaning of data depends on the models one uses to interpret them. These include models of psychological development, of the mind, and of data analysis. The models used by Bell, Weinberg, and Hammersmith appear to be different in some ways than models generally accepted by most psycho-dynamically oriented investigators. But, as with the Bieber study, Bell, Weinberg, and Hammersmith's data can be discussed independently from their conclusions.

The extensively cited research of Siegelman (1974) stands in contrast to many of the studies mentioned above. Siegelman questioned whether meaningful differences really exist in the patterns of familial interaction during childhood of non-neurotic homosexual men in comparison with non-neurotic heterosexual men. Siegelman replicated his initial investigation in a cross-national sample (1981).

Siegelman's original 307 homosexual subjects were recruited from non-criminal and nonclinical sources. The 138 heterosexual control subjects were students. The study was carried out in the New York metropolitan area. Family background was assessed through use of a short form (40 items) of the Parent-Child Relations Questionnaire (PCR-SF-2). Factor analysis of the responses was carried out. Additional information about parent-child history was obtained from a Biographical Questionnaire (BQ). Items assessed by multiple choice questions were grouped into three areas as follows:

1. *Close to Father:* "As a child, how attached were you to your father?" "While you were growing up, how did you and your father get along?" "How do you and your father get along now?" "How close are you to your father now?"
2. *Close to Mother:* Same items as in group 1 but referring to mother.
3. *Dominance of Parent:* "While you were growing up, who in your family had the final say about how the house was run?" "While you were growing up, who in your family took responsibility for discipline?" "While you were growing up, who in your family really had the final say about how the family's income was spent?" "Who in your family had the final say about your parent's social and recreational activities?" "While you were growing up, which parent was the more important in your family?"

The results on the PCR-SF-2 indicated that in contrast to heterosexual men, homosexual subjects reported both their fathers and their mothers to be more rejecting and less loving. On the BQ, the homosexual men reported less closeness to their fathers.

Data were then analyzed for the part of the sample with low neuroticism scores. When homosexual and heterosexual men were matched for low neuroticism, no significant differences were found between the two subsamples. Siegelman stressed that "the complete lack of significant differences in parental background between homosexuals and heterosexuals with low neuroticism scores is in sharp contrast to those studies supporting the 'triangular system' hypothesis" (p. 16). He pointed out that even in nonclinical samples, degree of neuroticism should be controlled for. The negative findings of this investigation, lucidly reported by Siegelman, have had major impact on many contemporary clinical theoreticians, including the architects of *DSM-III*. According to Siegelman, these findings "seriously question the existence of *any* association between family relations and homosexuality vs. heterosexuality. The evidence found in the past investigation is consistent with the belief of Hooker . . . 'that disturbed parental relations are neither necessary nor sufficient conditions for homosexuality to emerge'" (p. 16).

Siegelman went on to replicate the 1974 investigation with a British sample (1981). Eighty-four homosexual subjects were compared to 62 heterosexual, who were matched for a number of variables. On the PCR-SF-2, the homosexual men reported more often that their mothers were demanding. On the BQ, they noted less often than heterosexual men that they were close to their fathers. When the subsamples who scored low on neuroticism were compared on the PCR-SF-2, the homosexual men described their mothers as more demanding and on the BQ the heterosexual men reported that they were closer to their fathers.

In discussing the results of this investigation, Siegelman heavily stressed the negative results: "the overall findings . . . for all group comparisons indicate that the homosexuals and heterosexuals differed very little in the descriptions of how their parents acted toward them while they were growing up and on parent closeness" (p. 509). Siegelman interpreted the findings of both investigations as evidence against the existence of a particular type of parental configuration in the background of homosexual men. In stressing the multifactorial nature of the etiology of homosexuality, he felt that his data argued against the role of the family as a general influence.

> The data reported . . . raise serious questions about the existence of any association between parental background behavior and homosexuality vs. heterosexuality in males. . . . The evidence to date . . . does not indicate that any particular parental background is typical or generally present in the development of most or all homosexuals or heterosexuals. (p. 509)

Most of the studies described above suggest an association between certain parent–child configurations and the development of predominant or exclusive homosexuality in males. Some studies, however, have called this association into question. Bell, Weinberg, and Hammersmith found the protypical family pattern to be present but their path analysis led them to conclude that the family configuration did not directly contribute to the etiology of homosexuality. Siegelman's research suggested that there may not be a protypical family configuration leading to homosexuality per se, although this research still allows for the possibility that the pattern described by others occurs in the backgrounds of neurotic homosexuals.

Siegelman's work is not without its critics. Van Den Aardweg (1984) observed that questionnaires might not assess behavior in sufficient depth to allow adequate description of the complexities of parent–child relationships. A detailed examination of Siegelman's methods suggests that Van Den Aardweg's criticism has some merit. The Biographical Questionnaire used, for example, required respondents to make global judgments about all parent-child interactions. Questions like "*as a child,* how attached were you to _____?" and "*while you were growing up,* how did you and _____ get along?" force the respondent to consider childhood as one broad period. Phase-specific sequences of development cannot be described using such methods. Moreover, as Van Den Aardweg suggested, it is difficult to see how the subtleties of interactive patterns and attitudes can be detected by a relatively small number of multiple choice questions. It is also interesting that Siegelman's more recent investigation found that British homosexual subjects who scored low on neuroticism were more distant from their fathers during childhood than comparable heterosexuals. Like a number of earlier clinical investigators, Van Den Aardweg stressed that a combination of parental attitudes can create a certain type of configuration in the family that seems to be associated with the development of homosexuality. He found this pattern in almost all of the 200 Dutch homosexual men he saw in private practice over a twenty-year period.

Despite the limitations of Siegelman's approach from the point of view of the psychodynamic clinician, other aspects of his scientific design certainly warrant that his findings be given serious consideration. His studies remain an exception, however. Although most other studies did not control for neuroticism, they involved nonpatients as well as inpatients and outpatients, were carried out in diverse settings, and included (in toto) a large number of subjects. The weight of the evidence discussed here seems therefore to implicate a pattern of family interactions in the development of homosexual men. But a big leap is necessary in order to conclude that homosexuality is likely to be *caused* by exposure to this type of family situation. Marmor (1980) pointed out, "the difficulty with this [family pattern] as a specific cause of homosexuality . . . is that dominating and seductive mothers and weak, hostile, or detached fathers as well as variations of this constellation abound in the histories of countless heterosexual individuals also" (p. 10).

Many experienced therapists can attest to the accuracy of Marmor's point. The following history of a heterosexual man, a control subject who participated in a study of homosexuality I carried out, further illustrates Marmor's observation (Friedman 1980).

Ed is a twenty-seven-year old heterosexual writer. He experienced erotic arousal and erections at age four, self-masturbation at age thirteen, and first sexual intercourse at age seventeen. His father is a fifty-five-year-old retired soldier, his mother a fifty-three-year-old housewife. Ed is the youngest of four children. Apart from his mother, he was closest throughout his growth and development to a sister one year his senior. Another sister, six years older, is married and has three children. The oldest sibling is a brother, married and heterosexual. There is no known family history of psychosis.

Both parents were practicing Lutherans and Ed was raised devoutly. The father, originally rural lower class, was a high school dropout who enlisted in the army. He drank and gambled heavily and slept away from the home during most of Ed's formative years, claiming that he was "out with friends." Early in the juvenile period, Ed recognized that his father was "probably screwing around." Ed's mother, a high school graduate from a middle-class background, cried over the father's promiscuity, gambling, and abusive behavior. She frequently threatened to leave him but never did, for reasons unknown to the patient.

Ed's earliest recalled feelings toward his father were of terror. "He was so mean, so cold . . . there was no input, no communication." The father belt-whipped him at least once a month until Ed was thirteen. Ed believes he was beaten not because he violated rules but because he irritated his father. Ed was athletically awkward, whereas his father was a fine athlete. His father screamed at him for his poor performance: "Goddammit, can't you do anything right— can't you even throw a ball?" Occasional father–son athletic endeavors caused Ed to feel "dread and terror." Because Ed was clumsy and unable to learn athletic gracefulness, his father derisively labeled him a sissy.

During childhood, Ed's father never remembered his birthday. (Only his mother gave him presents, usually stuffed animals.) "My father was uneducated, dumb, uncompassionate, nasty. I can never remember in my whole life touching my father, other than being hit by him." Ed's mother was chronically depressed but managed to run the household. She disparaged men and actively discouraged Ed from dating. She appeared disinterested in the fact that he had bad relationships with his peers. Although not close binding, she did not teach him skills he could use to gain acceptance with peer groups, nor did she appear to value participation in such groups.

As is common in military families, there were moves every one-and-a-half to two years, leading to disruption of relationships during Ed's juvenile period. From age six to nine, living in Europe, Ed's only close relationship was with his sister. They spent much time together in shared activities of a neutral nature, for example, walking, talking, playing tag. Although Ed sometimes played with dolls, he was not really preoccupied with feminine games. Ed did not cross-dress, nor did he wish to be female; however, he did envy the social life of girls. Ed never related closely to his two oldest siblings, who were more involved with their peers than with the life of the family.

In Europe, Ed attempted to join a same-sexed peer group but because of his athletic awkwardness he was attacked and humiliated. He recalls coming home in tears on many occasions because of his ineptitude at soccer and other rough-and-tumble games. He felt chronically anguished during those years because of his sissiness. When he returned to the United States at age ten, he quit sports completely, refusing even to throw a ball. He was chronically frightened of fighting and fearfully avoided all social interactions which might lead to peer aggression.

During late adolescence and early adulthood, Ed became progressively socially integrated. He made friends, including a best friend, a married artist with whom he remains intimate today. Ed ascribes the onset of social relatedness to verbal skills and aesthetic interests which he and his friends share. Ed's developmental and family history is protypically that of a homosexual man, but in fact Ed has been a lifelong exclusive heterosexual. This type of history is not uncommon among heterosexual men.

As this case history indicates, considerable overlap between heterosexuals and homosexuals exists in family background, which seems to weaken the argument for the importance of a protypical family background in the etiology of homosexuality. Strengthening the argument for the influence of the family, however, is the likelihood that the overlap in family patterns is not uniform across a hypothetical spectrum describing "deviance" or "abnormality" of family background. Among stable, nontraumatic, well-adjusted families it seems likely that relatively little overlap exists: that is, an emotionally secure, nontraumatic, warm and supportive pattern has not been documented to occur with any frequency in the backgrounds of homosexual men. Such histories are alleged to occur in anecdotal reports but detailed anamneses are not presently available in the literature, especially the psychoanalytic literature.

The characteristics of such an ideal family might be as follows: The parents would be warm, would care about each other, and would be sexually well adjusted. Neither parent's attitudes toward gender-related behavioral traits would be excessively contemptuous or idealizing. The children would have been wanted and their arrival would not have placed excessive strain on the family. During the many years between the prehomosexual boy's conception and his emergence into adulthood, neither he nor his family would experience catastrophic stress of any type. The family would live in the same geographical area, at least through the subject's high school graduation. The boy would have friends of both sexes from early childhood on, and he would be an accepted and valued member of a peer group. His childhood would not be characterized by peer ostracism, scapegoating, or acceptance by members of the opposite sex and exclusion by members of his own sex. The family's attitude toward sexuality would be neither puritanical nor libertine. Privacy would be respected, including children's privacy with regard to sexual matters. The subject's homosexual erotic feelings would exist at least from juvenile years on. He would know by midadolescence that he was homosexual and would reveal this to his family by late adolescence. Although perhaps surprised, his family members would continue to love and accept him in a warm, supportive way. No family relationship would be adversely affected by the announcement of his homosexuality. Specifically, his warm and mutually respectful relationship with his father and brothers, present since his earliest years, would persist on as firm a foundation as ever.

This type of family setting, of course, cannot be considered normal in a statistical sense. Most families are not as stable and emotionally secure as this ideal family; nonetheless, it is important to appreciate that although most heterosexual men probably did not experience this type of secure family background, some did. If this is true for homosexual men it has yet to be convincingly demonstrated.

The literature reviewed in this chapter concerns psychosocial effects: the potential role of the family in the etiology of homosexuality. In contrast, the literature discussed in chapter 3 concerns predominantly cognitive effects: the potential association between a feminized or demasculinized self-concept and homosexuality. Representation of the self during childhood as not masculine enough (according to some internal standard) appears to provide a psychological environment conducive to the genesis of exclusively or predominantly homosexual fantasies. It is less clear whether certain familial interactions provide a social environment similarly conducive to the genesis of homosexual fantasies. The distinction between self-representation and family interaction directs critical attention toward the distinction between object relations development and interpersonal development. At issue are the processes of internalization as they unfold during childhood and as they influence and (ultimately) are influenced by sexual fantasies.

To place psychological development in an appropriately complex perspective we must evaluate the family studies together with the gender-behavior studies with regard to potential influence on sexual orientation. Both types of study are focused on the same phases of childhood. In almost all investigations of homosexuality that assess both family history and gender-behavior history, the latter is reported deviant more consistently than the former is.

A strong case can be made for the hypothesis that a feminine or unmasculine self-concept during childhood is not only associated with the emergence of predominant or exclusive homosexuality in men, it is the single most important causal influence. In the literature dealing with gender identity/role, on the one hand, and with the family in relation to sexual orientation, on the other, childhood gender disturbance appears to be a much more powerful predictor of predominant or exclusive homosexuality than does family constellation. This even seems to be the case with the Bieber study (1962), which has been most influential on thinking about the role of the family in the etiology of homosexuality.

A close look at the raw data published by Bieber and colleagues does not necessarily lead to the conclusion that a boy exposed to a certain type of family environment is likely to become homosexual. Although familial disturbances were frequent in the backgrounds of the homosexual patients, concurrent gender identity/role disturbances were equally or more frequent. Although Bieber's study does suggest that there are family influences on homosexuality, such influence may be exerted primarily on gender identity (i.e., on the childhood representation of the self in gender-valued terms) and only indirectly on sexual orientation per se. One interpretation of the findings of the Bieber investigation is that when the prehomosexual children were experiencing gender identity/role difficulties, key relationships within their families did not ameliorate their problems and in fact may have made them worse.

This hypothesis is compatible with the cross-cultural study carried out by Whitam and Zent (1984). (See chapter 3.) The investigators failed to find differences between homosexuals and heterosexuals in any of the four countries with regard to the mother's attitude toward sex, seductiveness or warmth of the mother, parents' desire for a girl, or the belief that the subject's family was "normal" (table 5.3). In the Filipino sample there were statistical differences with respect to puritanical father, absent father, and detached, distant father. In the American sample there were statistical differences between homosexual and heterosexual subjects with respect to detached, distant father, strong mother, and hostile father. The differences between American heterosexual and homosexual men with respect to the detached, distant father was the only difference significant at the .001 level. The hostile father was found only in the American homosexual sample. According to their data, the closest approximation to the classic family configuration described by Bieber appeared among American homosexual subjects, who reported strong mothers and detached, distant, and hostile fathers (table 5.3). Whitam and Zent suggested that the differences they found might be related to cultural differences in intrafamilial acceptance of cross-gender behavior.

The following speculations, emphasizing cognitive and social development, seem compatible with both the family studies reviewed here and the gender-behavior research discussed in chapter 3. Childhood gender disturbances occur for a variety of reasons, many of which are still not completely understood. Psychosocial interactions influence each other and have an impact on the inner world of self-representation. Parents and children act and react to each other, and children's mental apparatuses are differentially sensitive to different types of input at various phases of development. One can conceptualize a spectrum at any point in development with regard to the origin of a particular type of interaction (such as distant father, close mother). On one side, the impetus for the interaction might stem from the child; on the other side, it might stem from the parents. Most interactions, however, would involve more complex patterns of behavior and would fall in the middle of the spectrum. No matter what the causes of gender disturbance, however, unmasculine or feminine boys, at least in western European countries, are more likely to find social acceptance with females than with males. Gender disturbed juvenile boys (and often younger children as well) are likely to be rejected by males, both in and outside their families. The rejection of feminine or unmasculine boys by other males seems frequently to be reciprocal: that is, the gender disturbed child is sometimes the rejector, often because he finds stereotypically masculine ac-

TABLE 5.3 Differences between Heterosexuals and Homosexuals with Respect to Familial Factors

Group	Significant at .05?	Significant at .001?	Explanatory note
1. What was your father's attitude toward sex? Open and frank? Puritanical?			
American	NS	NS	—
Guatemalan	NS	NS	—
Brazilian	NS	NS	—
Filipino	.05	NS	Homosexuals' fathers more puritanical
2. What was your mother's attitude toward sex? Open and frank? Puritanical?			
American	NS	NS	—
Guatemalan	NS	NS	—
Brazilian	NS	NS	—
Filipino	NS	NS	—
3. Was your mother ever seductive with you?			
American	NS	NS	—
Guatemalan	NS	NS	—
Brazilian	NS	NS	—
Filipino	NS	NS	—
4. Was your father emotionally distant and detached when you were growing up?			
American	.05	.001	Homosexuals' fathers detached
Guatemalan	NS	NS	—
Brazilian	NS	NS	—
Filipino	.05	NS	Homosexuals' fathers detached
5. Was your father hostile to you when you were growing up?			
American	.05	NS	Homosexuals' fathers hostile
Guatemalan	NS	NS	—
Brazilian	NS	NS	—
Filipino	NS	NS	—
6. Which parent was the strongest when you were growing up?			
American	.05	NS	Homosexuals' mothers stronger
Guatemalan	NS	NS	—
Brazilian	NS	NS	—
Filipino	.05	NS	Homosexuals' mothers stronger
7. Which parent was the warmest when you were growing up?			
American	NS	NS	—
Guatemalan	NS	NS	—
Brazilian	NS	NS	—
Filipino	NS	NS	—
8. Was your family "normal" or in some way unusual?			
American	NS	NS	—
Guatemalan	NS	NS	—
Brazilian	NS	NS	—
Filipino	NS	NS	—

Table 5.3 continued

Group	Significant at .05?	Significant at .001?	Explanatory note
9. Were both parents present in the home while you were growing up?			
American	NS	NS	—
Guatemalan	NS	NS	—
Brazilian	NS	NS	—
Filipino	.05	NS	Homosexuals' fathers absent
10. When you were born did your parents want a boy or a girl?[a]			
American	NS	NS	—
Brazilian	NS	NS	—
Filipino	NS	NS	—

[a]This question was not included in the Guatemalan version of the questionnaire.
Source: Whitam & Zent 1984

tivities, such as rough-and-tumble play, repellent. The most important male in this rejected–rejector dynamic is of course the boy's father. Many different kinds of interaction could lead ultimately to a distant father–son relationship.

The prehomosexual boy's relationship with his mother is less likely to fall into a rigid pattern. As a general rule, however, the mother (who is sometimes too close to her son) is not likely to reject the boy and he, in turn, is not likely to find his mother's feminine traits repellent. From a cross-cultural perspective, mothers appear more tolerant than fathers of untypical sex role behavior in their sons.

The causes of feminine or unmasculine self-representation in childhood are variable; the relationships between predisposing constitutional factors and familial influences remain to be clarified. The specific psychological mechanisms by which predominantly or exclusively homosexual erotic fantasies take root in the soil of the self-representation also remain to be established. The self-concept is conceptualized as a final common pathway, itself influenced by (and influencing) other factors. For example, the childhood self-concept is most likely responsive to family dynamics. It appears, however, that gender-valuing of the self-representation changes as the child's cognitive and social worlds expand, particularly after adolescence. In many cases, individuals' concepts of masculinity and femininity change so that children who felt unmasculine become homosexual adults who consider themselves adequately masculine. Sometimes, however, the childhood gender disturbances persist.

From the clinical point of view it is important to keep in mind that even such widely quoted negative studies as Siegelman's (1981, 1974) found distant father–son relationships in the backgrounds of non-neurotic homosexual men in comparison to heterosexual men. Whitam and Zent's data (1984), which also appeared to weaken the case for familial determinants of homosexuality, nonetheless found the classic pattern of maternal overinvolvement and paternal distance and/or hostility among American homosexual men. Moreover, emerging research suggests that at least the more severe gender disorders of boyhood are associated with both global psychopathology and disturbed family relationships (Coates & Person 1985). Clinicians in the sexual orientation / gender area, particularly those working with younger patients, may expect to encounter the patterns of family interaction outlined in this chapter.

From the scientific point of view it must be noted that the body of literature concerning sexual orientation and the family is largely retrospective. The gender identity literature, in contrast, includes prospective studies; thus it rests on a stronger database than the family literature. The gender role behavior of a child may influence and be influenced by family interactive patterns in myriad ways. The mutual influences occurring over time are so complex that it is difficult, perhaps impossible, to infer which are primary from retrospective studies. Multiple levels of conscious and unconscious organization, both in the child and in the family, are involved in positive and negative feedback cycles leading to general patterns of behavior. In this introductory chapter I do not attempt to do justice to the individual and social dynamics that must be taken into account for an in-depth understanding of the developmental issues related to sexual orientation. I consider individual and family dynamics in more detail in parts 2–4.

PART TWO

Psychopathology
and Sexual Orientation
in Males

6

Character Pathology and Sexual Orientation: Introductory Concepts

Many psychoanalysts and psychotherapists see gay patients who have requested help because of impulsivity, compulsivity, and driven, frantic sexuality. Often the symptomatic behavior is attributed by the analyst, and sometimes by the patient as well, to homosexuality. It is important for clinicians to keep in mind that individuals at different points on the Kinsey scale can exhibit similar mechanisms of ego functioning and parallel types of sexual psychopathology. Conceptualizing sexual pathology in terms of the character pathology in which the sexual behavior is embedded frames questions of health and illness quite differently from conceptualizing homosexuality as a form of psychopathology per se. The clinical and psychoanalytic literature on homosexuality often suggests, subtly or openly, that patients' homosexuality causes extensive associated psychopathology. In scientific language, homosexuality is often treated in the literature as an independent variable, and disorders of sexual and personal relationships are treated as dependent variables. There are no studies, however, comparing patients of similar levels of ego integration and opposite points on the Kinsey spectrum.

Common sense and clinical experience suggest that the causes of most pathological sexual behavior are integrally related to the causes of disordered ego and superego functioning and disordered object relations. To understand sexual pathology, then, one must understand character pathology. There is no homosexual or heterosexual character type. In fact, it would appear that homosexuality, bisexuality, and heterosexuality are distributed across the entire range of character types and character structures.

Characterology has become a subspecialty of the clinical disciplines, and it can be approached descriptively in a number of ways. The approach used here is more or less traditionally psychoanalytic (with specified modifications). Character *type* is described in terms of character traits and defenses exhibited (e.g., obsessive, hysteric, paranoid, or narcissistic). In keeping with recent thinking on character, particularly that of Kernberg (1975, 1976, 1984), the *level* at which the personality is structured, conceptualized as an independent dimension of character functioning, is also described. I use the terms *character* and *personality* synonymously.

In chapters 7–11 case histories of individuals with various types of personality disorders are presented and discussed. Men at similar levels of character integration but at different points on the Kinsey scale are compared. Space does not allow for discussion of all personality disorders or for equally detailed treatment of all personality types. Since the idea that character type interacts with structural level is of great importance, however, it is presented in detail in a consideration of the obsessive-compulsive character. Many points about psychic structure in relation to sexual orientation and to psychopathology are illustrated in discussion of this topic. The paranoid personality is discussed in the context of the relationship between homosexuality and paranoia. Because of the historical importance of paranoia and masochism in relation to homosexuality, I devote a chapter to each of these subjects. First, however, I introduce Kernberg's theory of character integration.

KERNBERG'S THEORY OF CHARACTER PATHOLOGY

Kernberg's name more than any other is connected in the minds of most analysts with the concept of levels of character integration. Kernberg (1975, 1984) conceptualized character pathology in terms of what he called *structural characteristics*. He divided character pathology into three levels on the basis of instinct and superego development, defensive operations of the ego, and quality of internalized object relations. He theorized that at the higher level of character pathology (i.e., the least pathological), the superego is well integrated (albeit excessively harsh); repression and associated "advanced" defenses such as intellectualization, rationalization, and undoing constitute the defensive armamentarium; ego identity, self-concept, and representational world are all stable; and no pathology of object relations is present.

At the intermediate level of character pathology, pregenital fixation and regression points predominate, and superego functioning is less well integrated, although higher-level defenses are sometimes in use. Primitive defenses such as splitting and denial are also sometimes apparent, and object relations are more conflicted than at the higher level. At the lower (most pathological) level of character pathology, pregenital aggression predominates, the superego is poorly integrated and primitive superego precursors are manifested; defenses are also primitive and splitting, denial, projective identification, idealization–devaluation, and grandiose omnipotence predominate. At this level, defense and impulse expression are more directly linked, so that, in Kernberg's words, "the primal impulse expression shows through the defense" (1975, p. 29).

Kernberg (1975) describes splitting as

> the active process of keeping apart introjections and identifications of opposite quality. . . . The direct clinical manifestation of splitting may be the alternative expression of complementary sides of a conflict in certain character disorders, combined with bland denial and lack of concern over the contradiction in . . . behavior and internal experience. . . . One other direct manifestation of splitting may be a *selective* "lack of impulse control" in certain areas, manifest in episodic breakthrough of primitive impulses which are ego syntonic during the time of their expression (and splitting is prevalent in impulse neurosis and addictions). Probably the best known manifestation of splitting is the division of external objects into "all-good" ones and "all-bad" ones with the concomitant possibility of complete, abrupt shifts of an object from one extreme compartment to the other, that is, sudden and complete reversals of all feelings and conceptualizations about a particular person. Extreme and repetitive oscillation between contradicting self-concepts may also be the result of the mechanisms of splitting. (p. 29)

Splitting occurs in association with other lower-level defense mechanisms, primitive idealization (the perception of objects as all-powerful or all-good), and devaluation (the perception of objects as worthless or all-bad). Neither process is based on realistic evaluation of the attributes of external objects. Instead, these judgments are based on need satisfaction or frustration and the resultant fantasies generated. Individuals with lower-level character pathology also utilize projection and denial in a primary, basic way to a far greater degree than do most patients with higher-level organization.

At the lower level of character pathology, objects are not experienced as constant; the inner world of object relations is organized around part objects; and identity is diffused. These patients suffer from weak ego integration and are unable to integrate good and bad attributes of self and object representations. Instead, inner part objects are experienced as all good or all bad, and the individual is deficient in the capacity for empathy toward other people (i.e., he or she is unable to relate to others as complete personalities rather than as need-gratifying or threatening objects). Patients with a lower level of character pathology are chaotic, impulsive, and unable to tolerate guilt or anxiety. They manifest a shift toward primary process thinking, micropsychotic reactions, and psychotic reactions in the transference. They cannot tolerate sustained intimacy or ego boundary weakness; they lack the capacity to perceive other people as three-dimensional, seeing them as idealized or devalued objects; and they readily distort the perceived world by means of primitive introjects. All of these disorders lead to severe impairment in the ability to experience and sustain love relationships. Sexual relationships are often suffused with aggression and/or anxiety. Since these patients have global integrative deficiencies, they are unable to maintain a stable concept of an object world in relation to the self and they experience identity diffusion.

Kernberg suggested that most obsessive-compulsive and depressive-masochistic characters are structurally organized at the higher level, whereas infantile, antisocial, as-if, and inadequate personalities are at the lower level. In Kernberg's view, the borderline disorders, in general, are to be classified at the lower level.

Kernberg was not the first to point out that individuals may differ in level of personality integration, despite similarity in certain character defenses. Easser and Lesser (1965) illustrated this point elegantly with regard to hysterical defenses. For example, two patients may seem to manifest hysterical defenses. One demonstrates integrated ego functioning, intact superego functioning, object constancy, and the capacity to mentally represent whole objects with qualities and attributes, rather than part objects that are all good or all bad. This patient, despite experiencing various painful symptoms, has a well-differentiated, stable sense of identity. The second patient, superficially similar to the first in many ways, is quite different in others. She manifests weakness in ego integration and is incapable of tolerating guilt or anxiety. After doing something "wrong," for example, the first patient experiences a transient guilty depression, whereas the second experiences severe tension relieved only by cutting her arms with razor blades. The second patient lacks object constancy and cannot tolerate being alone even for brief periods. She experiences interpersonal relationships as either "wonderful" or "horrible" depending on their need-gratifying or frustrating characteristics. She feels empty and complains that she doesn't know "who she is."

Since both patients manifest dramatic mannerisms, colorful dress, seductiveness with men, shallow affect, somaticization, and sexual dysfunction, both may appear to suffer from hysterical character neurosis. In fact, the patient with adequate ego integration is considered hysterical. But the more impaired patient, phenotypically hysterical, actually suffers from a more severe type of character disorder, which Easser and Lesser termed *hysteroid*. Kernberg would consider the more impaired patient to manifest a pseudohysterical infantile character structure, a type of borderline disorder. The ability to diagnose based on level of structural organization in addition to types of defense is very useful in predicting the course, complications, and optimum strategy of psychotherapy.

Although Kernberg was not the first to classify patients according to their level of character organization, his systematic attention to object relations in such patients has been extremely thorough. The descriptive aspects of Kernberg's theory have proved most helpful. It seems to me, however, that the developmental aspects have not. Kernberg's hypothesis relating character pathology to instinct theory stands on weak ground. Concepts such as libidinal and aggressive drives and points of fixation and regression are of historical interest and may have limited application in some clinical situations, but I think they no longer have a place in a theory of development. Kernberg's description of levels of character organization can be retained, however, without retaining the aspects of his developmental model that call upon instinct theory. It is not necessary to refer to developmental traumata or obsolete concepts such as libido in order to describe present levels of personality functioning.

Kernberg's interpretation of homosexuality even more seriously limits his theory. Kernberg conceptualized homosexuality in terms of pathological object relations (1975, pp. 328–30). He arrived at this view through his model of the relationship between childhood development and adult functioning. Kernberg's model of homosexuality needs considerable revision and I do not use it in this book. Instead, I separate Kernberg's theory of homosexuality from his theory of levels of character organization and use the latter in creating my own model of sexual pathology and psychopathology.

CHARACTER PATHOLOGY AND HOMOSEXUALITY

The complexities inherent in describing character pathology in relation to aspects of homosexuality can be ameliorated to some degree by keeping a simple diagram in mind. The first part of this diagram utilizes Kernberg's concept of level of character integration (psychostructural level). This may be envisioned as a spectrum with the highest level of integration at one pole and the lowest level at the other.

Highest Level	*Lowest Level*
Neurotic character	Borderline syndrome
Repression is core defense	Splitting is core defense
No primitive idealization and devaluation occur	Primitive idealization and devaluation occur
Representational world is stable	Representational world is unstable
Self-representation is stable	Self-representation is unstable
Identity is solid	Identity is diffused

The concept that ego integrative functions can be represented on a spectrum *within each type of character organization* is illustrated above for the hysterical character. The concept is so central to further discussion that an additional illustration seems indicated. Let us consider three men, each with obsessional defenses. All use the defense of isolation to a great degree. The first man is a combat jet pilot with no evidence of character pathology; the second is a surgeon with a neurotic character disorder; and the third is a civil servant with a borderline personality organization.

I evaluated the pilot as part of a routine screening process. He had never been a psychiatric patient. Fit and trim, in his late twenties, he had the quietly commanding style of an effective decision maker. Captain X was friendly, respected by colleagues, and loved by his wife and children. When we discussed psychological conflicts, he smiled and pointed out that he had studied Freud and realized that everyone has conflicts—he had just never been aware of his, nor could he see evidence that internal psychological conflict had influenced his life. He felt solidly rooted in the traditional values of "God, Family, Country, Loyalty, and Honor." He had an excellent sense of humor, loved to ski, and enjoyed poker games with buddies and Scrabble with his wife.

The captain was seen as an unusually able combat pilot and was known for his reliable performance in dangerous situations. No matter how turbulent the situation, he always retained a clear mind, good judgment, and excellent psychomotor ability. "I guess I was born that way, my daddy was that way too," he said. The adaptive value of isolation of affect in this man's life is illustrated in the following interchange:

Q. What feelings do you have in combat?
A. Not many. There really isn't time to have feelings.
Q. Do you get scared afterwards?
A. [Laughs] Not really. Sometimes I think, "you sure are one lucky son of a bitch to see another day."
Q. What about your feelings before a mission?
A. Sure—sometimes I get tense but I push it out of my mind. I figure God either meant me to be a granddaddy or not. Actually, I figure he did. Anyway, I concentrate hard on what I have to do. I guess that's a feeling.
Q. What about other times?
A. I'm aware of having feelings, of course, like when I'm with my family for instance. But at work, I mostly keep the feelings out and have thoughts.

Captain X had never experienced symptoms of psychiatric disorder in any severity. He was coldly rational when necessary, "all thoughts"; yet his interpersonal relationships were deep and obviously full of feeling. His defenses operated flexibly in a manner that facilitated his capacity to work and to love.

The captain's character organization falls at the extreme left pole of the psychostructural spectrum. Psychoanalysts tend to have relatively little experience with people such as this since they do not require mental health services.

The surgeon in our example, Dr. Y, suffered from an obsessional character neurosis. He came for consultation because he had decided that his wife's and children's complaints about him "had merit." He said he felt chronically "lifeless." Immaculately groomed, before he related his history the doctor noted that the Venetian blinds in my office were dusty. An excellent surgeon, he was revered by patients, respected by peers and superiors, and feared by subordinates. Dr. Y's reputation as a perfectionist was well deserved. He was unforgiving of human error both in himself and in others. His harshness, even brutality, toward resident physicians and nurses seemed reasonable to him: "after all, life and death are at stake," he noted.

Unlike the captain, however, who commanded without intimidation, Dr. Y evoked anxiety and hostility in an interview situation. In the initial phase of our first interview, I found myself anxiously reviewing a list of things that I "ought to have done that day" (polish my shoes, change my trousers, instruct the maid to dust *carefully*)—until I realized that I was responding to the doctor's powerful, rigid persona. Like the captain, Dr. Y was aware of "no feelings in high-pressure, life-and-death situations." Unlike the captain, however, he seemed to experience few feelings at other times either, except for anger and depression. He displayed a dutiful posture toward his wife, but he was not "loving" and certainly not "passionate." He occasionally had brief extramarital affairs, "more or less to check the equipment out," but never engaged in a serious relationship. He felt distant from his teenage children, both of whom irritated him because of their "sloppy attitude toward life."

Dr. Y's life was his work, performing surgery. During leisure hours, work-related thoughts filled his mind. On the tennis court, at the dinner table, even during sex, his mind was always focused on "lists of things to do." The doctor realized that his preoccupation with surgery was not normal. He had long been unable to feel kindness, caring, warmth, or humor. Repetition had replaced curiosity and his aesthetic sense, once keen, was now confined to surgical matters.

The doctor's emotional constriction had begun shortly after the death of his father, also a brilliant surgeon, and the almost simultaneous death of a beloved older brother in an auto accident. These catastrophes had occurred at the same time that his participation in a major scientific discovery had resulted in considerable fame and rapid promotion to the level of full professor. Prior to these life events, Dr. Y had been a rigid, sometimes difficult, ambitious man with access to a full range of feelings. But since the events in question had occurred years before, he did not feel that they had influenced the gradual subsequent replacement of feelings by thoughts. He dismissed as "not significant" the fact that he had never experienced painful grief over the deaths of his father and brother, despite his love for them.

Dr. Y's rigidity, his inability to achieve satisfactory love relationships, his anger and depression, and his sense of an impoverished inner life were all manifestations of a character neurosis. His neurotic conflicts were motivated by unresolved oedipal guilt, which led to a pathological mourning reaction to the loss of his father and brother. Despite his inner pain, Dr. Y never experienced the ego fragmentation characteristic of the borderline syndromes. His obsessional defenses functioned in a rigid, hypertrophied way and, activated by unconscious anxiety, led to impairment in the capacity for intimacy and finally to the inability to experience any feelings. Psychoanalytic therapy helped Dr. Y to mourn. His capacities for love and pleasure returned and the defense of isolation lost its hypertrophied, maladaptive quality.

The level at which Dr. Y's character is organized can be represented toward the left side of the psychostructural spectrum, which depicts patients with character neuroses but not borderline syndromes.

Mr. Z, a middle-aged civil servant, exhibited a borderline level of integration. He came for consultation because of hypochondriacal worries. Although he realized that he was physically sound, Mr. Z had developed the terrifying thought that he might suffer from parasitic worms in his intestines and lungs. The image of sparkling cleanliness he initially conveyed was rudely dispelled by the appearance of a stained yellow handkerchief into which Mr. Z coughed spit during the session. At times, he scrutinized the expelled mucus. "I know this is disgusting," he apologized, "but I can't help myself." He later explained that he was "checking" for blood stains and "to see if I cough up anything that moves."

Mr. Z lived alone and had no friends. He was a reliable worker but despite working at the same job, at the same desk, in the same large office, for twenty years, he had formed no personal relationships at work. His manner toward co-workers was friendly but remote. Mr. Z contemptuously dismissed the possible rewards of closeness with others: "Who needs them—people are worthless shits. They don't read, they are ignorant—once you get to know them, they try to take you for all you're worth anyway."

Mr. Z saw himself as "possibly a writer in the making." He had been at work on an autobiographical novel for more than ten years. He did not consider himself a novelist, however, since he had not published anything. In fact, Mr. Z was hard put to describe his identity. He was certainly not to be defined by his vocation, since he felt contemptuous of civil servants. He had never married, had no children, and although he considered himself religious, he was not an identified member of an organized religion—"too primitive!" he complained. Mr. Z experienced frequent episodes of panic "because I lose track of where I am, or where I'm going." At those times, the world seemed unreal, and, as he put it, "I get numb, and can't tell where my body stops. I sometimes can't feel where my arms and legs are. My mouth and face feel numb too."

Mr. Z occasionally went to singles bars, and sometimes women became interested in him. Any possibility of intimacy, however, resulted in increased anxiety and hypochondriacal fears. Mr. Z had never been psychiatrically hospitalized, had never been delusional, and had never had hallucinations or compulsions. He suffered from repetitive "thoughts" that intruded against his wishes. For example, the words "mow the lawn" would unaccountably stick in his head to the point of producing a sense of torment. Sometimes Mr. Z found himself praying that these thoughts would "leave my mind alone." His goals in life were to achieve "inner peace" by becoming free of hypochondriacal worries and intrusive thoughts and "possibly finishing my novel." He had decided that if he accomplished this, he would "find" himself.

The level at which Mr. Z's character is organized can be represented at the right pole of the psychostructural spectrum. His obsessive defenses did not occur in the context of a well-organized ego structure. His obsessionality, which met the criteria for an obsessive-compulsive disorder, was experienced along with unintegrated ego functions. His self and representational worlds were unstable. Identity diffusion, devaluation of subjects, and inability to experience intimacy were all present.

These three men can all be described as obsessional. They illustrate the point that it is necessary to describe psychostructural level in addition to type of defense in order accurately to depict character pathology. The task of describing individuals is made even more difficult by the multiple *additional* factors that influence adaptation, the capacity to love and work, to cope with adversity, and to respond to psychotherapy. These factors include intelligence, ability to think psychologically, motivation, financial resources, and such difficult-to-measure qualities as courage and level of tolerance to pain. Practical necessity compels us to limit the universe of discourse to some degree. My focus is therefore on level of character integration in relation to homosexuality and heterosexuality. I assume that the qualities mentioned above (e.g., intelligence, courage) are disturbed without regard to sexual orientation.

The homosexual–heterosexual spectrum described by Kinsey can be represented by a line similar to that which represents Kernberg's psychostructural spectrum. At the extreme left we find people who are exclusively heterosexual in interest and/or activity. At the extreme right, we find people who are exclusively homosexual in interest and/or activity (see chapter 1).

If we rotate the line representing character pathology so that it becomes the ordinate of a hypothetical graph, the line representing homosexual-heterosexual activity becomes the abscissa (fig. 6.1). This simple notational scheme allows a clinician to describe both a person's level of character structure and his or her sexual behavior without condensing the two conceptual frameworks.

The notation for erotic fantasy and activity may be represented independently from the notation for identity. As I thought of depicting behavior this way I was reminded of a comment made by the (fictional) Mozart in the play *Amadeus*. The character points out that in a play, two people speaking simultaneously produce only noise. Add music, however, and both can be heard; they now create a duet. In fact, many aspects of human behavior can be thought of similarly. One task required of the modern descriptive psychiatrist /

Kinsey rating

| 0 | 1 | 2 | 3 | 4 | 5 | 6 |

psychoanalyst is creation of the right context (analagous to music) for the representation of complex dialectics of behavior, while avoiding the type of simplistic condensation that leads to confusion and cacophony.

The graphic model of character integration and sexual behavior can be used to depict or represent people in spatial fashion. To illustrate this I represent with triangles well-integrated people at polar opposites on the Kinsey scale, and with rectangles poorly integrated people who also are polar opposites with regard to sexual orientation (fig. 6.2). Different symbols could also be used to represent people in the middle of either spectrum.

We need an additional dimension if we wish to depict type of character defense. The diagram we are now obliged to use (musically analagous to a trio) was invented by Stone (1980). He pointed out that for adequate representation of the psychopathology of individuals with borderline syndromes a cuboidal diagram is necessary. He suggested that one side of the cube represent level of character integration (psychostructural level), the second side type of character defense, and the third side genetic predisposition to affective disorders or schizophrenia (fig. 6.3).

Stone's model has been found useful by clinicians working with borderline patients. Since my focus is on sexuality, I have taken the liberty of replacing Stone's dimension for genetic predisposition with the Kinsey scale. Of course genetic predisposition to affective disorders and schizophrenia is important for thinking about sexual pathology, but it is not central to our considerations here. The diagnosis cube for representing homosexual–heterosexual interest/activity, level of character integration, and personality type is shown in figure 6.4.

In considering interactions between psychostructural level and sexual orientation an observation is necessary about similarities and differences between men at opposite ends of the Kinsey scale. In adults, if homosexuality is not

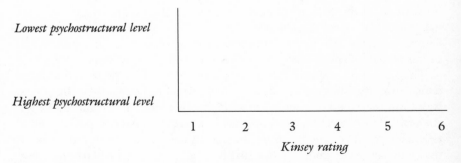

Fig. 6.1 Diagnostic schema for sexual orientation and psychostructural level.

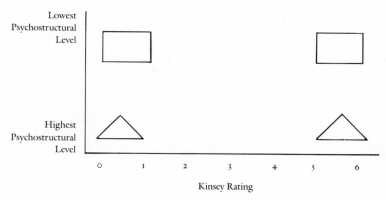

Fig. 6.2 Character structure and Kinsey rating

defined as pathological, the best evidence available indicates that no forms of psychopathology distinguish men at opposite ends of the Kinsey spectrum but with comparable higher levels of ego integration. It has not been demonstrated that so-called obligatory homosexuality leads to impairment in the capacity to love or work. Adults who behave and identify as homosexual do not appear to manifest significant psychopathology more frequently than heterosexual people do (DHEW 1972, Marmor 1980, Saghir & Robins 1973). In interpreting this data, of course, psychoanalysts recognize that certain types of character pathology that initially present in a subtle manner may actually be severe.

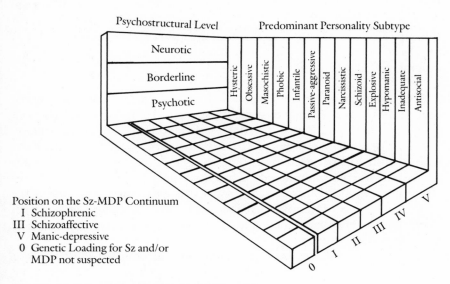

Fig. 6.3 The diagnosis cube (Stone 1980, p. 35)

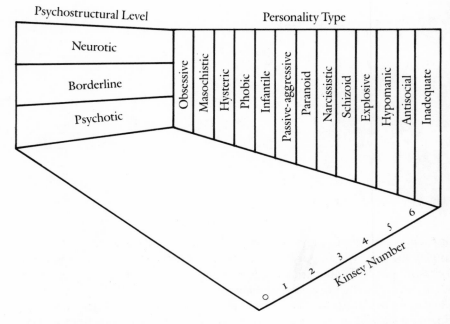

Fig. 6.4 Sexual orientation diagnosis cube

Patients with pathological narcissism, for example, have been used to illustrate this point. There is no scientific reason, however, to think that homosexual men are prone to suffer from such conditions any more than heterosexual men are. As an example, I present a more or less typical history obtained from a well-integrated individual.

Bob, a forty-year-old engineer, was seen in a research and educational context. Bob was a life-long 6 on the Kinsey scale. He had never experienced an erection in association with a consciously perceived heterosexual fantasy, nor could he recall ever having had heterosexual dreams. Homosexual dreams with orgasm had occurred from time to time during his life. From mid-adolescence to young adulthood, he had dated girls, hoping to become sexually aroused by them. Sexual activity was attempted a few times but never proceeded because of lack of sexual desire and any of the changes of the sexual response cycle. His sexual fantasies had emerged prepubertally, years before he knew what homosexuality was.

Bob's first sexual activity with another person occurred during young adulthood, more or less coincident with the recognition that he "must" be homosexual. Some people in his interpersonal network knew of his homosexuality, some did not, depending on his assessment of their attitudes and values. He had regular sexual activity with a few different partners but never cruised or visited gay bars or baths. He did not belong to a gay organization. As an adult, Bob had had a stable, productive work history. He had loyal, caring, durable friendships with both men and women and found pleasure in many aspects of his life. He had demonstrated the capacity for appropriate grief and appropriate feelings of depression.

The psychological problems of men whose egos are organized on the higher level, that is, those with nonborderline character neuroses, are quite similar regardless of sexual orientation. Just as psychologically healthy homosexual and heterosexual men can love expressively and work effectively, so neurotic homosexual and heterosexual men experience similar types of impairments in these vital capacities. The similarity in the internal psychological worlds of higher-level men at all points on the Kinsey scale is particularly striking in view of the facts that homosexual and heterosexual men often live in very different subcultures and that large segments of society are openly prejudiced against homosexual individuals.

At the lower part of the psychostructural spectrum, asymmetries between homosexual and heterosexual groups appear more pronounced. The subgroup of predominantly or exclusively homosexual men is probably weighted toward patients with gender role/identity disorders. This subgroup contains more effeminate men (for example, so-called "drag queens") than the heterosexual subgroup. It is important to keep in mind that gross gender pathology during adulthood is generally associated with global impairment of the sense of identity and ego functions; that is, with borderline pathology (Ovesey & Person 1973; Person & Ovesey 1974a, b, c). This does not mean that the borderline syndromes occur more frequently among homosexual men than among heterosexual men. It does seem, however, that the *form* borderline pathology takes may be a function of sexual orientation. The subgroup of exclusively heterosexual men with borderline pathology contains transvestites, that is, fetishistic cross-dressers, but there are probably far fewer of these, in number and percentage, than there are homosexual patients with gender disorders. The exact percentage of borderline homosexual and heterosexual men who suffer from gender identity/role disorders is not known: this question awaits systematic psychoanalytic investigation. As a general guideline, however, it seems safe to assume that the percentage of homosexual men who are entirely masculine (by usual cultural standards) increases as the level of global character pathology decreases.

It should also be noted that the types of sexual perversion (called paraphilias in *DSM-III-R*) are somewhat different at opposite ends of the Kinsey spectrum. For example, sexual sadism and masochism are more or less comparable in quality across the spectrum, but pedophilia is not (Mohr, Turner & Jerry 1964). Homosexual and heterosexual pedophilias differ in certain fundamental ways, not only in the gender of the erotic object. This is true of some paraphilias but not others.

MODELS OF HOMOSEXUALITY AND ISSUES OF COUNTERTRANSFERENCE

Multidimensional models of behavioral functioning protect the clinician (to some degree) from countertransference errors due to stereotyping. For example, let us describe two patients in multidimensional terms. Patient A has an obsessional personality type, low psychostructural level, and a Kinsey rating of 6 (exclusively homosexual). Patient B has a low level of integration, an obsessional personality type, and a Kinsey rating of zero. I have frequently heard the first type of patient described as a "very sick homosexual" by colleagues. The second type of patient is usually described as a "very sick obsessive" or a "very sick borderline," but never, in parallel fashion, as a "very sick heterosexual." This type of clinical shorthand expresses the countertransference error of clinicians who identify with the view of homosexuality present in the culture at large. It is probably for this reason that the Kinsey investigators opposed the use of the term homosexual as a noun. One must note, however, that the heterosexual patient in the above illustration is also dehumanized, since his identity is (casually) equated with his disorder (i.e., he is referred to as "an obsessive" or "a borderline"). This attempt to reduce the anxiety of interpersonal interactions by labeling patients is regretfully more prevalent in the medical world than it should be. ("I saw an interesting diabetic the other day"; "the M.I. [myocardial infarct] in bed 16 needs to be examined.") The problems therapists must cope with in conceptualizing homosexuality are unfortunately compounded by these inadequate medical models and the forces of social prejudice.

In the diagnostic scheme I propose there is no way of classifying homosexuality as a unitary entity. Instead, I suggest that it is more helpful for clinicians to describe sexual fantasy and activity, on the one hand, and identity in the context of character structure, on the other. This model of homosexuality is quite different from that used by most other psychoanalysts. For example, Socarides proposed five major forms of homosexuality—latent, variational, situational, preoedipal, and oedipal—based on his speculation about three areas of character development: (1) conscious and unconscious motivation, (2) developmental stage of nuclear conflict, and (3) the degree of pathology of internalized object relations. In Socarides' view (1978), preoedipal homosexuality is obligatory, oedipal is not. In contrast with schemas such as those proposed by Socarides and many other psychoanalysts, the classificatory model proposed in this chapter is atheoretical with regard to homosexuality. No assumption is made concerning the relationship between homosexuality–heterosexuality and preoedipal and oedipal developmental and motivational concepts. No assumption is made concerning relationships between homosexuality and psychopathology. The rationale for this alternative viewpoint is based on developmental and theoretical ideas discussed later.

7

Homosexuality–Heterosexuality and Obsessional Character Disorders: Character Neuroses

In chapters 7–9 I focus on homosexuality and heterosexuality in men with obsessional character types at different levels of structural organization. In this chapter I compare higher-level obsessional men at opposite ends of the Kinsey scale. I discuss men who experience homosexuality as a stable trait rather than as ephemeral or transient states. These men are homosexual, experiencing little or no heterosexuality during their lives. Presently 6 on the Kinsey scale, they would be rated 5–6 during the entire course of their lives. Heterosexual men discussed have a lifelong rating of 0; that is , they have never consciously experienced homosexual arousal or activity. In chapter 8 I compare men with low-level borderline pathology at opposite ends of the Kinsey scale. Finally, in chapter 9, I discuss bisexuality in obsessional men at higher and lower levels of structural organization.

The terms *obsessive* or *obsessive-compulsive* have been used in psychoanalytic writings to mean four different things: (1) a nonpathological personality style; (2) a character disorder; (3) a specific type of disorder, distinct from the character disorder, characterized by obsessions and compulsions; (4) a form of borderline syndrome. In the history of psychopathology, distinctions between these entities emerged rather recently: earlier descriptions tended to lump together these "obsessive-compulsive" categories of psychopathology.

In his classic paper "Character and Anal Erotism" (1908/1959), Freud observed that a group of individuals is characterized by the presence of personality traits formed as a result of conflict surrounding toilet training. The symptoms of obsessional neurosis and the traits of orderliness, frugality, and obstinacy were presumed to stem from anal regression. Freud particularly emphasized the importance of anal sadism in the genesis of obsessional psychopathology (1908/1959, 1917/1957). Many clinicians have replicated his descriptive observations, and a voluminous literature corroborates his claim that a large group of patients appears to share specific features of character style as well as specific types of defenses. By character style I mean aspects of behavior that are motivated in part unconsciously and in part by consciously perceived attitudes, values, and interests that provide meaning to the person's inner life (Shapiro 1965; MacKinnon & Michels 1971; Salzman 1980; Salzman & Thaler 1981).

Abraham (1921) used the concept of a "field of power" to depict obsessional people. He was impressed with the importance of territoriality and power struggles to obsessional individuals: "the sensitiveness of the person with an anal character to external encroachments of every kind on the actual or supposed field of his power is well known" (p. 171). Abraham pointed out that controlling and sadistic interpersonal behavior may be expressed by such people in diverse ways. For example, they "like to arouse desire and expectation in others and then to give them gratification in small and insufficient amounts" (p. 171).

Abraham observed that obsessional patients were avaricious and frequently displaced the value of money to the value of time. Saving money and/or time often assumed enormous significance in their lives. Like Freud and countless other analysts, Abraham noticed the central role of orderliness and frugality in the motivational systems of these patients. As Fenichel (1945) put it:

> Frugality is a contention of the anal habit of retention, sometimes motivated more by the fear of losing, sometimes more by erogenous pleasure. Orderliness and obstinacy are more complicated. Orderliness is an elaboration of the obedience and obstinacy of the rebellion against the environmental requirements covering the regulation of excretory functions. Under certain (constitutional and environmental) circumstances, obstinacy may become so extreme that the person in question is compelled always to do the exact opposite of what is required of him. (p. 279)

The image expressing the origin of anal character traits is that of a child in a power struggle with his or her parent, an adversary of incalculably greater strength. The obsessive person later in life characteristically sees him- or herself in power struggles, often against apparently superior opponents. He or she learns to persevere and to use guile and apparent passivity as weapons, and he or she comes to feel morally superior to those who attempt to impose their will on him or her. Obedience to authority is of central concern to the obsessional person. He or she is often (apparently) deferential toward superiors and harsh toward inferiors. He or she tends to be tidy, neat, and clean (although the defensive constellation may cause the obsessive person to be neat about some things and untidy about others or continually to struggle to clean up environments which were allowed to become messy). Punctuality is deeply meaningful to such people (MacKinnon & Michels 1971): most set great stock on arriving at appointments on time and often have little patience for those who do not. But depending on the relationships among conflict, defense, and symptom, the obsessive person may vary in his or her attitude toward time. Habitual lateness may be accompanied by anxious worries about being on time or extreme punctuality may alternate with apparent disregard for time.

Fenichel (1945) made some pertinent observations about the obsessional person's preoccupation with money:

> To understand the relation between feces and money operative in every compulsion neurotic, it is first necessary to have an understanding of the psychological significance of the concept of possession. . . . When the child realizes that he loves his feces, which represent to him a very special substance, a part of his own body, he feels, "this is something that ought to be in my body; but it is now outside and I cannot put it back." Again, he calls it "mine," which means "I should like to have it inside my body but that is impossible so I declare it 'symbolically-put-into-my-body.'" Thus "possession" means "things that do not actually belong to the ego but that ought to; things that are actually outside but symbolically inside." Though they are in the external world, they are cathected with "ego quality." Possessions as a rule are provided with attributes for the purpose of identifying them: "The blue one belongs to me." This, however, is not easily done with feces, which look the same in all human beings. Later on, the child learns that "money" exists, something which grownups esteem as a possession but which is not "blue" but always looks alike, no matter in whose possession. What money and feces have in common is the fact that they are deindividualized possessions, and deindividualized means necessarily losable. Thus money, in the same way as was feces previously, is estimated and watched over as a possession which is in constant danger of losing its ego quality. Money then becomes an object for pleasure (or for punishment), that is, a substitute for feces rather than an objectively useful thing. It may be irrationally retained or irrationally thrown away or these two contrasting behaviors may be combined in various ways. (p. 281)

Obsessive-compulsive people are often collectors, an attribute also thought to be derived from their anality. Every experienced analyst has known obsessive collectors. An informal survey of my colleagues produced the following list of things collected by their obsessional patients: stamps, coins, model cars, rare books, books about particular subjects (e.g., World War I, Greek vases, model boats, airplanes), boats, pistols and rifles, big game, photographs, paintings, furniture, perfume bottles, Coca-Cola memorabilia, baseball cards, doll houses, clothing with various particular attributes, boots, fishing flies and lures, butterflies, Tiffany lamps, musical instruments, wedding announcements, pens (I arbitrarily stop here lest I appear too obsessive).

The obsessive-compulsive person uses prototypical mechanisms of defense, including reaction formation, isolation, and undoing. The pressure to create dirty messes, for instance, can lead to its opposite as a reaction formation: a rigid attitude toward cleanliness often coupled with a sense of moral superiority towards those who do not consider "cleanliness" to be associated with "Godliness." In the defense of undoing, certain activities represent attempts magically to negate or wipe out earlier actions or subjective experiences. Undoing is often linked to obsessional "checking." For example, a patient who was conflicted about working and taking care of his home would start to drive to work, then become preoccupied by the worry that he had left the stove on at home. For reasons he didn't understand, he felt the need to retrace his route home as exactly as possible. Once there he "checked" to be sure that the stove was off and set out again, only to reexperience the same concern at the same point in his route. This patient actually "undid" his commute and symbolically "undid" his unconscious desire to start a fire that would destroy his home. Isolation, of course, refers to the separation of thoughts from the consciously perceived feelings that provide context and meaning to them. This characteristic makes the obsessional person appear excessively cold and logical.

Theoreticians and clinicians have been impressed with the central role of aggression and cruelty in obsessional phenomena. This association was originally attributed to fixation at an anal-sadistic level of development. Whatever the underlying reasons, the accuracy of the association from a descriptive point of view seems certain. Fenichel observed, "overt or concealed tendencies towards cruelty or reaction formations against them are constant findings in obsessional neuroses" (p. 273). Numerous examples of this phenomenon can instantly be summoned up by any experienced clinician. For example, one patient, after learning that I had to cancel a session because of an illness in my family, spent a few sessions discussing TV and news accounts of (what he imagined were) similar illnesses, all with extremely gory outcomes. Another patient, who obviously felt extremely frustrated in treatment, advised me with apparent concern that he had had a premonition that I would soon be afflicted with carcinoma of the pancreas, which would cause my rapid and painful demise. "I am worried about you," he said; "my premonitions are always correct." A surgeon became preoccupied with the thought that his scalpel might slip and "nick" a patient's intestinal wall. His associations were to disembowelment as a form of torture and to hara-kiri as an honorable form of suicide. An administrator complained that his role often "forced" him to behave cruelly. He was pained by the fact that he actually enjoyed his power and control over people and felt terribly guilty that at times he enjoyed inducing suffering. He had achieved his high administrative post as the result of expertise in ethics, a subject he had written numerous books on.

Shapiro (1965) emphasized the rigid cognitive style characteristic of obsessive thinking. What he called *principled inattention*—restriction of attention to areas of personal concern—causes obsessional individuals to be opinionated, dogmatic, and incapable of being influenced by others; this rigidity often coexists with indecisiveness. Preoccupied with technical details, obsessive people are often intolerant of global, intuitive thinking. They are work- and goal-oriented to the point that even play is often experienced as work. Obsessional people "keep score" and tend to turn spontaneous events into tactical maneuvers. As the wife of an obsessive attorney put it, "whether on the tennis court or in bed, he is always earnestly in pursuit of a performance goal. I used to love to play but when he is involved a pall gets thrown over everything." The man in question was thoroughly confused at his wife's inability to see that "good times get better when you work at them." The couple experienced sexual difficulties. When the obsessive husband learned that his wife frequently did not have orgasms during intercourse, he concentrated on maintaining intromission for as long as possible, simultaneously stimulating her clitoris. He was bewildered to find that his wife wished to feel loved and that she complained not about his technique or the physical aspects of sex, but about his inability to tell her that he loved her, either during lovemaking or at most other times. "Why must I *say* that?" he remarked exasperatedly; "she already knows it!"

The harsh superego of the obsessive person leads to preoccupation with duty and rules and makes him or her vulnerable to guilty depression. The well-documented relationship between obsessiveness and clinically severe depression may have psychobiological bases as well (see Mavissakalian, Turner & Michelson, 1985). The *DSM-III-R* criteria for compulsive personality disorders are perfectionism, preoccupation with detail, stubbornness, preoccupation with work to the point of impairment in interpersonal relationships or in the capacity to enjoy other activities, indecisiveness, overconscientiousness, impaired ability to express affection, lack of generosity, inability to discard worn-out or worthless objects.

OBSESSIVE-COMPULSIVE PERSONALITY STRUCTURE AND OBSESSIVE-COMPULSIVE DISORDER

The term obsessive, as noted previously, may be applied both to a healthy person and to one with a specific type of character neurosis or borderline syndrome. The term obsessive-compulsive disorder refers to a somewhat different category of behavior. The disorder is defined by the presence of obsessions and/or compulsions that cause significant distress or interfere with social functioning (Insel 1984).

Obsessions are ego-alien, intrusive, repetitive thoughts. The thoughts are unwanted, generally perceived as senseless and repugnant, and fought against. They lead to anxiety and a sense of inner pain. Obsessional thoughts tend to be about dirt, aggression, orderliness, sex, or religion. Compulsions are stereotyped repetitive acts, most frequently involving cleaning or checking, that are distressing because of their apparent irrationality. Obsessive-compulsive disorder usually begins in adolescence or early adulthood. The disorder is relatively uncommon: approximately 0.6–2 percent of psychiatric outpatients suffer from it (Rasmussen & Tsuang 1984). Most people with obsessive-compulsive disorder appear to have obsessive personality types. It is easy to see how the defense of isolation in severely pathological form can lead to obsessional thoughts that are ego-alien, persistent, and tormenting. "Why should I keep having the thought 'kill your son'?" a patient asked me: "I love my son!" The thought, divorced from consciously perceived aggressive affect, is experienced as if it were an affliction from without, yet the patient knows that it is from within. That some patients appear to develop obsessive-compulsive disorder without having an obsessive-compulsive personality stands as another example of how much remains to be learned about the mind (Mavissakalian, Turner & Michelson 1985).

Epidemiological data about obsessionality in relation to sexual orientation are extremely sparse. There is no evidence that healthy obsessional personality type, obsessive-compulsive character neurosis (or personality disorder), obsessive-borderline syndrome, or obsessive-compulsive disorder are unequally distributed among individuals along the Kinsey spectrum. In the following chapters, I compare people at higher and lower psychostructural levels. The middle level, where patients with severe character neuroses meet those with borderline syndromes, is not treated in detail in this book, because of space limitations. I present instances of the obsessive-compulsive disorder among patients in the borderline spectrum, but I do not assume that patients with obsessive-compulsive disorder must necessarily be borderline. Respecting the fact that no data address this point, however, I suspect that the majority of these patients are in fact at lower psychostructural levels.

HOMOSEXUALITY–HETEROSEXUALITY AND HIGHER-LEVEL OBSESSIONAL CHARACTER NEUROSIS

Patients suffering from obsessional character neurosis experience object constancy and a stable self-concept and sense of identity. Their ego functions are, for the most part, unimpaired. They have the capacity for deep, rich, object relationships. But unconscious conflicts cause their obsessional traits to impair their capacity to work, love, and/or feel fully alive. As both a consequence and a cause of their adaptive failure, they frequently become depressed. The traits that lead to misery in their hypertrophied rigid form include a rigid, controlling interpersonal style; perception of all interpersonal interactions as power struggles; excessive preoccupation with neatness, tidiness, cleanliness, money, and time; stubbornness, sadism, and cruelty; self-righteous pomposity; isolation of affect leading to emotional coldness; indecisiveness; doing and undoing, rationalizing, and hostile behavior—or the opposite—preoccupation with detail, duty, and work; performance orientation toward all experience; and a harsh judgmental posture toward the self and frequently toward others.

Obsessional men with higher-level character neuroses are common. Below I present two cases in some detail. Neither history illustrates every point about obsessionality, but each shows how obsessional character traits may impair the capacity for loving sexuality. I selected heterosexual and homosexual men at comparable phases of the life cycle. Both experienced their sexual orientation as a stable personality trait.

CASE HISTORY OF A HETEROSEXUAL OBSESSIONAL MAN

Carl, an accountant in his thirties, was accused by his wife, Cindy, of avoiding sex. At first he denied it. Irritated, he "retaliated" by sending her articles at her work address about "the new impotence." These articles portrayed women as demanding, dominating, and insatiable. Cindy pointed out that she had been aware of the problem for many months but had avoided confronting Carl because she feared his feelings would be hurt. Furthermore, Carl's busy schedule made it difficult for the couple to have private time to talk. Very successful at his work, Carl specialized in corporate tax issues. He restricted his social life almost entirely to colleagues, claiming that there was "simply no time" to be involved with someone he was not working on a project with. A "fitness addict" (in his words), Carl liked to tell Cindy about the "extreme efficiency" of playing squash with clients. "On the way to the court we talk shop, and in the locker room we talk shop after we beat our brains out. It's fantastic!" Cindy complained that Carl described his schedule in identical words, repetitively, and with a superior tone, as if he were lecturing to a teenager. Despite the fact that Cindy enjoyed aerobics and was a fine squash player herself, Carl's remarks, delivered with intensity, never failed to arouse anxiety in her: "He makes me feel like I am decaying on the spot!" Cindy described Carl as "a body fascist." He rarely deviated from his weekly exercise schedule, which included "working out" twice a week with free weights and a Universal machine. The time spent, the weight lifted, and the number of repetitions were recorded in a notebook. Three times a week, before leaving for work, Carl jogged six miles, always over the same route. He engaged in a "small ritual" the night before: his jogging shorts and T-shirt were laid out on a sofa in the bedroom, always with the shirt on the left. The athletic supporter, socks, sweatshirt, sweatpants, and hat were placed on a separate chair. If rain was suspected, Gore-Tex garb was placed on the same chair. Each evening Carl listened to the weather report ("Channel 7 is the most accurate") and checked it against the newspaper ("I hate surprises"). Because of his "training schedule," Carl was asleep by ten, to Cindy's progressively escalating distress. "Shower and brush teeth at nine, lay out clothes, watch TV and pop off," Cindy said; "you can set your watch by this man."

Since Carl often brought work home and Cindy's career as a real estate broker sometimes involved evening work, the couple rarely spoke to each other about anything but superficial matters during the week. "Make *love* to him?" Cindy complained; "I can't even hold his hand except on the weekend. Occasionally he asks how my day went, that's the extent of our intimacy. I don't feel like his wife. I don't even feel like his roommate. I feel like a piece of furniture in the house."

In Carl's view, Cindy was being unfair. For one thing, she seemed to him "excessively emotional," which he felt was a sign of weak character. Even more important was Carl's "irritation" that Cindy was attempting to interfere with his training schedule. Cindy's complaints seemed "almost disloyal; after all, I'm doing all this for our future. It's combat out there. I have to keep fit." Carl felt "betrayed" by Cindy because she seemed to be "backing out of goals we set when we got married." The goals Carl referred to were financial. Five years previously, Cindy had been given a lecture, including tables and graphs, outlining the family's financial growth rate. According to Carl, money was building up according to plan and in two more years, at the time agreed upon five years earlier, they could have a child. Cindy felt that in two years they might be divorced. She resented Carl's obstinate refusal to allow her to have her own charge cards or checking account. "I can't believe, in this day and age, that I turn over my money to him and he doles it out as an allowance. I try to argue with him about this but he's so damn logical."

Carl was adamant that he control the couple's finances. He explained that his insistence was entirely logical. He was a professional money manager, "one of the best." "Why should I dot the i's and cross the t's for *other* people, and not for my own wife." This might seem sexist, Carl explained, but "it's really *not!* If Cindy were the accountant she would manage the money. It's not because I'm a *man;* it's because I know how to save money." Carl prided himself on his ability to give Cindy the money she wanted and yet continue to put away a quota of savings. Even though he rarely denied Cindy money, he insisted that she explain the reasons for every significant purchase and discouraged spontaneous spending ("things dribble away"). To Cindy's anguish, he often claimed that this would provide an excellent example for their children.

Cindy looked forward to vacations as the only time when Carl "loosened up." But even vacations were associated with requirements, rules, and rituals. Carl decided that he and Cindy would alternate in choosing their vacation site. "My only requirements are that there must be a six-mile jogging route nearby, and the hotel must have a gym so I don't break training." Despite these restrictions, the couple did a fair amount of traveling. On vacation, Carl kept a financial notebook in which he recorded all daily expenses. He made detailed preparations for visiting new places, including bookwork, lists of supplies, and phone calls to people who had been there. His anxiety and irritability about potential hazards and obstacles "took the fun out" of shared experiences for Cindy. "I have the feeling that I'm always struggling with him and I don't know why." Even when Carl appeared to agree with Cindy, a struggle inevitably ensued as to exactly how an experience would unfold. For example, Carl would agree to go to a museum. Once inside, he would suggest a sequence for viewing exhibits. As they began to get underway, however, he would hesitate. "I wonder if that's *really* the best—what do *you* think?" he would ask. Cindy felt trapped at such moments, when her strategy of agreeing to avoid conflict seemed doomed because of his indecisiveness. When she committed herself, Carl's response was invariably "But . . ." Even if she agreed ("whatever you say, dear"), his response was "but . . ."

Early in their relationship, Carl and Cindy enjoyed an active, spontaneous sexual life. Both were fully sexually responsive and they made love many times a week. Cindy pointed out that during the early years of their relationship, Carl's rigidity had not been fully expressed. He had been less controlling of money and not so frantic about exercise. He had been more spontaneously affectionate and the couple's life had not been rigidly scheduled. Roughly coincident with a dramatic upturn in Carl's career, the rigid behavior gradually emerged.

Although Carl initially resented Cindy's confrontation about their sexual life, he soon realized that she "had some right on her side." Because he loved Cindy and wanted to preserve his marriage, Carl agreed to (couple) consultation, although he had never before seen a mental health professional. Carl had been aware of sexual frustration during recent years, which he did not attribute to difficulties in his relationship with Cindy. He had developed an interest in pornography and was particularly stimulated by stories in which women submitted to men who controlled them sexually. To his shame, he occasionally found himself masturbating to fantasies in which he seduced famous women, such as movie and TV stars. Both Carl and Cindy felt that their lovemaking had become unimaginative, repetitive, and ritualized. Carl felt that this was due to Cindy's inhibited, puritanical sexual outlook. Cindy told quite a different story. She related that Carl insisted their lovemaking follow a rigidly prescribed routine. The type of foreplay was specified, timed, and followed by coitus. If Cindy became sexually excited at unanticipated times, Carl either lost his erection or suddenly ejaculated.

Despite Carl's symptoms, he had numerous strengths. From a lower-class background, he had distinguished himself via his flawless performance in school and at work. Not everyone perceived him as emotionally cold. His mother, a widow, found him a considerate, thoughtful, loving son who not only provided for her financially but was emotionally supportive as well. Carl inspired loyalty in others because of his ethical stance and leadership capacities. He counted a number of people who were honored to consider him a friend. His nieces and nephews adored him. He never forgot a birthday and always personally selected tasteful, meaningful gifts. He was seen as a source of quiet strength. Although Carl prided himself on socializing only with business associates, in fact he had quietly kept up a friendship of twenty-five years with a childhood pal who was now a policeman. Carl's assets had drawn Cindy to him, and she felt alarmed that they had appeared to wither away in the marriage.

Carl and Cindy underwent marital therapy, and Carl's obsessional symptoms responded to psychotherapy. Carl, in his relationship with his alcoholic, weak, but loving father, had experienced severe guilty anxiety at being placed in an "oedipal victor" situation. His career success was accompanied by superego retaliation, and obsessive symptoms that had been relatively quiescent since childhood had been exacerbated. He unconsciously felt the need to atone for his (unconscious) aggression by giving up his wife. Carl unconsciously perceived an adult, satisfying sexual relationship with a loved one to be unacceptable. In psychotherapy, as Carl learned to distinguish between assertion and (unconscious) aggression, and as he recognized the self-destructive aspects of his behavior toward Cindy, his inner life became richer. Warmth soon returned to his marriage.

CASE HISTORY OF A HOMOSEXUAL OBSESSIONAL MAN

Robert, the forty-five-year-old president of a large corporation, consulted me because his lover, Thomas, had threatened to leave him unless he did so. Robert was respected and feared at work. Meticulously neat, he insisted on a dress code in the office, and he often cancelled his conferences with and publicly humiliated subordinates whose attire was sloppy. He had fired students on summer jobs who appeared at work in blue jeans.

Robert dressed only in pinstripe suits during the week. Each day he wore a different shade of grey or blue and sparkling black wing-tip shoes. Robert prided himself on his large collection of paisley and regimental striped ties (stored in two separate closets). He carried a nail clipper in his pocket, and his staff had learned to make themselves scarce when he began clipping his nails during meetings. As Thomas put it, "he always clips his nails before he reams someone out." Robert's office was arranged as meticulously as his person. If his secretary let any disorder appear, he became angry. He had his home cleaned daily. "I can afford it," Robert observed; "why should I have to put up with dirt when it makes me tense?"

Because of his brilliance, Robert enjoyed an international reputation in his area of expertise. His ability to analyze complex situations in terms of component parts was second to none. With a photographic memory for statistics and the ability to perform complex computations in his head, Robert had no difficulty chairing meetings. Although he never used notes, he was always one step ahead of executives who were presenting material. He was renowned for his ability to listen attentively to detailed presentations and make brilliant summaries after others had proved unable to integrate the material. Always prefacing his remarks with "it seems to me that . . . ," he crisply reviewed, criticized, and suggested options, each with its associated risks and benefits.

Robert was known in the industry as "the man who never blinks and never sweats."

Like many obsessional men, Robert was involved with a lover whose personality style was virtually the opposite of his own. Thomas, a filmmaker, was creative, expressive, and spontaneous. He described Robert as "an obnoxious s.o.b. I don't know why I love the guy." Robert, whose social role was that of an eligible heterosexual bachelor, had been "fascinated" with Thomas from the start. He found Thomas's capacity to function at a "nonlogical" level particularly intriguing. Whereas Robert collected art, Thomas was an accomplished painter, and Robert derived great pleasure from watching him create a painting. Particularly "wonderful" to Robert was Thomas's capacity to create without "knowing why." "It feels right that way," Thomas often said about a painting or film he made. Robert critically analyzed why these creative enterprises worked, and usually Thomas agreed in amazement. Robert's verbal facility complemented Thomas's intuitive synthetic ability, and each was deeply impressed with the other's talents.

The tendency of gifted, somewhat lonely people to find each other led initially to Robert and Thomas's friendship. Although both men had narcissistic tendencies in that they felt special, neither was organized in terms of object relations at a pathologically narcissistic level. Robert and Thomas were both capable of meaningful, rich object relationships. Each man perceived his superiority in his chosen world as both enjoyable and something of an affliction. Robert often felt impatient because he was brighter than most people. He likened usual social discourse to "living in a slow-motion movie." But his cold, haughty facade masked an underlying need for intimacy that he usually felt was frustrated by his high standards.

People often sought Robert out. He was charming when he wanted to be, but he found the endless cocktail parties at which he was matched up with eligible women superficial and trying. Furthermore, he was angered by the fact that many men and women who were his social and even intellectual peers seemed to lack scruples. Despite his reputation for being a tough-minded business executive, Robert considered himself completely ethical. He held himself up as an incorruptible role model for ethical business behavior. Because of his position of power and influence, Robert had been approached many times with bribes and gifts. Cynical about human nature, he was rarely surprised and never tempted. His stubborn refusal to lie (if at all possible) made him particularly unpopular in the corporate world. Robert was especially amused that at least a few times a year he was offered the sexual favors of a young woman for his cooperation in some business deal.

Thomas was also seen as a leader in his field and, like Robert, inspired awe. He had an unerring sense of "precisely how a film should unfold." Like Robert, he often experienced himself as an outsider because, as he put it, "other people seem to live in the present; I'm always one frame ahead."

Thomas met Robert a year after the end of an affair with a chess player of international renown. Although Thomas experienced deep feelings toward his previous lover, he claimed that he had fallen "truly in love only once in my life, with Robert." Robert too, had had affairs, although without the same sense of passion. This time, though, Robert to his surprise fell deeply in love with Thomas. The two men had developed a brief, intense friendship before becoming lovers. Thomas had not been sure whether Robert was gay and had not wanted to make an embarrassing overture. Robert, on his part, had wanted to "test out" his feelings before acting on them. He never became sexually involved with someone he did not know well—an attitude he had held long before fear of disease became endemic in the gay community. For Robert, sexuality was associated with intimacy. He found his own "prudishness" somewhat amusing but nonetheless did not frequent gay bars or baths. Robert disliked anonymous sex: "If I'm going to have sex with someone, I want to be sure they have a personality." Thomas had experienced an "experimental-adventurous phase" as a teenager, during which he had had sex with many partners in numerous places. As he got older, his need to integrate sexuality with love had become more compelling. "I was ready for Robert when he came along."

The two men, who had been lovers for five years when I met them, had briefly lived together but found it more satisfying to maintain separate apartments. They spent nights together frequently, always at Robert's place because Robert felt more comfortable sleeping in his own bed. ("Besides, *his* bathroom is always full of hair," Robert pointed out.) After about two years Robert and Thomas began to squabble, then to have more serious arguments. Robert became more and more controlling; Thomas felt constricted. "I feel like I'm living with Hitler!" he once said. Power struggles appeared in every area of interaction. Their sex life became constricted and ritualized. In bed, as in the rest of their relationship, Thomas felt confined. Robert, meanwhile, needed more and more control over "who touched whom where and with what."

Robert experienced a release of tension after sex, whereas Thomas felt depressed. Although they had experimented, their preferred sexual act had always been mutual masturbation, eventually, however, their sexual activity had become entirely restricted to mutual masturbation. To his dismay, Robert sometimes found himself fantasizing about other men during sex in order not to lose his erection. He felt terribly guilty about this "disloyalty." Robert organized "communication times" during which he interrogated Thomas, explaining, summarizing, and discussing options as if he were at a board meeting. Thomas began staying out at night, missing appointments with Robert, and inciting jealousy. Once he provoked Robert into a frenzy of rage by photographing the contents of his apartment, without Robert's knowledge, for use in a film.

Robert and Thomas had broken up four times, but the anguish of being apart had proved unbearable. Their difficult relationship continued, with islands of caring expressed amid an ocean of hostility, until Robert, desperate and depressed, sought counsel from a life-long friend, a professor at a European university, who was the only heterosexual person Robert had told of his homosexuality. After many hours of frank discussion, his friend concluded that Robert and Thomas loved each other but that Robert, at least, was too neurotic to cope with the sustained intimacy of a love relationship. He recommended psychoanalytic consultation. Robert worried that psychoanalysts were homophobic and might make things even worse. Nonetheless, he returned to the United States determined to get professional help. He procrastinated for a few months but finally, after a screaming fight during which Robert and Thomas almost came to blows, Robert felt so guilt-ridden and "horrified" that he suggested they seek help together. Thomas then revealed that he had recently begun psychotherapy on his own and he suggested that Robert do the same.

After an initial evaluation (including an interview with Thomas), I recommended intensive psychotherapy. It rapidly emerged that Robert felt chronically guilty and unconsciously believed that sexual intimacy was unacceptable because of his unworthiness. Robert's father, a passive, hostile bookkeeper, had never achieved the vocational success Robert had. Robert experienced chronic guilty fear at having surpassed his father. He also unconsciously equated Thomas with a childhood friend who had been killed in an accident forty years earlier. Robert's controlling behavior was an attempt to protect a "possession" that had become most dear. His obsessional traits and symptoms were attempts to undermine a love relationship Robert felt he did not deserve. During some years of intensive therapy, Robert and Thomas have remained together, and the destructive aspects of their relationship have abated to a large degree.

These two cases, although only examples of a few of the sexual difficulties experienced by higher-level obsessional people, illustrate some basic issues. Regardless of the gender of the love object, the interpersonal aspects of sexuality—the capacity to be loving and sexually expressive—may be impaired. Whether one is homosexual or heterosexual, the loving, caring aspect of the self can fall prey to an obsessional character neurosis.

Higher-level obsessional men, regardless of their rating on the Kinsey scale, experience all types of sexual dysfunctions and (in *DSM-III-R* terminology) other Axis 1 disorders. They are at risk for clinical depression, as are all individuals with obsessional traits. The two cases presented above stress the similar impact of obsessional character neurosis on the meaning of sexuality to gay and straight men. In addition, the men's psychodynamic conflicts were similar in certain ways, and in both cases interpretation of rageful, competitive feelings toward males was essential. Both men experienced grief and mourning as part of working through, but their sexual orientation remained completely stable.

This should be particularly emphasized with regard to Robert, the gay patient. Interpretation of the unresolved oedipal conflict (associated with the ineffable experiential aspects of therapeutic process) freed this man of his blocked capacity to love, but his homosexuality never altered. This is compatible with recent observations about male homosexuality, particularly those of Isay (1985) and Leavy (1985).

8

Homosexuality–Heterosexuality and Obsessional Disorders: Borderline Syndromes

No reliable epidemiological data reveal the frequency of lower-level obsessional character disorders, but clinical experience suggests that they are common. A substantial number of sexually pathological patients are found in this group. The combination of obsessive-compulsive defenses and impairment of the ego mechanisms that regulate impulse gratification results in the impulsive-compulsive behavior characteristic of sexual perversion (paraphilia). The mechanisms of splitting and dehumanization (viewing people as part objects and in terms of need satisfaction) are also associated with paraphilias (Stoller 1975). Both homosexual and heterosexual lower-level obsessional men manifest the symptoms of borderline personality disorder as defined in *DSM-III-R*. These include such activities as unstable intense interpersonal relationships; self-destructive impulsivity involving such activities as sexual interactions, gambling, substance abuse, shoplifting, overeating; affective instability; inappropriate anger, recurrent suicidal threats or behavior or self-mutilating behavior; identity disturbance, intolerance of being alone and chronic feelings of emptiness, frantic attempts to avoid abandonment. From the point of view of *DSM-III-R,* these patients are diagnosed as suffering multiple disorders (e.g., obsessional personality disorder, borderline personality disorder, and so on). From the point of view of psychodynamic object relations, they share the features of lower-level borderline patients, but symptom expression is shaped by the obsessional character type.

As previously noted, the types of pathology occurring in homosexual and heterosexual men at this psychostructural level are not completely parallel. The gender role/identity disorders almost certainly occur more often in homosexual men, and some types of paraphilia are asymmetrically distributed. Both heterosexual and homosexual borderline obsessional men manifest antisocial sexual behavior including rape, incest, and paraphilias such as sexual sadism and masochism. Both experience driven, dehumanized sexual activity; sexual dysfunctions; and other psychiatric symptoms, syndromes, and disorders, such as depressive disorders and panic attacks.

It is impossible to describe here all types of obsessional symptoms and syndromes at the lower psychostructural level. In the cases to follow the relationships between obsessionality, borderline pathology, and sexual orientation illustrate the similarity between men at opposite ends of the Kinsey spectrum but at the same psychostructural level. The differences between homosexual and heterosexual men particularly with regard to gender dysphoria are also illustrated. In these cases, sexual orientation itself is a stable trait.

SEXUAL ASPECTS OF BORDERLINE OBSESSIVE DISORDERS

The first case, James, shows the contrast between the quality of life experienced by men at lower psychostructural levels and that of higher-level patients with character neuroses. This patient's sexuality reflects the primitive fragmentation characteristic of his general functioning. The history illustrates, in particular, excessively controlling interpersonal behavior, inability to tolerate being alone, failure to achieve sexual intimacy, primitive and rigid preoccupation with cleanliness, and fetishistic cross-dressing (transvestism).

Heterosexual

James, a forty-year-old attorney, sought consultation for depression after his second wife left him. His work was intermittently excellent but variable enough that he had never achieved partnership in his law firm. When he "felt well," James was logical, clear, well-organized, industrious, and attentive to detail. However, James did not understand why he sometimes had "weird feelings of numbness" during which the world seemed unreal to him. At such times, he became anxious that he had a serious disease. He was not reassured that frequent physical examinations by several competent internists revealed no positive findings. When James experienced depersonalization, derealization, or anxious hypochondriacal worries, he became distracted and was unable to function effectively. He misread and misplaced documents, was late for appointments, and seemed unrelated and detached. James frequently wanted to change professions but had no idea of what he wished to do. He had fantasies of being "on a desert island, doing nothing, content, alone."

James's first wife left him because she found aspects of his obsessive behavior too restrictive to bear. He was preoccupied with cleanliness to the point that he refused to travel in foreign countries ("you never know what the food or water or bathrooms will be like"), refused to walk on certain streets in the city ("too much dog shit"), even refused to let her wear perfume ("a disgusting habit"). James became unaccountably "tense" when physically separated from his wife. He insisted that they speak on the phone many times a day and had temper tantrums if she tried to attend leisure activities without him. When he wanted to go somewhere she didn't want to go, he insisted that she accompany him "out of love."

While married to his first wife, James refused to socialize with others. In his view, the streets were dangerous, and one could get mugged "trying to be friendly." Furthermore, he believed that married people should "be for each other" and that friends interfered with closeness. When James insisted that his mother-in-law wear only freshly laundered clothing because her usual attire had an "odor," his first marriage for all intents and purposes ended.

James's second marriage lasted only a few weeks. His bride, a religious Catholic, forbade all premarital sexual activity other than kissing. On their wedding night James was horrified to discover that she had a vaginal mucus discharge and a characteristic vaginal odor. He insisted that she douche before intercourse, and he avoided manual or oral stimulation of her genitalia. For the first two weeks of their marriage, the couple engaged in sexual activity only once: James's wife masturbated him to orgasm (after first positioning towels to avoid the "mess" of the ejaculate). The couple finally had sexual intercourse on one occasion. There was no foreplay; James rapidly mounted his partner (who experienced dyspaureunia) and ejaculated. After James criticized her for "not doing better," his wife decided to leave him, despite religious interdictions.

After his wife moved out, James briefly considered celibacy; however, he experienced sexual desire and frequent erections. He felt furious at his wives for treating him unfairly. One night he discovered some undergarments that his second wife had left behind. "On an impulse," he masturbated with her panties and, after he ejaculated, threw them away. He then began to experience his estranged wife's underwear as sexually stimulating, and he searched "every nook and cranny of the house" for additional garments. He discovered a garter belt and a bra, and again "on an impulse" he put them on and masturbated to orgasm while staring at his reflection in a mirror. After ejaculating into a towel, James threw away the undergarments. James remembered where his wife had purchased her lingerie, and he bought underwear there. When he discussed with the matronly saleswoman details of the type of lingerie that would make the best "surprise gift" for his wife, James became sexually excited.

James embarked on a secret sexual life that caused him great guilt and anxiety. His ritualized scenario was repeated as precisely as possible. He threw away his kitchen garbage and installed a fresh plastic bag in his wastebasket, folded a black towel and placed it on his bed, closed the window blinds, and turned off all the lights but one night lamp. Staring at his shadowy reflection in the mirror, James dressed in bra and panties and masturbated into the towel. He placed the garments and towel in the plastic garbage bag, tied it closed, and threw it down an incinerator. He then showered and went to sleep. James could not understand what it was that stimulated him about wearing women's undergarments, since he was perceived by others (and at the conscious level by himself) as masculine. Severe guilt about this sexual ritual compounded the depression James was experiencing as a result of losing his wife. His chief complaint upon seeing me did not concern his sexuality but rather his depression: "I feel like shit!" Only after establishment of a therapeutic relationship did the complete sexual history emerge.

Although James obviously manifested obsessional defenses, his core problems involved lack of object constancy, primitive projection, failure of ego integration, and identity diffusion. His sexual activity was impulsive, compulsive, and depersonalized. James was treated with supportive psychotherapy and medication. Low-dose neuroleptics, tricyclic antidepressants, and protracted psychotherapy led to some symptom improvement. Some transvestism has persisted, however, and sexual activity in the context of a relationship has not occurred.

Homosexual

The case of Fred illustrates the relationship between lack of object constancy, obsessionality, and global impairment in the capacities to love and work. This man experienced both identity diffusion and a gender role/identity disorder. He participated in the type of driven, frantic sexuality that some clinicians erroneously attribute to homosexual men in general.

Fred, a forty-five-year-old executive, sought consultation for depression after his lover "dumped" him. Fred was simultaneously in the process of dissolving a lucrative business partnership that had broken up because of a "personality conflict." Fred had been the so-called inside man, responsible for bookkeeping, accounting, and internal organization. His lifelong preoccupation with details, lists, and numbers made him an outstanding accountant, and his stubborn insistence on keeping track of "every penny spent" meant that any office he managed was meticulously organized. Fred's capacity to tolerate human error was minimal, however. Subordinates perceived him as a martinet, and he had trouble keeping a secretary for more than a few months. Fred had no durable, caring friendships because of his hypercritical, accusatory stance toward ordinary human foibles.

Fred's partner, Tony, had been the outside man in the business, responsible for sales and acquisitions. Fred was unable to function without checking up on Tony many times a day, and often he called him late at night and early in the morning. Despite conscious acceptance of Tony's attitude that vocational success should be evaluated by income generated, not by the number of hours worked, Fred attempted to keep a schedule of Tony's work hours. At first Tony, an affable entrepreneur, had been amused by Fred's "hysteria." A heterosexual (and sexist) hedonist, he attributed Fred's intrusive, controlling behavior to his homosexuality. "You gays are like women," Tony told Fred; "you can be counted on to be hysterical." After a while, however, Tony found Fred's urgent, pressured discussions and interrogations at all hours less amusing. Although there were times when Fred knew it was wrong to telephone his partner, he felt compelled to call, "as if an outside force were making me." Fred's inability to function independently and his frantic, accusatory stance led Tony to decide regretfully to put an end to their association. Tony expressed sincere sorrow because he believed that Fred's detailed, orderly approach perfectly complemented his own global, somewhat impulsive style. But he felt that the additional money to be made as Fred's partner was not worth the stress of "not being able to lead my own life."

Fred's lovers had the same complaint. Initially they were attracted to Fred's good looks and cultured, charming manner. Soon, however, Fred became unable to tolerate even brief physical separations from his lover. He complained that he felt "empty" when the lover was not with him. "I need you to fill me up," he told each one. The scenario was always the same: he began to phone his lover frantically many times a day, he made jealous accusations without substance, and he had temper tantrums until the lover felt "hounded to death" and broke off the relationship. Fred was cautious in his choice of lovers, taking great care to be involved with someone appropriate. He saw himself as a dignified person and, as he put it, he "naturally started relationships in an appropriate way." He was also worried about AIDS ("these days you can't be too careful!"). After a relationship had ended, however, Fred engaged in frenzied sexual activity with strangers at pornographic gay movies. He had a mild gender role/identity disorder that became more pronounced during these intervals, which lasted from a few days to many weeks. He felt "swishy" and took to wearing silk shirts open almost to the waist, black leather pants, and shoes with high heels (never women's clothing, however). On a typical night he got dressed up, had a few mixed drinks alone, then went to a pornographic movie. There, he was fellated and performed fellatio, usually more than once and with different individuals. He felt driven to do this for a few consecutive nights until the "fever died down." When the episode of driven, anonymous sexuality had subsided, he felt less "swishy," for reasons he did not understand, and found himself ready to start a new relationship. The cycle then began anew.

Fred experienced chronic feelings of "terrible loneliness." He was terrified that he would become ill and die alone, uncared for, and unremembered. Associated with his depression, he developed insomnia, which he treated with alcohol and valium. He became so hung over in the morning that he couldn't function. He perceived himself as playing Russian roulette with the whiskey and pills, since he knew he might die from respiratory depression. Fred came to see me in consultation after reading an article stating that suicide attempts are "cries for help." "Save me from suicide," he sobbed during his initial visit. Fred's treatment has been painful and difficult, and the outcome is uncertain.

ANALITY AND LOWER-LEVEL OBSESSIONAL
CHARACTER STRUCTURE

The following two cases focus on anality. Although psychodynamic theoreticians often stress the relationship between homosexuality and anality (Fenichel 1945), in fact both heterosexual and homosexual men can be preoccupied by the anus and its contents. Anality, in its most concrete form, serves various functions. Anal intercourse and anal exploration occur frequently in sexual activity regardless of the Kinsey rating of the participants. But anal intercourse (as common sense would suggest) is probably practiced more frequently by homosexual than heterosexual men.

The functions served by sexual activity, in a context of adequate ego integration, seem similar regardless of the gender of the sexual object or the parts of the body involved. Pathological anality, therefore, is pathological not because the anus is sexualized, but rather because of the relationship between the anal imagery associated with sexual arousal and the integration of the total personality. Thus it is only when anal preoccupation meets criteria for paraphilia or perversion, or when it is clearly an integral part of a larger symptom picture (i.e., compulsion, phobia, delusion), that it should be considered important in clinical terms. This is the type of anal behavior found in lower-level obsessional men regardless of the gender of their sexual objects.

Heterosexual

Harry, an executive, had become bored with his predictable, constricted marriage. Although he felt loyal to his wife of twenty-five years and devoted to his children, he experienced nagging discontent with every aspect of his life. He had sexual relations with his wife every month or two, always without passion. Every Friday night he played poker with friends. His stamp collection provided another source of pleasure, but his relationship with his children was distant and he had no intimate friends.

One night a stranger came to the poker game and "hit if off" with Harry. To Harry's surprise, he offered him the opportunity to snort cocaine. Harry accepted "just for the hell of it." Shortly thereafter he was introduced to women "who would do anything for cocaine." Harry bought the drug and was soon involved in "cocaine orgies" instead of poker games on Friday nights. Without fanfare, Harry had slipped into a double life. His associates now included "cocaine whores" and members of organized crime.

At first under the influence of cocaine, then while drug-free as well, Harry became obsessed with anal sex. He had fantasized about anal intercourse previously but had never tried it either with his wife or with the few other sexual partners he had had before marriage. Harry now discovered that all aspects of anal functioning were intensely sexually stimulating to him. He engaged in manual exploration, analingus, and anal intercourse, and he became preoccupied with (heterosexual) anal pornography, which he often used during masturbation. Frequently impotent, Harry used a dildo to have anal sex with multiple partners, usually under the influence of cocaine. He also became fascinated with feces and had his partners defecate and give him and themselves enemas during sexual activity.

For more than a year, Harry's double life remained secret, probably due to his wife's denial and/or disinterest. But finally he began staying out late on other nights. His new acquaintances began calling his home at all hours. One night his wife told Harry that she believed he was having an affair. Tearfully, he confessed his cocaine abuse, whereupon she promptly attempted suicide by injecting barbiturates. Consumed with remorse, but unable to give up either cocaine or his driven need to engage in orgiastic anal sex (which he had kept a secret from his wife), Harry sought psychiatric consultation. He said that in recent months he had developed a habit of smelling his fingers. He did this many times a day, often against his will, "feeling silly," and with the expectation that his fingers might smell of feces. Harry washed his hands many times a day, but the compulsion to smell his fingers persisted. At times, he burst into tears because he felt that his life was "totally out of control." "If psychiatry can't help me," he said, "I might throw myself out of a window." Harry's case was referred to a colleague. He ultimately discontinued treatment and was lost to follow-up.

Homosexual

Timothy, a librarian, loved his work because of its "tidy aspect." "Plus," he said, "I love the smell of books." He was openly gay and had for years led a decorous, predictable life. He had sex with one of a few partners, cultivated a small garden, and collected rare books. At about the same time as Timothy's superior at work developed cancer of the rectum, Timothy fell in love with and was rejected by an opera singer younger than he. Timothy ruefully recognized that he had begun a "mid-life slide." He became depressed and began drinking regularly at gay bars, then he began picking up sexual partners at bars and baths. He discovered that engaging in anal intercourse (insertee) with men the age of the man who had rejected him provided extraordinary sexual pleasure. He never had sex twice with the same partner.

Timothy came for consultation because his life had taken on a frantic, driven quality, and he was afraid of contracting AIDS. In the month prior to consultation, he had had sex with twenty different men. Timothy wondered whether a brain tumor might be causing his frenzied behavior, and he had even consulted a neurologist, keeping his sexual life secret but complaining of headaches. He did not fully believe the negative report. He related that, for reasons he did not understand, he had taken to relaxing at home in a woman's nightshift (never with sexual arousal). At times when alone he dressed in women's skirts, which made him feel less tense. Timothy continued to function well at work, and no one in his circle of casual friends knew of the change in his personality. He was treated with supportive psychotherapy and low doses of neuroleptics, and he showed some improvement.

COMPULSIVE SEXUALITY

The cases below further illustrate compulsive sexuality. Sexual compulsions, although similar to nonsexual compulsions such as checking or cleaning, are somewhat different in that the intensity of the compulsive urge is related to the intensity of the experience of sexual affect. Like nonsexual compulsions, sexual compulsions are experienced as ego-alien urges and cause anguish. No data indicate the degree to which sexual compulsions coexist with obsessive-compulsive disorder. The two cases that follow differ in the content of compulsions, but in both cases repetitive, irresistible acts were carried out against the dictates of conscience. The acts produced anguished guilt and occurred in the context of lower-level obsessional character organization.

Heterosexual

This army drill sergeant was feared by his men because of his brutality, although they grudgingly admitted that he was "fair" in that he only punished men who had indeed committed an infraction. Sergeant Jestins's uniform was always spotless and perfectly pressed. Sloppy attire enraged him and on more than one occasion he had been unable to restrain himself from physically assaulting subordinates. He was so feared and respected as a soldier, however, that his career had never been jeopardized by his punitive rages.

Sergeant Jestins's interpersonal relationships within the military were regulated "by the book." He had no friends, believing that affection was weak. Any open display of emotion (other than anger) aroused contempt in the sergeant. He took pride in his work and never questioned his duty to God and country. His men were combat ready at all times. Those that couldn't meet his rigid standards were shipped out or derided until they went AWOL or became psychiatric casualties.

Sergeant Jestins had married a divorced woman with two teenage daughters. He was as much a martinet at home as at work. He doled out allowances to his wife and the girls, demanding an account of every penny spent. He was harshly critical of the boys that the girls dated and of his wife. He was particularly disgusted by the fact that she did not exercise and had allowed her body to become flabby. Sergeant Jestins found himself avoiding sexual relations with her and seeking out prostitutes. His wife became depressed and alcoholic and withdrew from all family interactions.

When the sergeant's stepdaughters went out on dates, he waited up for their return, insisting that they be home by eleven. Once one of the girls was a few minutes late, and the sergeant punished her by turning her over his knee and spanking her. To his surprise and consternation, he found that this punishment sexually aroused him. He began to have unwanted, distressing fantasies of sexual relations with both stepdaughters. He condemned himself and sought to distract himself by frequently having sex with prostitutes. This failing, he turned to prayer and intense exercise. But nothing worked. By day Sergeant Jestins was the living embodiment of a harsh superego. He became even more cruel in his insistence on cleanliness in the barracks and, to enforce discipline, forced errant soldiers to clean the latrine with toothbrushes. Once the day's activities were over, however, he experienced tormenting desires to have sex with his stepdaughters. He found these urges "disgusting" and "evil" and prayed to God for deliverance from them.

After one particularly agonizing struggle with the conflict between impulse and conscience, Sergeant Jestins entered the bathroom as one of his step-daughters was showering. According to him, she was anxious but nonetheless seductive and willing to have sexual intercourse with him. For two years, Sergeant Jestins frequently had sex with both stepdaughters, leading to intense feelings of guilty depression. The sergeant wondered whether he had commit-ted some terrible crime earlier in his life, for which he was condemned to live in hell. He swore both girls to secrecy and begged their forgiveness. He contem-plated suicide and practiced putting an empty revolver to his head and pulling the trigger.

Finally, one of the girls confessed to her mother. After some denial and delay she went with the grim story to Sergeant Jestins's commanding officer, who arranged for psychiatric treatment. "Do something to stop me," Sergeant Jestins pleaded at the initial consultation; "I cannot stop myself." Extensive psychiatric treatment of all the family members was ultimately undertaken. The sergeant's wife and both stepdaughters chose to leave him. He was able to achieve some measure of self-awareness, and he ultimately remained in the armed forces, functioning adequately in his military role, and maintained a stable sexual adaptation based on frequent sex with prostitutes.

Homosexual

Kirk, a thirty-five-year-old attorney, sought consultation because he was con-cerned that he might murder someone by acting on sexually sadistic fantasies. Completely homosexual in his fantasy life since the age of nine, he became aware during adolescence that he was sexually excited by sadistic homosexual pornography. He collected detective and pornographic magazines containing sadistic stories, which formed the basis of his masturbation fantasies of a man being bound, tortured, and killed. Sometimes the man was someone he knew, sometimes a movie star, sometimes a stranger. Kirk became "wildly aroused" when he read in a local newspaper a detailed account of a homosexual lust murder. The period of intense arousal lasted for weeks, during which he masturbated many times a day to the scenario described in the newspaper.

Kirk became sexually active with other males at the age of sixteen and discovered S&M gay bars at eighteen. He frequented them regularly and picked up masochistic partners whom he tied up and whipped. He also had a number of long-term liaisons, and for the most part his sexual life followed a predictable pattern.

When Kirk was thirty-three, his mother died. He experienced profound grief and then chronic depression. After several months of decreased sexual desire, he returned to S&M gay bars, hoping to regain interest in sexual activity. Soon this occurred, but a new element had appeared. Instead of feeling relief of tension associated with his old fantasies, Kirk became preoccupied with the impulse actually to kill someone. This notion initially came to him in the form of a question he asked himself: "what if you were to kill someone? No one would know!" He tried to push the question out of his mind, but it recurred frequently, intruding even during the work day. Kirk fully realized the difference between fantasy and reality, but his guilty anxiety increased when he recognized that these thoughts seemed more of a rehearsal for reality than imaginary stories which, as he put it, "actually hurt no one." To his horror, during sexual activity he experienced an intense desire to plunge a knife into his partner's chest. At first this fantasy occurred during sex with an overtly masochistic partner, then with others as well. It soon became the focus of his inner sexual life. He masturbated to it frequently and occasionally had nightmares in which a man's being stabbed was a prominent theme. Sometimes these frightening dreams were accompanied by nocturnal emissions.

At about the same time as his murderous desires increased in intensity, Kirk experienced the sense that he was no longer himself. He felt that his personality had been taken over by some monstrous outside "agency—possibly the Devil!" When not sexually aroused, he experienced his homicidal fantasies as alien—"not me!" When aroused, however, the fantasies provided intense pleasure until orgasm was reached.

Kirk befriended a messenger boy at work who soon became his sexual partner. One night, Kirk hid a kitchen knife under his bed so that he could reach it during sex if he wanted to. The next day, overwhelmed with guilty anguish, he bought a shotgun with which to kill himself. At this point he sought psychiatric consultation. He was hospitalized and received extended treatment, improving to the point where he was no longer a danger to others or himself.

MULTIPLE SYMPTOMS OF OBSESSIVE CHARACTER STRUCTURE

Patients at the lower level of psychostructural integration often exhibit multiple symptoms. In the following cases many symptoms are illustrated, and relationships between affective disorder, obsessional personality type, borderline level of integration, and sexual orientation receive particular attention. Depression and all varieties of obsessionality are associated. Many patients with the more severe depressions (psychotic or endogenous) have obsessive character structures. Obsessive-compulsive disorder becomes worse with depression and can be ameliorated to some degree by the use of antidepressants (Insel 1984; Mavissakalian, Turner & Michelson 1985). Depression may also be associated with sexual dysfunction, as both a cause and an effect. The following cases illustrate similarities and differences in gay and straight men with lower-level obsessional character structure, expressed via obsessions, phobias, sexual impotence, major depression, suicide attempts, hostile dependent unstable romantic liaisons, and identity diffusion. The gay patient described also has a severe gender role/identity disorder.

Heterosexual

Arthur, a thirty-year-old schoolteacher, had been raised as an Orthodox Jew. From post-oedipal latency-age years he had fought with his mother, who suffered from obsessive-compulsive disorder characterized by compulsive checking and phobic avoidance of doorknobs and other things and situations in which exposure to germs was, in her view, possible. Arthur's father was a Talmudic scholar whose relationship with his son was distant and severe. He often verbally expressed compassion for Arthur's plight with his mother ("I know she's a difficult woman") but never became involved in the struggle between mother and son. Indeed, according to his son, he firmly believed that disobedience to either parent was sinful.

Arthur's mother had been frantic about toilet training and unforgiving of the occasional accidents Arthur had with urinary control prior to his latency-age years. His parents, especially his mother, were relentlessly strict in their observance of Orthodox ritual. Housecleaning in preparation for the Passover holiday, for example, assumed gargantuan proportions as the family scrubbed and searched for forbidden bread crumbs that might have dropped behind, under, and between things. The family was sexually repressive and sex roles were rigidly differentiated, prescribed by tradition and law.

In the home, family members frequently did not observe privacy about bodily exposure. Arthur's mother and his younger sister frequently walked around in undergarments. Bathroom doors were left open during showers and while family members were using the toilet. Arthur recalled that on more than one occasion during adolescence and adulthood his mother accosted him in the hallway, asking for help clasping her bra. Arthur was forbidden to date girls until age nineteen. Against great inner feelings of resistance, he began to masturbate at puberty. He lived in dread that a nocturnal emission would stain the sheets and lead to a humiliating confrontation with his mother.

During adolescence Arthur became involved with pornography in a frenzied way. Every day he felt compelled to buy new pornographic magazines and pictures. Some he discarded, some he gave to friends, some he stored at a friend's home. For reasons he did not understand, he began anonymously to mail pornographic pictures and magazines to girls he found attractive. His masturbation fantasies focused on the girls' shock and horror at seeing the genitalia of the men in the pictures. During his adolescence Arthur engaged in no sexual activity with partners. He felt such guilty anguish about his sexual fantasies and activities, particularly the mailing of the pornography, that he tried to "erase" lustful feelings and imagery by piercing his palms with thumbtacks and burning his arms with cigarettes. At times he experienced a sense of pride about how much pain he could endure. But the sexual fantasies and activities continued.

Although Arthur attended a parochial high school (Yeshiva), he was allowed to attend a secular college. There he experienced chronic anger, which he attributed to the slovenly dress, cigarette smoking, and drug and alcohol abuse of students and teachers. Where previously he had felt too busy to make friends, now, in college, he felt there was no one "worthy" of his friendship. Arthur developed chronic, severe headaches and persistent hostile depression. He continued to live at home and the rageful confrontations with his mother worsened. Their battles were usually verbal, but sometimes physical, and Arthur (to his subsequent guilt) told his mother that her obsessive-compulsive symptoms meant she was "crazy."

Arthur was by and large an indifferent student but he excelled in mathematics and physics. He had been identified as a brilliant mathematician from his earliest years. His only avocation was chess, at which he achieved a national ranking. Although his mathematics experience at college paralleled his earlier outstanding experiences, and he was immediately seen as the most powerful player in the chess club, Arthur's experience with physics was somewhat different. Whereas his mathematics professor was reserved, even remote, but respectful of his students, his physics professor was flamboyant, caustic, and contemptuous. He had made substantial contributions to the field and apparently enjoyed singling out the better students and jousting with them in front of the class. Any hesitancy, imprecision, or inarticulateness invited ridicule. Following such a contest and despite acquitting himself well in the eyes of others, Arthur's tension increased. Daily headaches were associated with the physical sensation that his skull was expanding. He felt that strangers at school and on the street could see that there was something wrong with him. At night before sleeping he sometimes heard a man's voice saying "stupid, stupid."

Arthur found a young woman in his physics class particularly attractive. Following the incident with his professor, his sexual feelings, always powerful, became even more insistent and persistent. To his consternation, he developed a repetitive fantasy in which he approached the woman from behind in a dimly lit hallway and coughed to announce his presence. She would turn around to see his pants unzipped and his fully erect penis. Shocked, she would scream or faint. Arthur was sometimes unable to resist masturbating to this fantasy during the class.

Arthur came to my attention following a second arrest for exhibitionism. He had been unable to resist the impulse to act out a scenario in which he exposed his penis to a solitary female whom he felt he was "sneaking up on." The act was erotically arousing and he would masturbate to orgasm later when alone. Arthur acted out the scenario repetitively for about six months before he was apprehended for the first time. He experienced his sexual activity as "horrible, beneath contempt." He felt "insane" since he could not resist his impulse despite his suffering, and he entertained the notion that his soul was possessed by a demon. He developed anorexia, terminal insomnia, nightmares, pessimism, helplessness, and hopelessness, and he seriously contemplated suicide. After being arrested, his emotions were obviously complex, but one of them was a strong sense of relief. The second time he was caught, he attempted suicide, discovered by prison guards as he was putting his head in a noose he had contrived from his belt, while blood flowed from both wrists.

With extensive mental health intervention Arthur's major symptoms remitted. The prolonged treatment included supportive psychotherapy, group psychotherapy, pharmacotherapy and social work intervention with the family. Although such dramatic symptoms as exhibitionism and suicidal depression did recede, other impairments associated with low-level obsessional character structure remained.

Homosexual

Didi, a thirty-five-year-old "drag queen," was the fourth of five children born to a Portuguese-American working-class family. Didi's father was a fisherman, his mother a housewife. The oldest sibling, Didi's brother, worked on the father's boat and was a happily married father of four. The next two siblings were girls, both of whom, in Didi's words, "adored me my whole life." The youngest child in the family, also a girl, had died tragically at the age of two, when Didi was three. The children had been crossing a street with their mother when a truck careened out of control, killing the little girl, Diane, while leaving the others unscathed. Both parents experienced painful grief, but the mother's response was especially prolonged and agonized. A simple, uneducated immigrant woman, she had lost her own mother in an accident during her early childhood. She refused to give up Diane's highchair or crib and kept her clothing in a special chest. The profound depression she experienced following the loss became chronic, and throughout Didi's childhood she was tearful, bitter, and ruminative about God's injustice. She was overprotective of her son and forbade him to engage in any physical activities. Didi was rarely allowed out of her sight. She lived in dread that he would fall and injure himself and instructed him not to climb or participate in rough-and-tumble or athletic play.

During Didi's preschool years, his mother sometimes dressed him in girl's clothes, hugged and rocked him, and cried. The child seemed interested in female clothing. He especially enjoyed wearing women's hats and shoes and playing with ribbons provided by his sisters and mother. Whereas the females in the family felt that his behavior was "cute," the males perceived it as "unnatural," and both his father and his brother withdrew from Didi as his behavior became more feminine. But his father felt that since his wife had suffered the catastrophic loss of a child, he could not place limits on her conduct toward the boy. By the time he began kindergarten, the child had acquired the name Didi, although his given name was Robert. First his mother, then his sisters had begun calling him "little Di," emphasizing his similarity to his dead sister, and this had been transformed to Didi, although he continued to be called Robert in school. (As an adult, he legally changed his first name to Didi.)

Didi's mother and sisters were Catholic, believing in the literal truth of the Bible and living in dread of damnation. They practised numerous rituals to undo or ward off sin. A particularly feared sin was sexuality. Women were assumed to be chaste in body and mind, but men were prone to evil lust, which dominated the culture in which they lived. During Didi's early school years he avoided other boys. He was identified as a "sissy" and a "faggot" quite early but was never physically assaulted by other boys, who perceived Didi's effeminacy as "weird" and tended to withdraw from him.

Didi made friends with some girls and occasionally played with them at his home. His mother forbade him to visit their homes, lest he get sick from their "germs." Didi and his friends painted, colored, and played hopscotch. They also played house, during which Didi, like his friends, fantasized being a mother. Didi's favorite after-school activity, however, was housecleaning with his mother and sisters. He contentedly scrubbed windowpanes, washed silverware, and polished furniture for hours. Didi was very clean, and any hint of dirtiness or messiness made him anxious and angry. He rigidly demanded that others be neat as well. He insisted that pictures hang perfectly straight, that papers on desks be neatly stacked by size, that his environment be organized and under his control. He collected miniature dolls and animals, a hobby that persisted into adulthood. By late adolescence Didi's collection of ceramic, wood, glass, metal, plastic, and wax miniatures took up virtually the entire wall space of two rooms. He was unable to discard figures that were damaged, for reasons of which he was unaware.

Didi's extreme effeminacy attracted notice at school and his parents were advised to seek professional help on many occasions. They steadfastly refused, however, believing that mental health professionals were only for insane people. Didi knew that he was a boy, with male genitalia, who would (to his consternation) grow into a man. Didi never believed that he was a girl trapped in a boy's body; he realized that he was a male who felt and wished to be female. Prior to puberty Didi had reached the conclusion that his life was a punishment for a terrible sin that he did not consciously conceptualize. He had poor self-esteem, was prone to tearfulness, and felt that he was worthless, ugly, stupid, and, because of his effeminacy, a "freak."

Puberty for Didi was catastrophic. He hated his penis and frequently taped it to his thigh to hide it. Erections terrified him, yet he was stimulated by pleasureful imagery of homoerotic activity. He fantasized amputating his penis with a razor, or watched it in fascination as he masturbated to orgasm, always with homoerotic imagery. Such fantasies typically involved fellating or being anally penetrated by a male classmate or celebrity. Didi became severely depressed at puberty. He felt "sinful," "evil," and "dirty." At school he developed severe anxiety, particularly when called upon to recite. His anxiety, still intense when he returned home at the end of the school day, was relieved by dressing in woman's clothing. He did not experience this as sexually arousing. "It made me feel like a whole person," he said.

Following puberty, Didi, still called Robert at school, felt "like a girl" at home. In the privacy of his room he wore female clothing, developing a preference for loud colors, satiny fabrics, and bras that were dramatically unlike the clothing worn by women in the family. Didi's effeminacy attracted the attention of gay men from his latency age years, but he remained a virgin until age fifteen, since he had been taught that sex was evil. Finally, he was unable to resist an overture from a neighbor, with whom he established a sexual liaison.

Chronically depressed, Didi also became chronically angry in late adolescence. He had little conscious awareness of the reasons for his anger. He realized that he felt resentful of his mother's hypercontrolling, intrusive behavior, but he did not identify this as the reason for his hot temper or persistent feelings of resentment. Nor did Didi attribute to his rage or anxiety the motivation to perform sexual activity with men for money. He did not identify himself as a prostitute, but he did not object to the label. He relished the power of setting a high price for sexual desirability. During sex with men Didi rarely became sexually aroused; his erotic excitement was confined to self-masturbation in privacy.

By his early twenties Didi was making an average of two hundred dollars a month for sexual activity. He had moved to his own apartment and had also attempted suicide twice, once by slashing his wrists and once by taking an overdose of Valium. Didi was ultimately approached by an agent and decided to become a female impersonator. He captured a substantial salary at a nightclub where he impersonated a female rock singer and stripper. Didi's chronic anxiety had never abated, and the need to dress in women's clothing to relieve it remained intense and persistent. He insisted on being identified as male ("he") on some occasions, female ("she") on others. He knew of the sex change operation but did not want it; he had taken estrogen experimentally but had not found a female-like habitus congenial. As an adult Didi still found solace in cleaning window panes, furniture, and Venetian blinds. He had also become more rigidly perfectionistic about cleanliness than he had been as a child. Sloppiness irritated him, and the presence of dirt in his surroundings provoked temper outbursts. He had never fallen in love or formed a durable intimate friendship. He experienced himself as cold, excessively logical, and unable to love.

I saw Didi in an educational context, not a clinical one. He insisted on a male gender label. Because of his chronic depression, he was considering whether to undertake psychotherapy. Didi was bright, cynical, and worldly-wise. "Why should I talk to a shrink," he said; "what can it do for me?"

Relationships between effeminacy, obsessionality, and homosexuality can be complex. Recent research on effeminacy carried out by Coates and colleagues at Roosevelt Hospital in New York suggests that effeminacy frequently originates in a setting of individual and familial psychopathology (Coates & Zucker 1986). In this case of a child predisposed to obsessionality, we can only speculate about the possible synergistic effects that influenced cross-dressing. The act of cross-dressing might have assumed unusual power to organize the child's self-concept because it took on a sense of compelling urgency. This urgency hypothetically resulted not only from the child's wish to replace the dead sister but also from the amplifying effect of obsessive-compulsive defenses operating in the context of a poorly integrated character structure.

The preceding clinical illustrations focused on men at opposite ends of the Kinsey spectrum. Histories of men with obsessional character neuroses were contrasted with histories of men with obsessional borderline syndromes.

The obsessional character neuroses involve interaction between two sets of behaviors. On the one hand there are behaviors explicitly concerned with sexuality: sexual attitudes, values, fantasies, dreams, activity with others, sense of identity, social role, and interpersonal relations organized by and organizing the relational, recreational, and procreational aspects of sexuality. On the other hand are obsessive defenses and traits, including denial, undoing, externalization, reaction formation, rationalization, isolation, checking, orderliness, obstinacy, frugality, moral sadomasochism, controlling behavior, and preoccupation with work and duty. The interactions vary greatly from person to person and are influenced by other individual characteristics such as intelligence, insightfulness, financial resources, courage, and so on. The obsessional borderline syndromes also involve interaction between sexual and obsessive behavior, but in addition they are characterized by numerous symptoms associated with impaired ego integrative capacity and primitive object relations. The clinical model becomes even more complex as we turn our attention to the relationship between bisexuality and obsessionality in various forms.

9

Bisexuality, Obsessional Character Neurosis, and Borderline Syndromes

Bisexuality, no matter how defined, is not considered a form of psychopathology in this book. The issues discussed here concern only those aspects of bisexuality and obsessionality commonly encountered in psychoanalytic and psychotherapeutic practice. My impression that these problems are common derives from personal clinical experience; no published data adequately substantiates my belief. Individuals such as the ones described below probably represent only a small percentage of bisexual men.

Just as there are no universally accepted definitions of homosexuality, so there are none of bisexuality. Much confusion has resulted from the fact that some authors group bisexuality with homosexuality while others group it with heterosexuality. Discussions of the psychological or sociological aspects of sexual orientation often lump together men who are "homosexual or bisexual" by some criteria. Many psychobiological studies, however, (such as those described in part 1), treat exclusive homosexuality separately from bisexuality and heterosexuality. The area is further complicated by Freud's model of constitutional bisexuality and by imprecise use of the concepts of latent and unconscious homosexuality (discussed in chapters 11, 15, and 18).

In chapter 1, I divide homosexuality into four dimensions: erotic fantasy, sexual activity with others, sense of identity, and social role. The term bisexuality likewise may connote the simultaneous experience of heterosexual and homosexual erotic fantasies and/or a sense of bisexual identity. The term is also used to refer to sexual activity with members of both genders and to public declaration of a bisexual social role. The issue of time frame has generated much confusion with regard to bisexuality. Consider, for example, someone whose fantasies are sometimes exclusively heterosexual and sometimes exclusively homosexual. Would one describe this person as homosexual, hetero-sexual, or bisexual? Obviously this depends on the convention one adopts for describing sexual orientation as a function of time. Once again, there are no universally accepted guidelines. The diagnosis cube (see chapter 6) can be used for any time frame specified.

Bisexuality, like homosexuality, is not explicitly defined in this book. I hope the meaning expressed by the term will be clear in the contexts in which it is used.

Numerous interactions may occur between bisexuality and obsessionality. For example, all forms of bisexuality (i.e., sexual fantasies, sexual activity with others, identity, and social role) may influence and be influenced by the key obsessional mechanisms of ambivalence, splitting, and undoing. A formidable array of symptoms can be produced as a result. For example, a man might compulsively engage in sexual activity with numerous women as a reaction against unacceptable, consciously perceived homosexual feelings. Another might depersonalize and phobically avoid women in reaction to unwanted heterosexual desires that threaten his already fragile sense of gay identity.

In bisexual obsessional patients, sexual fantasies may lean toward either heterosexuality or homosexuality. Individuals equally aroused by imagery of males and females seem rare, at least in the psychopathological groups de-scribed here: I have never seen a neurotic or borderline male patient who manifested equal preference for males and females as a stable trait over time. Since neurosis is conceptualized as the result of numerous intrapsychic com-promises, true bisexuality might seem to be a splendid compromise for a neurotic person (Brenner 1973). In fact this does not appear to be the case.

BISEXUALITY AND OBSESSIONAL CHARACTER NEUROSES

The heterosexual bisexual obsessional patient is illustrated in the next two clinical vignettes. These individuals experience homosexuality as incompatible with the dictates of conscience. A full range of obsessional neurotic symptoms can be intertwined with the homosexual component of their sexual fantasies, which may or may not be acted upon. These individuals' homosexual activities can assume the quality of a sexual compulsion: frantic, driven, and irresistible, carried out against conscious will. During the altered state of consciousness in which the compulsive urge dominates, the person is flooded with lustful feel-ings joined to the consciously perceived stimulus. At that time the defense of isolation of affect may be applied to other feelings. The person may or may not be aware of anxiety and guilt as he engages in the compulsive sexual activity. The thought that he is doing wrong often persists, however, and painful guilt and anxiety typically follow the compulsive act.

Jim, a thirty-five-year-old married attorney, Catholic, the father of four, sought consultation because of depression. It rapidly emerged that his depression surrounded guilt about homosexual fantasies, which he had experienced for many years but had never acted upon. He now felt compelling pressure to begin a homosexual liaison. Jim had been a stubborn, oppositional child, who had from his earliest years been deeply concerned with neatness and cleanliness. As an adult he displayed the coldness, perfectionism, work orientation, and hyperattentiveness to detail characteristic of obsessional character neurosis.

As a child Jim experienced only heterosexual fantasies prepubertally and during early adolescence. Beginning with late adolescence, however, and coincident with leaving home, he began to have homosexual fantasies, although they were not as intense or pleasureful as his heterosexual fantasies. Jim believed homosexuality to be a sin and he never doubted as a teenager that he was heterosexual. He first had sexual intercourse at age seventeen and he found the experience intensely pleasureful. Subsequently, he had satisfying relations with a number of young women. He fell in love with Polly at the age of twenty-one and they married.

Jim's feelings of guilt and shame about his constant homosexual fantasies were not intense until Polly's first pregnancy. An infection led to her hospitalization, during which Jim experienced homosexual fantasies somewhat more intensely. His guilt and shame increased markedly and he became noticeably depressed. Family and friends attributed Jim's depression to worry about Polly, but Jim felt afflicted by a "horrible, disgusting secret." When Polly returned home, Jim's homosexual fantasies lost their urgency, and his depression and associated guilt and shame remitted. A few years passed, then the scenario was repeated: unwanted homosexual urges led to guilt, shame, and depression. In this case, the precipitant (not identified as such at the time by Jim) was Polly's two-week visit to distant relatives. The homoerotic imagery was associated with urgent, frantic masturbation, many times a day. During masturbation, sometimes the imagery was homoerotic, sometimes it changed to Polly. Upon Polly's return, the psychic status quo returned: Jim had a satisfying sexual life with Polly; his homosexual fantasies were constant, not intense, but accompanied by guilt and shame.

One month before Jim's third episode of distress, Polly's mother developed a terminal illness. After much discussion, Polly and Jim mutually decided that she should take the children and move in temporarily with a friend near her mother. Jim had encouraged Polly to fulfill her responsibilities, so he felt bewildered by the intense anxiety he experienced when she departed. To his consternation, he became flooded with homosexual feelings. He still found women erotically arousing and he attempted to displace the homosexual imagery by increasing heterosexual stimulation. He bought heterosexual pornographic magazines and viewed pornographic movies, but to no avail.

Jim never realized the meaning of the relationship between Polly's absence and his homosexual feelings. Instead, he felt bewildered and anguished that he, an obviously heterosexual man, should be afflicted with these "vile desires." When the compulsive desire to go to a gay bar became overwhelming, Jim began to drink himself to sleep, consuming up to half a bottle of gin per night. He became severely depressed and had nightmares. Jim decided to seek professional help when he had to overcome the impulse to commit suicide by taking sleeping pills along with the gin.

Jim was one of two children born to a truck driver and a nurse. Both parents were observant Catholics and openly disapproved of sexuality. Jim's mother was depressed and abused alcohol; gin was her favorite drink. His father was a hot-tempered, hypercritical man who verbally and physically abused his wife and anyone who crossed his path on a bad day. He had been arrested for assault. He beat the children with a strap when they misbehaved. Jim shared a room with a brother, one year younger, until he left home at eighteen. The brothers were best friends, and both experienced the separation during late adolescence as traumatic.

When Jim was four, his mother left the home after a violent argument with her husband. The children became even more terrified when their father stormed out of the house, leaving them alone. They huddled on the floor together until he returned, drunk, hours later. Their mother returned the next day. The parents separated for a few weeks when Jim was five, and again when he was six. Both times his mother took the children with her to a hotel and left them locked in a room with the TV on for hours at a time.

Jim never understood or integrated these events, which contributed to the extreme sense of vulnerability that overwhelmed him when Polly left. His homosexual fantasies appeared to be caused by a variety of factors. One influence was his close childhood relationship with his brother, which was more difficult during adulthood—in fact, friction between the brothers had been severe since Jim's marriage to Polly. His brother remained single, without a loving sexual relationship, for many years, but finally married in his thirties. Jim responded well to supportive psychotherapy. He learned to recognize his vulnerability to separations from Polly and to cope more adequately with such separations. He did not engage in homosexual activity and his homosexual fantasies lost their urgent, compelling quality.

Unlike Jim, Charles did not experience homosexual fantasies constantly. Charles was a 0 on the Kinsey scale except for discrete intervals during which persistent, insistent homosexual fantasies existed side by side with heterosexual fantasies. The homosexual fantasies were intense and ego-alien. They had a compelling quality and occasionally motivated homosexual activity, carried out with gay acquaintances, which was followed by remorse and anguish.

Charles, a married Episcopalian, had experienced transient homosexual fantasies since puberty, but they were inconsequential in comparison with powerful heterosexual fantasies. He first had intercourse at sixteen, fell in love with a woman at twenty-one, and married at twenty-four. Charles divorced at twenty-seven, remarried at thirty, and was happy until he and his wife realized that they had a fertility problem. An evaluation revealed that Charles had a low sperm count. During the examination process he and his wife had difficulty carrying on with their normal sexual activity and he became preoccupied with homosexual fantasies that were for the first time intense. They lasted for a few weeks and gradually subsided. Charles's homosexual fantasies returned when the couple was considering artificial insemination and adoption. When his wife went to another city to ask her mother for advice, his fantasies recurred. He engaged in sexual activity, which led to feelings of guilty anguish. Charles wondered whether he was "a homosexual" and, in a state of torment, decided that he "couldn't be." He was bewildered by his fantasies and wondered whether they represented a form of punishment for past "sins."

The couple decided to adopt a child. Almost as soon as they obtained the baby, Charles's homosexual fantasies subsided and then vanished. Sex in the marriage again became mutually satisfying.

Charles eventually undertook psychoanalysis for characterological manifestations of obsessionalism. These, particularly rigidity and isolation of affect, were a source of concern because his emotional coldness was negatively affecting his family life. During psychoanalysis, Charles's homosexual feelings recurred. He acted them out with gay partners, to his consternation. The feelings were analyzed and they again subsided.

Charles came from a middle-class family. His father, although not violent or physically abusive, was cold and often harshly critical. His mother was depressed and the parents were stably but unhappily married. Charles had urethral stricture as a child and needed dilatation at age five, then yearly until age ten. He had nightmares before and after the procedure. He never fully understood why dilatation was necessary or what a urethral stricture was, and as a boy he decided that he had a seriously damaged penis. He never discussed this belief with anyone and, although he learned differently later, he never entirely believed that he was not damaged. As a teenager, Charles felt that his penis was small but was reassured when he compared it to a friend's. He participated in mutual masturbation with this boy, who became the object of Charles's homosexual fantasies. His friend was more athletic, handsome, and successful with peers than Charles. In mid-adolescence Charles experienced a growth spurt, became more socially successful, gave up his relationship with this friend and moved on to develop other friendships. These were deeply satisfying and sustaining, as was his relationship with his wife, whom he called his "best friend."

Homosexual fantasies in both cases presented above appeared to function as sexualized defenses. Jim's intense homosexual fantasies appeared to be triggered primarily by separation anxiety. Charles viewed his infertility as symbolic castration. His homosexual fantasies appeared to express symbolically the types of conflict about masculinity that have been observed by many psycho-analysts (Ovesey 1954).

Both of these patients experienced ego-alien homosexual fantasies in the context of a sense of heterosexual identity. In one instance the unwanted homosexual fantasies were constant; in the other they were intermittent but when present they remained continually in awareness for weeks. These cases are examples of two types of bisexual phenomenon. In one category, homosex-ual and heterosexual erotic fantasies are continuously present in consciousness. In the second category, the homosexual component is intermittent. In both categories, the personality structures of the individuals are probably compara-ble. Why some people apparently have the capacity to repress homoerotic imagery while others apparently do not remains to be clarified.

BISEXUALITY AND BORDERLINE SYNDROMES

The cases discussed below display the fragmentation of self and object worlds and the impaired ego functioning characteristic of the borderline syndromes. The interaction between bisexuality and borderline obsessional pathology is common and occurs in many people who complain of feeling unsure whether they are homosexual or heterosexual. Identity diffusion is a prominent part of the clinical picture and patients commonly feel bewildered about the meaning of sexual fantasies in relation to their sense of identity (i.e., they wonder "am I gay or straight?"). I present patients with various sexual fantasy and identity combinations here without categorizing them as homosexual, bisexual, or heterosexual as is the convention elsewhere in this book. Each patient present-ed below experienced a variety of symptoms in numerous combinations.

Klaus, a divorced forty-year-old administrator, father of two, sought con-sultation because of anxiety, depression, depersonalization, and derealization associated with changing erotic fantasies and perceived sense of identity. In addition his frantic sexual activity, experienced as uncontrollable, led him to fear that he was losing his mind.

Klaus's background was extremely traumatic. A refugee whose parents and siblings were casualties of war, he had witnessed many atrocities during child-hood and adolescence. After being orphaned, he had been brutalized in nu-merous ways before puberty, including homosexual rape and forced sexual encounters with adult women. He saw himself as heterosexual during adoles-cence and young adulthood. Despite intermittent intrusive, intense homosex-ual fantasies he did not participate in homosexual activity. Klaus came to the United States in his twenties and soon married. Although he had never fallen in love, he quickly proposed marriage to an American woman, reasoning that an American wife would help him fit into American society. Klaus "went along" with his wife's desire to have children. He felt no love for his two daughters, who arrived within the first three years of the marriage, only resentment at having to care for them.

The marriage was fraught with overt conflict which gradually worsened with time. His wife complained that Klaus had no understanding of her emotional or sexual needs. Lovemaking was mechanical. Klaus usually ejaculated prematurely after minimal foreplay and then fell asleep. Klaus viewed his wife as sexually and interpersonally demanding, describing her as "the kind of woman who will suck out your marrow if you let her." During the marriage, Klaus began visiting prostitutes. He preferred sex with two partners, preferably one male and one female. Klaus experienced anxiety as "a sense of tension" and orgasm brought relief of tension. His need for sexual activity assumed an insistent, persistent, compelling quality. Klaus felt progressively anxious about his inability to control his sexual impulses. He frequently dashed out of his house to cruise the streets for prostitutes. He often left business meetings to masturbate, fantasizing sexual activity with both male and female partners. Frequently, Klaus had many orgasms a day, usually via self-masturbation. He felt that his urgent need for orgasm impaired his social and vocational functioning, yet it seemed irresistible. Klaus felt depressed, empty, and unreal following orgasm, but the activity also relieved tension, for which he felt grateful.

In the fourth year of the marriage, Klaus's wife left him, moving with their two daughters to a distant city. Klaus began to experience states, lasting for weeks, in which his sexual fantasies were mostly homosexual. He attended gay baths and had anonymous sex with numerous partners. On many occasions he tentatively decided that he was gay, but when he was on the verge of coming out, his homosexual fantasies would diminish and heterosexual fantasies would gain ascendancy. He would then tentatively decide that he was straight. Gay sexual activity would be replaced with sex with female prostitutes. Gradually homosexual fantasies would return and the cycle would begin again.

Klaus lived alone in the apartment where he and his family had resided. He let the place deteriorate. He described it as dusty and dirty, with dishes frequently unwashed and clothing on the floor. Yet Klaus remained meticulously neat about his person and flew into a rage if his clothing was not perfectly cleaned and pressed.

Klaus sought consultation following an incident at work in which two workers announced their homosexuality. This precipitated a crisis of indecision in Klaus about whether he was gay or straight. Following the incident, he experienced persistent derealization and depersonalization. Numerous rituals he had performed during childhood again became part of his life: he refused to walk under ladders and felt it necessary to step on every crack in the sidewalk and to wipe the telephone with a handkerchief before speaking into it. Klaus's work performance remained reasonably satisfactory, but he had no friends and no social support network. He felt so anxious and depressed that he sought professional assistance, despite negative feelings towards psychotherapists. As had been his pattern with previous therapists, Klaus was unable to sustain a therapeutic alliance with me and dropped out of treatment before it could get underway. In his history we see a person whose urgent attempts to base a sense of identity on erotic fantasies and activities were defeated by severe psychopathology associated with a fragmented personality structure.

Toni, a twenty-seven-year-old male prostitute, requested surgical procedure for sex change at a medical center where I saw him in consultation. Toni stated as a chief complaint, "I am a woman trapped in a man's body." He interrupted the initial interview in order to phone a friend, whom he asked to check his apartment to be sure the door was locked. Toni admitted that he often had the urge to "check," although he recognized that it was "silly." When asked what would have happened had the friend not been home, Toni answered that he would have had to terminate the interview to go home and check. Toni's social functioning was greatly restricted because of this problem.

Toni had desired a sex change for about a year. Previously he had perceived himself as gay. Toni's former pimp, Carlos, had beaten him frequently and sometimes burned him with cigarettes; nonetheless, Toni claimed that he had been in love with Carlos. Carlos threatened on occasion to leave Toni, which led Toni to threaten and sometimes attempt suicide by overdosing on drugs or slashing his wrists. He had been a psychiatric inpatient three times, but each hospitalization had lasted for less than a week.

After a raging fight, Carlos and Toni split up for good. Carlos had apparently complained that Toni's looks were deteriorating with age, and he replaced Toni with a teenage boy. Toni developed a severe depression. He lost interest and pleasure in all activities, had crying spells, was preoccupied with suicide, lost his appetite, lost ten pounds in twelve weeks, and felt agitated, sleepless, unable to concentrate, and confused. Toni believed that strangers stared at him because he gave off a foul odor. He heard a man's voice saying "ugly, ugly."

Toni sought psychiatric help and his depressive symptoms improved with tricyclic medication. After he had begun feeling somewhat better, he dropped out of treatment. Shortly thereafter, he experienced a powerful, illuminating sense of insight while watching a TV show on transsexualism. For the first time in his life, Toni felt a sense of "true inner direction." He decided that he was really a transsexual and that his life would gain true meaning only if he could obtain a sex change. Toni began to insist on being addressed as "she." He obtained estrogens on the black market and used them briefly but discontinued them because of hot flashes and headaches. Once he had decided to become "completely female," life seemed more hopeful. To be sure that the desire for sex change surgery was not transitory, Toni waited for many months before seeking to implement the plan. He realized that many people who applied for sex change were not accepted, and he fantasized that if this catastrophe should occur, he would amputate his penis.

Except for the brief interval in which he used estrogens and some episodes of severe depression, Toni experienced sexual desire and fantasies in normal intensity. Although sexual imagery was predominately homosexual, hetero-sexual fantasies sometimes occurred, accompanied by severe anxiety and self-loathing. He had engaged in intermittent heterosexual activity from early adolescence, until he decided that he was basically female. During Toni's late adolescence and early adulthood, he served as a prostitute for women as well as men. His sexual performance with males and females was adequate, but Toni only experienced pleasureful sexual activity with males. When he had sex with women, he denied experiencing a feeling of pleasure even during orgasm. Although some of these (invariably older) women wished to befriend him, Toni was unable to accept their help. His only "friends" were other gay prostitutes, none of whom functioned as intimate confidants or provided social support.

Orphaned at birth, Toni had been raised in institutions. As a teenager he was taken into a dormitory by Carlos, who had noticed Toni's effeminacy, present from early childhood. Toni had never had a caring relationship with an adult during childhood and adolescence and had never formed positive peer relationships with boys or girls. The only adult to take an interest in him prior to psychiatric treatment was Carlos.

Toni did not receive the sex change procedure. Extensive inpatient and outpatient psychiatric services were provided, and after about a year and a half of treatment, Toni came to see himself as male (although effeminate) and gay. He began attending secretarial school and continued to work as a prostitute (for males) occasionally. Toni's prognosis is guarded—it is not certain how much therapeutic improvement is possible. But Toni does recognize to some degree that his fantasy of penile amputation (which underlay his desire to change gender) reflected a pathological desire for self-mutilation, as a result of low self regard. When he was able to discuss his feelings about Carlos his wish to change genders subsided. The transient conviction that he was transsexual seemed at the time to protect Toni from being overwhelmed by the painful feelings associated with identity diffusion.

Kenneth, a middle-aged civil servant, was referred because of affliction with unwanted, ego-dystonic, guilt-inducing heterosexual feelings. This man, dap-per, intellectual, and superficially good-humored, was attractive to women. To his dismay they often attempted to seduce him. Kenneth felt that he had been "truly homosexual" from the age of five, and he experienced anxiety and severe guilt over his heterosexual feelings. He liked women and empathized with their predicament at being attracted to "a gay." In addition, for reasons he did not understand, the heteroerotic feelings women's seductive maneuvers aroused in him caused shame, guilt, dysphoria, and depression. "It is not me!" he explained. If he experienced an erection in response to a woman's sexual advances it was associated with a sense of horror. Kenneth did not spontaneously fantasize about sex with women. Following overtures by women, however, heterosexual fantasies would last for weeks before they subsided. Kenneth would then become anxious and depressed and would worry that he was not truly gay. As his heterosexual fantasies subsided, his self-esteem rose, associated with a feeling of "being in control again."

These matters were a source of concern for Kenneth, but they paled beside a terrifying prospect of retirement. He had been a civil servant for twenty-five years and was approaching the mandatory retirement point. Kenneth had no future plans and depended completely on his vocational setting for social structure. Despite the duration of his employment and his reliable performance, he had formed no personal ties at work. He realized that he would be missed there because of what he could do, not because of who he was. Kenneth saw himself as a civil servant. Other than that, he felt he was virtually nothing. Although he felt proud to be gay, he did not think that gayness could be his sole identity. Kenneth was openly gay only with select people. He was not politically or socially active in the gay community. At work, he was known as a heterosexual bachelor.

Kenneth experienced intense feelings exclusively toward his lovers. They tended to be late adolescent or young adult men, who after a few months (or sometimes longer) rejected him. During the initial phase of a relationship Kenneth showered his lover with gifts and attempted to play the role of mentor and guide. But soon he became hypercontrolling, jealous, and unable to tolerate being alone; this behavior provoked rejection. Kenneth had lost his father as a teenager. A solid athlete and student who had been accepted by his peers, he experienced the loss as a total catastrophe. He gave up sports, friendships, and all group activities.

Kenneth responded positively to supportive psychotherapy. It should be emphasized that without specific, concrete intervention by the therapist directed at his heterosexuality, Kenneth came to recognize that heterosexual fantasies and activity were incompatible with his preferred self-concept. In a therapeutic environment of empathic listening and gentle exploration, Kenneth was able to renounce the likelihood of acting out his heterosexual impulses. This reassured him and his self-regard increased with the conviction that he could master heterosexual impulses should they arise. To his considerable relief, Kenneth was also able to decide upon a post-retirement vocation. Insight about the nature of his sexual attachments (i.e., why he chooses young men and provokes them to reject him) awaits further therapy.

Arthur, a forty-two-year-old curtain salesman, separated, the father of two, had had bisexual fantasies since the age of nine or ten. He also manifested severe hypochondriasis and was preoccupied with the size of his penis and testes and the volume of his ejaculate (all of which he feared were too small). He insisted on cleanliness and neatness in dress but his private personal habits were slovenly (i.e., he never made his bed, he threw underwear on the floor at night, his desk drawers were a disorganized mess). His persistent problem with lateness nearly resulted in his expulsion from college and cost him many business accounts. Friends routinely invited Arthur to social events an hour early and expected him an hour late, and he frequently lost jobs because of procrastination.

Arthur had been married for fifteen years prior to his separation. To his shock and surprise, his wife left him for another man. Arthur knew that his wife had been unhappy with their relationship for years. She complained that Arthur never expressed affection in any way, never told her he loved her, routinely forgot her birthday, and never hugged her or took her hand on the street. She was bitterly disappointed that virtually his only involvement with their two sons was to insist that they be quiet when he wanted to watch TV. Curiously, it never occurred to Arthur that his wife might leave him. Although he recognized at an intellectual level that she was attractive to men, he did not integrate this information in a meaningful way. Until his wife left him, when he was thirty-five years old, Arthur had experienced her as "a nothing." Subsequently, her value escalated, and Arthur suffered a major melancholic depressive episode in response to the dissolution of his marriage.

Arthur responded positively to tricyclic medication prescribed by his family physician. His depression subsided, but he persistently worried that there was something wrong with his lower intestinal tract and sought out gastroenterologists and proctologists on numerous occasions. He did not tell the physicians about his previous examinations, so that in one year Arthur had had twelve complete lower GI workups. Although the negative findings were temporarily reassuring, his worries recurred and he felt compelled to repeat the procedures on the average of every two months.

Arthur's sexual life following separation was at first with female prostitutes and women he met at bars. On the verge of beginning a serious relationship with one such woman, he began to worry that she might carry a venereal disease. Despite lack of evidence for this and persistent sexual activity with prostitutes who *were* at high risk for venereal disease, he broke off relations with the woman. Shortly thereafter, Arthur developed rectal bleeding from hemorrhoids, and he became convinced that the blood on his toilet tissue was a sign of malignancy. He believed that the physicians who reassured him by telling him the correct diagnosis were either missing something or deliberately lying. He became preoccupied with his mortality and, positive that his life expectancy was limited, he ruminated about how to spend his remaining days.

Arthur's only confidante was his mother. His father had died when Arthur was seven, and there were no siblings. Shortly after Arthur developed hemorrhoids, his mother had a stroke which led to hemiparalysis, aphasia, and chronic organic mental syndrome. Arthur visited her daily and desperately tried to communicate with her. His route to the hospital took him past a gay bar, and one evening he impulsively stopped in. He had never before participated in homosexual activity. He met a man there with whom he engaged in mutual masturbation later that night. During this encounter Arthur experienced "a spectacular sense of ecstasy." He began to frequent gay bars and baths and found that intensely pleasurable homosexual activity helped take his mind off his mother. When he was unable to avoid his worries about her, however, he became terrified. He could imagine no life for himself if she died.

One evening Arthur met some gay activists and was not only persuaded of the justice of their cause but experienced a sense of belonging. He joined their organization and decided to "come out of the closet totally." He informed everyone who knew him that he was gay. Reaction tended to be polite but cool. Open discrimination against gay people was not practiced at Arthur's place of employment, but other gay workers there, to Arthur's bewilderment, did not seek him out. Arthur felt comforted that his future would be devoted to gay causes, and he seemed reasonably stable until his mother suddenly died of a pulmonary embolus. Crazed with grief, Arthur threatened to jump from the Brooklyn Bridge. The police took him to the emergency room of a local hospital, where I first saw him. He was briefly hospitalized but soon dropped out of treatment following improvement in his suicidal depression. At that point he appreciated that his suicidal agitated depression was a reaction to the loss of his mother. His sexuality, although discussed to some degree in the context of the AIDS epidemic, was not a topic that he was able to relate to with insight.

I felt that Arthur's enthusiastic pursuit of a gay identity appeared to be an attempt to cope with diffusion in his sense of identity generally. This attempted solution allowed him to maintain sexual satisfaction while renouncing heterosexuality. Unresolved preoedipal and oedipal conflicts produced anxiety which, when added to the emotional pain resulting from his mother's illness, led him to avoid heterosexuality and to amplify the sense of pleasure from homosexual fantasy activity as a symptomatic attempt to cope. Interestingly, despite Arthur's (hypothetical) maternal identification, he did not become overtly effeminate following her illness and death.

Jerome, a twenty-five-year-old Catholic grade-school teacher, said when consulting me, "tell me if I'm gay so that I can decide whether to live or die!" Jerome was raised in an environment that was hostile toward homosexuality to an even greater degree than is usually the case in the United States. His father, a construction worker, was bigoted, derisive toward women, contemptuous of minority groups, homophobic, and xenophobic. His ideas of solutions to social problems consisted of statements like "Beat the shit out of them!" "Nuke the bastards!" "Line up every motherfucker and blow their balls off." From his earliest years, Jerome hated his father and avoided him as much as he could.

Jerome's mother, a grade-school teacher, was a constricted, depressed, highly obsessional woman. She confided to Jerome as a boy that she remained with his father only because divorce was prohibited by the Catholic church. The family was very religious, and each of the five children, of whom Jerome was the oldest, attended parochial school. Jerome recalls being taught that masturbation and premarital sex were sinful, and he felt guilty fear when he was unable to resist the temptation to masturbate as a teenager. Although he confessed this activity to his priest, he was never able to confess the "terrible secret" that his fantasies on occasion were homosexual.

Jerome's fantasies were actually predominantly heterosexual, and his homosexual fantasies were relatively rare. They were usually precipitated by a humiliating encounter with a male authority figure, following which Jerome would imagine that he was "screwing an older man up the ass." This fantasy was sexually arousing and usually subsided after masturbation to orgasm. It first occurred after Jerome and his high school basketball coach had a raging argument. Jerome recalled him screaming, "you shit! When I tell you to *do* something, you *do* it. If I tell you to cut your goddamn testicle off, you pull it out of your pants and cut it off!" In a fury Jerome stormed off the court and was thrown off the team. That night, for reasons he was unaware of, the homosexual masturbation fantasy appeared. Following orgasm, Jerome experienced "disgust, repugnance, and depression." Not only was he shocked and frightened by the gender of the sexual object, but the idea of anal penetration also seemed especially repellant to him.

Jerome had been close to his mother during his childhood. He described her as being "fanatically neat, frenzied by the threat of dirt." Not only did she inspect her home with ruthless efficiency for the merest hint of untidiness or messiness, she treated her children in the same way, and they endured frequent inspections of parts of their bodies for dirt. Ears were attacked with Q-tips, dirty necks with washcloths. The younger children had to display their underpants to determine whether they had "wiped themselves" adequately to avoid fecal staining. Offenders were spanked on the bottom and sent off to the bathroom to wipe themselves again. The children invented a term with multiple uses in their home: "shiny asshole."

Jerome's teachers throughout his juvenile years and adolescence described in him contradictory attributes and abilities that they found difficult to understand. An excellent athlete and fighter who was respected and feared by other boys, he nonetheless often complained of not getting the "respect" of peers. His school performance was extremely variable. Teachers could not get a grasp on Jerome's capacities and were frequently surprised by a good or bad score on an exam. Although Jerome was voted into school office, he had no close friends and was not close to members of his family. He was withdrawn from his brothers and sisters at home, seeking out his mother's company until adolescence, then preferring solitude. Some people felt that Jerome was quiet and withdrawn; others experienced him as labile and full of rage.

Jerome had a long-lasting sexual relationship with a woman, beginning at the age of eighteen and continuing until he was seen in psychiatric consultation. He found their sexual activity intensely satisfying but felt little positive emotion toward his partner. He felt contemptuous of her for being sexually "loose." During their four-year relationship, she experienced a number of serious stresses, including the death of a sibling and her father's illness. Jerome expressed sympathy but, to his surprise, felt "nothing inside." As far as he was aware, he had never loved anyone; the only feelings he was aware of experiencing in any sustained way were rage, anxiety, depression, and sexual lust. Other than his isolated homosexual fantasy of penetrating an older man anally, Jerome never had homosexual fantasies, and he never engaged in homosexual activity. He had profuse masturbation fantasies of having intercourse with women and was sexually aroused by heterosexual but not homosexual pornography.

Unlike his brothers, who became construction workers like their father, Jerome became a teacher like his mother. His choice aroused his father's contempt since it seemed unmasculine. Despite his seething hatred for his father, Jerome had always withdrawn from arguments with him, until an eventful family dinner. Following consumption of a large amount of beer, Jerome's father began to become surly toward his mother. After she had left the table, he turned his attention to various minority groups who he felt were destroying America. After dispensing with blacks, Jews, Asians, and Latins, he turned his attention to homosexuals, "the worst of the lot." During his father's tirade against "queers" Jerome experienced intense anxiety, which he attempted to alleviate by drinking whiskey. He felt unreal and "absentmindedly" wondered if he were dying from a heart attack. Suddenly, and with a feeling of intense relief and inner clarity, he decided that his father was talking about him and that in fact he was "queer." His anxiety subsided, and he quickly excused himself from the table and left home. Shortly thereafter, Jerome broke off his relationship with his girlfriend, explaining that he was gay. He "came out" at school and joined a gay political organization. He had a sweatshirt made that pronounced in pink lettering, "I am Gay and proud of it!"

Despite experiencing a sense of inner contentment, Jerome avoided sexual contact with gay men. He explained that although he was privately gay, he was considering becoming a priest and had therefore decided to abstain from sexual activity. Actually, Jerome experienced no sexual attraction for men, and was confused because his fantasies were predominately heterosexual. But he dismissed this inconsistency as being of "no significance." Jerome avoided contact with his family at first but finally sent them a letter advising them that he was gay. As expected, his father and brothers rejected him completely. His mother did not, but neither did she sanction homosexuality or make any effort to understand her son. She spoke with him from time to time and pretended that nothing unusual had happened.

Following his loss of contact with his girlfriend and with the men in his family, Jerome became progressively depressed. Gradually he became convinced that his father's views about homosexuality were correct. He burned his sweatshirt in a furnace. Consumed with self-loathing, he began to drink heavily, primarily to combat insomnia. Jerome read books about homosexuality and learned that "it is untreatable." He decided that he was "doomed" and determined to hang himself. During an unexpected visit, however, his old girlfriend persuaded him that he couldn't be "100 percent gay" in light of their sexual relationship. At her behest, he sought psychiatric consultation, which led to extensive outpatient and inpatient treatment. Ultimately, Jerome's isolated homosexual fantasy subsided and he was able to fully experience a sense of heterosexual identity and social role. without irrational anxiety. (Ovesey's description of pseudohomosexuality, discussed in chapters 11 and 18, is particularly relevant with regard to Jerome's psychodynamics.)

EROTIC FANTASY AND SENSE OF IDENTITY IN OBSESSIONAL BISEXUAL MEN

Men who are afflicted with obsessional psychopathology can be uniquely perplexed by bisexual phenomena. In such men sexual experiences, be they fantasies or activity with others, cannot be understood in any simple way. Key interactions occur between bisexual phenomena, obsessional character defenses and symptoms, and the perception of the self as homosexual or heterosexual. Pathologically obsessional men often experience bisexuality as an assault on their sense of identity. Despite this, higher-level bisexual obsessional patients do not experience identity diffusion the way borderline patients do.

Erik Erikson (1959) originally reported that people who suffer from identity diffusion fail to achieve a stable self-concept, differentiated object world, and relationship between themselves and some greater social unit. Subsequent psychoanalysts describing identity diffusion have focused on a profile of traits and symptoms associated with it, including inner shallowness and emptiness and impaired capacity to love others maturely (Akhtar 1984). Despite experiencing an inevitable sense of identity strain, bisexual obsessional neurotic men retain the richness of an organized inner world. Their capacity to love and work is not any more impaired than is that of other patients who suffer from character neuroses.

Identity diffusion is the hallmark of the bisexual obsessional borderline syndromes. Although identity diffusion is present in all borderline conditions, the variety of forms it takes in bisexual obsessional borderline conditions is often especially dramatic. The most frequent symptoms involving the sense of identity are uncertainty about whether one is gay or straight; selection of a gay identity as a compromise solution to anxiety generated by identity diffusion; and choice of a negative gay identity for pathological reasons usually involving unconscious hostility toward important objects and the self.

The concept of negative identity was also initially described by Erikson as the choice of an identity based on roles, presented as undesirable by authority figures, that fulfill unconscious, irrational, and pathological needs experienced by the growing child (1959, p. 129). Jerome, the last patient described above, experienced this symptom. Because of the frequent negative response to male homosexuality in this culture (particularly on the part of males), homosexual identity/social role assumes a negative valence far more frequently than heterosexual identity/social role. On the other hand, the case of Kenneth illustrates someone for whom a gay identity is clearly adaptive and a sense of being heterosexual is symptomatic. I have not had clinical experience with this in higher-level obsessional men, which is why both cases of character neurosis presented above (Jim and Charles) involved ego-dystonic homosexuality. I suspect that higher-level men with ego-dystonic heterosexuality will be described in the future: ego-dystonic heterosexuality does not necessarily occur only in borderline patients.

The symptoms of patients in whom bisexuality interacts with obsessionality can be particularly difficult to conceptualize clinically. Both the erotic fantasy component and the identity component of the person's total sexual self may or may not represent the maladaptive consequence of unconscious irrational anxiety (i.e., may or may not be psychopathological). Usually both erotic fantasy and the perceived sense of identity are influenced similarly by unconscious conflict, but there can also be some degree of independence. Thus, an individual's symptoms can primarily take the form of sexualization, while in another case the sense of identity may be symptomatic. An individual can organize his or her life around a particular identity, viewed as "the real me." In pathological instances of this phenomenon, the identity is selected on the basis of unconscious irrational conflict and its choice is associated with unconscious (and frequently conscious) fantasies of retaliation. In these cases, reduced anxiety associated with a particular identity is similar to the anxiety reduction that accompanies cross-dressing in a gender-dysphoric individual. To make matters more complex, sexual activity with others and social role may result from similar determinants.

Like all people who have obsessional character types, bisexual obsessional patients are prone to phobias and depression (Insel 1984). These patients' bisexuality lends a distinctive form to the associated problems. They may, for example, phobically avoid potentially erotic situations, which can lead to development of more generalized phobic avoidance patterns. Depression is often directly attributable to the patients' guilt and shame surrounding their sexual fantasies. Usually the self is attacked because of the symbolic negative meanings attributed to homosexual imagery. The psychological mechanisms of the depression are essentially those described by Freud in "Mourning and Melancholia" (1917/1957).

The types of patient described in this chapter illustrate the importance of avoiding reductionistic, dichotomous approaches toward nosological problems in the field of psychopathology. These patients are not usually helped by simple reassurance about the normalcy of "sexual preference." The clinician's expressed conviction that homosexuality is a disease or disorder will generally not be greeted with enthusiasm either. If the clinician is observant of the interactions between the four major dimensions of sexual orientation (erotic fantasy, erotic experience with others, sense of identity, and social role) and the personality organization of the patient, sound treatment plans may be formulated despite the complexities described in the cases presented here. Of course it is important to avoid inappropriate reductionism with all patients. But obsessional bisexual patients seem as a group to be especially likely to stimulate such responses. The clinician who responds to these patients prematurely, rigidly prescribing a desirable sexual orientation, is rarely helpful. Such intervention is probably often due to countertransference difficulties, although this has yet to be empirically validated. (The interaction between countertransference and sexual orientation has been understudied to date.)

10

Masochism and
Sexual Orientation

Of the remaining major types of psychopathology, three have attracted the special attention of psychoanalysts because of their hypothesized association with homosexuality. These three broad categories are masochistic character disorders, paranoid disorders, and pathological narcissism. This chapter and chapters 11–12 review these areas from historical and contemporary perspectives.

The term masochism was introduced into the psychiatric nomenclature by Krafft-Ebing (1898), who was impressed with a novel by Leopold von Sacher-Masoch in which characters were motivated to experience suffering, enslavement, and humiliation. Like de Sade, Sacher-Masoch was soon granted the distinction of his name's connoting a type of pathological character, a sexual perversion, and a general tendency in human motivation. Sacher-Masoch's name now stands alongside Krohn's (ilietis), Hashimoto's (thyroiditis), Wegner's (granulomatosis), Tay-Sachs's (lipid storage disease) and many others. (Naming a disease after a person's name has traditionally been a way of immortalizing medical scholars. The appropriation of a fiction writer's name for dubious immortality suggests that writing has its hazards.) In this chapter I describe the features of masochistic character disorder and present an overview of psychoanalytic models of masochism. Aspects of masochism particularly relevant to homosexuality are illustrated, and I contrast clinical manifestations of masochistic character disorder in individuals at different points on the Kinsey scale and at different psychostructural levels.

FEATURES OF MASOCHISTIC CHARACTER PATHOLOGY

The term masochism has traditionally been used to connote both a sexual perversion or paraphilia and a form of character organization. In the former,

143

sexual excitement is produced by the person's own suffering. Fantasies of being bound, beaten, humiliated, enslaved, or tortured motivate sexual activity. The diagnosis of sexual masochism is made if intense masochistic erotic fantasies have been present for at least six months and the person has acted on masochistic urges or is markedly distressed by them. Very little is known about this condition but it is generally accepted that such individuals constitute a small minority of people with masochistic character disorder (Reich 1949; Asch 1985). Most people with the latter condition do not have masochistic sexual fantasies; their masochism is expressed in the way other areas of their personality are organized. This has been called moral or psychic masochism (Freud 1924/1961).

The key feature that masochistic patients share is repetitive motivation to experience various types of suffering. Reich (1949) noted that such patients tend to complain, to be self-deprecatory, and to damage themselves. A number of clinicians point out that masochistic people are exhibitionistic. As Fenichel (1945) puts it, "masochistic characters customarily derive pleasure from exhibiting their misery. 'Look how miserable I am' typically stands for 'look how miserable you made me.' The masochistic behavior has an accusing blackmailing tone" (p. 363). Shapiro (1981) described the traits of exaggerated self-depreciation, exhibitionism, display of old misfortunes, injustice collecting, "demeaning humility," and deferentiality as prototypical of the masochistic character. Asch (1985) stressed the need to fail in all major areas of functioning as the hallmark of people with masochistic character disorders. The word *provocative* recurs over and over in the clinical literature on masochism, referring to masochistic people's tendency to provoke responses from others that lead to their own suffering. This tendency is described by many analysts who have to cope with masochistic provocation in the analytic situation. Countertransference errors may stem from unconscious sadism in response to the patient's masochism.

Patients with masochistic character disorders are usually depressed, but not all people with chronic depression are masochistic. New research in the affective disorders suggests that many people with chronic, persistent depression suffer because they are ill, not because of an unconsciously determined need to suffer. These people, who are categorized in various subgroups depending on the phenomenology, etiology, course, and complications of their depression, can all be described as having so-called depressive characters. Their depression often results from biological influences, and appropriate treatment leads to dramatic improvement in the quality of these patients' lives. Typically this type of patient is grateful to be able to reexperience pleasure and enjoy life again. The tenacious, repetitive need to experience unpleasure, always found in masochism, is not a prominent feature in many individuals with depressive characters. What distinguishes masochistic depression from other depressions is not its chronicity or severity but rather the degree to which the depressive affect is associated with masochistic fantasies and the degree to which the (depressive-masochistic) complex is a response to unconscious irrational conflict.

PSYCHOANALYTIC MODELS AND MECHANISMS OF MASOCHISM

Freud's early view of masochism was that it represented a turning inward of hostile, sadistic impulses originally generated in reaction to a frustrating environment. The strictures of society embodied in aspects of the parents become internalized and contribute to the genesis of a harsh superego (1915/1957; 1919/1961). Later, Freud hypothesized the existence of a powerful primary self-destructive motivation in human beings, which he developed into the concept of the death instinct (1920/1955; 1924/1961; 1937/1964). This view, although supported by abundant data, was found distasteful by optimists. Some theoreticians struggled to save the concept of the death instinct, but it was ultimately abandoned, not only because it was disquieting but also because it lacked power as a general theory of motivation. Freud's clinical observations stood up well, however, and subsequent clinicians have generally been impressed with superego and ego-ideal pathology in masochists. Engel (1962) pointed out that patients who have excessively harsh superegos can suffer from painful guilt, which leads them to use techniques of self-punishment and atonement in an effort to palliate the guilt. This can result in "a predilection for painful, disagreeable, humiliating and defeating situations, a proneness to accidents, injury or surgery, and an intolerance of success and good fortune" (p. 337). Fenichel (1945) discussed various symbolic functions of masochistic activity. He summarized Freud's notion that masochistic suffering might symbolically represent both ingratiation intended to obtain the father's forgiveness and defiance in exhibiting to the world how terrible the father is. He also speculated that masochistic activities might represent an alternative to castration, hypothetically avoided as a result of engaging in masochistic activity. Many clinicians suggest that the masochistic person actually controls the interaction with the environment—thus the masochistic activity might actually represent a misguided attempt to master pain and suffering (Reik 1941; Shapiro 1981). Others stress that the need to be abused may mask a wish to be loved. The abuse occurs in a context of attachment and presumably reenacts a childhood tie to a sadistic or brutal parent (Berliner 1958).

Cooper recently approached the problem of models and mechanisms somewhat differently (1964; 1980; 1984; in press). He was impressed with Bergler's hypothesis that very early disruption in the mother-child relationship (i.e., in the "preoedipal" or "oral" stage) influences the genesis of the masochistic character. Bergler (1952) suggested that in provoking humiliation and rejection, the masochist is unconsciously motivated to repeat an infantile relationship with the preoedipal mother. Cooper noted that a satisfactory model of masochism could not be found within the structural theory. Grounding his views in recent object relations theory and self psychology, he suggested that in normal development, separation-individuation damages the sense of magical omnipotence and is perceived as a narcissistic injury. The infant copes with this frustration "by making suffering ego-syntonic. 'I am frustrated because I want to be. I force my mother to be cruel'" (Cooper in press). Psychopathology results when the object is perceived as excessively cruel and frustrating and the self is perceived as so helpless that "the gratifications obtained from disappointment take precedence over genuine . . . assertive satisfactions. Being disappointed or refused becomes the preferred mode of narcissistic and masochistic distortions that dominate the character" (ibid.). Cooper noted that superego distortions, which usually dominate the clinical picture, are an inevitable consequence of this type of early miscarriage of development. He conceptualized masochistic and narcissistic character disorders as different aspects of a single entity.

Although agreeing with Cooper about fundamental similarities between severely masochistic and narcissistic individuals, Rothstein (1981) pointed out that they appear to differ in certain aspects, particularly in the way they experience humiliation.

> Masochistic characters are pessimistic and defend against their fear of humiliation, as Edelberg and Loewenstein suggest, by fantasies of seduction of the humiliator. They seek humiliation as one of their aims and gain the unconscious narcissistic gratification of controlling the insult they feel is inevitable. Persons with narcissistic personality disorder are consciously more optimistic. Although they fear humiliation they have the sense that they can master this fantasied danger by active identification with the humiliator. The defensive identificatory process motivates these analysands to fantasize and/or enact the humiliation of others. (p. 104)

Kass, MacKinnon, and Spitzer (1986) carried out an empirical study of the masochistic personality. They collected therapists' ratings of the masochistic personality traits of patients in psychotherapy. These traits, found to be common and to have good internal consistency, are as follows:

1. Remains in relationships in which others exploit, abuse, or take advantage of him or her, despite opportunities to alter the situation.
2. Believes that he or she almost always sacrifices his or her own interests for those of others.
3. Rejects help, gifts, or favors so as not to be a burden on others.
4. Complains, directly or indirectly, about being unappreciated.
5. Responds to success or positive events by feeling undeserving or worrying excessively about not being able to measure up to new responsibilities.
6. Always feels pessimistic about the future and preoccupied with the worst aspects of the past and present.
7. Thinks only about his or her worst features and ignores positive features.

8. Sabotages his or her own intended goals.
9. Repeatedly turns down opportunities for pleasure.

In an appendix for proposed diagnostic categories needing further study, *DSM-III-R* includes Self-defeating Personality Disorder. Although the descriptive features of this disorder overlap with those discussed by Kass et al. (1986), *DSM-III-R* explicitly avoids the term masochistic personality disorder. The authors of *DSM-III-R* wished to avoid suggesting that self-defeating traits are motivated by unconscious factors and also did not want to revive the historic association between the term masochism and outdated psychoanalytic ideas about female sexuality.

The psychological mechanisms involved in sexual masochism are unknown at present. The observation that some people exhibit what seems to be a conditioned association between images of self-humiliation and suffering and erotic excitement is an empirical finding, not an explanatory model. Freud hypothesized in his famous paper "A Child Is Being Beaten" (1919/1961) that the unconscious fantasy behind the child-beating fantasy is actually that of beating a rival. Whether this is so as a general rule, however, has never been conclusively demonstrated. Moreover, the mechanism by which pain is transformed into sexual pleasure is not known, nor is it clear why masochistic character traits are apparently so common but the consolidated perversions so rare. Although masochistic traits are common in both genders, sexual masochism (like all the perversions) seem to occur most frequently in males, also for unknown reasons.

MASOCHISM AND HOMOSEXUALITY

Bergler hypothesized that male homosexuality is a response to unconscious masochism. He suggested that a male's erotic tie to a male is a symbolic representation of the cruel mother image. The homosexual male simultaneously gratifies and does penance for the aggressive-erotic primitive tie to the cruel mother (1944; 1951; 1956; 1959; Bergler & Kroger 1954). Other analysts note that the submissive, feminine aspects of homosexuality in any of its forms might symbolically express a retreat from oedipal aggression, with concomitant feminine identification (the negative oedipus complex). Identification with the woman in labor and with the female's behavior during coitus, both images conceptualized as involving powerful masochistic components, have been implicated as important psychodynamic influences in homosexuality (Fenichel 1945; Loewenstein 1957). Many case reports illustrate Bergler's model in individual patients (e.g., Socarides 1978). Nevertheless, today there is no more scientific evidence pointing toward a general relationship between masochism and homosexuality than there was in Bergler's day.

Freud believed that masochism is an "integral part of female psychology," an idea that is no longer generally accepted today (Asch 1985). One wonders to what degree the tendency to equate male homosexuality with masochism may have been influenced by Freud's notion that femininity, passivity, and masochism are generally associated. Bergler's theory equating homosexuality with masochism lacks an empirical foundation and seems to me incorrect. Specific subgroups of masochistic men, however, probably do manifest the mental mechanisms suggested by Bergler.

In order to determine whether masochists are unequally distributed across the Kinsey spectrum, systematic clinical research is necessary. For example, sexual behavior might be assessed independently of character pathology, diagnosed by means considered reliable by contemporary standards. Associations could be tallied up and compared (i.e., masochistic characters among lifelong 0's and 6's on the Kinsey scale). Such clinical investigations have not yet been done. Next I describe interactions between masochism and homosexuality that seem common in clinical practice.

CLINICAL MANIFESTATIONS OF MASOCHISM AND HOMOSEXUALITY

In some people the homosexual component of sexual fantasies and/or sexual activity with others, and/or the sense of identity, and/or social role appear to be motivated by unconscious masochistic conflicts. This association varies greatly and no data shed light on its frequency, but it seems clear that masochistic motivation may lead some people to publicly declare that they are gay, that is, to "come out."

The term coming out is used by some investigators to refer to a person's first public identification of him- or herself as homosexual to other homosexuals (Hooker 1965). Other scholars emphasize recognizing oneself as homosexual more than letting others know that one is gay (Dank 1971). The most common usage of the term among gay people I have spoken with is simply to connote the announcement of being gay. This announcement need not be to other gay people and need not be coincident with the private recognition that one "is" gay. I use the term in this way. Private recognition that one is gay is not generally a matter of choice. Ideally, the decision to tell others should be, particularly in a potentially aversive social climate (unfortunately, this is not always the case).

The process of coming out has received some attention from the psychoanalytic community, but it is such an important landmark in the lives of so many patients that additional investigation is needed (Gershman 1983). It seems clear that the decision to let others know about one's homosexuality may involve realignment of profoundly important relationships, such as those with parents, siblings, and employers. It would be clinically naive always to accept the reasons people give for coming out as the actual reasons motivating the behavior. Whereas emotionally healthy people come out for healthy reasons, people who suffer from psychopathology often come out for reasons that cannot be considered healthy, even given a generous margin of neutrality with regard to judgments about healthy and unhealthy behavior. One common maladaptive, irrational reason for coming out is to satisfy masochistic needs. In these cases the sadistic aspects of homophobic society prove impossible for the masochistic person to resist. I am not suggesting that masochism provides a psychological model for coming out. I am pointing out, however, that gay masochistic patients may use coming out in ways that have no real equivalent in heterosexual social-role behavior.

In trying to assess the potential masochistic contribution to coming out, the degree of suffering resulting from the decision cannot be the sole indicator, since great suffering can occur as a result of courage as well as masochism. It is important to keep in mind that the climate of belief in our culture positively sanctions narcissistic-hedonistic values. Anti-narcissistic activities, in which the welfare of the group is placed before the welfare of the individual, or anti-hedonistic behavior, in which immediate pleasure is willfully put aside, can be misinterpreted in such a climate. Some therapists may feel that a wide variety of such acts, if they involve apparent suffering, are masochistic. In fact, it is impossible to comment on motivation without understanding the meaning of actions to the people that carry them out. This is true of activities that cause pain, even of repetitive patterns of behavior associated with deprivation and suffering, such as the training of professional athletes or ballet dancers. Some of these people may be masochists but most appear to be primarily motivated by the pursuit of excellence. This is even true of some behavior that leads to death. Altruistic suicide, for example, cannot be understood simply as masochistic (Durkheim 1897/1951): some martyrs may be masochists, others probably are, but many may be heroic idealists.

In evaluating the adaptive significance of a particular act, such as coming out, distinctions between idealism and masochism must be respected. As with most clinical phenomena, gray zones exist, and with them uncertainty on the clinician's part. In general, however, the evaluating therapist should be able to ascertain when heroic self-sacrifice is legitimately high-minded and when it is primarily motivated by the individual's unconscious need to suffer. Two clinical vignettes are presented below. In the first, the motivation to announce homosexuality appeared to be masochistic. In the second, the motivation appeared idealistic, not masochistic, although personal suffering was great.

COMING OUT AS A MANIFESTATION OF MASOCHISM

Dominic, a thirty-five-year-old executive, exclusively homosexual in fantasy and activity from childhood, maintained a heterosexual social role. He realized he was gay during adolescence. Raised in an extremely homophobic family and subculture, he had for many years maintained a double life as an eligible bachelor and a sexually active gay man. This decision seemed good judgment in light of the prejudicial feelings of those in his environment. But Dominic's double life caused him great bitterness. He complained unceasingly about the homophobic attitudes at work and in his family and fantasized that a day would come when he would win his parents and employers over by revealing his true gay identity.

Dominic's parents were Sicilian immigrants who owned a grocery store in upstate New York. Observant Catholics, they were scarcely able to accept Dominic's refusal to become a priest. Ultimately, however, they became proud of his vocational success. Dominic's two older sisters were nuns. The third sister, to whom he was closest, was a nurse, married to a fireman.

Dominic had worked his way up to a position of responsibility in a large insurance corporation. He was liked because of his reliability, willingness to work hard, readiness to cancel vacations and weekend plans as needed, and eagerness to follow orders. Dominic had never been involved in an overt conflict during his years at the firm. He was known by his superiors as a "true company man." Dominic had long recognized that the company was racist, sexist, and homophobic—there were no blacks or women, for example, in managerial positions. Behind closed doors, the higher executives, recognizing that they would soon be forced to liberalize, agonized about which type of tokenism would be worse. It was a sign of the inner circle's acceptance of Dominic that he had been allowed to hear these frank discussions. Homosexuality was never brought up as a work-related issue, but in the macho "locker-room" atmosphere that prevailed at committee meetings, pejorative remarks about male homosexuals were made as a matter of course. Men who failed at sex-typed tasks were routinely labeled as "faggots." Dominic was ambitious and slated for success. He had mastered a vital area of logistics, understood by no one else, and was considered indispensable. There was widespread talk of creating a vice-presidency for him.

After years of maintaining a successful social role as a bachelor, Dominic decided to "become more openly honest." This decision followed a series of stressful life events: his father had a stroke, resulting in aphasia and hemiparesis. His mother, unable to maintain the grocery store alone, sold it and developed a severe depression. Dominic's beloved sister Lisa confided to him that her husband was an alcoholic. Despite her parents' absolute interdiction against divorce and the opposition of her priest, she was planning to leave him. She told Dominic that their mother confessed to her that she had never loved their father but had stayed with him out of duty, and she advised her daughter to do the same.

These events, all of which happened within a few months, affected Dominic deeply. For reasons unknown to him, he began to ruminate about the "immorality" of leading a double life. "How can I be true to myself when I am living a lie?" he asked. At work he became distracted and anxious. Soon his superiors expressed concern, and finally he was called in for a review. After much praise of his excellent record, his boss confided avuncularly that something was obviously disturbing Dominic, and the time had come to discuss it openly. He would find himself among supportive friends. The firm had a fine record of looking after its own, and Dominic, who had worked there for many years, was considered "family."

Dominic admitted that he had been depressed and discussed the unsettling events that had recently occurred in his family. Then, against conscious misgivings but feeling suddenly trustful, he confessed that the real problem was that he was gay. His boss thought he was joking. When it became apparent that he was not, he listened with courteous reserve and reassured Dominic that things would "all work out." Dominic initially felt relieved at his honesty and castigated himself for having been "paranoid" and not having come out earlier.

During the ensuing months, Dominic was treated politely by upper-echelon executives, but he soon realized that he was no longer privy to their confidences. Soon the firm announced to his shock that a vice-presidency was being created for someone from outside whose area of expertise was the same as Dominic's. Dominic was asked to donate part of his secretary's time to the office pool. As part of a general "renovation," he was moved to an office without a window. At no time was the subject of Dominic's homosexuality ever discussed again, but after a number of similar incidents, Dominic realized that he was being extruded from the firm because he had revealed he was gay. He resigned and moved to a small company in San Francisco, where he functioned well but missed the challenges of a large corporation. Dominic returned to New York, accepting a lesser position. Bitter that his professional status was incompatible with his abilities and aspirations, he sought psychiatric consultation. He complained of chronic depression, feelings of failure, and pervasive cynicism about the unfairness of life. Deeply resentful of homophobic society on the one hand, he had also become ashamed of being gay.

Therapeutic exploration revealed that Dominic's predominant unconscious motivation for public declaration of his homosexuality, at the time that he did so, had been masochistic. His unconscious self-destructive impulses in part resulted from guilt stimulated by his father's stroke, in part from identification with his masochistic mother, and in part from his sister's decision to leave her husband, which he perceived as idealistic. An important treatment goal was to help him experience a sense of pride in being gay. Other complex tasks of long-term therapy involved distinguishing masochistic from nonmasochistic functions of homosexual phenomena. Analysis of the masochistic components underlying manifestly experienced homosexual phenomena resulted in diminished masochism, while nonmasochistic components of homosexual life were preserved. I suspect that this is generally true in similar clinical situations; however, literature in this area is extremely sparse.

The case below tells a story superficially similar to the preceding one but with profound underlying differences. In this case the decision to come out appeared to be motivated by courageous idealism, not masochism.

COMING OUT AS A COURAGEOUS EXPRESSION OF IDEALISM

Luke, a forty-five-year-old career army officer and a life-long exclusively homosexual man, had weighed the pros and cons of coming out since he had realized as an adolescent that he was gay. A graduate of West Point, he knew he had no future in the military as an acknowledged homosexual. Early in his career, vocational ambition was his most important consciously perceived motivation. He aspired to be a general by the age of forty-five. An honors student and a track star, he had every reason to believe he would be successful. He had no living relatives and as far as he was concerned the army was his family.

Luke volunteered for duty in Vietnam. Although his military record was superb, his two years there changed his philosophy of life. The death of friends in Vietnam, the wholesale destruction he participated in, the recognition that his superiors had lied to him and that they had been lied to about the conduct of the war all led him to question his beliefs and attitudes. On one occasion, Luke was the sole survivor of a bombing attack. He had been in a briefing room that had taken a direct hit by a shell. Many men were killed but he had somehow miraculously survived unhurt. Following this incident, his priorities changed, and he decided that it was more important for him to live according to an inner moral code than to pursue worldly success. Luke achieved the rank of Lieutenant Colonel and, following rotation back to the United States, he continued to be a successful and popular officer. He read avidly and organized a philosophical discussion group on post.

Luke elected to give up his social role as the most eligible bachelor following an incident in which an enlisted man suspected of being homosexual was scapegoated by noncommissioned officers. Luke had already decided to come out and was deliberating about the right time to do so when the incident occurred. He announced to his immediate superiors that he was homosexual, then let it be known publicly. He agreed to psychiatric consultation, and I had the opportunity to interview him.

Luke's decision to come out had been well thought out and its consequences were fully appreciated. He felt it was urgently important for him to live according to the dictates of conscience. He knew that his career in the military was essentially over because of his decision and this saddened him, but he also felt proud of his courageous stance in keeping with his perceived role as a leader of men. Luke's psychiatric profile revealed no pathology by *DSM-*

III-R criteria. He decided to resign his commission quietly after making a personal statement of conscience. He left the military shortly after his forty-fifth birthday, returned to graduate school, acquired a doctoral degree, and went to work as a college teacher.

I had occasion to speak with this former officer some years after he left the military. He seemed neither bitter nor depressed. He freely discussed the unfairness of homophobia but pointed out that since his tour in Vietnam he had changed his notions about the role that fairness could be expected to play in political and social life. He expressed gratitude that he was able to live in an open society where as a gay activist he could have a positive impact on the cultural climate. Luke, regretful about the high level of what he termed "primitive prejudice" in society, did not see himself as a failure or a victim. In fact, he felt that he had managed to accomplish a relatively difficult psychological task, namely, to live in a way compatible with his values and his aspirations.

Other individuals seen not infrequently in clinical practice are patients who have had predominantly or exclusively homosexual fantasies during their entire lives who nevertheless relentlessly pursue heterosexuality and fear and avoid all aspects of homosexuality. Gay patients whose attitudes and values are incompatible with being gay and who seek therapy hoping to become straight are at particular risk from masochism. These patients, whose consciously perceived attitudes toward homosexuality echo those of the culture at large, and usually those of their families and religions as well, hate themselves because of their homosexuality. Many develop consolidated masochistic character structures and use treatment as a way of exhibiting self-hate to another person and attempting to provoke condemnation. Should such patients find therapists who are willing to take their wish to become heterosexual as a treatment goal simply on face merit, unfortunate miscarriage of therapeutic effort may result. The (naive) therapist may come to symbolize layers of punitive rejecting authorities, including "society," the oedipal father, and the preoedipal mother. Patient and therapist may collaborate in a repetitive masochistic ritual not only without therapeutic movement but damaging to the patient's already fragile sense of self-esteem. Isay (1985) describes such situations:

> In my practice I have seen a number of homosexual men who have returned for further help after interrupting treatment with other analysts, whose goal, either explicitly stated or implicitly guiding the treatment, had been to help the patient change his sexual preference. This clinical material suggests that such efforts may cause symptomatic depression by contributing to an already diminished and injured self esteem, and in some cases it may produce severe social problems in later life. My conclusion from listening to these patients is that the analyst's internalized social prejudice produces a countertransference readiness that interferes with the proper conduct of an analysis by causing the analyst not to be able to convey an appropriate positive regard for his patient or to maintain therapeutic neutrality. (p. 241)

Patients with lifelong predominantly or exclusively homoerotic fantasies who enter psychoanalysis or intensive psychotherapy with the desire to "become" heterosexual are at risk for setting unrealistic therapeutic goals. Although inter-individual variability may be expected and each person must be evaluated separately, no adequate data to date suggest that such change is usually possible. Although some patients can add the capacity to perform heterosexually to their behavioral repetoire, that is quite a different matter from totally replacing homosexual with heterosexual fantasies.

Psychotherapy and psychoanalysis are time-consuming and expensive. Some masochistic homosexual patients use the pursuit of heterosexuality as a reason for enduring hardship in order to undertake treatment. They may, for example, undertake consecutive analyses involving many years and large sums of money. Some masochistic patients, analogous to surgical patients who have multiple operations without organic cause, are motivated to experience the adversity of the psychotherapeutic or psychoanalytic situation as an end in itself. This type of masochism can be difficult to detect, particularly if the analyst believes that the patient's expressed desire for change in sexual orientation need not itself be analyzed. Since Isay (1985) and Leavy (1985) discuss the clinical phenomena described above, no clinical illustrations are presented here.

Another phenomenon, not confined to the homosexual community but relevant for a subgroup of masochistic gay men, is the motivation to engage in so-called opportunistic sexual activity in order possibly to contract AIDS (Flavin, Franklin & Frances 1986). The masochistic fantasy motivating this type of sexual activity is that of playing Russian roulette. The case presented later in this chapter of a masochistic borderline bisexual man illustrates episodic opportunistic sexual activity motivated by a sadomasochistic desire to contract AIDS.

PSYCHOSTRUCTURAL LEVELS, MASOCHISM, AND SEXUAL ORIENTATION

People with predominantly masochistic conflicts are distributed across the full spectrum of psychostructural levels. This may seem surprising given that the theories of etiology of masochism so heavily involve very early (preoedipal) experiences with cruel, rejecting maternal figures. One might expect masochistic people to be integrated at a borderline level as a result of early traumata, and many are. The fact that well-consolidated masochistic character neuroses also occur frequently suggests that the character type is multideter-mined and the influence of component factors varies from case to case. At higher psychostructural levels, at which self and object representations are solid, the sense of identity is sound, and ego mechanisms function well, masochistic tendencies are likely to be revealed in structured interpersonal and vocational situations. In these cases, work and attachment occur in a consolidated masochistic context. At lower psychostructural levels, masochistic behavior is more likely to be impulsive, flamboyant, and bizarre. The chances that self-destructive activity will get out of control and seriously damage the person are greater at the lower levels. This is particularly true of masochistic perversions, which at the lower levels may involve being urinated or defecated on, being wounded, or even being killed (e.g., by acting out a fantasy of being hanged).

The case illustrations below contrast masochistic men at opposite poles of the Kinsey spectrum and at higher and lower levels of psychostructural integration. A masochistic borderline bisexual man in whom pursuit of AIDS was a prominent motivation is also presented.

Masochistic Character Neurosis: Heterosexual

Mr. White, a fifty-five-year-old architect, sought consultation for depression. He portrayed himself as a martyr and an innocent victim constantly used and abused by others. He was second in command of a large firm and collected injustices allegedly carried out against him by the chief executive officer. For example, when his superior was away, Mr. White was expected to carry out the CEO's functions. Despite wielding great authority at these times, on other occasions he performed menial tasks such as setting up chairs for meetings or pouring coffee. He had policy-making powers but allegedly his superior reversed all his decisions. Mr. White had never discussed his complaints with the CEO: he was waiting for his resentments to "be noticed." It turned out that he performed menial functions entirely on his own, supposedly to illustrate the firm's need for more personnel. He had never explicitly outlined such needs in memos or presentations. He had also never objected to his low salary, accepting 5 percent yearly increases with profuse thanks while privately expressing bitterness to his wife and friends about being exploited. Mr. White refused many opportunities to work elsewhere, arguing that all work situations were fundamentally similar.

Mr. White's litany of injustices was lengthy and persuasive. So-called friends borrowed money and never returned it. His teenage children were openly disrespectful: they played their stereos at all hours, refused to use earphones, and dominated the family TV. They entertained friends in their rooms until the wee hours of morning and smoked marijuana in their rooms. "I can't do anything with them," he complained, "they don't listen to me!"

Mr. White had been in a stable, loveless marriage for thirty years. His wife, never employed, lost no opportunity to berate him because of his low income. She was expressly contemptuous of his general ineffectuality, dull style, and poor physical condition. She frequently raged at him and he would typically scream back, "I am doing all I can. What do you want of me?" At times, particularly when inebriated at parties, Mr. White's wife complained to anyone within earshot of his lack of prowess as a lover. She attributed her own lack of sexual desire to his poor lovemaking technique. He admitted that her complaints had merit, yet he did nothing to alter his approach. He complained to friends about feeling "love-starved and sex-starved," but never considered leaving his marriage because he felt that there was no hope of improvement with anyone else, citing as evidence the fact that he knew of no one with a happy marriage. He had brief extramarital sexual relationships which invariably ended because of his need to discuss his wife endlessly with his lovers.

Mr. White perceived himself to be a helpless victim in virtually all meaningful situations. Without insight, he attributed his chronic resentment to the meanness of those around him. He had been raised by a brutal, extractive father and a masochistic, depressed mother with whom he strongly identified. His request for psychiatric assistance followed her death. He responded well to tricyclic medication but refused long-term psychotherapy, believing that his problems were caused by others.

Masochistic Character Neurosis: Homosexual

George, a forty-five-year-old copyeditor, sought consultation for depression following an eye infection which left him unable to work. The patient did freelance copyediting at home, six days a week, twelve hours a day. The hourly wage was low, and he had to work long and hard to maintain an adequate standard of living. Prior to his eye infection, George had struggled with slowly progressive myopia and chronic headaches. Friends had commented on the poor lighting in his office but he refused to improve it, stating that bright light produced unpleasant glare.

George had great intellectual gifts in both the arts and the sciences. A Phi Beta Kappa graduate of an Ivy League college, he was sought after by graduate schools and corporations. One computer firm offered him, as a recent college graduate, a starting salary higher than his present earnings. But George felt disdainful of "contemporary philistine society." He "endured" being something of a campus celebrity with anxiety and a sense of foreboding that he did not understand, and following graduation he decided to "shun the trappings of success" and live in anonymity. He found an apartment in a slum area of New York and settled down to a routine that continued unchanged for twenty-five years. He found his daily toil excruciatingly boring. He spent much time editing texts in various self-help areas—gardening, boat repair, weaving. He rationalized the low pay and dullness of his work as "society's problem." George believed that if "society" truly valued books and reading, his job would be more lucrative. He felt deeply resentful at having to endure a financially deprived lifestyle and often compared his earnings to those of "sanitation workers, nurses' aides, dogcatchers." Despite having voluntarily chosen a low-paying job, George had expensive tastes that were continuously frustrated. He loved opera, theater, and gourmet food. Constantly complaining of the inequities of a culture that "was indifferent to talent," he was avoided by ex-friends of higher means who found his scathing cynicism and self-deprecating manner difficult to tolerate. George had no hobbies. Since college graduation he had taken only two brief vacations. The reason for this was what he termed his work ethic. The fact that the significance of his vocational enterprise was of distinctly limited value troubled him episodically.

George had been moderately effeminate as a youngster. Sent away from his Midwestern home to a military school at age fourteen, he had experienced a lonely, anguished adolescence. Exclusively homosexual in erotic fantasies, George had never engaged in sexual activity with another person. He had been raised in a strict Calvinist environment. During his childhood he had been taught, and continued to believe, that homosexuality was sinful. Not only did George abstain from sexual activity with others, he was also consumed with guilt because of his homosexual fantasies and his yearning for a sexual/love relationship with a man. He resisted masturbation as much as possible, but when he succumbed or experienced a nocturnal emission during a homosexual dream he felt intense guilty depression. He then had the thought that he was hopelessly evil and that his life was a punishment because of "horrible" sexual urges.

George had avoided psychiatric consultation since he believed he was evil and not psychiatrically impaired. When he became anorectic, insomniac, and had fantasies of hanging himself, however, a neighbor prevailed upon him to seek professional assistance. Pharmacotherapy successfully led to amelioration of endogenomorphic symptoms. Crisis intervention psychotherapy was directed at diminishing his guilt at being homosexual. Interpretation, support, and education ultimately led George to join a psychotherapy group for gay men. His desperate loneliness abated: he achieved a measure of self-acceptance and was able at least to consider sexual activity with other men as a possible way of improving his life. Individual psychotherapy was also initiated and other aspects of George's masochistic stance are presently being explored. Whether he will achieve insight and give up other aspects of a lifelong masochistic position is impossible to predict at this time.

In the preceding cases, despite crippling masochistic difficulties, the men did not manifest the impulsive self-destructiveness, affective liability, or identity instability of low-level borderline individuals. Such patients are presented below.

Masochistic Borderline Syndrome: Heterosexual

A forty-five-year-old married attorney sought consultation because of alcoholism, multiple drug abuse, and marital difficulties. His wife threatened to leave him unless his drunken debauches and perverse sexual activity stopped. He felt unable to live without her and was terrified that she might carry out her threat. He advised her that if she left him he would blow his head off with a shotgun. She was concerned that he might do this, but she felt that her own sanity was threatened by his behavior.

Mr. Doe functioned as a responsible husband and attorney for intervals lasting as long as many months, but ultimately he would not be able to resist getting drunk. During binges, he engaged in sexual activity with prostitutes, insisting that they wear masks and spike-heeled shoes. They participated in a stereotypical masochistic scenario in which he was handcuffed to the bed in his underwear and flogged with a leather strap. He then performed cunnilingus on one partner while being whipped by another, during which he masturbated to orgasm. Mr. Doe also abused many other drugs, including amyl nitrate, cocaine, amphetamines, and barbiturates. During binges he stayed away from home for days at a time without telephoning or letting his whereabouts be known. Upon returning, he begged his wife's forgiveness, supplicating her to "be loyal," "stand by him in his hour of need," and "allow him" to be a husband. Mr. Doe had a violent temper and when his wife confronted him about the necessity to take responsibility for his behavior, he often smashed furniture and had screaming rages.

Mr. Doe had no intimate friends despite many casual acquaintances who liked him. As soon as a relationship became emotionally close, he found fault with the person, made impossible demands, or became overtly abusive. He was once jailed for assaulting a friend. At times, when alone, Mr. Doe became overwhelmed with feelings of dread and what he described as emptiness. Sometimes, for reasons he couldn't understand, he felt better only after he burned his arms with cigarettes. Grinding out lit cigarettes on his forearms, he experienced a sense of pride at being able to "bear the pain."

Mr. Doe had been raised in an impoverished family. His father had died of complications of alcoholism when he was five. His mother worked from dawn to dusk as a cleaning woman, leaving the boy in the care of two older sisters who abused him, forcing him to do menial chores and frequently beating him on his bare buttocks with a strap. Mr. Doe's high level of intelligence and determination to avoid poverty had carried him through college and law school. His episodic alcoholism and drug abuse began in his teenage years; in law school, masochistic sexual activity became part of the binges.

Handsome and articulate, Mr. Doe had "a way with women," but he was often impotent. His wife, ten years older and a fellow attorney, knew of his alcoholism when she married him. He had promised to seek treatment but kept procrastinating. Early in their marriage his wife also discovered his masochistic sexual activities, when he had a panic attack while being whipped and at his behest, a prostitute had called her. Their relationship was then understandably marked by crises as he put off seeking psychiatric treatment. Mr. Doe, a member of the bar, had never worked for any firm for more than one year. He was often unemployed for months, supported by his wife, but his charm, good looks, and intelligence always led him to be hired again by a new employer. After a brief interval of normal functioning, he either failed to appear at work or got into a violent altercation with a superior. Mr. Doe had no religious or political affiliation and did not see himself as a member of any identifiable social group. He felt utterly dependent on his wife and often told her that he would be "nothing" without her. At times he also accused her of being a "dominating bitch" who deprived him of a sense of manliness. Her own psychiatric difficulties did not allow her to set limits on his behavior. Finally, Mr. Doe's wife insisted that he seek psychiatric help, and he recognized that he would not be able to change her mind. The ensuing therapeutic intervention, involving Alcoholics Anonymous, hospitalization, marital therapy, Antabuse, and extended psychotherapy, was unsuccessful. Mr. Doe dropped out of treatment and was lost to follow-up.

Masochistic Borderline Syndrome: Homosexual

A forty-year-old manicurist was treated for penile lacerations in the emergency room of a metropolitan hospital. Psychiatric consultation was requested when it was discovered that he had inflicted the injury with a broken bottle. The breakup of a "love affair" with a pimp and drug dealer had precipitated the self-injury. The patient felt that his penis had gotten him into so much trouble that it deserved punishment. He became frightened at the ensuing bloodshed, however, and sought medical aid.

This lifelong exclusively homosexual man had a history of multiple psychiatric hospitalizations, each following attempted suicide by ingestion of drugs and alcohol. Twice he had been comatose and had required life support assistance. All of his suicide attempts were precipitated by unsatisfactory love affairs. In addition, the patient's record indicated numerous visits for rectal lacerations and other anal and rectal difficulties. On one occasion a metal drinking glass had to be extracted from his anus. He complained vociferously about how "lousy" his ex-lovers were but denied that his own selection of partners might have led to his difficulties. He admitted, however, that he was exclusively attracted to violent men, often ex-convicts, usually sadists. "I'm a pushover for a tough guy," he said. This man had no friends or family and had been raised in foster homes and reform schools. He lived in a furnished room and barely supported himself. His only aspiration was to "find true love." He refused psychiatric treatment and was lost to follow-up.

Masochistic Borderline Syndrome: Bisexual

A forty-five-year-old professor was seen in consultation because of marital discord. Dr. Smith had experienced both homosexual and heterosexual erotic fantasies from childhood. His heterosexual fantasies were more pleasureful and profuse, and during adolescence he developed a heterosexual sense of identity without consciously perceived conflict. He had no homosexual experiences until after his marriage at age twenty-five. His wife was a graduate school classmate, and the couple married shortly after they received their Ph.Ds. The marriage was stormy from the beginning. Both sets of in-laws were intrusive, guilt-provoking, and controlling. Husband and wife soon began keeping count of whose parents were entertained more frequently. The tendency to quantify favors spread to other areas of the relationship: each felt that because he or she had done certain specific things for the other, certain specific responses from the mate were required in return. Progressively frequent and intense arguments revolved around demands by one that the other make sacrifices to preserve their relationship.

Initially of equal promise academically, Dr. Smith's wife dropped out of academia to become a mother. Within five years the couple had four children and found themselves financially stressed, chronically overworked, and exhausted. In marital fights Dr. Smith's wife pointed out that she had given up an academic career for their family and that he hardly appeared grateful. The couple's sexual life dwindled to the point where sexual relations occurred only every few months.

In this setting, Dr. Smith found himself experiencing homosexual fantasies that were more and more frequent and intense. One night he and his wife had a screaming fight in which they slapped each other. She threatened suicide, he slammed his fist into a mirror. He stormed out of the house, his hand bleeding, and after hours of walking through the city, he went to a gay bar. He left without having a sexual encounter and returned home to find his wife inebriated, reading a bedtime story to their children. Overwhelmed with guilt, he begged her forgiveness. After a brief improvement in their relationship, the fights began again. Soon Dr. Smith episodically sought out gay bars and began having brief homosexual liaisons. He had increasingly intense masochistic fantasies of being tortured by men in leather coats and being forced to engage in anal sex with gangs of men. These fantasies alarmed him and he resisted his impulses to act on them. He kept his homosexual life secret, and his wife accused him of having a mistress, which he denied.

Dr. Smith's work began to deteriorate. He missed classes and committee meetings and was reprimanded by the dean. He came to feel that he had been pushed into an academic career by his parents and that he had never wanted to be a professor. He accused his wife of coercing him into marriage and forcing him to maintain employment in order to support their family. He aspired, "like Gauguin, to leave everyone and go off to the South Seas." He thought of himself as a novelist although he had never published a piece of fiction. He experienced profound feelings of emptiness and uncertainty about who he really was and what he wanted from life. Initiated into cocaine use by students, he began to borrow money from his mother to obtain the drug. Initially he told her the money was for his children, later that it was to pay a therapist.

One night, Dr. Smith and his wife had a particularly vitriolic fight. She accused him of ruining her life, opened the windows of their home and screamed insults about him to their neighbors, tore up books in their library. In a frenzy, Dr. Smith ran out of the house, after informing her that it was she who had destroyed him, as she would soon learn. For the first time he went to a gay bath. In an agitated, depressed rage, he decided to have as much sex as possible in order to expose himself to AIDS. During a thirty-six-hour period he had six orgasms with six different men. By month's end he had had oral and anal sex with about twenty additional partners. He experienced a sense of triumph at having a weapon with which he could finally defeat his wife. He waited until a quarrel was beginning. His wife once again accused him of having a mistress. "It would be pretty silly for me to have a mistress," he replied, "since I am gay!" In the shocked silence that followed the patient confessed that not only was he gay but he "probably had AIDS." Dr. Smith's wife reacted with horror and disbelief. She telephoned the news to both sets of parents. A lengthy conference followed involving the in-laws, during which Dr. Smith confessed that he had used the money given him by his mother to buy cocaine. Under pressure from both sets of parents, Dr. Smith and his wife sought psychiatric consultation. Despite the fact that both had come to believe he actually had AIDS, repeated blood tests for HIV antigen were negative.

Psychiatric evaluation revealed that both partners in this marriage had predominately masochistic character structures integrated at a borderline level. Each needed extensive individual treatment. They soon decided to separate and divorce. During individual therapy Dr. Smith's homosexual fantasies subsided, he became involved in sexual relationships with women, and he no longer believed that he was gay. In fact, he looked back on the episode of his life when he had decided he was gay as "a bad dream." In retrospect, it appeared that Dr. Smith's homosexual activity with others during adulthood, and to a great extent his homosexual erotic fantasies, were predominately motivated by sadomasochistic fantasies, as was his sense of gay identity. The motivation to contract AIDS had suicidal and homocidal components, since his wife's death from AIDS was part of the motivating fantasy.

DIRECTIONS FOR FUTURE RESEARCH

There is no evidence to date indicating that consolidated masochistic motivation is aggregated among men at any point on the Kinsey scale, nor is there empirical support for the view that most masochists are predominately or exclusively homosexual or that most homosexuals (however defined) are masochistic.

The patients discussed in this chapter are difficult to treat. They often seek professional assistance because an acute crisis leads to sudden escalation of psychic pain beyond bearable levels. Some patients drop out of treatment as soon as the unusually intense state of suffering is relieved. Others settle into lengthy, arduous therapeutic relationships that they use for masochistic purposes. Psychotherapy or psychoanalysis is thus converted into yet another life situation in which the person feels deprived and victimized. The features distinguishing patients who improve as a result of treatment and those who do not have yet to be specified.

Of all men with masochistic character neuroses and borderline syndromes, many do not symbolically represent their masochistic conflicts with homo-erotic imagery. Those who do can be conceptualized as falling into several major subgroups. Some bisexual men appear to experience homosexual erotic fantasies primarily as a defense against masochism. These patients, similar to the bisexual masochistic man discussed above, appear to change their position on the Kinsey scale (becoming more heterosexual in fantasy and/or activity) as their masochism subsides. Other bisexual men, who often appear initially similar to those in the subgroup above, remain stable in their position on the Kinsey scale as their masochism waxes and wanes. The features distinguishing these groups are not presently known. In men who are predominately or exclusively lifelong homosexual, the position on the Kinsey scale is probably constant irrespective of the severity of masochistic impairment. The theoretical rationale underlying this clinical hypothesis is put forth in part 4 of this book.

Many other questions about masochism and its relation to sexual orientation remain open. For example, the attributes and developmental experiences that distinguish characterological masochists without masochistic paraphilia from those with the sexual disorder have not been described. An anecdotal clinical literature suggests that there may be sex differences in masochistic psychopathology. Presumably males experience the paraphilia more frequently, despite the fact that females exhibit the spectrum of characterological disturbances at least as often as males do. But these clinical impressions are not supported by a firm database. It would be interesting to compare men and women of predominantly masochistic character type and comparable levels of psychostructural integration to determine whether the masochistic paraphilia is more common in one gender than in the other.

As pointed out earlier, clinical experience suggests that in some subgroups of bisexual men, homosexual imagery may serve a defensive function, disguising unconscious masochism. I suspect that there are also bisexual men in whom heterosexual imagery serves a similar masochistic function, but this phenomenon has yet to be well described. As noted previously, however, the relentless pursuit of heterosexuality by some gay psychoanalytic patients may be the manifest expression of underlying masochism.

It is generally accepted that masochism in any of its forms is difficult to treat, but there are no follow-up studies on the effects of psychoanalytic treatment. It is also not known whether sexual orientation influences treatment outcome.

As with many aspects of psychoanalytic psychology today, critical overview of this area points to an urgent need for systematic clinical investigation. Such research should involve extensive data pooling. In the instance of masochism, for example, only small numbers of patients within specific subgroups are likely to be treated at a given center. If one wished to compare the frequency with which the masochistic paraphilia occurs in borderline homosexual and heterosexual masochists, several treatment facilities would have to work together in a collaborative investigative effort.

11

Homosexuality and
Paranoid Psychopathology

The relationship between homosexuality and paranoid phenomena is uniquely important in the history of psychopathology, primarily because of theories advanced by Freud in his discussion of the Schreber case (1911/1958). Many psychoanalysts and psychiatrists once accepted Freud's model as if it were based on solid evidence. In 1955, for example, Ovesey wrote, "the theory has found widespread acceptance in psychiatric circles and most psychiatrists today would probably subscribe quite uncritically to the Freudian proposition that there is an exclusive etiological relationship between paranoia and homosexuality" (p. 341). Although Dr. Schreber suffered from a psychotic condition and Freud's discussion focused on delusions, the posited relationship between unconscious homosexuality and paranoid phenomena has been extended to include nondelusional paranoid phenomena and paranoid traits as well. The extension of this model of unconscious homosexuality from delusions to paranoid traits and symptoms generally, coupled with the tendency to consider unconscious homosexual conflict a universal psychodynamic in males, has led to substantial confusion in the way generations of psychodynamically minded clinicians have thought about homosexuality.

In this chapter I discuss descriptive aspects of paranoid psychopathology and focus on Freud's paper on Dr. Schreber. Models of paranoia contributed by more recent theoreticians are also reviewed, including Ovesey's (1955) suggested modification of Freud's theory, Cameron's (1959, 1967) view of paranoia, and Frosch's (1983) discussion of unconscious homosexuality, which I use as a point of departure for my own comments on unconscious and latent homosexuality. Since distinctions between categories of paranoid psychopathology are often blurred, I begin by reviewing briefly the common paranoid conditions.

DESCRIPTIVE FEATURES OF PARANOID PSYCHOPATHOLOGY

Severe paranoid psychopathology is characterized by delusions. The *DSM-III-R* categorizes Delusional (Paranoid) Disorder according to type of delusion: erotomanic, grandiose, jealous, persecutory, or somatic. Paranoid delusions are a common feature of organic mental disorders and substance abuse disorders; they sometimes occur in schizophreniform and mood disorders as well. Schizophrenia also occurs in paranoid form. The *DSM-III* noted that patients with paranoid schizophrenia may be unsure of their gender identity and may fear being thought of as homosexual or being approached by homosexual people. This clinical phenomenon is not alluded to in *DSM-III-R*. Many clinicians observe that fear of homosexuality is not infrequent among males, whereas paranoid schizophrenic women tend more often to worry about being perceived as prostitutes ("sluts," "whores," etc.). I know of no reports of paranoid males fearing being thought of as heterosexual or being accused by hallucinations of heterosexuality.

Interviewing a paranoid schizophrenic male who thinks *you* think he is homosexual can be most distressing. I recall a number of frightening encounters with paranoid schizophrenic men, but the most terrifying one, which involved homosexual ideational content, occurred when I was in the army. The interaction went something like this: I introduced myself; he said, "Hello sir." We shook hands. I was positively impressed with his correct manners, somewhat formal stance, clean uniform, and penetrating gaze. I said, "Have you come a long way?" He said, "Yes *sir*" and fell silent. His gaze seemed most penetrating. I was absentmindedly thinking about this when the corpsman accompanying him requested permission to leave to go to the bathroom. I agreed and then offered the patient a seat.

"A *seat*," he said, staring at me. "A fucking seat!" He sat down tensely, then leaned forward and snarled, "*So,* you think I'm a queer, do you? Why you Communist prick!" He stood up and I pressed an emergency button on the wall. The patient slammed my desk with his fist. "My knuckles are bleeding, you sonofabitch!" he said, glaring at me with focused hatred. I was reminded of animals whose hypothalamic rage centers had been stimulated by intracerebral electrodes.

"So you think I'm *queer,* you fucking asshole, you dipshit pig. Well, die then!" He spat at me and was moving to attack when four burly corpsmen burst into the room. The patient quieted down as soon as he was restrained, but he ultimately required large doses of chlorpromazine. I quieted down after some weeks, not without ingestion of substantial doses of gin. The encounter occurred in 1970, but it remains as vivid in my mind as if it had happened yesterday.

Consideration of the relationship between homosexuality and paranoid psychopathology was not the first thing on my mind immediately after this encounter. Subsequently, however, I wondered why the soldier mistakenly decided that I thought he was homosexual, and why it seemed to bother him so much. These questions have been addressed by Freud, Ovesey, Cameron, and Frosch (among others). Before reviewing their thoughts some mention should be made of the nondelusional paranoid person.

People with paranoid character structures have a number of traits that determine a characteristic life stance. They attribute malevolent motivation to others and are suspicious, mistrustful, resentful, and litigious. Convinced of the truth of their beliefs and the justice of their causes, they are always rigid (Shapiro 1981). Hypervigilant patrol of the boundaries of the self is unceasing: paranoid individuals act as if they were watchdogs of their own souls. They are secretive, guarded, and tend to perceive kindness as weakness. They usually seem cold; they are angry, unaffectionate, and humorless. Paranoid people tend to misinterpet the external environment and to be prone to ideas of reference (MacKinnon & Michels 1971). Their misinterpretations of the innocently intended behavior of others can trigger violent rage. The potentially violent paranoid person is frequently male and is not necessarily hallucinating, delusional, or psychotic.

Many an innocent person has been the object of paranoid referentiality. Often this occurs when men come into contact with other men at bars, on athletic fields, in schoolyards, on city streets. An accusation is suddenly spit out—"Hey you! You looking at me?" "You talking to [i.e., about] me?" "You laughing at me?" This challenge is sometimes a prelude to violence. Often the perceived insult involves overt homosexual content: "You think I'm a fag?" Women may be the object of paranoid rage as well and may be attacked if the paranoid male's sense of masculinity is threatened by them. Such naturalistically occurring social behavior and similar fantasies described by many men have led clinicians to question whether there is a relationship between a homosexual psychodynamic complex and paranoid psychopathology.

FREUD'S MODEL OF PARANOIA AND HOMOSEXUALITY

Freud's article "Psychoanalytic Notes on an Autobiographical Account of a Case of Paranoia (Dementia Paranoides)" (1911/1958) was based upon the *Memoirs* of Dr. Jur Daniel Paul Schreber. Dr. Schreber, an appeals court judge in Dresden, was hospitalized in his fifties with a paranoid illness. His book, published in 1903, provided a remarkable account of the development of paranoid delusional thinking. Freud never interviewed Schreber, basing his article entirely on Schreber's book.

The article, central in Freud's evolving concept of the libido theory, hypothesizes that delusions are a reaction to (i.e., a defense against) unconscious homosexual wishes. Freud was aware that his theory was risky:

> In Schreber's system the two principal elements of his delusion (his transformation into a woman and his favored relation to God) are united in his assumption of a feminine attitude toward God. It will be a necessary part of our task to show that there is an essential *genetic* relation between these two elements. Or else our attempts at elucidating Schreber's delusions will leave us in the absurd position described in Kant's famous simile in *The Critique of Pure Reason*: "we shall be like a man holding a sieve under a he-goat while someone else milks it." (p. 132)

Although his discussion of Schreber's autobiography is dazzlingly brilliant and seductive, Freud was not entirely successful in demonstrating an essential relationship between unconscious homosexuality and paranoid psychopathology. Because of the powerful impact of this paper on psychoanalytic thought about homosexuality, however, I treat it in detail.

Freud noted that a few months before the delusions began, Dr. Schreber, "in a state between sleeping and waking," had a fantasy that "it must be very nice to be a woman submitting to the act of copulation" (p. 108). Dr. Schreber apparently had not consciously experienced such thoughts earlier in his life. This nondelusional thought, in the light of subsequent developments, seemed to Freud a manifestation of the illness that soon evolved in full form. Freud claimed that the fantasy suggested psychodynamic influences of central importance in determining the form of the disorder. He observed that Dr. Schreber would ordinarily have rejected the idea expressed in his dreamlike fantasy; during his subsequent psychosis, however, he embraced it.

In the fall of 1893, Dr. Schreber experienced an episode of insomnia for which he sought treatment from a Dr. Flechsig. Schreber's condition soon deteriorated. He developed a delusional disorder that, in its early phase, was agonizingly painful: "He believed that he was dead, and decomposing, that he was suffering from the plague! He asserted that his body was being handled in all kinds of revolting ways. . . . he longed for death. . . . and made repeated attempts to drown himself in his bath" (p. 109).

Schreber felt that he was being persecuted and abused by certain people, including Dr. Flechsig. It ultimately dawned on him that there must be a hidden reason, "a sacred cause," for his suffering. Subsequently his mental functioning in most areas improved dramatically, but he developed a consolidated, well-structured delusional system. During the persecutory phase of his illness Schreber believed that he had been emasculated for the purpose of homosexual abuse. Later, he believed that the emasculation was simply part of the process of sex change necessitated by his unique relationship to God. In Freud's words, "a sexual delusion of persecution was later on converted in the patient's mind into a religious delusion of grandeur" (p. 114).

Schreber's core delusion was of gender change: "The idea of being transformed into a woman was the salient feature and the earliest germ of his delusional system" (p. 117). The delusional change in gender was accompanied by Schreber's belief that he had a uniquely close relationship to God. This relationship was an erotic one; the state of "heavenly bliss" in which Schreber felt closest to God was described as "voluptuous." Freud asserted that the erotic component to the illness was not entirely surprising from the psychoanalytic point of view:

> This instance of sexualization will . . . give us occasion to examine the patient's general attitude to the erotic side of life and to questions of sexual indulgence. For we psychoanalysts have hitherto supported the view that the routes of every nervous and mental disorder are chiefly to be found in the patient's sexual life; but whereas some of us have done so merely upon empirical grounds, others have been influenced in addition by theoretical considerations. (p. 127)

It bears some emphasis that Freud's (then new) psychoanalytic approach was biased toward a theory of sexual etiology of psychopathology. The theory connecting paranoia to unconscious homosexuality fit nicely with the general orientation of emerging psychoanalytic psychology.

Freud observed that prior to his illness, Schreber was a sexually ascetic agnostic. During his illness, however, he became a believer in God and a sexual hedonist of a special type: "The sexual enjoyment which he had won for himself was of a most unusual character. It was not the sexual liberty of a man, but the sexual feelings of a woman. He took up a feminine attitude towards God; he felt that he was God's wife" (p. 129). In discussing the underlying mechanism of paranoia, Freud first outlined the libido theory. This famous theory posited normative developmental phases of the infant in which a stage of autoeroticism was followed by narcissism, homosexuality, and then heterosexuality. Freud's comments about manifest adult homosexuality in this paper, the goal of which was to relate unconscious homosexuality to paranoia, are as follows:

> There comes a time in the development of the individual at which he unifies his sexual instincts (which have hitherto been engaged in auto-erotic activities) in order to obtain a love-object; and he begins by taking himself, his own body, as his love object, and only subsequently proceeds from this to the choice of some person other than himself as his object. This half-way phase between auto-erotism and object love may perhaps be indispensable to the normal course of life; but it appears that many people linger unusually long in this condition, and that many of its features are carried over by them into the later stages of their development. The point of central interest in the self which is thus chosen as a love object may already be the genitals. The line of development then leads on to

the choice of an outer object with similar genitals, that is, to homosexual object-choice, and thence to heterosexuality. Persons who are manifest homosexuals in later life, it may be presumed, never emancipated themselves from the binding condition that the object of their choice must possess genitals like their own. (p. 163)

This quotation illustrates the beguiling arrogance of Freud's genius. In the middle of an article on the analytic investigation of paranoia, in a section entitled "On the Mechanism of Paranoia," we find, taking up less than one page, an entire theory of overt homosexuality. This theory, which Freud claimed was based upon "recent [i.e., prior to 1911] investigations," allegedly "enables us to understand the part played by a homosexual wish in the development of paranoia" (p. 163). Freud clearly meant that the evolution of Dr. Schreber's illness was compatible with the libido theory and could be taken as clinical evidence in support of it. It appeared to Freud that most paranoid illnesses, perhaps all, were explicable via the model developed to describe Schreber's illness. Freud felt that prior to the occurrence of a paranoid illness, vulnerable people are predisposed to regress to a narcissistic homosexual stage of development. They struggle continually with unacceptable unconscious homosexual impulses, which threaten to erupt into consciousness. When something disturbs this fragile equilibrium, these impulses, no longer contained by normal psychological defensive processes, must be disguised by delusions. The homosexual impulses determine the content of delusions. Once the delusional illness has appeared, as in Schreber's case, numerous sublimations and restitutive processes determine its subsequent form.

Three ideas about homosexuality stemmed from Freud's comments in this paper: (1) that homosexuals are paranoid; (2) that rageful men are afraid of being homosexual; and (3) that homosexuality reflects arrested development. The first notion is of course false (Hooker 1956; Saghir & Robins 1973). The second, although common enough, is not applicable to most cases of male aggressivity. The arrested development theory is complex, and it is given more complete consideration in part 4. (In my opinion it too is incorrect.)

In closing his article, Freud once again stressed that it was meant as illustrative of a theory *already formed*. He also made one of his many appeals for the need for empirical validation:

I can . . . call a friend and fellow specialist to witness that I had developed my theory of paranoia before I became acquainted with the contents of Schreber's book. It remains for the future to decide whether there is more delusion in my theory than I should like to admit, or whether there is more truth in Schreber's delusion than other people are as yet prepared to believe. (p. 182)

Other than the criticism that Freud's hypotheses were not derived from the Schreber autobiography (instead, he used the book to illustrate an already formed subtheory of paranoia, part of his larger libido theory), his article raises a number of questions and problems, many of which have been addressed by psychoanalysts. For example, the conversion "I love him" to "I hate him" seems plausible in the Schreber case. In other instances, however, "I hate him" could simply mean "I hate him" ("and have always hated him"). The paranoid form "he hates me" can arise as a result of projected (but not necessarily homosexual) impulses—the tendency to project the unacceptable would therefore be applied to unconscious homosexuality only when the core conflict is a homosexual one. Blum (1980) argued that hostility, rather than defense against unconscious homosexual impulses, is the core influence in paranoid conditions. He suggested that unconscious homosexual conflict, if present, is of secondary importance, and he stressed the role of ego fragility and the organizing function of beating fantasies in the etiology of paranoid disorders.

But Freud's theory of paranoia exhibits an even more fundamental problem. As noted earlier, modern concepts of gender identity differentiation were developed after Freud's lifetime. In his article about Dr. Schreber (as elsewhere in his writing), Freud did not use the term homosexuality as it is used today: he condensed the concepts of sexual (i.e., erotic) behavior and gender-related behavior. Modern theories and findings in developmental psychology draw a clear distinction between gender identity differentiation and sexual orientation, whereas Freud did not. Suppose that Dr. Schreber was not a delusional psychotic patient but was convinced that despite his having male genitalia, he was female. Today he might complain, "I am a woman trapped in a man's body," which would be taken as evidence of a basic gender identity disorder. His desire for partners of the same sex could be understood in the context of the incongruence of his anatomy with his sense of gender identity. Dr. Schreber's manifestly experienced "homosexuality" always occurred in the context of a primary psychotic gender identity disorder. Freud's theory of delusions as presented via the Schreber case, therefore, primarily related *gender* confusion to paranoia. Niederland (1984) noted that following partial recovery from his illness Schreber retained the conviction that he was a woman "with female breasts and other feminine attributes." A similar view was presented by MacAlpine and Hunter in 1953 and by Stoller in 1974.

OVESEY'S CONCEPT OF PSEUDOHOMOSEXUALITY

Although Freud's model of paranoia achieved widespread acceptance and unparalleled influence, it had critics. Ovesey (1955b/1969) offered an especially lucid revision of Freud's theory.

Ovesey drew on research by Klein and Horowitz (1949) on delusional psychotic patients in psychotherapy. The defensive operations of these regressed individuals were completely fragmented. If unconscious homosexual wishes had caused their delusions, evidence of this would have been noticed by therapists. Homosexual impulses previously repressed would presumably be overtly expressed as a consequence of defensive failure. This was not the case.

Ovesey described the distinction between homosexuality and what he termed pseudohomosexuality (1954; 1955a, b). Pseudohomosexual conflicts, he claimed, are intimately related to insecurity about one's masculinity. Some men develop in such a way that they fail to live up to societal standards for masculine performance—they cannot be appropriately assertive. A subgroup of such men experiences significant pseudohomosexual conflict, which is expressed ideationally in the form of the equation:

I am a failure = I am not a man = I am castrated = I am a woman = I am a homosexual

In Ovesey's view, the pseudohomosexual conflict can motivate hypercompetitive activity or the search for a powerful, protective father figure. But both stances are doomed to failure because of internal psychological conflict. Hypercompetition is associated with defeat conceded in advance and with chronic (pseudohomosexual) anxiety. Pursuit of a powerful male protector is associated with anxiety that one may actually be homosexual (even though the perceived motivation is not associated with sexual excitement). Ovesey explained this by hypothesizing yet another equation: penis = breast. The conscious experience of wishing to incorporate the penis (or a barely disguised variant, the fear of penile penetration) may symbolize the wish to be nurtured and protected. The underlying concrete expression of this wish is the child sucking at the mother's breast.

Ovesey noted that pseudohomosexual conflict occurs in both psychotic and nonpsychotic people. Psychotic individuals, however, express the conflict in delusions and hallucinations. Ovesey applied the adaptational theory of motivation of the Rado-Columbia school to the material at hand. He defined *true motivation* as teleologically determined in terms of the ultimate adaptational goal. This true motivation may be hidden from awareness via defensive processes. The *apparent motivation,* which is consciously perceived, can be projected by paranoid people. Whereas true homosexual anxiety stems from conflict about true homosexual motivation, pseudohomosexual anxiety stems from conflict about motivation that is *apparently* homosexual but is *truly* about power and dependency.

In Ovesey's view, true homosexual conflict can trigger the paranoid constellation, but pseudohomosexual conflict does so more frequently. In many cases, neither component seems to be present: instead, rage is directly projected and the related anxiety is survival anxiety. Ovesey's view is compatible with the empirical data: homoerotic fantasies and/or activities do not appear to be unusually common among delusional men. Preoccupation with homosexual imagery without associated erotic arousal is quite common but by no means universal (Klein & Horowitz 1949; Klaf & Davis 1960; Planansky & Johnston 1962). For example, it often happens that a delusional man whose erotic fantasy life and activity with others is completely heterosexual nonetheless hears voices calling him "queer." In suggesting that homosexual imagery may symbolically express motives that are not sexual (i.e., power and dependency), Ovesey anticipated the notion that these images might really communicate gender insecurity. In fact, he pointed out that "the pseudohomosexual conflict can develop only in those men who fail to meet successfully the societal standards for masculine performance" (1955b/1969, p. 56) and explained, "the pseudohomosexual conflict represents a failure in 'masculine' assertion, and each idea in this equation reflects a social value judgment" (p. 57).

Ovesey makes the distinction between gender-related behavior and explicitly sexual behavior even more clearly in his work on the psychodynamic aspects of transsexualism (Ovesey & Person 1973; Person & Ovesey 1974, a, b, c, 1983).

CAMERON'S CONCEPT OF PSEUDOCOMMUNITY

Cameron, like Ovesey, felt that Freud was wrong to emphasize the centrality of unconscious homosexual impulses in paranoid reactions: "A great number of overtly homosexual persons never develop paranoid delusions and a great many people are paranoid without being homosexually oriented" (1967, p. 668). Cameron felt that the most common developmental problem leading to paranoia was a failure to develop basic trust in early life. During the infancy of paranoid people, their caretakers are rejecting or undependable. The child feels anxious and unloved and cannot feel secure that nurturance and safety will be provided. Cameron emphasized the impact of hostility, social isolation, and cognitive distortion on the paranoid constellation. The paranoid adult is suspicious and mistrustful of others. Chronically angry but threatened by the conscious perception of his or her rage and by the superego anxiety it engenders, he or she denies anger and projects both anger and anxiety. Instead of feeling guilty about being angry, he or she feels frightened of others who are angry at him or her. Aggressive responses are justified as legitimate self-protective efforts in the face of external danger. Cameron pointed out that the final crystallization of persecutory delusions—the point at which paranoid people conceptualize the unifying purpose behind frightening events—involves the creation of a pseudocommunity (1959). This is a group of real or imagined people united in a plot against the paranoid individual. Authority figures are usually prominent in the pseudocommunity, since the paranoid person has felt slighted and humiliated by such figures since childhood.

Cameron noted that in normal day-to-day functioning, basic trust is necessary for consensual validation (e.g., "Is that a table there?" "Is the traffic light green?" "Did you see that?—Thank goodness; for a second I thought my eyes deceived me"). Basic trust is also central in the working of complex psychological processes that allow adults to experience day-to-day life as moderately secure. Cameron's emphasis on the abused and neglected backgrounds of paranoid people, their interpersonal deficits, and their desperate attempts to maintain interpersonal contact, even of a tormenting kind, conveys a sense of pathos. Abused as children, paranoid people recreate an atmosphere of abuse in adulthood by provoking others to mistreat them.

Cameron's model is basically compatible with that of Sullivan, who also disagreed with the unconscious homosexuality theory of paranoia. Sullivan emphasized the interpersonal determinants of paranoia, which he felt was a response to profound feelings of inferiority. Sullivan also asserted that it was incorrect to condense paranoid men's fragile sense of masculinity with homosexuality (1953; 1956; 1962).

FROSCH'S MODEL OF UNCONSCIOUS HOMOSEXUALITY

Frosch's book *The Psychotic Process* (1983) presents an integrative review of the psychoanalytic literature on homosexuality and paranoia. Frosch's treatment deserves attention not only for its scholarly overview but also for its provocative claim: "Many of the more recent contributions view the unconscious homosexual features in the paranoid constellation as secondary to other factors, as pseudo-phenomena. I intend, however, to reaffirm the role of unconscious homosexuality as the organizing principle in the paranoid constellation" (p. 65).

Before developing his thesis, Frosch distinguishes between latent and unconscious homosexuality. In his view, latent homosexuality means that "the potential for becoming an overt, practising homosexual" is present (p. 65). To illustrate the difference, Frosch presents the case of a twenty-three-year-old man who requested help because of anxiety that he might be homosexual.

> During a course on psychoanalytic concepts, he became very tense and anxious when the concept of unconscious homosexuality was discussed. When I saw him he was panicked by recollections of incidents in his life that pointed in the direction of overt homosexuality. For instance, as an adolescent he had found himself fascinated by the genitals of the other boys while taking showers at the gym. On occasion he had erotic feelings, had begun to have an erection, and had rushed out of the shower in embarrassment. Other experiences also suggested a homosexual orientation, which if not overt, nonetheless had the potential of becoming overt. The patient had not recognized the homosexual nature of his feelings until he took the course and the subject of unconscious homosexuality was discussed. (p. 65)

The man soon became an overt homosexual: "Over a short period of time he began to accept this as his preference; his latent homosexuality became overt" (p. 66). Frosch emphasizes that this case does not illustrate unconscious homosexual wishes: the individual's homosexual desires were conscious but not cognitively integrated.

In the notational scheme I propose earlier in this book, there is no place for latent homosexuality. I agree with Frosch that unconscious homosexuality must, by definition, be excluded from conscious awareness. However, I take issue with his emphasis, in the so-called latent form, on the potential for homosexuality to become overt. A person can experience conscious homosexual feelings but engage predominately in heterosexual activity; or he or she can engage predominately in homosexual activity but label him- or herself heterosexual. Finally, someone can experience homosexual fantasies and even identify as homosexual but never have the potential to become an "overt" (i.e., practicing) homosexual for reasons that are predominately conscious. I see no need for the category of latent homosexuality. I would describe the experience of Frosch's patient as follows: Exposure to males in certain social situations → erotic arousal → anxiety and denial of the meaning, but not repression, of homosexual arousal → learning about homosexuality in a course → cognitive reintegration, diminishing of denial, acknowledgement of the meaning of homosexual stimulation → homosexual activity → self-identification as homosexual → assumption of homosexual identity and presumably social role.

Frosch's emphasis on sexual activity with others (what he means by overt) seems to me excessively narrow and more confusing than helpful from a clinical point of view. I do feel that the concept of unconscious homosexuality (discussed later) is helpful in a circumscribed way in understanding certain behavior. But unconscious homosexuality has no place in a *diagnostic* classification method. It seems practical to diagnose on the basis of reportable or observable phenomena that can be assessed with reliability and validity. Unconscious homosexuality is not such a phenomenon.

After explaining the difference between unconscious and latent homosexuality, Frosch discusses psychoanalytic theories and evidence relating unconscious homosexuality to paranoid phenomena. He notes that a number of investigators—including White (1961), MacAlpine and Hunter (1953), Fairbairn (1956), and Niederland (1968)—reinterpreted the Schreber case, emphasizing very early "pregenital" traumata and taking issue with the primary role of unconscious homosexuality. Niederland also brought forth material about Schreber's father, a prominent physician and educator. (Schreber's father ran an orthopedic institution. He believed that physical restraining devices worn by young children assisted in the learning process. It would appear that he had a rigid, sadistic character structure which influenced the later development of his son's illness.)

Summarizing the work of other psychoanalysts who felt on clinical and theoretical grounds that Freud's exclusive emphasis on the unconscious homosexual dynamic in paranoia phenomena was incorrect, Frosch discusses Federn (1952), Grauer (1955), Sullivan (1956), Ovesey (1955a, b), Meissner (1978), and Blum (1980). He points out that many clinical psychiatric (i.e., nonpsychoanalytic) studies have been carried out attempting to test the hypothesized relationship. Frosch observes that in these studies the "persecutor" of patients of both genders is generally male. He suggests, however, that lack of psychoanalytic sophistication may have led to methodological problems in some of the studies.

Turning his attention to anal sadism and aggression, Frosch observes that Freud returned to the problems raised in the Schreber article later in his career, after he formulated the dual instinct theory.

> On the one hand [Freud] depicts the use of overt aggression as a defense against unconscious homosexuality and indicates that ambivalence is always present in the persecuted paranoid as a defense against the homosexual conflict. On the other hand he speaks of overt homosexuality as a defense against overt aggression. He points to a form of overt homosexuality that arises out of the repression of hostile, aggressive feelings and death wishes, directed toward other family members of the same sex, usually brothers. With repression these impulses undergo a transformation so that the earlier rivals become the first homosexual love objects. Here we see the opposite dynamics from the paranoid in which the original love object later becomes the hated object. (1983, p. 84)

Frosch cites a number of other investigators who stressed the primary role of aggression in paranoid phenomena, including Baumeyer (1956), Numberg (1938), and Knight (1940). He notes also that a number of reports stressed the role of anality and anal sadism in paranoid disorders, including those of Ferenczi (1911), Van Ophijsen (1920), Klein (1932), Arlow (1949), and Starcke (1920).

Interwoven with discussion of the psychoanalytic literature are many clinical illustrations from Frosch's extensive experience. The clinical material includes nonpsychotic individuals as well as delusional ones, and, taken with the critical review of other work, leads to Frosch's own formulation, which I summarize as follows:

1. The preparanoid child is humiliated by a same-sex parent. The humiliation, profoundly meaningful and protypical of the father–son relationship, occurs early in development prior to the formation of what Frosch terms "sexual identity."
2. The actual humiliating experiences are, in Frosch's words, "tied to the child's fantasies." I take this to mean that they are experienced as dreaded fantasies come true and that they influence the development of subsequent fantasies.
3. The experience of perceived enforced passivity continues to be traumatic after the event and may be catastrophic.
4. This experience is interpreted by the paranoid adult as a humiliating anal sadistic assault. The assailant replicates the original childhood object, and the anality reflects a regression to the anal phase of development during which the original traumata occurred.
5. The unconscious homosexual component actually expresses a wish for and a fear of adopting a passive-feminine posture toward an ambivalently perceived same-sex authority figure. The paranoid constellation involves denial, repression, and projection; positive feelings are repressed and denied; rage is denied and projected.

Frosch's theory integrates abundant data suggesting that preoedipal rage is of central importance in paranoid phenomena. This is compatible with evidence that paranoid people are often found to have been mistreated during childhood. Their early traumatic experiences are not simply the product of fantasy and retrospective distortion. Frosch's theory does not stress oral aggression, a recurrent theme in many of the works he cites. I can only assume that Frosch's personal clinical experience is more compatible with the notion of anal persecution than with that of poisonous nurturance. But there are two portals of entry into the male body, the mouth and the anus, and penetration may be symbolically expressed in terms of either one. Presumably the early humiliating experiences Frosch discusses often occur during both oral and anal phases of development. Clinically, oral and anal aggressivity (both preoedipal) seem to influence the paranoid constellation, and Frosch's lack of stress on orality seems to be a limitation in his theory. If the concept of oral aggression received more emphasis, his theory would integrate even more data, in my view.

Does Frosch accomplish what he set out to do, however—does he reestablish the importance of unconscious homosexuality in producing the paranoid constellation? The answer to this depends on the meaning of the term homosexuality as used by Frosch. In contrast to his careful definitions of *unconscious* and *latent,* Frosch never defines *homosexuality.* As he uses it, the term connotes gender-related behavior (i.e., passivity, femininity) as well as behavior that is explicitly sexual. It is gender-related behavior, not sexual behavior, that is central in the paranoid constellation, and Frosch recognizes this:

> The term "unconscious homosexuality" applies to the conflict in paranoid symptomatology, and it has very specific connotations of dangerous and unacceptable passivity which must be rejected and disavowed. *Perhaps the term "homosexual" should not but used, but rather the passive-feminine position, insofar as it applies to the male.* (Emphasis mine.)

Frosch's model directs attention to the following facts and ideas: Early in development, when gender identity is not yet fully differentiated, traumatic experiences of a particular type may influence psychological systems of organization concerned with regulation of affect, secure gender identity, and sexual and aggressive fantasies. In Frosch's view these traumata create a link between rage and experiences that are perceived as threatening to gender identity and gender self-esteem. His model does not suggest, however, that homosexual phenomena produce the paranoid constellation.

Many people who read about homosexuality are not psychoanalysts. Behavioral scientists, sociologists, anthropologists, and so on might not fully appreciate that the causal relationship Frosch delineates is between paranoia and the gender-related component of "unconscious homosexuality"; sexual behavior is not primarily involved. It is particularly important to emphasize this in light of Frosch's assertion that his chapter purports to "reaffirm the role of unconscious homosexuality as the organizing principle in the paranoid constellation."

ADDITIONAL COMMENTS ON PARANOIA AND HOMOSEXUALITY

The model of psychostructural levels is not usually used in discussing paranoia: there are some personality disorders that never occur in the context of a healthy level of functioning. In paranoid individuals, although ego defenses may seem to operate smoothly enough and the self-concept is not necessarily manifestly fragmented, characterological rigidity is always severe, and defensive operations and the level of object relations are always primitive. The well-integrated obsessional person or the individual with a masochistic character neurosis is capable of experiencing love, warmth, and a range of other positive attributes; the apparently well-integrated paranoid person cannot.

From a purely descriptive point of view, some analysts find the model of psychostructural levels useful in working with paranoid patients, in the same way that it may be useful in describing the narcissistic disorders (i.e., paranoid personality type at a borderline level of integration; narcissistic personality type at borderline level of integration). In the case of the paranoid disorders, however, those that operate more smoothly are not necessarily healthier.

Many other investigators have discussed the relationship between unconscious homosexuality and paranoid mechanisms. For example, Salzman (1960) noted the interaction between basic grandiosity and realistic rejections and failures, and Sappenfield (1965) was impressed with the importance of conflict about incest. Walters (1955) criticized the inadequate empirical basis for Freud's theory. Some other clinical investigators supported Freud's view (Rosenfeld 1949, Meketon et al. 1962). It is sometimes difficult to interpret attempts to conduct controlled investigations of Freud's hypothesis, since descriptive psychiatrists often seem to disregard the distinction between conscious and unconscious homosexuality. No particular type of paranoid pathology has been demonstrated to aggregate at any point on the Kinsey scale.

The body of material discussed above discourages simplistic, mechanistic interpretations of the relationship between unconscious homosexuality and paranoid phenomena. Freud's theory of a universal homosexual dynamic in paranoid conditions does not rest on a firm empirical base. The psychodynamic and developmentally oriented reports do suggest that gender identity, gender security, and gender self-esteem figure prominently in paranoia. Clinicians working with adult paranoid patients agree that these patients fear attack and tend to be insecure in their sense of masculinity. The psychotic person often represents abstract ideas concretely. The paranoid psychotic individual in particular is likely to experience or envision hostile intrusion as penetration of the body through an orifice (mouth or anus).

It is also generally agreed that paranoid people project extreme hostility, which they experience but deny. In the view of many investigators, this hostility is engendered in early childhood. The child is brutalized during the oral and anal phases (using the libido model) and during separation-individuation, self-definition, and gender identity differentiation (using modern terminology). Under the impact of the disorganizing affects of anger and anxiety, self-definition is fragile and gender identity differentiation occurs in an atmosphere of danger and insecurity. Later in life, the paranoid person may have an apparently solid recognition that he is male, but this recognition may be associated with extreme anxiety. When the integrity of the self is perceived to be in danger, the paranoid person often consciously experiences a threat to the *gender* self. In most cases, the paranoid male appears to process anxiety as if an external assault on the integrity of the gender self were imminent. Whereas self-dissolution anxiety is common in many forms of severe psychopathology, the consciously perceived experience of gender self dissolution fused with rage is unique to the paranoid conditions.

Nonpsychotic paranoid individuals may cope with and repress the image of the fragmented gender self. In psychotic paranoid people, however, the image is likely to be experienced as reality. Since intimacy cannot occur without infringement of (or impingement upon) the self boundary, true intimacy is impossible for the paranoid person. But impairment of intimacy occurs for a variety of other reasons as well. Abused children do not tend to become warm, affectionate adults. I agree with investigators who suggest that the primary affective problem in the paranoid constellation is with rage; the primary structural problems are with ego integration and persistent, rigid utilization of primitive denial and projection; the primary interpersonal problem is with trust and love; the primary organizing need is to reexperience an ambivalently perceived infantile relationship with a humiliating caretaker to whom one is attached, but from whom one continually retreats. The image of gender-self fragmentation and its related anxiety is frequently but not universally associated with paranoid phenomena. In many men the psychological experience of rage and threatened gender dissolution or humiliating failure of gender self-esteem are so intertwined that it appears as if one causes the other. In fact this probably occurs often. In a particular patient the perceived threat of homosexual assault may specifically cause rage and fear. Every clinician learns this early in training, and many have had frightening experiences with paranoid patients similar to the one I describe. When a paranoid male experiences fear of homosexual assault, he may manifest what has been termed homosexual panic (Glick 1959, Kendler 1947). It bears emphasis, however, that not all decompensating, dangerous paranoid patients have homosexual ideation. The term homosexual panic is often used imprecisely and inferentially to refer to all rageful, decompensating paranoid males. This usage is incorrect and perpetuates the notion that unconscious homosexuality causes paranoia.

The contributions of numerous investigators have replaced one question about the association between homosexuality and paranoia by another. The contemporary clinician no longer need consider why homosexual men are paranoid, since there is no evidence that they generally are. It now must be asked why homosexual males are not more often paranoid. Homosexuality begins in childhood, and many gay people grow up in environments that are virulently homophobic and sexist. One might expect that as a result of exposure to hostile, severely stressful interpersonal environments, homosexual males would tend to develop paranoid psychopathology. Since this does not occur with unusual frequency, we must ask whether unusually adept coping mechanisms coexist with homosexuality in many individuals. Innately powerful internal balancing mechanisms would allow people to preserve the capacity for basic trust despite being surrounded by an atmosphere of rageful rejection. This possible mechanism of psychological health among homosexual men is discussed more extensively in part 3.

12

Psychopathology
and Sexual Orientation:
Further Reflections

The preceding chapters illustrate that interactions between sexual orientation and psychopathology are complex. Nonetheless, they may be approached logically and systematically by the contemporary clinician. Since all facets of sexual orientation are embedded in personality structure, psychopathology involving sexual orientation can best be understood within the context of character pathology. All personality disorders, or mixtures thereof, at all levels of character structure integration, are exhibited by men from all parts of the Kinsey spectrum. (All types of psychotic disorders also occur in men from all parts of the Kinsey spectrum.) The *Diagnostic and Statistical Manual* (*DSM-III-R*) lists eleven personality disorders (not including the mixed, atypical type): paranoid, schizoid, schizotypal, histrionic, narcissistic, anti-social, borderline, avoidant, dependent, compulsive, and passive aggressive. It would be redundant to present cases of all types of disorders, at all levels of character structure integration, from both poles and the middle of the Kinsey spectrum. The basic descriptive approach toward psychopathology advocated in this book is put forth in previous chapters and I hope by now it is clear.

The biopsychosocial advances of sex research during recent decades suggest that the degree to which adult homosexuality (in any form) is associated with compromised ego and superego functioning and impaired capacity for object relations varies along a spectrum. A psychoanalytic model of the adult mind in which heterosexuality is taken as an integral component of health seems excessively rigid, out of touch with modern sex research, and of potential disservice to some patients.

There are many subgroups of homosexuality, phenotypically similar but with different origins, mental functions, courses, and responses to psycho-

180

therapy and psychoanalysis. One subgroup, understudied by psychoanalysts to date, is made up of men who have always been predominantly or exclusively homosexual in fantasy and/or activity and whose character structure is integrated at a high level. As noted previously, these men appear to have character neuroses comparable to those of heterosexual men. Other homosexual men, integrated at an even higher level, find their way to a positive sense of gay identity. These men experience stable representational worlds, empathic object relationships, and highly functional ego mechanisms. Psychoanalysis as a form of education about the self is, of course, not contraindicated for such people. However, in some of these cases a psychoanalyst, if consulted, should recommend no treatment because there is no evidence of pathology.

One qualification must be made with regard to the potential pathological significance of homosexual phenomena. Thus far my discussion of psychopathology has focused on adults. The relationships between homosexuality and psychopathology during childhood are different from those during adulthood and are discussed extensively later; developmental phenomena are considered and reviewed in parts 3–4.

HOMOSEXUALITY AND NARCISSISM

The link between narcissism and homosexuality is particularly important in the history of psychoanalysis. Freud hypothesized that homosexuality and narcissism were intimately related, suggesting in *The Three Essays* that narcissistic object choice was a key psychological mechanism in the etiology of inversion (i.e., homosexuality). As he saw it, the prehomosexual child identifies with a woman and takes himself as a sexual object. He then searches for a love object like himself whom he can love as his mother loved him (1905/1953). Later, in "On Narcissism," Freud developed more fully his theory of narcissistic object choice and its effect on producing homosexuality (1914/1957). The influence of this model has been as powerful as Freud's influence in other areas of psychoanalytic thought. Thus, in a chapter on narcissism published in a recent textbook, Kernberg wrote:

> A second more severe but relatively infrequent type of pathologic narcissism was first described by Freud as an illustration of narcissistic object choice. Here, the patient's self is identified with an object while at the same time, the representation of the patient's infantile self is projected onto that very object, thus creating a libidinal relation in which the functions of self and object have been interchanged. This is often found among male and female homosexuals: they love another the way they would have wished to be loved. (1985)

It stands to reason that if traumatic psychic input during very early development is so severe as to alter the (hypothetically) normal course of sexual object selection, then other areas of the personality must be compromised as well.

Childhood stress powerful enough to produce narcissistic fixations leading to future narcissistic regressions would be unlikely to affect only sexual object choice. If Freud's hypothesis about narcissistic mechanisms in homosexual object choice is correct, and if his model of development in relation to present psychological functioning (i.e., the fixation-regression theory) is also correct, then a person with lifelong predominant or exclusive homosexual erotic fantasies and activity and a gay identity might be likely to manifest the characterological symptoms of narcissistic personality disorder. These include grandiosity, self-centeredness, exhibitionism, emotional shallowness, dependency on others, extreme envy, contemptuous devaluation and exploitation of others, a sense of entitlement, a tendency to transiently overidealize others, inability to empathize or make deep commitments, profound impairment in the regulation of self-esteem, lack of an internalized, differentiated value system, a tendency to experience realistic restraints and limits as humiliations, a need to experience the self-representation as perfect. Some analysts believe this personality configuration is associated with homosexuality. A model proposed by Socarides as recently as 1978 equates exclusive homosexuality with severe narcissistic pathology (1978). Socarides earlier suggested that "obligatory" (exclusive) homosexuality is due to preoedipal fixation. In his initial view, individuals with this type of homosexuality manifested severe gender identity disturbance, intractable anxiety "leading to an overriding, almost continual search for sexual partners" (p. 93), persistence of primitive and archaic mental mechanisms causing incorporation and projection anxieties, additional anxiety due to fragility of self-boundaries and ego functions, and predominance of pregenital characteristics of the ego. This model conceptualized homosexuality as a subtype of borderline psychopathology. Socarides subsequently modified this model and suggested that two forms of obligatory, exclusive homosexuality actually occur: a mild form and a form associated with the severe global impairment he initially thought was universal among homosexual people (1978). Although individuals who experience the milder form of homosexuality have good self–object differentiation, according to Socarides, they suffer from impaired ego functioning. Reality testing is often "ignored to serve the pleasure principle"; thinking, although clear, "reflects projective anxieties" and is dominated by the pleasure principle. Impulse control is "incomplete . . . leading to acting out of impulses and pursuit of instantaneous gratification." Other deficits supposedly manifested by these individuals include "elevated sense of self-esteem bordering on omnipotence, alternating with feelings of self depreciation"; need for narcissistic supplies; intolerance of frustration; and substitution of action for "normal anxiety or depression" (1978, pp. 487–88). The so-called mildly impaired individuals, according to Socarides' description, are actually severely impaired and would best be described as suffering from pathological narcissism. The assumption that global psychopathology must be present in homosexuals (even if it is not immediately apparent) led Socarides

(1974) and some other analysts to take issue with the nonpathological view of homosexuality presented in *DSM-III*.

Most behavioral scientists, however, and many psychoanalysts reject the hypothesis that predominant or exclusive homosexuality is associated with pathological narcissism. The basis for this rejection is not only that scientific studies do not support the association but also that personal experience provides meaningful evidence to the contrary. The personal experience of informed professionals carries special weight in this area because the narcissistic person often appears deceptively normal in social situations. It is virtually impossible, however, to maintain a durable, caring relationship with a narcissist. Many mental health professionals do have lasting friendships with gay men, have shared happiness and sorrow with them, offered support to and received support from them. These professionals dismiss the idea that their friends must be pathologically narcissistic because they are gay.

Kohut (1971) hypothesized that narcissistic patients develop idealizing and mirror types of transference reactions. The analyst becomes a "self-object," symbolically representing an idealized mother in whose presence and for whose approval exhibitionism occurs. The patient therefore enters analysis at a stage of arrested psychological development. During analysis it becomes apparent in the transference that he is substituting the analyst for a missing segment of his psychic structure. If the analysis is successful, a process that Kohut called *transmuting internalization* occurs, leading to normal structural differentiation of superego and ego ideal. This is accompanied by amelioration of narcissistic symptoms, particularly by the internal, adaptive regulation of self-esteem (Kohut 1977). At present, no data indicate the frequency with which idealizing mirror transference reactions occur in predominantly or exclusively homosexual patients, and there are no data about the frequency of this reaction in patients at opposite ends of the Kinsey spectrum. I speculate that when psychoanalytic data do become available, they will indicate that many lifelong predominantly or exclusively homosexual men develop transference neuroses, not narcissistic transferences. The distribution of men from various parts of the Kinsey spectrum who develop transference neuroses instead of narcissistic transference reactions remains to be established.

HOMOSEXUAL PHENOMENA AS NEUROTIC SYMPTOMS

In some subgroups of men, homosexual phenomena per se (i.e., erotic fantasies, sexual activity with others, sense of identity, social role) should in my view be considered as symptoms. Clinical experience suggests that under certain circumstances homosexual imagery may serve psychopathological functions. When this occurs, conscious perception of the imagery is presumably motivated by unconscious irrational anxiety. The symbolic meaning of the imagery is often masochistic, or, as Ovesey pointed out, it can relate to conflict about power or dependency (1954; 1955a, b). My impression is that during adulthood this phenomenon occurs predominantly among men who are not at the extreme right end of the Kinsey spectrum (i.e., who are not lifelong predominantly or exclusively homosexual). Many men in this symptomatic group experience homosexual phenomena in a state-related way, rather than as a trait analogous to a personality trait. Put differently, I suggest that homoerotic fantasies motivated by unconscious irrational anxiety and symbolically expressing unresolved conflict occur predominantly in bisexual adults. I use the word bisexual here to refer to the erotic components of behavior. Such men may identify themselves as gay, heterosexual, or bisexual. This does not mean that homoerotic phenomena in bisexual men are generally motivated by unconscious irrational anxiety. It simply means that if homoerotic fantasies primarily serve maladaptive functions that are compromise solutions to unconscious conflict, the patient is likely to have a history of meaningful heteroerotic fantasy or activity. My impression of the types of patient who use sexualized homosexual imagery in a neurotic way derives from my experience with the psychotherapeutic and psychoanalytic treatment situation. Whereas such homosexual fantasies commonly remit following interpretation, there is no adequate clinical evidence that this usually occurs unless the patient is or has been heterosexual to some degree.

Despite the heated assertions of some practitioners, psychoanalysis does not usually (if ever) lead men who have been predominantly or totally homosexual throughout their lives to become predominantly or totally heterosexual (Panel 1983). There are a number of possible explanations for this. The hypothesis that makes most sense to me is that homosexual phenomena are motivated by unconscious irrational anxiety in some people but not in others, especially not in adults who have been predominantly or exclusively homosexual during their lives. In some men at the homosexual end of the Kinsey spectrum, *heterosexual* imagery may be similarly motivated by unconscious irrational anxiety and therefore may be understood as symptomatic. But this has yet to be described.

The view of psychopathology in relation to homosexuality presented in this book is different from the perspective provided by *DSM-III*. The position about homosexuality taken in *DSM-III*, in turn, was radically different than that taken in the previous two editions of the manual. The *Diagnostic and Statistical Manual* published by the American Psychiatric Association in 1952 lists homosexuality in the "Sexual Deviation" category included under "Sociopathic Personality Disburbances." The prevailing psychiatric opinion at that time suggested an intrinsic relationship between a person's sexual object preference and conscience structure, and homosexual activity was thought to be associated with superego defects. In the second edition of the *DSM,* published in 1968, homosexuality was no longer placed in the sociopathic category, but it was still considered a mental disorder and an example of sexual deviation. Heterosexual intercourse was taken as a standard for sexual health.

Eight specific disorders are named in the "Sexual Deviation" section of *DSM-II*. Homosexuality leads the list, followed by fetishism, pedophilia, transvestism, exhibitionism, voyeurism, sadism, and masochism.

Shortly after the publication of *DSM-II*, the idea that homosexuality per se was a form of psychopathology came under widespread criticism. A series of dramatic and astonishing events occurred, including acrimonious debates between proponents and opponents of the pathological view of homosexuality, a poll of the members of the American Psychiatric Association, and disruption of scientific meetings by gay activists. In the third edition of the manual, homosexuality was deleted as a mental disorder. The category "Ego-dystonic Homosexuality" was reserved for individuals who experience unwanted, distressing sexual arousal to homosexual stimuli and who wish to desire or increase heterosexual arousal. This revised judgment about the pathological significance of homosexual behavior is one of the most dramatic reversals of opinion on a health–illness issue in the history of medicine (Bayer 1981).

In the revised edition of *DSM-III* (*DSM-III-R*), even ego-dystonic homosexuality was dropped as a diagnostic category. Some psychoanalysts privately feel that the decision to drop the category was primarily political. I believe that the decision was sound clinically and scientifically.

There are difficulties with the concept of ego-dystonic homosexuality as a category of psychopathology. First, many patients experience ego-*syntonic* homosexual phenomena (in the sense meant by *DSM-III*) that are clearly pathological. According to the *DSM*, these patients arrive at a therapist's office "well" and are made "sick," since in the course of therapeutic work their homosexual fantasies become ego dystonic. The *DSM-III* view of homosexuality required analysts to accept their patients' initial manifest presentation as healthy. The analyst who agrees with such patients that their homosexual experiences were normal is as remiss, in my opinion, as the analyst who agrees with other subgroups of patients that their homosexuality is pathological and should be changed to heterosexuality.

Second, the *DSM-III* excepted as qualifying for the diagnosis of mental disorder patients who experienced ego-dystonic homosexuality as a consequence of major depression. This reflected an awareness that the primary underlying problem for some patients may not be homosexuality per se but rather pathological self-hatred because of homosexuality. Unfortunately, the manual did not extend this concept far enough. Psychoanalysts commonly work with gay patients whose pathological self-hatred is hidden by character armor (Reich 1949). These patients may never experience major depression, but their identification with homophobic authority figures is clearly maladaptive. In short, many patients request analytic intervention because they experience homosexuality that is "ego dystonic." Nonetheless, in these patients the core psychological difficulty really involves an excessively rigid and harsh superego. These patients are ill not because of their homosexuality but because

of their perception of ego dystonicity. Appropriate psychotherapeutic intervention leads to diminishment of self-hate and acceptance of oneself as homosexual.

Ego dystonicity is not helpful in evaluating whether homosexual patients
should be considered healthy or unhealthy. There is no more of a logical basis
for considering ego-dystonic homosexuality a mental disorder than there is for
considering homosexuality itself one. I therefore believe that dropping the
category ego-dystonic homosexuality from *DSM-III-R* showed sound clinical
reasoning. When homosexual phenomena are symptoms of a primary psychiatric disorder, such as a gender identity disorder, they should of course be so
specified in the manual. By taking this position the *DSM* is not promulgating
the view that homosexual phenomena are always normal and innocuous forms
of mental activity and behavior. It is, however, endorsing the position that
homosexual individuals should not be considered psychologically ill simply
because of their perceptions of and judgments about their homosexuality.

Many important interactions between homosexuality and psychopathology
require systematic investigation at this time. One of immediate public health
significance concerns so-called opportunistic homosexual activity. Men who
have frequent sexual contacts with multiple partners, particularly partners they
don't know well, are at risk to contract AIDS (Nichols and Ostrow 1984).
People with all forms of severe psychopathology are prone to use primitive
denial and poor impulse control. Such men, when engaging in homosexual
activity, may be likely to deny the clear need for safe sex practices.

Discussion of the association between homosexuality and AIDS leads to a
final thought about the necessity for research on virulent homophobia, since
because of that association gay men are once again potential targets for
irrational hatred and scapegoating (Altman 1987). Interactions between individual psychodynamics and psychopathology and social dynamics are of particular relevance here. For example, when one meets a person one assumes to
be heterosexual, one does not customarily attend to his or her sexual history. In
fact, the heterosexual social role functions interpersonally in a manner analogous to clothing. In order to appreciate the significance of this, one need only
reflect on the conventional format for introducing a stranger to a group in a
nonsexual setting in our society—that is, the type of social situation in which
the business, scholarly, and religious activities of society are carried out (and
most leisure activities as well). The introduction does not specify the person's
sexual object, nor does it describe the individual's sexual behavior generally.
This omission, far from accidental, is an essential aspect of the introduction
ritual in our culture. Omission of sexuality in the labeling process by which a
stranger is introduced to a group allows the introductory situation itself to be
nonsexual.

The gay person, like the heterosexual "straight" person, experiences being
gay as a cognitive-social phenomenon, not a sexual phenomenon. The strang-

ers to whom the gay person is introduced, however, are forced to attend to his or her sexual behavior at the moment of introduction. Attention toward a stranger's inner sexual life leads to attention toward one's own. Because of the way the human mind works, the focus of such attention is on imagistic concrete experience (the fantasy of the person engaged in sexual activity). The gay social role is therefore analogous to being undressed. The introductory situation becomes sexualized, violating a social taboo. This distinction between heterosexual and homosexual social role is important with regard to both the determinants of identity in the individual and the social unit's response to the individual. Space does not allow for a lengthy discussion of homophobia here. I note in passing, however, that irrational, anxious, hostile responses may be activated not only among people who are threatened by their own homosexual impulses, but also in anyone whose oedipal and preoedipal aggressive and sexual feelings are barely repressed. Every potentially gay individual must take this into account in deciding whether to advertise his or her gay identity.

The interactions outlined above are only a few of those of potential interest with regard to homophobia. The understudied subject of homophobia requires research as much as or more than the area of homosexuality. Some investigation has recently taken place in this area. For example, Douglas, Kalman, and Kalman (1985) carried out a study of homophobia among physicians and nurses at a large urban teaching hospital. Thirty-seven medical house officers and ninety-one registered nurses completed questionnaires. One physician and eleven nurses responded that homosexuals who contract AIDS are getting what they deserve; twelve physicians and twenty-seven nurses indicated that they had more negative feelings about homosexuality since the emergence of the AIDS crisis. This observation, appropriately described as "alarming" by the authors (p. 309), indicates the necessity for studies of homophobia at other medical centers and for education and counseling about homophobia directed at health care professionals. This is only one of numerous manifestations of homophobia requiring systematic investigation. Of the two types of behavior, homosexuality and homophobia, it appears unfortunately that the latter may be sanctioned by the social climate more often than the former. The aspects of homophobia that belong in the clinical domain remain to be definitively described.

In conceptualizing the origins and function of homosexual fantasies, sexual activity, sense of identity, and social role in the mental apparatus, the whole patient must be evaluated. This requires a model of the mind that takes the whole person into account. In my view the best paradigm put forth to date is the biopsychosocial model described by George Engel (1962). This perspective of the mind and of the total functioning of the human being in health and illness is based on the idea that systems of biological, psychological, and social levels of organization continually and actively interact to influence and be influenced by overt behavior. Neglect of any of these systems of organization leads to reductionism. Engel's view of people in terms of systems that freely communicate and interact with each other is ideal for conceptualizing the vicissitudes of homosexual phenomena in a clinically helpful way. The biopsychosocial model, taken in conjunction with Stone's (1980) view of psychopathology as a multidimensional matrix, leads to the conclusion that there are many subgroups of homosexuality. Among the numerous behavioral parameters requiring systematic evaluation before reaching a diagnosis of psychopathology are history of sexual fantasy, activity, identity, and social role in relation to life-cycle phases; stressful life experiences; personality type; level of character integration; history of attitudes and values about sexuality; constitutional predisposition to schizophrenia and affective disorders; predisposition to certain temperaments; and assets, such as the capacity to cope with adversity, to reason, and to experience affection, kindness, and humor.

PART THREE

Developmental
Considerations

13

Childhood

Parts 1 and 2 of this book include considerable developmental data and concepts, but even more emphasis on psychological development is needed to understand male homosexuality from a contemporary psychoanalytic perspective. A number of recent research and clinical contributions dealing with children and adolescents are clearly relevant to understanding male sexual orientation during adulthood as well as earlier in life. Some of this recent work raises important questions about traditionally accepted psychoanalytic models of the origins and consequences of homosexuality. Other modern contributions seem to be more compatible with older psychoanalytic constructs. Additional materials need to be made available to the psychoanalytic community.

Chapters 13 and 14 are primarily descriptive. Theoretical issues concerning the structure and function of the mental apparatus, raised by the descriptive material, are taken up in part 4. This chapter begins with consideration of effeminacy. The discussion is limited to very young children with effeminacy because of the empirical finding that extreme childhood effeminacy is often followed by adult homosexuality. I do not consider the preoedipal phase of life in toto; I restrict myself here to discussion of a behavioral syndrome which, despite its infrequency, is especially important to understanding sexual orientation.

My discussion of effeminacy is followed by consideration of homoerotic and heteroerotic fantasy and activity and gender disturbance in older, juvenile-age boys. The crystalization or differentiation of erotic fantasy prior to adolescence has consequences for the concept of sexual preference, which is critically considered below. This chapter is concerned with childhood as it pertains to predominant or exclusive homosexual fantasy and activity. Because of extremely scanty data on bisexuality in childhood, bisexual fantasy and activity are considered only with regard to adolescence (chapter 14).

Chapter 3 reviews the evidence that predominant or exclusive homosexuality is usually preceded by childhood gender disturbances. These appear to fall into three major subgroups: (1) extreme boyhood femininity, (2) mild to moderate boyhood femininity (i.e., an attenuated or less than full form of boyhood femininity), and (3) unmasculinity. I suggest that the last syndrome is characterized chiefly by juvenile-age avoidance of rough-and-tumble activities, low masculine self-regard, and poor relationships with males generally.

Research certainly does not prove that every instance of homosexuality originates in childhood gender identity/role disturbances. But a theoretical model derived from this research does not have to be based on 100 percent association. Certainly those few instances of male homosexuality that may not derive from childhood gender identity/role disturbances deserve careful investigation. Since the available data from all sources indicate that in most cases the association does exist, however, the psychodynamics and pyschopathology of gender identity/role differentiation and pathology are central in understanding the beginnings of predominant or exclusive male homosexuality. Since a substantial amount of empirical research has been done on extreme boyhood femininity, this syndrome is discussed below. It should be noted that extreme boyhood femininity is hypothesized to occur in only a relatively small percentage of the larger group of gender-disturbed children who become homosexual adults.

CHILDHOOD EFFEMINACY

Childhood effeminacy syndrome usually eventuates in homosexuality. The descriptive aspects of this syndrome are therefore relevant for clarifying the early development of one subgroup of homosexual men.

Severe, chronic gender pathology in very young children is quite rare. Although epidemiological data are lacking, it appears that individuals who manifested severe, persistent childhood effeminacy make up but a small fraction of predominantly or exclusively homosexual men. Coates and Zucker (1988) describe most lucidly the characteristics of children with severe gender identity pathology:

> Children with gender identity disorders most often have disturbed gender role identity. Invariably they know that they belong to their own sex, and therefore they do not have disturbance in core gender identity. They can be said, however, to have a disturbance in gender role identity, since they feel they possess the qualities of the opposite sex. In gender role behavior, their interests and activities are typically associated with the opposite sex. Thus, gender-disturbed boys wish to be girls, prefer feminine interests and activities, and express a dislike of their male anatomy.

These boys are typically fascinated with heroines in stories and on TV. They see girls and women as better in every way than boys and men. They prefer stereotypically feminine toys such as dolls and like feminine clothing and ornaments (ribbons, jewelry, etc.). The families of these children often seem strikingly similar to the families of homosexual men described in much of the literature. Thus, father absence or detachment, negative maternal attitudes toward men and particularly toward male aggression, and active maternal overinvolvement with discouragement of separation and individuation of the child are prominent features of a common type of family configuration of extremely effeminate boys. Coates and Zucker's observations about mothers' reactions to the rough-and-tumble activities of their toddlers are particularly revealing in light of the line of reasoning presented in chapter 2 of this book.

> These mothers' fear of male aggression often led them to confuse normal boyhood assertiveness and rambunctiousness (rough-and-tumble play) with aggressive and destructive behavior. Many of them commented on how nice, gentle, or good their sons were ("priestly" in the case vignette) and how different their sons were from other boys, who were typically mean, aggressive bullies. These mothers were often proud of their sons' nonviolent qualities and saw their sons as special and better than the neighborhood boys, whom they considered roughnecks. (p. 18)

In addition to family pathology, effeminate youngsters often manifest diffuse psychopathology, indicating that the effeminacy syndrome is part of a global psychiatric disorder (Coates & Person 1985). Projective psychological tests are frequently abnormal in characteristic ways, indicating that the syndrome involves not only cross-gender social behavior but also the internal self-object world of the child. Empirical studies of effeminate children have uncovered in many individual patients and their families the very symptoms that were once hypothesized by influential psychoanalysts to occur in the backgrounds of most homosexual adults. One wonders whether these psychoanalysts' database contained disproportionate numbers of children who in early life experienced full or partial effeminacy.

The concept of phase-specific *critical timing* suggests another way of looking at some of these data. As noted earlier, although adult homosexuality does not seem to be part of a global psychiatric disorder (in contrast to childhood effeminacy), the evidence about familial influence on homosexuality is complex and certainly not easily dismissable. It is possible that the family patterns directly observed in effeminate children and retrospectively reported by many homosexual men are in fact similar. The difference might be *when* this family pattern occurs during development. A certain type of family dynamic might lead (or predispose) to *both* effeminacy and homosexuality, if it occurs during a critical interval prior to age three or so, but might lead only to homosexuality if it occurs later. Put differently, it is possible that persistent, extreme effeminacy is rare because the critical time interval during which the (predisposed?) child is at risk is quite brief and occurs early in life. Homosexuality, on the other hand, might be common because the time interval during which influences may exert their effects is protracted. Whereas the critical time frame for extreme effeminacy may be days or weeks or even months, the corresponding interval for influencing homosexuality is probably many years.

The question arises whether descriptive features of childhood effeminacy are compatible with psychoanalytic theories of the etiology of male homosexuality. It seems to me that the cross-sectional and prospective studies of effeminacy pose problems for psychoanalytic theoreticians (such as Socarides and Bergler) who propose that predominant or exclusive homosexuality *in general* is related to preoedipal traumata. Socarides, for example, equates so-called obligatory homosexuality with preoedipal influences:

1. The preoedipal form (of homosexuality) is due to a fixation to the preoedipal phase of development during the first three years of life.
2. It is unconsciously motivated and arises from anxiety.
3. Severe gender identity disturbance is present. (1978, p. 92)

Modern research indicates that only subgroups of homosexual men manifest histories of severe boyhood effeminacy (see chapter 3). Socarides' model may describe those subgroups, but it does not seem to apply to the entire group of predominantly or exclusively homosexual men (obligatory homosexual in Socarides' language). Most of these men have not experienced extreme, persistent boyhood effeminacy (Bieber et al. 1962; Saghir & Robins 1973; Friedman & Stern 1980b; Bell, Weinberg & Hammersmith 1981). If Socarides' theory were generally valid, then severe childhood effeminacy would be much more common than it is, and many more homosexual men would report that they were feminized children. Admittedly, partial effeminacy during childhood may be underreported. Meyer-Bahlburg (1985) suggested that childhood gender identity disorder may be more common than is generally appreciated. Retrospective distortion by homosexual men might also lead estimates of effeminacy in their backgrounds to be too low. Nevertheless, the disparity between the occurrence of severe, persistent childhood effeminacy and that of adult homosexuality is so great that Socarides' theory seems, on this basis alone, inapplicable to the majority of homosexual men.

Another problem for the preoedipal theories of etiology of homosexuality concerns associated psychopathology during adulthood. If the time frame were as Socarides and Bergler propose, then most adult homosexual men would have severe borderline and/or narcissistic-masochistic psychopathology. The evidence is compelling, however, that this is not so (Hooker 1967; DHEW 1972; Saghir & Robins 1973; Siegelman 1974, 1981; Clark 1975).

SEXUAL ORIENTATION AND EROTIC LIFE IN CHILDHOOD

This section concerns erotic fantasy, not gender identity, and includes all males, not just those with childhood effeminacy.

Whereas childhood effeminacy has been investigated directly, the onset of erotic fantasy and activity in children in general has not. Although there has been some direct study of childhood sexuality (including research in the psychoanalytic sector, particularly by Galenson and Roiphe [1981]), it has for the most part not focused on sexual orientation. Data about the onset of erotic life in men are largely retrospective (Kinsey 1948; Manosevits 1970; Gebhard 1972).

At some point, usually prior to puberty, boys become aware that they are sexually excited by certain types of imagery. The age at which men report first awareness of this phenomenon varies greatly. Many relate that they experienced sexual fantasies or sexual excitement from earliest childhood. Others recall onset of specifically sexual fantasies later, in the oedipal or postoedipal period. There is no evidence that sexual orientation is related to the age at which sexual excitement is recalled to have begun. For example, in an investigation that compared the sexual histories of lifelong, exclusively homosexual, nonpatient men and heterosexual controls, no differences (except for gender of sexual object) were found (Friedman & Stern 1980a). All homosexual subjects recalled being sexually interested in males during their earliest years, although the intensity of interest was highly variable. The onset of erotic arousal was defined in this investigation as the time in life when sexual fantasies associated with erections began. The mean age of onset of erotic arousal was 9.5 years (the range was 4–13 years). In fifteen cases, erotic arousal began spontaneously, not stimulated by contact with another person. In one case, arousal followed the stimulus of sleeping in the same bed with same-age relatives. In one case, arousal began in a setting of peer mutual masturbation. In no case did arousal begin with contact, either sexual or nonsexual, with a known homosexual. Most subjects knew little, if anything, about homosexuality at the time of initial erotic arousal.

All heterosexual subjects also recalled being more or less interested in females during their earliest years, although the intensity of the interest was highly variable. Mean age of first erotic arousal in heterosexual subjects was 9.9 years (the range was 5–13 years). All cases of heterosexual arousal occurred more or less spontaneously, without being stimulated by sexual activity with another person. In both groups, first orgasm occurred coincident with puberty and usually as a result of self-masturbation (table 13.1).

Once sexual fantasies appear in a consolidated way and as a significant motivating force they result in further developmental differences between homosexual and heterosexual males. Often boys experience consolidated homosexual fantasies as shameful. These fantasies are not communicated to family or friends and are disavowed as part of the self system. The juvenile-age boy often does not interpret the presence of homosexual fantasies and the absence of heterosexual fantasies as evidence that he is gay. This is consistent with the fact that many of the psychological processes involved in identity formation normally occur years later, during adolescence and young adulthood. The

TABLE 13.1 First Sexual Arousal and Experience in 17 Homosexual and 17 Heterosexual Males

Subject Number	Age of Onset of Erotic Arousal		Age and Method of First Orgasm			
	Homosexual	Heterosexual	Homosexual		Heterosexual	
1	9	13	13	self-masturbation	13	self-masturbation
2	11	6	13	mutual masturbation peer	12	sexual intercourse same-aged girl
3	9	11	13	self-masturbation	14	self-masturbation
4	8	12	12	mutual masturbation peer	12	sexual intercourse same-aged girl
5	13	8	13	mutual masturbation peer	13	self-masturbation
6	13	12	13	self-masturbation	12	self-masturbation
7	8	13	11	self-masturbation	13	self-masturbation
8	12	6	12	self-masturbation	13	nocturnal emission
9	13	9	13	self-masturbation	12	self-masturbation
10	10	8	13	self-masturbation	13	self-masturbation
11	12	12	12	nocturnal emission	13	self-masturbation
12	8	9	13	self-masturbation	13	self-masturbation
13	9	9	13	self-masturbation	13	self-masturbation
14	6	13	11	self-masturbation	13	self-masturbation
15	11	5	12	mutual masturbation peer	13	self-masturbation
16	4	12	12	nocturnal emission	13	self-masturbation
17	6	11	11	self-masturbation	13	self-masturbation
Mean	9.5	9.9	12.3	self-masturbation: 11 cases nocturnal emission: 2 cases mutual masturbation: 4 cases	12.0	self-masturbation: 14 cases nocturnal emission: 1 case sexual intercourse: 2 cases

Source: Friedman & Stern 1980a, p. 180

prepubertal boy who experiences exclusively homosexual arousal and who knows nothing of homosexuality often does not realize that he "is" homosexual. The child does experience himself as "different," however (Isay 1985). Often this sense of being different precedes onset of homosexual arousal, but the homosexual fantasies increase it.

In contrast to their gender experience, the erotic experience of homosexual boys is in certain important ways typically boylike. Most boys, no matter what their sexual orientation, experience intense sexual desire (i.e., lust) by puberty, and most masturbate to orgasm. Girls' stance toward sexuality, on the other hand, is primarily influenced by menstruation (and therefore procreation) and only secondarily and variably by masturbation and orgasm. Depending on sociocultural experience, girls may experience sexual arousal and orgasm during or prior to puberty or may experience no sexual arousal or desire. In most females, maximal sexual interest and frequency of sexual activity occur much later in the life cycle (Kinsey et al. 1953).

Although boys with consolidated homosexual fantasies often continue to resemble girls with regard to activities, interests, and gender of erotic object, the quality of their inner erotic experience is so different from that of girls that a sense of distance can be produced. This may contribute to a more global feeling of confusion and dissonance. Often the homosexual youngster experiences erotic fantasies that he recognizes are neither completely girllike nor boylike. He feels that he can discuss these with no one in the heterosexual culture around him. The presence of consolidated homosexual fantasies usually increases the boy's sense of himself as being unlike other boys and not masculine. The feeling of being different is a reaction to a variety of difficulties with gender-related behavior as well and is associated with a fundamental sense of discomfort about the self.

Homosexual fantasies also often have deleterious consequences for self-esteem. Social acceptance is frequently contingent on keeping the homosexual fantasies hidden. This produces guilt, shame, and an increased sense of isolation.

> The protection of self-esteem is one of the central developmental tasks of childhood. . . In the child's eyes his sense of self-worth is essential to his survival. The child who does not experience his value in the eyes of his parents will fear their abandonment and its attendant dangers to his existence. The older child and adolescent may even contemplate suicide. The maintenance of positive self-esteem is so fundamental a task that all of the structures of personality contribute to its organization. (Mack 1983, p. 12)

Positive self-esteem normally emerges in a secure family context. Later, acceptance in nonfamily groups becomes paramount. During the post-oedipal, prepubertal juvenile years the sense of fit between a group's purposes and an individual's attitudes and values is central for the evolution of a sense of belonging and a feeling of positive self-regard.

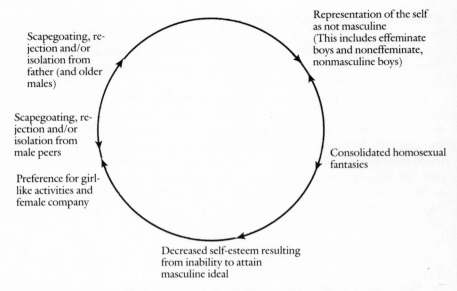

Fig. 13.1 Psychosocial interactions in gender-disturbed juvenile boys

In many prehomosexual boys, the sense of not belonging, often great prior to the full emergence of homosexual fantasies, becomes exacerbated by these fantasies. Obviously, the assault on self-esteem is often brutal. Consolidated homosexual fantasies and psychological sequences frequently experienced and participated in by boys with juvenile-age gender disturbance may be diagrammed as an ongoing cycle in which sexual fantasy influences and is influenced by self-representation, which influences and is influenced by social interactions (figure 13.1). Representation of the self as not masculine influences and is influenced by consolidated homosexual fantasies. These fantasies in turn negatively influence self-esteem, resulting from inability to attain the masculine ideal. This in turn influences and is influenced by preference for girllike activities and female company. This influences and is influenced by scapegoating and rejection by males, which influences and is influenced by representation of the self as unmasculine.

JUVENILE UNMASCULINITY

Before proceeding further, a brief summary of gender disturbances in relation to homosexuality is indicated. Children with gender disturbances associated with predominant or exclusive homosexuality appear to fall into several subgroups. As noted earlier, I find it helpful to conceptualize three major categories of childhood gender disturbance. Category 1 consists of boys with extreme femininity that persists throughout childhood. Category 2 consists of boys who manifest clinically significant effeminacy but who do not have the severe effeminacy syndrome in full form throughout childhood. During juvenile years these boys still display some girllike behaviors and traits, however. Category 3 is fundamentally different from the first two categories. It consists of boys whose primary problem is not that they are feminine but that they are unmasculine.

Often beginning during the juvenile years, that is, latency age (in contrast to severe effeminacy, which begins much earlier), this type of gender disturbance has been understudied and criteria for it are not defined in *DSM-III-R*. Its fundamental characteristic is a persistent, profound feeling of masculine inadequacy which leads to negative valuing of the self. Research on patients and nonpatients (reviewed in chapters 2, 3, and 5) suggests that the following additional features are present:

1. Poor ability at and avoidance of rough-and-tumble play activities.
2. Fears of injury to the body and strong feelings of body fragility.
3. Extreme aversion to aggressive interactions with other boys and avoidance of social activities in which such interactions might occur.
4. Extremely low male peer group status.
5. No positive, persistent interpersonal relationships with male peers.
6. No compensatory positive, persistent interpersonal relationships with older male authority figures (fathers or father surrogates). Such men as the boy has contact with (including his father) are likely to value the very rough-and-tumble activities that he is innately poor at.

These behavioral features may coexist with positive relationships with females, but not necessarily so. Many of these youngsters turn to girls for companionship but others remain loners. Femalelike symptoms in such youngsters tend to be secondary. For example, a lonely nine-year-old boy, driven away by other boys and shunned by his father, may play with girls and enjoy participating in feminine activities with them. But this type of youngster is quite different psychologically from a nine-year-old who has been fascinated with ribbons, jewelry, and lipstick and has cross-dressed whenever possible from earliest childhood. By juvenile years, both boys may play only with girls and both may avoid male sex-typed activities. Overt abnormality in the second case, however, consists of abnormally girllike behavior from preoedipal years. Overt abnormality in the first case may not have been apparent until the child was seven or eight years old. This type of child may not have manifested grossly abnormal femalelike behavior at ages two through five. It is hypothesized, therefore, that many juvenile-age boys with the gender disturbance I term unmasculinity do not experience severe feminization preoedipally.

SEXUAL PREFERENCE: A CRITICAL CONSIDERATION

The popular concept of sexual preference is important particularly with regard to adolescence because of its emphasis on the identity/role dimension of sexual orientation. The concept of sexual preference may be applied appropriately to some subgroups of adolescents, but it is clearly not applicable to others.

Male sexual orientation often begins with sexual fantasies prior to puberty and remains fixed for life. When sexual orientation differentiates, just as when gender identity differentiates, behavioral options become limited. Differentiation of gender identity is not described in terms of "gender preference": the maleness of men is not depicted as "gender preference" because two- to four-year-old children do not freely choose their gender lifestyle. Similarly, ten- to twelve-year-old boys do not freely choose their sexual fantasies. Lust happens to them and they masturbate. Their sexual fantasies subsequently shape the boundaries of their lives. Furthermore, the imagery that determines sexual orientation is rooted in the concrete mental representation of the human body, just as core gender identity is. This concrete quality makes the notion of preference incongruous. We *choose* social roles (more or less) but not most aspects of our body-selves. We do not, for example, describe people as having an "Oriental preference," a "tall preference," or even an "obese preference." (These issues are discussed further in part 4.)

The notion of sexual preference is therefore inapplicable to the majority of males, most of whom are heterosexual from early childhood, but some of whom are predominantly or exclusively homosexual since early childhood. Only when bisexuality is considered does the concept of sexual preference seem appropriate (in some subgroups). Sexual orientation differentiation differs from gender identity differentiation in that there are only two genders, but there are more than two ways in which these two genders can be arranged in erotic imagery. Thus someone may be entirely homosexual or heterosexual or in between in a variety of ways. Adolescent boys who experience bisexual erotic imagery or who have the potential to do so have more behavioral options than individuals at either pole of the Kinsey scale. For some of these bisexual individuals, the idea of preference or choice may fit their psychobiological potential. This group has received scant attention to date and virtually none from psychoanalysis.

It is clinically important to distinguish between patients who manifest one of the many varieties of bisexuality and those who are exclusively homosexual in erotic fantasy. No epidemiological data indicate what percentage of the male population progresses through adolescence with sexual imagery that is coded either as homosexual and *not* heterosexual (i.e., no heterosexual behavioral option available) or as heterosexual and *not* homosexual (i.e., no homosexual behavioral option available). Studies primarily of adults suggest that a large number of males (although a small *percentage* of the male population) develop the exclusively homosexual behavioral constellation described in chapter 14. The percentage of these patients in clinical practice might be higher than in the population at large, but this remains to be established.

FUTURE RESEARCH

There is great need for longitudinal study of children who do not manifest gender disturbance but who become predominantly or exclusively homosexual adults. Some retrospective investigations suggest that this group, although containing a minority of prehomosexual males, nonetheless may be fairly large (Saghir & Robins 1973). Some investigators suggest, to the contrary, that gender disorder invariably precedes predominant or exclusive male homosexuality (Zuger 1984). The characteristics of the non-gender-disturbed group remain to be described.

Another important question requiring systematic investigation concerns the prevalence of depression in gender-disturbed youngsters. The existential plight of these children is often so painful that clinical depression should be expected to occur among them. Childhood depression has been understudied in this group, so this inference awaits future validation. (Depression has been demonstrated in the subgroup of children with extreme effeminacy [Coates and Zucker 1988].)

The issue of coping in gender-disturbed boys also requires detailed investigation. Although symptomatic, these children often continue to function. It is possible that, for reasons that have not yet been well described, their mechanisms for coping with anguish and adversity are unusually effective.

14

Adolescence

In chapter 1, I note that erotic fantasy, erotic activity, sense of identity, and social role are all important dimensions of sexuality. Prior to adolescence the sense of identity (as gay/homosexual, heterosexual, or bisexual) is not yet formed. During adolescence the interplay between the erotic and identity/role components of behavior often becomes particularly complex. As noted in chapter 1, the erotic dimensions of experience and behavior may be described in terms of the Kinsey spectrum. The spectrum model is not suited for description of the identity/role dimensions of behavior, however. Consideration of the interplay between erotic and identity/role behavioral elements requires the use of both a spectrum and a categorical frame of reference.

Part 1 of this chapter focuses on exclusive homosexuality, part 2 on bisexuality. Because sexual orientation during adolescence is of intense interest to contemporary clinicians, I discuss clinical issues somewhat more extensively here than elsewhere in this book.

The Homosexual Adolescent

The boy who enters adolescence having experienced exclusively homosexual fantasies is often even more isolated from others than he was in childhood. During and immediately after puberty, his guilt and shame increase as his sexual feelings become more intense. The boy now feels different from peers, who seem unaware that when dating girls they are actually participating in role rehearsal for the adult heterosexual world. Unlike other social roles, which are more or less verbally taught during adolescence, the heterosexual role is simply assumed. This type of boy, in early and mid-adolescence, continues to believe that he is moving toward a heterosexual identity despite his homosexual sexual fantasies. As he becomes older, the disparity between sexual fantasy and expected role behavior becomes more of a problem. Now with progressive worry, he engages in heterosexual role behavior not only as a form of social deception but often in the hope that this type of activity will lead to heterosexuality. The boy tries to defer establishment of a sexual identity while rehearsing a consciously preferred social role and waiting for heterosexual desires to emerge. They never do.

Martin (1982) emphasizes the impact on the developing child of the absence of positive homosexual role models and the negative effects of being forced to conceal homosexuality from family and friends.

> Heterosexual adolescents have a multitude of role models for all possible social identities which may touch on their sexual orientation, but homosexual adolescents have no constructive models and indeed are led to believe that their sexual identity precludes other roles. This denial of role models is an essential part of the total stigmatization process. The young gay person is forbidden the opportunity to develop that personal identity which Erikson . . . defined as "the sense of ego identity." (p. 55)

Similar observations have been made independently by an increasing number of psychoanalysts. In a 1983 symposium on male homosexuality sponsored by the American Psychoanalytic Association, Leavy made the following remarks:

> Words of obloquy usually enter the vocabulary of youth long before their meaning becomes plain. There are mysterious allusions to queers, queens, fags, fairies, pansies, nanny-boys . . . but rarely as signifiers designating members of the intimate or familial social situation. The bearers of these ignominious names abide supposedly on a remote periphery, carrying out their shady and sinister existence as at best figures of fun, at worst, corrupters and criminals. The homosexual youth, despite frantic efforts to meet the social order, held to be "straight" while knowing that he is deviant, succumbs to the injunctions that attack his sexual disposition root and branch. (Leavy 1985, pp. 143–44)

Leavy astutely observed that the homosexual youngster, desperate to feel that he belongs to society (i.e., heterosexual society), is apt to agree with the extreme devaluation of homosexuality. He hates himself because of his homosexuality and believes that the negative opinions of homosexuality he hears everywhere are accurate and justified. Leavy pointed out that many of these youngsters seek solace in religion, but to no avail: both testaments of the Bible view homosexuality bleakly, from the dire punishment of the men of Sodom to Paul's pronouncement that no homosexual shall inherit the Kingdom of God.

Following upon observations of Troiden (1979; Troiden & Goode 1980) and Cass (1984), Isay described from a psychoanalytic perspective the stages of acquisition and consolidation of a homosexual identity (1985). Isay too reported that recognition and acceptance of homosexuality are usually delayed until late adolescence or early adulthood. Often not until then does the homosexual boy have the life experience and cognitive capacity to relinquish the intense need to deny the significance of his differentiated sexual fantasies. Isay suggested that "the integration of one's homosexuality into a cohesive and positive self-image is part of the normal development of a healthy homosexual man" (p. 19). Isay focused on low self-esteem, resulting from childhood and ongoing trauma, as an influence impeding healthy homosexual identity integration. In Isay's view, the consolidation and integration of a positive homosexual identity is generally associated with social integration in both straight and gay communities and with expressive and supportive homosexual relationships.

In a sense, clinical problems in this group of adolescents—particularly in later stages of adolescence—are the easiest to grasp, because they are so well defined. Once a clinician has assessed the patient as a lifelong predominantly or exclusively homosexual male, the clinical task is usually to facilitate the development of a positive self-image as homosexual. The patient must be protected from those in his social environment who attack him because he is gay (e.g., his parents) and from aspects of his own personality that may attack him for similar reasons. Usually the patient's antihomosexual attitudes and values can be diluted by energetic therapeutic intervention.

Group support by other gay males is generally much appreciated by the homosexual adolescent. Group therapy, often with gay therapists and patients, may help diminish social isolation and wounded self-esteem. Family therapy is frequently useful as well. Many patients need support and guidance in the task of confronting their families with the facts about their homosexuality. Others may choose to hide their sexual orientation from their families or break with them altogether. There is no guideline for normalcy in situations like these; the attitudes and value system of the individual patient determine his course.

This is also true with regard to accepting a homosexual identity. There is no "health guideline" suggesting that it is necessary to accept a gay identity and/or social role simply because one experiences exclusively homosexual fantasies from early childhood. Acceptance of being gay may conflict with profoundly meaningful values and beliefs (religious, for example). Sometimes these values are used in the service of masochism, but this is by no means always the case. People in this situation often have to make difficult choices: aspects of their lives sometimes have to be given up. Although some individuals seem able to add heterosexual behavior to their repertoires, many cannot. The topic of changing sexual orientation has been discussed in many forums (Acosta 1975). It is unclear how often even motivated adults can accomplish enduring change. It is safe, however, to conclude that total replacement of lifelong, exclusively homosexual fantasies by exclusively heterosexual fantasies is probably impossible for most people. Therapeutic issues in homosexuality require a book in their own right. As a general guideline, however, if altering differentiated sexual orientation seems to be the only path acceptable to a patient, psychoanalysis is not the primary treatment of choice. Isay discussed the complications involved in using psychoanalysis to accomplish this goal (Panel 1983). This guideline seems applicable to adolescents, about whom there are few pyschoanalytic data, as well as to adults.

Looking at predominantly or exclusively homosexual adolescents, one of the most striking findings is that there is no evidence at present that these young people experience persistent devastating psychopathology associated with their sexual orientation. This is in itself remarkable in light of the chronic, prolonged social stress they so frequently experience. In fact, the virulence and chronicity of this stress puts homosexuality in a unique position in the human behavioral repertoire. No other relatively common form of behavior is associated with such a degree of stress during formative years. The adaptational tasks required of the homosexual adolescent appear so extraordinary that it is easy to see why some clinicians assume that they cannot be accomplished and that the entire character structure must be devastated. Psychopathology associated with homosexuality during adolescence has been understudied to date. Nevertheless, the fact that severe, persistent morbidity does not occur more frequently is compatible with the hypothesis that factors associated with the etiology of homosexuality may also be associated (at least in some subgroups) with increased capacity for coping with adversity. These might include mechanisms influencing ego resiliency, growth potential, and the capacity to form intimate relationships.

In outlining the preadolescent experience of homosexual boys, gender disturbance and frequently associated feelings of anguish have been stressed. The pathway diagrammed in figure 13.1, although common, is also extreme. Gender disturbance during juvenile years can be subtle, yet with powerful psychological effects. Below I present the life history of a man I met in an educational–research context, focusing on the way his differentiated erotic imagery influenced his experience of adolescence. This man's subsequent life included a number of features commonly described by gay men with good coping skills and a generally high level of ego functioning.

THE DEVELOPMENT OF A WELL-ADJUSTED HOMOSEXUAL MAN

Tim recalled first becoming aware of strong sexual feelings at the age of eight or nine. He was raised in a rural setting and had never heard of homosexuals or homosexuality. He felt confused that he was aroused by males, but he never doubted, at that age, that he would one day marry. Inasmuch as Tim thought about the meaning of his sexual arousal pattern, he dismissed its consequence for his sense of identity; that is, he assumed that he was heterosexual (although he probably didn't know the word heterosexual at that time in his life).

Tim spent his early childhood and juvenile years doing solitary heavy labor on an isolated farm. He did well in school but had no time for afterschool activities because of the amount of work he had to do. Tim had no friends at this age, and although he enjoyed solitude, he was often lonely. His family ate dinner together every night, an event Tim enjoyed greatly. He particularly liked discussions about politics and books with his mother and older sister. His father and younger brother talked about cars, hunting, and the mechanical aspects of heavy farm machinery, all subjects which held no interest for Tim. Tim's father was outspokenly sexist in his views of work and leisure activities. He claimed that "reading was for women; guns and trucks were for men." Tim's mother, in contrast to her husband, whose economic circumstances had not permitted him to graduate from high school, was a college graduate and an intellectual. She particularly loved poetry and passed this love along to her children Ruth and Tim (one year younger). She was good humored about her husband's and youngest son's sexist attitudes. "Steven is your father's son," she often told Tim, "but you are like me."

From early childhood Tim felt allied with the women in his family and estranged from the men. The basic familial configuration—Tim's emotional closeness to his mother and sister and distance from his father and brother—remained in effect for life. Consciously, Tim did not consider himself unmanly. He was burly, strong, and could work side by side with anyone at the most strenuous jobs. Nor did his father and brother label him unmasculine or "sissy." But Tim felt profoundly more similar to the females than the males in his family, not only because of his intellectual interests but also because of his attitudes about life. In a level just below awareness but not truly unconscious, Tim considered himself unmasculine—but consciously this held no pejorative connotation for him.

During his long hours of solitary manual labor, Tim often daydreamed about having nonsexual friendships with boys his own age who were more emotionally and aesthetically sensitive than his father or brother. By early adolescence he began to feel guilty about his homosexual feelings. His family was puritanical and Tim could recall no discussions about sexuality. Sex was omitted from his school curriculum as well, and Tim was left to his own devices to acquire sex education. His parents had twin beds, but he assumed that they had sexual intercourse, which he had learned about from books. The same books taught him that homosexuality was sinful and perverse. At age thirteen Tim experienced his first orgasm-ejaculation via self-masturbation. His fantasies were of participating in mutual masturbation with a male classmate. Tim's guilt was severe and he believed that he would be "weakened," perhaps "hurt," if he masturbated too frequently. He struggled to exercise restraint but to his chagrin he was sometimes unable to resist temptation. Tim occasionally experienced nocturnal emissions, always with homosexual imagery.

By mid-adolescence Tim had become quite popular in school and had prevailed upon his parents to allow him to take part in afterschool activities.

Gregarious and likeable, he was elected president of the student organization. He was also captain of the wrestling team and editor of the school newspaper. During his high school years Tim made life-long friends of both sexes. These friendships were durable, intimate, and caring. An excellent athlete, Tim was chronically anxious in locker-room situations, fearing he might get an erection. He dated frequently and girls considered him one of the most desirable boys in school. Tim participated in petting, mutual caressing, and nudity. Much to his dismay, he never experienced sexual excitement in a heterosexual situation, although he was not consciously repelled. During these years, Tim gradually became aware that his sexual fantasies were exclusively directed at males; therefore, he decided, he must be homosexual. It dawned upon him gradually that his homosexuality might persist and he might not be able to be a father or husband. This possibility dismayed and terrified him.

By Tim's junior year, he fully appreciated his painful dilemma. Although he had never engaged in sexual activity with males, he apparently (as he put it) "suffered from homosexuality." He was unable to discuss the problem with friends, family, or teachers. There were no known homosexuals in his town, and Tim quietly decided that he "was the only boy who had ever had a problem like this." The disparity between his heterosexual role playing and homosexual erotic fantasy life troubled his conscience. Tim felt guilty about hurting girls' feelings when he failed to respond to their sexual advances. He felt guilt and shame at deceiving his family about his inner life. Despite these sources of distress, Tim was a well-organized young man who functioned at a consistently high level. Because of his ability to cope with difficulties, overcome obstacles, and negotiate conflicts, he was a leader and a role model for other students. He prided himself on his honesty and integrity—traits which were, however, associated with constant guilt about his homosexual fantasies.

Because of his academic and athletic abilities, Tim won a scholarship to college. Once there he consulted a therapist, who advised him that he was not really homosexual because he had not participated in sexual activity with males. He was cautioned never to do so. The therapist also told him that he suffered from "arrested development." As Tim recalls, the consulting psychiatrist was warm and friendly. He suggested that Tim should not be too discouraged by his lack of heterosexual arousal and advised that in the context of a loving, committed relationship with a woman, Tim's anxiety about sex might well subside. Should that not occur within the next few years, he counseled Tim to begin psychotherapy.

Tim felt bewildered and overwhelmed. He had already tried to experience heterosexual arousal but had not been able to do so. He decided that since psychiatrists were experts, he should probably follow the advice. But Tim determined to get a second opinion about his condition and its treatment, and he sought out an eminent psychoanalyst with a reputation for particular expertise in the area of homosexuality. This analyst advised Tim that homosexuality was due to an unconscious, irrational fear of heterosexuality. The potential to experience fulfilling heterosexual activity was present but would not emerge without psychoanalysis. Because Tim was intelligent, insightful, and emotionally sensitive, his prognosis was good. The outcome, however, would depend on Tim's motivation. Tim seriously considered undertaking pyschoanalysis. In order to do so, however, he would have had to leave college, which was in an area without psychoanalysts, and move to a large city where he knew no one. Moreover, Tim did not have financial resources to pay for treatment. His consultant advised him that assuming responsibility for the financial aspects of psychoanalysis was an important part of the treatment. Since Tim's psychological health was at stake, the consultant said, he recommended that Tim "beg, borrow, or steal to raise the money somehow."

With trepidation Tim chose a different course. He did not see how he could raise the money for treatment without giving up school, taking a full-time job, and going into debt. The prospect of living alone in a large city filled him with dread. He decided that the only hope he had of elevating himself from his poor rural background was to acquire a college degree. He returned to college and determined to "cure himself" of his homosexuality by following the first therapist's suggestion.

With considerable misgivings, Tim allowed a warm friendship with a woman to blossom into a deep romance. Because he had chosen a partner who was deeply religious, premarital sexual intercourse was interdicted. The couple participated in heavy petting, however, and after one year of steady dating they became engaged. During Tim's senior year at college he felt more and more guilty about deceiving his fiancée. He liked her very much, "loved her in many ways," but recalled that, "as much as I tried, I could not get sexually turned on." As graduation approached, Tim broke off the engagement with great anguish. He described the encounter with his fiancée as the most painful experience of his life. Unable to find a reason to end the engagement, since warm, loving feelings were obviously present, Tim finally confessed his homosexuality. His fiancée, however, did not believe him and remained convinced that Tim had invented a lie to spare her feelings. She was unable to be friends with Tim, since she felt that he had "broken her heart." Years later, long after she had married, Tim learned from a mutual friend that she had never believed Tim's confession of his homosexuality: she had decided that he had fallen in love with another woman.

Tim went on to attend graduate school. In his mid-twenties, he met a fellow graduate student with whom, after considerable delay, he had a homosexual love relationship. His lover, Bob, had believed like Tim that he was "the only homosexual person in the world." Together Bob and Tim read biographies of homosexual men who had contributed to society. They decided that homosexuality was not a perversion but that it was "probably sinful." The fact that they had found each other, however, led for both to a sense of increased self-esteem and diminished anxiety. Tim and Bob remained lovers after acquiring their degrees and until they found work in separate locales. They remain friends, although they are no longer sexually involved.

Tim made important contributions to his field after graduation. He fully acknowledged his homosexuality but never came out publicly. As far as Tim was concerned, the causes of homosexuality were unknown and the social responses to it were primitive and cruel. Rather than risk censure, he adopted a social role as a bachelor and pursued his sexual life in private. Tim felt that he experienced a (consciously) unconflicted sense of gay identity beginning in his thirties.

When I met Tim he was in his mid-forties. He had never in his life experienced an erection in response to a heterosexual stimulus. He watched the progress of the gay rights movement with interest but did not participate. He did not believe that he was ready to take a public position that he was proud to be gay, but he did feel proud to be himself and being gay had become a central part of his self-concept.

By middle age, Tim was highly regarded in his field and had deep friendships among both heterosexual and homosexual people. He had a few sexual relationships with partners that he knew well and had been affectionately involved with for years.

In considering the adolescent and postadolescent years of this man, Erikson's (1959) insights about the phase-specific aspects of psychological functioning during adolescence provide a thought-provoking backdrop.

> The period can be viewed as a psychosocial moratorium during which the individual through free role experimentation may find a niche in some section of his society, a niche which is firmly defined and yet seems to be uniquely made for him. In finding it, the young adult gains an assured sense of inner continuity and social sameness which will bridge what he was as a child and what he is about to become, and will reconcile his conception of himself and his community's recognition of him. If . . . we speak of the community's response to the young individual's need to be "recognized" by those around him, we mean something beyond a mere recognition of achievement; for it is of great relevance to the young individual's identity formation that he be responsible to, and be given function and status as a person whose gradual growth and transformation make sense to those who begin to make sense to him. It has not been sufficiently recognized in psychoanalysis that such recognition provides an entirely indispensable support to the ego in the specific tasks of adolescing which are: to maintain the most important ego defenses against the vastly growing intensity of impulses (now invested in a matured genital apparatus and a powerful muscle system); to learn to consolidate the most important conflict-free achievements in line with work opportunities and to resynthesize all childhood identifications in some unique way, and yet in concordance with the roles offered by some wider section of society. (p. 111)

During the time that sexually mature heterosexual adolescents experience a psychosocial moratorium so that they can search for a niche, Tim was required to live as if he were such a youngster. Had he been an "as if" personality (Deutsch 1942) or a sociopath (Cleckly 1964), Tim might well have suffered less. Tim's ego and superego capacities, however, appeared to operate at a high level. His well-developed conscience is attested to by the way he conducted his life. As an adolescent and young adult, he was guiltridden at having to live a lie. He suffered deeply when he deceived his fiancée about his sexuality. When he lost people he loved he grieved appropriately. This man never cheated at anything during a lengthy academic career. Deception was inimical to him and he tried to live according to an ethical code on a day-by-day basis. He applied his work ethic to academic endeavors at which he was productive. Tim's ego defenses operated smoothly. His affects, judgment, interpersonal relationships, time sense, reality testing, and so on all functioned at a high level as well. Tim fell in love (with a young man), another indication of his capacity for deep, higher-level object relationships.

In Erikson's words (slightly altered), what Tim was as a child was *irreconcilable* with what he was to become during adolescence. His conception of himself (decent, hardworking, loving, a committed leader) was irreconcilable with his community's recognition of his homosexuality (perverse, weak, evil, sick). Tim was "recognized" by the greater community only insofar as he kept his inner life secret. Tim negotiated adolescence and adulthood and ultimately synthesized an effective sense of identity in which valued attributes could be integrated with homosexuality. In Tim's case, probably similar to that of others like him, personal strengths—the capacity to endure, independent judgment, idealism, curiosity, flexibility, courage, and intelligence—appeared central in affecting survival of a relatively unimpaired mental apparatus despite extreme obstacles. Erikson's description of the adaptive value of a fit between inner life and social niche dramatizes the poignancy of the plight of homosexual boys who experience adolescence as Tim did.

Tim's brush with the world of mental health professionals is also revealing. One cannot help but observe that his consultants were not helpful to him. The first encouraged him to pursue heterosexuality, which Tim tried to do with disastrous consequences for himself and others. Tim's second consultant, a well-recognized authority on homosexuality and psychoanalysis, seemed even more sure of the validity of his concepts. It is fortunate that Tim retained the ego capacities of independent judgment and assertiveness in order to reject this consultant's advice. Had he been more passive and masochistic, he might have given up school and bankrupted himself in a (probably) unsuccessful pursuit of heterosexuality.

Before leaving the topic of exclusive homosexuality during adolescence, it is important to stress that people like Tim are unusually resilient and intrinsically sturdy. As noted, abundant psychopathology can also coexist with adolescent homosexuality. Sometimes this is directly or indirectly "caused" by the poor fit between sexual fantasy and social environment, sometimes not. I present the developmental pathway of a boy who grew into a psychologically healthy homosexual man because this pathway has been underemphasized in the psychoanalytic literature until recently. Tim's psychobiography also raises important questions about psychodynamics and psychological development. His preadolescent life was characterized by focal impairment in peer relations because of the constraints of rural life. Simultaneously, there was marked alignment of members of his family along gender lines, but Tim crossed the gender boundary, placing himself primarily with the females. This appeared to influence his internal self-representation without producing overt feminization of behavior. Furthermore, although Tim's self-representation was influenced by gender valuing, it is by no means clear that he suffered from a gender identity disorder, that is, a psychiatric illness of gender identity. The data necessary for such a diagnosis would have to include material that tapped Tim's unconscious, such as Rorschach responses or transcripts or psychoanalytic sessions. Tim was not a patient and this type of material was not available.

Tim's history illustrates an important characteristic of sexual fantasy in relation to sexual orientation: many adolescents have well-consolidated erotic fantasies prior to participating in sexual activity with others. The differentiation of sexual fantasy does not depend on sexual activity with other people. This point cannot be emphasized too strongly. Tim's history reveals that at least one of his consultants seemed not to believe this. Research investigators particularly interested in social-sexual behavior often underemphasize the distinction as well. More detailed consideration of questions raised by Tim's history requires a model of the mind in relation to sexual orientation. This is discussed in chapter 18, where Tim's case is again considered from a theoretical perspective.

OPEN QUESTIONS ABOUT ADULT SEXUAL ORIENTATION AND CHILDHOOD PSYCHOPATHOLOGY

The literature suggests that as one moves down the chronological line, from older to younger, the likelihood of encountering gender identity pathology, family pathology, and social maladaptation among males who are meaningfully homosexual increases. Whereas during adulthood psychopathology is not aggregated among homosexual men in comparison to heterosexuals, this has not been demonstrated to date in early and mid-adolescent and younger patients. At present there is no evidence that devastating global psychopathology regularly occurs among homosexual adolescents. If such were the case, differential rates of psychopathology would probably still be detectable between adult men of divergent sexual orientation. Saghir and Robins (1973) demonstrated that there are no such differences in psychopathology between homosexual and heterosexual adults, but there are no similar studies of psycho-pathology among adolescents. Nor are there comparisons of projective test data between homosexual and heterosexual adolescents similar to Hooker's (1956) investigation with adults. Until such research is carried out, the question remains open whether differences in focal psychopathology exist between boys of divergent sexual orientation.

It is disconcerting that no studies assess sexual orientation longitudinally, either in naturalistic situations or among adolescent patients in therapy. Neither the conditions that might alter sexual orientation early in life nor the time frame during which this alteration might be possible are known. There is no database for sexual orientation comparable to that which has been provided for gender identity differentiation. From the naturalistic point of view, for example, we may wonder whether Tim's homosexuality would have differentiated as such if he had been more like the males than the females in his family or if he had had acceptable male playmates during his preadolescent years. We can also ask whether Tim's homosexuality would have differentiated as such if he had had therapy during his childhood and adolescent years. That is, if Tim began therapy with apparently consolidated homosexual fantasies, would these have been supplemented with or replaced by heterosexual fantasies in the context of a therapeutic relationship (either one with a male or one that fostered Tim's relationships with males)? If so, is there a time frame after which such change could not occur (by age fifteen, for instance)? These are thorny questions that have no easy answers.

A clarification about sexual values in relation to therapy is also needed here. If someone like Tim enters treatment, the therapeutic issues are diverse, but the therapist's posture toward such a person's homosexuality should be neutral. The questions asked above are not value-laden with regard to sexual orientation. The question is, if Tim's need for acceptance by and closeness with males had been met, would his sexual orientation have shifted *on its own* as a consequence? The answer to this type of question is not known.

An overview of the developmental issues discussed above suggests that relationships between homosexuality, gender identity disorders, and other syndromes of psychopathology during childhood, adolescence, and adulthood pose formidable problems for a modern psychoanalytic theory. The major findings requiring theoretical integration are as follows:

- Most childhood effeminacy results in homosexuality.
- Most adult homosexual males are not effeminate, and many experience themselves as adequately masculine and are so experienced by others.
- Most adult homosexuality is not preceded by childhood effeminacy syndrome in full form.
- Most adult homosexuality is, however, preceded by some type of prepubertal gender disturbance of childhood. In some cases, this may best be conceptualized as childhood effeminacy in partial form. Probably more often, childhood unmasculinity is a

separate syndrome, beginning later in development and characterized primarily by inadequate interpersonal relations with males and a sense of the self as inadequately masculine. (There are no prospective studies analogous to those on effeminacy indicating the percentage of boys with prepubertal unmasculinity who later become homosexual adults.)

- Childhood effeminacy is associated with global psychopathology and marked disturbance in family dynamics as well.
- Pervasive childhood unmasculinity is probably also generally associated with psychopathology and familial pathology. This area has been understudied to date, and this assumption must be treated with caution, but numerous retrospective studies suggest that this is the case.
- Studies of adult homosexual men indicate that global psychopathology is not more common among them than among heterosexual controls.

These apparently contradictory facts provide the background for discussion of theory in the chapters that follow.

The Bisexual Adolescent

Among the components of bisexuality during adolescence, the history of erotic fantasy is particularly important, because of the frequency with which apparently "homosexual" experimentation occurs. Boys often engage in sexual activity with other boys during adolescence without thinking of the experience as homosexual. The psychobiographies of the twins discordant for sexual orientation (discussed in chapter 2) illustrate this point. In early adolescence these two boys, along with several others, collectively masturbated while looking at a heterosexual pornographic magazine. Each twin engaged in mutual masturbation with another boy. The heterosexual twin interpreted this experience as heterosexual, in light of the visual imagery that stimulated his fantasy. The notion that the activity was homosexual did not occur to him, and he was quite sure that the interest of the other boys was heterosexual as well. The homosexual twin agreed that the other boys involved seemed to display intense heterosexual interest. For him, however, the experience was a homosexual one. The magazine was not a meaningful part of his sexual experience, which revolved around homosexual fantasies that had been present for years. This example illustrates that homosexual experimentation and play during adolescent years is the expression of true bisexuality only in a subgroup of boys. Most of the others are heterosexual, and some are exclusively homosexual. The heterosexual youngster who engages in sexual experimentation with other boys maintains an exclusively heterosexual fantasy world and soon gives up homosexual activity. The homosexual boy is described in chapter 13. The truly bisexual boy continues to enjoy homosexual activities and engages in homosexual erotic fantasies, but he also enjoys heterosexual fantasies and activity.

Chapter 13 describes the early history of the exclusively homosexual adolescent. The truly bisexual boy, that is, one who will become a man capable of experiencing consciously meaningful bisexual erotic fantasies, has been understudied. Bisexuality in the earlier phases of childhood awaits systematic investigation, and the childhood histories of such individuals are not well described to date. Because of an extremely sparse database, this chapter on clinical aspects of bisexuality emphasizes adolescence. Given the paucity of data, clinicians have tended to rely on theoreticians for a conceptual frame of reference in which to interpret adolescent bisexuality. A particularly influential clinical theoretician in this area is Erikson.

ERIKSON'S VIEW OF BISEXUALITY: CRITICAL CONSIDERATIONS

Erikson's (1959) basic concepts about bisexuality and identity have influenced many analysts' perspectives on homosexual phenomena. Erikson considered bisexuality a pathological variant of adolescence. In his famous diagram of the life cycle, Erikson suggested that during adolescence a homosexual identity or "bisexual diffusion" may occur as a consequence of impaired identity formation, leading to deleterious effects (fig. 14.1).

> In Box V, 5 we again meet the diagonal and the over-all focus of this paper; crossing it we enter the area of psychosocial elements which are not derivatives but precursors of future psychosocial crises. The first such element (V-6) is Sexual Identity vs. Bisexual Diffusion, the most immediate precursor of Intimacy vs. Isolation. Here the sexual mores of cultures and classes make for immense differences in the pyschosocial differentiation of masculine and feminine . . . and in the age, kind and ubiquity of genital activity. These differences can obscure the common fact discussed above, namely, that the development of psychosocial intimacy is not possible without a firm sense of identity. Bisexual diffusion can lead young adults toward two deceptive developments induced by special mores, or otherwise seduced they may foreclose their identity development by concentrating on early genital activity without intimacy; or, on the contrary, they may concentrate on social or intellectual status values which underplay the genital element with a resulting permanent weakness of genital polarization with the other sex. (p. 145)

Erikson conceptualized homoerotic fantasies and acts as occurring due to impaired processes of ego development. This model is often interpreted by psychodynamically oriented clinicians as follows: The postoedipal-prepubertal phase of development is one of latency. During this latency phase, repression keeps consciously perceived sexual fantasies at a low level of intensity. Latency is followed by adolescence, normally a time of turbulence (A. Freud 1965). The changes associated with puberty cause sexual and aggressive feelings to be experienced intensely. In some individuals, phase-specific ego weakness can lead to previously unconscious primitive oedipal and preoedipal fantasies' erupting into awareness. Conscious awareness of forbidden fantasies is both an effect of defensive failure and a cause of anxiety and further fragility of ego mechanisms. Because of the special nature of adolescence, fantasies that normally would ultimately be repressed may be actualized. If forbidden pleasures are acted out with others, the vulnerable adolescent's life course may be permanently altered.

Erikson's and similar models (e.g., Blos 1962), while applicable to subgroups of adolescents, are not inclusive models of either homosexuality or bisexuality. The group of adolescents discussed earlier with early, fixed, exclusively homosexual imagery stands as an exception to Erikson's model, which also leaves no room for equation of bisexuality with psychological health.

If one asks the same question about bisexual men as researchers have asked about homosexual men—is there increased psychopathology in this group?—the literature is too scant to provide an answer. In view of what is known about sexual pathology, however, there is no reason to assume that there is. I do not consider the capacity to experience bisexual fantasy in itself a form of psychopathology. The phenomenon of bisexuality in males has been understudied by clinicians and researchers and its underlying mechanisms are not clear. Nonetheless, it makes sense that many men have bisexual potential. The time interval during which erotic imagery is encoded on the conscious part of the mind is protracted. There is ample room for numerous positive as well as pathological experiences to exert influence. The positive influences might include many that are not overtly sexual, such as intense affectionate experiences with brothers, fathers, and male friends. One only has to think of the enormous amount of time preoedipal children spend with women and the universal tendency for identifications to occur during this phase of life to wonder why *all* males are not bisexual. Whereas reason may suggest that bisexuality should be the norm, the facts in our culture suggest that there really is no norm. The exclusively heterosexual group appears to be very large; the bisexual group is probably larger than the exclusively homosexual group but smaller than the exclusively heterosexual one (Kinsey, Pomeroy & Martin 1948; Gebhard 1972).

Bisexuality may perhaps be easily effected in children by cultural experience and expectation. Numerous cultures have been described, for example, in which youths that later become predominantly heterosexual are expected to and routinely do engage in homosexual activity with older men (Ford & Beach 1951). In contemporary American culture, however (and in similar societies), it is possible that by the end of adolescence a large group of males has no homoerotic fantasy option, a small group has no heteroerotic fantasy option, and a perhaps relatively large group has both homoerotic and heteroerotic fantasy options. The size of these groups during adolescence remains to be determined.

	1.	2.	3.	4.	5.	6.	7.	8.
I. INFANCY	Trust vs. Mistrust				Unipolarity vs. Premature Self-Differentation			
II. EARLY CHILD-HOOD		Autonomy vs. Shame, Doubt			Bipolarity vs. Autism			
III. PLAY AGE			Initiative vs. Guilt		Play Identification vs. (oedipal) Fantasy Identities			
IV. SCHOOL AGE				Industry vs. Inferiority	Work Identification vs. Identity Foreclosure			

	Time Perspective vs. Time Diffusion	Self-Certainty vs. Identity Consciousness	Role Experimentation vs. Negative Identity	Anticipation of Achievement vs. Work Paralysis	Identity vs. Identity Diffusion	Sexual Identity vs. Bisexual Diffusion	Leadership Polarization vs. Authority Diffusion	Ideological Polarization vs. Diffusion of Ideals
V. ADOLESCENCE					Identity vs. Identity Diffusion			
VI. YOUNG ADULT					Solidarity vs. Social Isolation	Intimacy vs. Isolation		
VII. ADULTHOOD							Generativity vs. Self-Absorption	
VIII. MATURE AGE								Integrity vs. Disgust, Despair

Fig. 14.1 Erikson's diagram of the life cycle (1959, p. 120)

PSYCHOPATHOLOGY AND BISEXUALITY

Many teenagers who experience bisexual fantasies, often associated with sexual activity with others, properly belong outside the clinical domain. This discussion applies only to those within it. As with all patients, the sexual behavior of these individuals must be conceptualized using the multidimensional biopsychosocial framework outlined in chapter 6. These patients pose an additional problem, however, in that some aspect of their sexuality may be amplified because of character pathology and/or other psychopathology, usually interacting with pathological family situations. Often a homosexual component is chosen for amplification, because of the negative valence of homosexuality in the culture. This may occur with any dimension of sexual behavior and may lead to increased homosexual fantasy as a result of symptomatic sexualization; increased homosexual activity as a result of decreased impulse control and the adolescent tendency to act on impulse; driven heterosexual activity as a reaction to unwanted homosexual fantasies; increased sense of being homosexual; or flamboyant and provocative social role expressions. Many of the types of impulsive-compulsive sexual pathology and gender pathology described in part 2 frequently occur during adolescence. The dimension of negative identity takes on added importance in adolescent patients. Space does not allow clinical illustrations of the many constellations of bisexual adolescent pathology, but many of the conceptual issues are illustrated in the case presented below.

BORDERLINE BISEXUAL ADOLESCENT

Don, a nineteen-year-old college sophomore, sought consultation because he felt confused about the meaning of his life and about his future plans. The patient saw himself as homosexual and was sexually active with men. He denied that he experienced internal conflict about his homosexuality; it was a source of great pleasure to him, and he matter-of-factly observed that his sexual orientation would never change.

Don's sexual fantasies began at about the age of five. They were predominantly heterosexual but occasionally homosexual. Puberty at the age of thirteen was associated with greatly increased, predominantly heterosexual fantasies of "girls from *Playboy* magazine." Self-masturbation began then and occurred many times a week.

At age fourteen Don formed the only intense relationship of his entire life: he fell deeply in love with Lois, a girl one year older. They had an intense love relationship with much sexual activity often leading to orgasm, but no sexual intercourse. (Don had never experienced sexual intercourse with a female.) His heterosexual fantasies increased during this period, although some homosexual fantasies were also present. It was through Lois that he became committed to yoga. "Prior to meeting Lois I knew nothing about yoga. She had two interests, sex and yoga. I was already interested in sex and I took up yoga too." Following Don's junior year in high school Lois went to college out of town. She became emotionally distant, broke off the relationship, and ultimately married someone else. Don found that his sense of emotional commitment to yoga greatly increased after he broke up with Lois. At about the same time, his homosexual fantasies began to assume predominance over his heterosexual fantasies. Between then and the time I saw him, his fantasies had been predominantly homosexual. At about age seventeen, he began to engage in homosexual activity with people he met casually.

Don denied having experienced a sense of grief after the relationship with Lois broke up. He began college and initially did well. For reasons he did not understand, however, he lost motivation to study. His apathy and desultory participation in seminars led to a visit to the school guidance counselor, who referred him to me. Neither he nor the consultant felt that his homosexuality was a problem—they had agreed that "being gay shouldn't be touched" in psychotherapeutic exploration. Don merely felt that his only interests, homosexual activity and yoga, were not enough to serve as a foundation for life goals.

Don was the oldest of three children raised in a blue-collar environment in the South. His parents were fundamentalist Christians and the home environment was highly religious. The family's attitudes and values were harshly antisexual. Because of his father's work, they moved every few years. Don had no sustaining friendships during childhood. At about age four or five, he began to play exclusively with females. Shortly thereafter he became aware that his father, although actively involved with his younger sisters, seemed relatively indifferent to him. "All I remember is that I wanted something from him and he wouldn't give it to me." He did not participate in rough-and-tumble activities, was naturally awkward, temperamentally unassertive, and unaggressive. His father, however, was very interested in sports.

Don's mother was only passively involved with his development, being quite busy both at home and at work. Don denied feeling emtionally close to her or his sisters. From about age seven until his prepubertal years, he recalls experiencing episodes of intense anxiety that were relieved when he dressed in his mother's dresses. This was always done in secret. He put on her outergarments and sometimes jewelry, without a sense of sexual excitement. Don gradually lost the motivation to cross-dress, however, and stopped doing so by puberty. Don describes his juvenile years as isolated and painful. "I got through those years by not focusing on the humiliations." Always the last chosen for team sports, he was a loner. Don felt unmasculine during this period, but these feelings subsided (at the conscious level) by early adolescence.

Don suffered from severe character pathology, with narcissistic and schizoid features, at a borderline level of integration. The similarity of his early childhood gender disturbance to that described so often in the backgrouds of exclusively homosexual men illustrates that this type of background is best conceptualized as an influence that affects the probability of certain types of behavior within groups, not as a necessary and sufficient cause of these behaviors in individuals. Don's prepubertal history of erotic fantasy was bisexual, but much more heterosexual than homosexual. The reasons for this are not clear. Chapter 2 described genetic and psychoneuroendocrine influences on sexual orientation: perhaps Don was constitutionally predisposed towards heterosexuality.

Given the present stage of our knowledge about sexual development and differentiation, Don's sexual history seems to raise unanswerable questions. In early adolescence, his erotic fantasy life became even more heterosexual than it had been earlier. Faced with the phase-specific adaptive task of creating an identity, it appeared for a time that Don would be assisted by his relationship with Lois. Rather than the relationship's buttressing his sense of identity as heterosexual, however, the reverse ultimately occurred. Don's conscious feeling of love actually seemed to express his unconscious, profound need for symbiotic attachment. Loss of the relationship was not accompanied by a healthy sense of grief; rather, Don experienced "little" at the conscious level. But subsequent psychotherapeutic work with him suggested that he unconsciously interpreted the loss as punishment for heterosexual fantasies and strivings. In keeping with a dynamic well described by many analysts, Don appeared to give up heterosexuality altogether in response to irrational, unconscious fear. In his case, the fear was represented by predominantly pre-oedipal fantasies condensed with oedipal fantasies. The negative oedipal component, although present, expressed the wish to fuse with the mother. Don's primary fear seemed to be self-annihilation. He initially attempted to deal with the threat of identity diffusion by making a sexual attachment to a girl. After this failed, he attempted a homosexual solution.

Don attempted to deal with his self-identity problem by means of sexual solutions. He amplified consciously perceived homosexual feelings and adopted a homosexual identity. Don's isolation of affect and repression of large conflictual areas of his mental life led him to present himself, to himself and others, as calm and contained. But his adaptation at our initial meeting seemed to me obviously symptomatic. For example, despite his consciously professed sexual orientation, Don retained the aspiration to be a (biological) father. He fully intended to accomplish this "someday" and denied the contradiction between his belief about his enduring homosexuality and the necessity of having sexual intercourse with a female in order to become a father. He found the social role of being gay distasteful for reasons he could not articulate. Because of shame, Don hid his homosexuality from his family. He had never been in love with a male and, for reasons he could not put into words, doubted that he ever would. He described himself as "a homosexual with straight ideals, who is doomed to be alone by age fifty." Although never suicidal, Don regarded his future as hopelessly bleak, yet he denied feeling depressed about this.

For patients like Don the most helpful therapeutic attitude toward sexual orientation is one of neutrality. This neutrality should not, of course, be confused with a cold, nongiving, pseudotherapeutic posture. Warmth, kindness, and empathy can all be conveyed without the therapist's making the countertransference error of prescribing the solution to such a patient's profound self-identity difficulties as "either heterosexuality or homosexuality." A strong indication that Don's ultimate path might be toward heterosexuality lies in the fact that he seemed to be on a predominantly heterosexual track prior to his attachment with Lois. Even so, the vicissitudes of Don's future growth, including his sexual growth, cannot be predicted on the basis of his history. The argument might be made, for example, that Don's basic and primary feelings were really homosexual and were defended against by neurotic amplification of heterosexual fantasies and activity. There is no logical counterargument to this view: this type of debate about psychodynamics and psychopathology is decided on an empirical level, not an exclusively theoretical-logical one. Each psychotherapeutic session is evaluated in terms of a model of the mind and the adaptation of the whole patient. The therapist can usually make appropriate interpretations and confrontations without directing the patient toward any particular sexual orientation.

Don's case illustrates only some of the common clinical problems involving bisexuality. Many males have bisexual potential by the time they reach early adolescence. Still others may develop bisexual erotic imagery in early and mid-adolescence as a result of experiences that occur under the influence of the androgen surge of puberty. Bisexuality may frequently be flamboyantly expressed during adolescence as a result of the numerous vicissitudes influencing adolescent identity/social role. There is no validating evidence, however, that the incidence of bisexuality increases during adolescence or that pathological identity weakness associated with adolescence causes bisexuality. It may frequently happen that one component of already existent bisexual erotic fantasy is amplified or repressed, or the significance of one component may be denied.

CLINICAL ISSUES IN ASSESSING ADOLESCENT
PSYCHOPATHOLOGY

In part 2 of this book, it is emphasized that evaluation of clinical problems involving sexual orientation necessitates consideration of multiple dimensions of behavior. As difficult as it may be to conceptualize adult psychopathology as a multidimensional matrix via the diagnostic cube, diagnosis of adolescent psychopathology may pose even more complex problems. For one thing, personality type must be assessed, but the younger the patient the less history of patterned behavior there is to document. Ambiguous outlines of personality disorders are frequently encountered in adolescents. Nonetheless, the classic personality disorders for the most part make their characteristic appearance prior to adulthood. Many personality disorders begin prior to puberty and roughly overlap the age at which sexual fantasy differentiates. The interactions between character type and sexual fantasy and activity are difficult enough to assess during adulthood after some years of patterned sexual behavior. It is frequently even more difficult to appreciate clinically the key interactions when they first make their appearance during the juvenile period or early adolescence.

Clinical judgments about identity are a requisite for accurate assessment of the structural level of character integration during adulthood. But the phase-specific tasks of adolescence sometimes make it difficult to distinguish borderline level of character integration from superficially similar but relatively innocuous expressively labile behavior involving the sense of identity. In the process of forging an identity, normal teenagers may try on and discard social roles, including sexual/social roles, as if they were costumes (Erikson 1959, 1968; Blos 1962, 1979). The clinician confronted with a problem involving sexual orientation must therefore conceptualize interactions between sexual fantasy, sexual activity, phase-specific identity / social role problems, and personality type. It is also necessary to diagnose the level of structural character pathology; that is, to determine whether patients are borderline, higher-level neurotics, experiencing adjustment reactions, or on a temporarily camouflaged pathway to health (Stone 1980; Kestenbaum 1985). As noted in part 2, clinical problems involving sexual orientation are common among borderline adults. In my experience, they are at least as common among borderline teenagers (although less often written about to date).

The issues outlined above are only some of the many associated with sexual orientation during adolescence. An important additional dimension of behavior involves the family. Adolescence, with its adaptive requirement that the person separate and differentiate from his or her family, mandates evaluation of the family as well as the individual in order to understand the patient's psychopathology. Numerous difficulties involving the total family system can present as problems attributable to an adolescent's sexual orientation. Character pathology in individual family members and "system pathology" can interact in a variety of ways. The most common interaction probably involves scapegoating the identified patient, who then becomes the repository of family difficulties. Crisis intervention therapy usually accompanies diagnostic intervention in such situations.

Organization of data along the lines suggested above depends upon skillful interviewing of the adolescent patient. The inner psychological life of teenage patients is usually accessible to direct inquiry about both gender-related fantasies and activity and erotic fantasy and activity. In taking the sexual history it is important for the interviewer to keep a structured set of questions in mind and to ask these questions in such a way as to maintain rapport with the adolescent patient. A model for sound interview strategy may be taken from the field of affective disorders of adolescence. Only relatively recently has it been established that major affective disorders frequently occur in adolescence. This was overlooked for many years because it was believed that adolescent depression is generally masked and cannot be directly elicited in a psychiatric interview (Carlson & Cantwell 1980) and that adolescence is normally a time of such extreme lability and turbulence that normal teenagers may seem virtually psychotic (A. Freud 1965). These erroneous clinical assumptions were discarded when researchers, using structured instruments, meticulously documented the symptoms of major affective disorder in adolescents (Puig-Antich 1980). It became apparent that a structured format, appropriately utilized in the psychiatric interview, could provide clinically meaningful data that might otherwise go unnoticed. The sexual history must be approached as straightforwardly and specifically as the history of depressive symptomatology. When this approach is used, the therapist usually finds that adolescent patients are relieved to be able to discuss their sexual lives openly and directly with a nonjudgmental adult.

Adolescence, while frequently discussed categorically (as it is here), is a protracted interval involving many years and subphases. It is important to stress how little solid information there is about sexual orientation in adolescence, particularly in younger patients. No prospective investigations have studied dimensions of sexuality in children followed through puberty. Because huge areas of behavior are still unstudied, the best information available to psychoanalysts is often circumstantial. Even larger uncharted areas exist with regard to the dimensions of boyhood and adolescent bisexuality than with regard to exclusive homosexuality. The need for ongoing research on all aspects of childhood and adolescent sexuality is evident.

PART FOUR

Theoretical Issues
and Conclusion

15

Gender Identity
and the Sense
of Masculinity

The data and concepts discussed in this book suggest that common psycho-analytic assumptions about the unconscious, particularly about the rela-tionship between the childhood and the adult unconscious, are in need of modification. In this chapter aspects of the theory of unconscious mental functioning are critically considered in the light of modern research and theory.

Many psychoanalytic revisionists have suggested modifications in Freud's theories. All important psychoanalytic theories, however, continue to share fundamental assumptions about the way the past is related to the present. To put the key concept in almost absurdly simple form, the inner world of child-hood continues to retain motivational power during adulthood because of the way the unconscious works. For a time, widespread belief in the validity of psychic determinism made it appear that psychoanalysts knew how the uncon-scious influenced motivation. But models based on psychic determinism, once invoked to explain many symptoms and syndromes of pyschopathology, now seem outdated. Clinical psychoanalytic theories must respond today to the fact that models of psychic determinism are inadequate to explain most forms of psychopathology.

This point deserves particular emphasis. On the one hand, it appears self-evident in view of research in the behavioral sciences during the past twenty-five years. On the other hand, theoretical discussions in psychoanalysis often still sound in many quarters as if psychic determinism can be used as an explanation for behavior, including psychopathology. Once it is fully acknowl-edged that psychoanalytic theory deals with influences much more frequently than causes, the importance of modern research on other behavioral influences becomes immediately clear.

For example, a simple model once used to explain a variety of forms of psychopathology involved unconscious, irrational anxiety. This anxiety was assumed to motivate pathological behavior and was considered a final common pathway in diverse forms of psychopathology. A tendency existed to view symptoms that resulted from predominantly biological influences as manifestations of severe illness and not of central interest to psychoanalytic theory. Theorists drifted away from biopsychosocial-integrationistic models of the mind and toward models that treated biological, psychological, and social influences on mentation as if they operated independently. The relevance of biological and social influences and interactions to psychoanalysis was often denied. Some analysts seemed to believe that the only segment of the biopsychosocial spectrum directly germane to psychoanalytic theory and practice was a narrow subdivision of the psychological domain: the immediate causes and consequences of unconscious conflict.

The unconscious irrational anxiety model was widely invoked by psychoanalytic clinical theoreticians. The model was felt to be helpful in clarifying the mental mechanisms underlying most forms of behavior that analysts saw as pathological (Alexander & Selesnick 1966). Homosexuality was generally considered such a form of psychopathology (Bieber et al. 1962).

In the 1940s, 1950s, and 1960s, when less was known about behavior than is known today, the validity of psychic determinism seemed evident. But subsequent advances, particularly in psychobiology, have critically weakened this model. The symptoms of endogenous depression, for example, as well as those of mania, the anxiety disorders, and numerous other forms of psychopathology, cannot be explained satisfactorily, let alone fully, using an etiological model of unconscious conflict. Similar criticisms of determinism and of the unconscious anxiety model of motivation and symptom formation have resulted from advances in other large areas of behavior, for example the psychobiology of sleep and dreaming, the regulation and behavioral consequences of circadian and other rhythms, and so on. Psychoanalysis today therefore finds itself grappling with a perplexing problem. On the one hand, it is generally agreed that the concept of unconscious motivation is not only helpful but necessary in order adequately to conceptualize human behavior. On the other hand, the mental mechanisms by which the unconscious functions have become less discernible and more puzzling as knowledge of human behavior has increased. Accurate description of the factors regulating the gateway between the unconscious and the conscious—particularly the factors influencing the motivation to behave in specific ways—remains to be effected by future generations of psychoanalytic investigators.

The retreat of psychoanalysis from psychobiology has also involved important aspects of human sexual behavior. Masters's investigation of human sexual response, for example, challenged the dual orgasm theory and rendered traditional psychoanalytic concepts of female psychosexual development and functioning obsolete (Masters & Johnson 1966). The recently acquired clinical and research data discussed in this book that (directly or indirectly) relate to sexual orientation are also of importance for placing theory about human sexuality on a sound footing. These data, and inferences from them, are also relevant to more general aspects of psychoanalytic theory. They call into question psychoanalytic theory of symptom formation during adulthood and basic psychoanalytic assumptions about similarities of male and female mental functioning. Parts 1–3 of this book focus directly on scientific and clinical data. This chapter discusses the relevance of this material for psychoanalytic developmental theory. The significance of modern concepts about sex and gender are considered with regard to the preoedipal, oedipal, and postoedipal phases of childhood.

THE PREOEDIPAL PHASE: GENDER IDENTITY DIFFERENTIATION VS. HOMOSEXUAL STAGE OF DEVELOPMENT

Modern gender theory necessitates abandoning a number of Freud's hypotheses still cherished in certain psychoanalytic quarters. One such hypothesis is Freud's idea that a homosexual phase of development is normative and that unconscious homosexuality is universal.

Stoller's basic concept that core gender identity differentiates during early childhood is generally accepted by contemporary behavioral scientists. Once the sense of being male or female has evolved, it becomes an irreversible part of the person's self-image. Money and Ehrhardt (1972) define core gender identity as "an infant's developing sense of self in the second year of life, well in advance of the classic oedipal phase to which the origin of differences in the psychology of sex is attributed in traditional theory" (p 182).

> Despite great variability between cultures in the prescription of gender-dimorphic behavior in childhood, adolescence and adulthood, the existence of gender-dimorphism of behavior is itself invariant. . . . In the final analysis, culturally prescribed (or prohibited) gender-dimorphic behavior stems from the phyletic verities of menstruation, impregnation, gestation and lactation. (p. 145)

Money and Ehrhardt also emphasize the necessity to distinguish between psychosexual development and psychosexual differentiation with regard to establishment of gender identity. "In developmental psychosexual theory it is no longer satisfactory to utilize only the concept of psychosexual development. Psychosexual (or gender-identity) differentiation is the preferential concept, for the psychodevelopment of sex is a continuation of the embryo-development of sex" (p. 7).

In describing the psychobiological sequences before and after gender identity differentiation, Money and Ehrhardt use the analogy of a relay race. The program carried by either the XX or XY chromosome pair, passed to the undifferentiated gonad, determines whether it becomes a testis or an ovary. The program is then passed to testicular hormone, which is required for male differentiation. If no hormone is secreted, differentiation is basically female. Androgen secreted by the fetal testis influences both the genitalia and the brain. The appearance of the genitalia leads to assignment of the infant as male or female. The program is passed from the internal, biological environment to the external, psychosocial one. As the result of complex interactions, many of which are not yet understood, gender identity differentiates during early childhood. The fixed core gender identity, in interaction with other aspects of the total person and the environment, influences innumerable behavior sequences. These occur both within the individual and between the individual, other people, and the nonhuman environment. These behavioral sequences lead to further behavioral dimorphism during subsequent phases of life (Friedman, Richart & VandeWiele 1974; Huston 1983; Stoller 1985). This is not to suggest that all behavioral dimorphism is a consequence of gender identity formation. The construction of the gender-self concept as male or female certainly synergizes and amplifies cycles of behavior leading to such dimorphism, however.

At this point questions may arise about the extent to which core gender identity (CGI) is the result of biological influences, on the one hand, and psychosocial influences, on the other. Some of these questions are touched on in part 1; some additional review is offered here as well.

It is best not to conceptualize the establishment of core gender identity in terms of dichotomous categories (nature vs. nurture, psychology vs. biology). Instead, an interactionist model should be used. In "normal" boys and girls (the vast majority of people), complex interactions between constitutional predisposition and cognitive, social-learning, and psychodynamic factors (i.e., identifications) lead to a final end product, core gender identity. Constitutional predisposition has been investigated primarily through study of the psychosexual aspects of hermaphroditism. Recent work in this area is well reviewed by Hoenig (1985). Important questions about the establishment of gender identity in hermaphrodites (as well as normals) remain open. Furthermore, it is not clear to what degree the findings from investigation of hermaphrodites are generalizable to nonhermaphroditic individuals. Hoenig devoted particular attention to Money's hypothesis that gender identity is "largely the result of gender assignment and rearing even when constitutional physical aspects are in discord with the assigned sex." This hypothesis is not unanimously accepted by contemporary researchers. (See Diamond 1982; Imperato-McGinley et al. 1974, 1979a, b, 1981; and Zuger 1970 for further discussion.)

In most normal children, and probably in most hermaphroditic individuals as well, the effect of postnatal learning on the establishment of CGI is extremely powerful and probably frequently determinative. Nonetheless, it seems reasonable to conclude that as a general rule, prenatal programming of the central nervous system by sex steroid hormones influences constitutional predisposition toward a variety of gender-dimorphic behaviors. Gender-shaping interactions occur postnatally, involving sequences of signals transmitted between the individual and others and within the individual. During a critical time interval in early childhood, a psychological construct, CGI, is formed. This is a permanent label indicating that the self is male or female. It is analogous to a cellular structure that has differentiated from a multipotential precursor. Although the experience of the self as male or female occurs postnatally, it is helpful to conceptualize CGI on a continuum with the prenatal differentiation of physical structures such as the genitalia. The precise age at which differentiation of CGI is completed remains to be definitively established. It is generally believed to occur prior to the oedipal phase of childhood (Money & Ehrhardt 1972; Hoenig 1985).

Core gender identity is a remarkably sturdy psychological construct. Once differentiated it does not fragment except under extraordinary circumstances. Although ideas about gender identity normatively become more and more abstract and sophisticated with cognitive development, ideas about *core* gender identity do not. Intelligent adults with the most sophisticated concepts of masculinity and femininity still retain concrete, physically rooted, and in a sense primitive beliefs that they are either male or female and will be so long as they live. The concrete, body-rooted nature of CGI has its parallel in the concrete, body-rooted nature of most erotic imagery.

In a series of papers on gender theory from a psychoanalytic point of view, Fast (1984) notes that the notion of belonging to one gender or the other is necessarily associated with the idea of a limit on behavior.

> As with other differentiations, gender differentiation is hypothesized to begin with recognition of a limit. It begins as the boy gradually becomes increasingly aware of the meanings of sex differences. He notices that some capacities and attributes (expressed in self representations or as identifications) that he assumed for himself cannot be his.
> . . . Sex differences means a move from the narcissistic assumption that all sex and gender characteristics are open to him to a recognition of the limits imposed by his body's structure and function. (p. 52)

One corollary of the idea of CGI that has received little attention from psychoanalysts is the fact that CGI differentiation imposes a limit on regression. For example, most and perhaps all people with character neuroses and borderline syndromes never regress to an undifferentiated gender state during psychoanalysis or psychotherapy. As a general rule, no matter how intensely involved in the analytic process a patient is, no matter whether the transference is narcissistic or neurotic, no matter how apparently regressed, CGI is retained. That this is true of narcissistic and lower-level borderline patients is particularly worthy of emphasis: despite identity diffusion, CGI remains as a unified psychological construct. It is also retained in cases of regression and personality fragmentation as a result of psychosis or extreme trauma. The fascinating area of gender identity in psychosis has been understudied to date. In the nonparanoid psychotic disorders, however, despite loss of reality testing in many areas and loss of the ability to think and speak logically and coherently, clinical experience suggests that CGI tends to be preserved. This is probably usually true in the paranoid disorders too, although (as noted in chapter 11) the gender self is often threatened.

Conservation of CGI thus appears to be a fundamental attribute of human behavior even in the face of extreme damage. It is part of the bedrock of the self. Yet it is presumably not determined biologically (in any simple, immediate way), and moreover, its form is not always the result of unconflicted social learning. Admittedly, there are rare cases, usually involving hermaphrodites, in which core gender identity is indeterminate or ambivalent (Money & Ehrhardt 1972). But boys almost always develop a lasting sense of being male and girls female, whether or not this psychological construct is born amid conflict. Once CGI is formed, there is no evidence that the previous undifferentiated state influences unconscious motivation in any way. As discussed below, the structuralization of gender identity has relevance for understanding the later structuralization of sexual orientation in males.

A few points about CGI require summary:

Differentiation of CGI alongside other fundamental differentiation (i.e., as alive vs. not alive, human vs. nonhuman) marks the beginning of a fundamental process of organization of all future experience.

Differentiation of CGI may occur in an atmosphere of interpersonal conflict. During the differentiation process, the organization of the mental apparatus into its tripartite structure is also proceeding. It is not clear to what degree the concept of internal psychological conflict is applicable to CGI, since the final organization of the mental apparatus into superego, ego, and id is completed after CGI differentiation has occurred. It is clear, however, that CGI must often differentiate in a dysphoric psychological climate that contains the anlagen of internal conflict. All preoedipal conflicts, for example, hypothetically emerge during the early and middle phases of CGI differentiation. But there is no evidence that once differentiated, CGI itself is subject to the vicissitudes of psychological conflict. In a sense, then, CGI may be thought of not simply as a psychological structure, but as a boundary of the entire mental life, including the unconscious. Subsequent psychological life (excepting in the few individuals with uncertain CGI), occurs within this boundary. This means that conscious and unconscious fantasy is limited by CGI. The importance of this hypothesis for understanding sexual orientation will be stressed in subsequent discussion.

Freud's hypothesis of a homosexual stage in the development of the sexual instinct and his theory of constitutional bisexuality attempted to integrate many of the same aspects of behavior that modern gender theory addresses. Gender theory, for example, supports Freud's idea that sexual orientation is usually not determined at birth. Freud suggested, however, that there is a normative homosexual developmental phase which provides a nidus for fixation. He also believed that "the existence of homosexual tendencies is permanent since a portion of the libido is assigned to this component of the sexual constitution" (Bieber et al. 1962, p. 4). In Freud's view, therefore, the potential to develop conscious homosexual or heterosexual fantasies is universally present. The heterosexual developmental track is only a conscious one, and unconscious homosexual potential remains. But modern concepts indicate that gender experience precedes and organizes erotic experience, not the reverse, as Freud thought. In this respect, the link that Freud proposed between the past (early childhood) and the present (adult functioning) was based on erroneous premises. The fundamental task of psychoanalysis has often been characterized as making the unconscious conscious. In order to do this, we must have a sound idea of the limits of unconscious motivation. Exactly what can emerge from the unconscious? An accurate model of the unconscious underlies the central psychoanalytic technique of interpretation.

The relation of limits to Freud's model of a homosexual phase of development may be stated as follows: There is no evidence to suggest that all males negotiate a homosexual phase of development. Thus, there is no reason to hypothesize a universal, unconscious homosexual dynamic in males. Put another way, there is no longer any reason to assume that all heterosexual men have made unconscious homosexual object "choices." The issue of homosexual fantasy in heterosexual men is a complex one, to be taken up later. Suffice it to say here that males should not be conceptualized as universally capable of homosexual "regression," since there is no universally experienced homosexual phase of early childhood. In the course of analytic work, it should be fully appreciated that the inner world of fantasy, including unconscious fantasy, is limited by psychosexual differentiation. Gender theory has rendered obsolete central features of Freud's theory of constitutional bisexuality.

THE OEDIPUS COMPLEX AND HOMOSEXUALITY

A particularly clear overview of Freud's theories of the developmental vicissitudes leading to male homosexuality is provided by the Society of Medical Psychoanalysts:

> Cathexis is partially accomplished, but on a narcissistic level. As a consequence, the individual seeks a love object representing himself and, therefore, necessarily having to possess the male genital. The individual is thus sexually involved with himself and his own genital in the form of another male who symbolizes himself.

Mental attitudes that exist during the phallic phase:
Here the male child reaches a stage where sexual impulses formerly expressed through other zones and instincts now become organized, so that the penis becomes the principal organ of discharge and pleasure. The boy begins to place enormous value on the male organ as the chief executor of the sexual function. As a result of earlier experiences with deprivation of other sources of pleasure (breast, feces, etc.), there develops during this (phallic) phase an unconscious fear of the loss of the prized organ. And, when the male child discovers the absence of the penis in the female this knowledge confirms the fear that the penis can be lost or removed. Females are consequently avoided to prevent the arousal of castration anxiety and are devalued because of their lack of the narcissistically overvalued male genital.

Difficulties associated with the Oedipus phase:
A second type of castration anxiety fostering homosexuality is associated with unconscious incestuous feelings for the mother, later transferred to all women. The castration anxiety in this context derives from fear of retaliation for wishes to castrate the father who is perceived as a sexual rival for the mother.

Freud believed that the sexual practices in the homosexual relationship symbolize regressions to developmental fixation points. For instance, if there is an anal fixation, the individual may identify with his mother and then attempt to play the mother's role through the symbolic equation of the anus with the vagina. On the other hand, if there is stronger identification with the father, the homosexual might subject other males to a passive role in the sodomitic act, which symbolically transforms these men into females and at the same time covertly expresses hostility towards them as males. Homosexuality therefore becomes one way of coping with rivalry with the father while at the same time gratifying sexual wishes. (Bieber et al. 1962, pp. 5–6)

In reviewing and elaborating upon Freud's developmental model, Fenichel (1945) stressed the mechanism of maternal identification as basic and primary. "Following the loss of an object or disappointment in an object, everyone tends to regress from the level of object love to identification; he becomes the object he cannot possess. Thus the homosexual individual identifies himself with the object after having been disappointed by its genitals" (p. 331). The maternal identification does not depend on a warm, loving relation with the mother. If the mother is abusive, for example, the mechanism of identifying with the aggressor might operate. For homosexuality to occur, "pregenital fixations, especially anal ones, and the readiness to substitute identifications for object relations are the necessary prerequisites. This readiness must be combined with intensity of secondary narcissism, of self love, that is." Other mechanisms that are less central include "enjoyment of the passive pleasures of pregenital times at the hands of a man instead of a woman," and defensive substitution of homosexual love for hatred of a sibling" (p. 337).

Fenichel's comments suggest that he probably equated pathological maternal identification with childhood gender identity disturbance. Although the language is somewhat archaic, a case can be made for the applicability of the concepts of narcissistic impairment and substitution of identification for object relatedness in boys who manifest effeminacy in full form. (Even so, Fenichel's formulation would concern psychodynamics and psychopathology, not etiology. If effeminacy were shown to result primarily from biological determinants, the psychological mechanisms described by Fenichel might still exist.) A part of Freud's theory of development does seem applicable to the subgroup of homosexual men who experience childhood effeminacy.

The role of the oedipus complex in sexual orientation comes in question at this point, given the history of Freud's model of development and psychoanalytic thought. The hypothetical relationship of the oedipus complex to the developing personality has also been modified by gender theory. This is perhaps best summarized by Fast:

> The differentiation model suggests that identification and rivalry with the same sexed parent are normally involved for both boys and girls and that identification does not only occur at the close of the oedipus complex. It suggests that before awareness of sex difference, children have established many identifications with their same sexed parents. With recognition of sex difference these must be redefined in gender terms and gradually integrated into a subjective construct of masculinity or of femininity. (1984, p. 103)

> Gender differentiation theory suggests . . . that the processes of the oedipal period are initiated by children's interest in sex difference, not by biological changes in penile or clitoral sensation. The observed intensification of interest in the genitals is not due to physical changes but to children's involvement in categorizing their genitals in gender terms. The restructuring of children's relations to their parents is not the product of a biologically patterned oedipus complex. It is the result of children's new perceptions of both themselves and their parents in gender terms, and the consequent elaboration of same-sex and cross-sex relations to them as specifically masculine and feminine in relation to the children's own masculinity or feminity. (p. 107)

Space does not allow an in-depth critical reevaluation of the oedipus complex. It must be emphasized, however, that failure of oedipal resolution refers to a developmental dynamic mechanism, not an etiological one. It is also important to distinguish between studies of the psychodynamics of adults and the development of children. Hooker's classic research, for example, demonstrated that blind judges could not distinguish homosexual men's responses on projective tests from those of heterosexual men (1965, 1967, 1972). This elegant research, plus abundant data from the clinical situation, indicates that the psychodynamic conflicts of adult homosexual and heterosexual men may be strikingly similar. Research of this type has not yet been carried out with children.

As Fast's remarks indicate, the meaning of the oedipus complex to contemporary scientists is different from that originally proposed by Freud. One might say the oedipus complex has aged but, unlike constitutional bisexuality, it has not died. The potential vicissitudes of failure of oedipal conflict resolution are many. Numerous symptoms, syndromes, developmental arrests, inhibitions, and so on, may result from such failure, and often they occur in children who become heterosexual adults. Failure of oedipal conflict resolution cannot *predict* the developmental track common for prehomosexual boys. The descriptive developmental data presented earlier in this book, however, do not call into question the oedipal theory. From the developmental point of view, it is compatible with classical psychoanalytic theory that boys who fail to resolve oedipal conflicts should then develop the very types of gender identity disturbances described earlier in this book.

Thus, as noted in chapters 3 and 13, two major types of gender disturbance in childhood seem to be associated with homosexuality in the adult. (Chapters 3 and 13 actually describe three groups, but for the line of reasoning developed here, the first two groups discussed there are considered one major group.) Effeminate boys obviously negotiate the oedipal phase of development in a disturbed way. From preoedipal years they develop along a specific track including a negative oedipal "way station," as it were. This track includes homosexuality during adulthood. It is hypothesized, however, that most homosexual adults do not start out on the effeminate developmental track. In the second group, gender disturbance probably begins later than in the first, and its manifestations are prominent during the oedipal and postoedipal juvenile phase. The behavioral disturbances of this group also suggest the importance of the oedipus complex in male development. Whereas many aspects of psychoanalytic theory have been weakened by modern empirical studies of sexual orientation, the central role of the oedipus complex during childhood has not.

The question remains, however, why neurotic disorders and symptoms of all types are not grouped on the homosexual side of the Kinsey spectrum. If neurosis stems from unresolved oedipal conflict, then it should be epidemic among homosexual adults. The empirical evidence indicates that this is not the case. How can we account for this inconsistency? A number of possible explanations arise, but one seems particularly likely to me: namely, that homosexuality is associated with some psychological mechanism, not understood or even studied to date, that protects the individual from diverse psychiatric disorders.

In considering psychoanalytic theory from a developmental point of view, we have critically discussed the idea of a normative homosexual developmental phase and the oedipus complex in relation to male sexual orientation. The following section focuses on the postoedipal-prepubertal period. The issues bearing on the sense of masculinity during these years have not been emphasized in the psychoanalytic literature, perhaps because it is assumed that the structural aspects of the self are already formed by the juvenile years. I do not believe that this is so. Gilligan's (1982) contributions to the psychology of sex differences seem particularly relevant for understanding masculinity in juvenile boys. Below I suggest a modification of her model concerning the development of boys' sense of masculinity.

THE POSTOEDIPAL PHASE: ON THE DEVELOPMENT OF MASCULINE SELF-ESTEEM

Empirical studies of sexual orientation implicate the postoedipal or juvenile phase of life as crucially important for the development of a sense of masculine adequacy in all boys (not just in gender-disturbed children). Furthermore, these studies suggest that self-judgment of masculinity usually seems to depend on positive social relationships with other males, both peers and adult authority figures. This may have to do with the way cognition operates at this age. Boys measure themselves in relation to others whom they estimate to be similar. Similarity of self-assessment depends on consensual validation. The others must agree that the boy is and will remain similar to them. The boy must also view both groups of males (peers and older men) as appropriate for idealization. Not only must he be like them in some ways, he must want to be like them in others. They in turn must want him to be like them. Unconsciously, they must have the capacity to identify with him. This naturally occurring fit between the male social world and the boy's inner object world is the juvenile phase-specific counterpoint to the preoedipal child's relationship with the mother.

Of the theoreticians that have discussed childhood masculinity, Gilligan's (1982) observations are particularly helpful. Emphasis on the importance of the relationship between the inner world of boys and the social world of other males, however, adds a dimension to Gilligan's insights about masculinity. Gilligan suggests that the fact that all children are cared for by women during early childhood has consequences for gender-dimorphic attitudes toward later intimate attachments. She quotes Chodorow's formulation:

> Girls, in identifying themselves as female, experience themselves as like their mothers, thus fusing the experience of attachment with the process of identity formation. In contrast, mothers experience their sons as a male opposite, and boys, in defining themselves as masculine, separate their mothers from themselves, thus curtailing their primary love and sense of empathetic tie. Consequently, male development entails a more emphatic individuation and a more defensive firming of experienced ego boundaries. (p. 8)

Gilligan proposed that at the same phase-specific critical period of childhood that gender identity differentiates, a *different* set of psychological processes simultaneously becomes established dimorphically. Girls become positively sensitized to the processes involved in attachment. For females, interpersonal intimacy becomes associated with a sense of strengthened gender security and self-regard. However, boys develop their gender identity in the context of separating from the mother. Males are prone therefore to gender insecurity, triggered by interpersonal intimacy and attachment. "Since masculinity is defined through separation while femininity is defined through attachment, male gender identity is threatened by intimacy while female gender identity is threatened by separation. Thus males tend to have difficulty with relationships, while females tend to have problems with individuation" (p. 8). Gilligan outlined the path that leads boys to become men who tend to define themselves in terms of separation, autonomy, individuation, and natural rights. Since male gender identity differentiates in a "holding environment," largely provided by the mother, a number of analysts have also hypothesized that successful male gender identity differentiation must occur against a gradiant of potential female identifications (Greenson 1968). Following gender identity differentiation, the mother–son relationship in actuality and in fantasy has been hypothesized to place a strain on gender identity perception, associated with a characteristic type of primitive symbiosis anxiety normatively experienced by males (Stoller 1974). These observations are compatible with Gilligan's view that masculinity is defined "through separation." Psychological movement away from intimacy stems from the necessity to create distance from the mother.

While Gilligan's insights are helpful for understanding how different attitudes about caring, love, competition, and aggression develop in men and women, I modify her hypothesis about male development in one key respect. Gilligan proposed that males tend to have difficulty with intimate relationships in general. This formulation is too global: in fact, males tend to have difficulty specifically in relationships that are defined in female-valued terms as being intimate. In boys, one axis of psychological movement appears to be away from the world of females. Simultaneously, however, and underemphasized by Gilligan, boys move toward the world of males. During preoedipal years cognitive, social, and psychodynamic processes interact to push the boy toward involvement with males. The process of cognitive categorization (i.e., "I am male") is generally associated with positive valuing of gender-specific experience (i.e., "I am male and therefore I wish to pursue male activities"). Characteristic cognitive social interactions are set into motion simultaneously (i.e., "I am male, and therefore other people treat me in a malelike way, and I respond to them as a male") (Kohlberg & Ullman 1974).

Subsequent biopsychosocial interactions involve not only the sense of maleness but also the sense of masculinity. As the boy grows older, particularly following the oedipal period when phase-specific adaptation necessitates involvement in groups outside the nuclear family, positive involvement with specifically male groups becomes increasingly important for establishment of masculine self-esteem. The self-assessment of masculinity requires evaluation by the mental apparatus at an even greater level of complexity than is required for gender categorization. The self-evaluation "I am not masculine" derives in large measure from a cognitive assessment of similarity and difference between the boy and other males. This cognitive judgment is not necessarily associated with a *negative* value judgment about the self. Whitam and Zent's (1984) research (reviewed in chapter 5) suggested that homosexual orientation may be associated with nonmasculine gender identity/role even in societies in which homosexuality and gender disturbance are not negatively valued. In the United States, however, and probably in many other societies, the judgment "I am not masculine" generally carries with it the additional judgment "I am not adequately masculine, and therefore I feel like an inadequate boy."

This negative judgment involves measurement of masculine-self adequacy according to a meaningful internal standard. The key part of the mental apparatus involved in this self-assessment is the ego ideal, the contents of which are of central import in conceptualizing the psychology of masculinity. The contents of the ego ideal during the juvenile phase are presumed to be the product of learning, introjections, identifications, and partial identifications. The disparity between the masculine self and the ideal masculine self is associated with painful affect, predominantly shame.

Male–female differences probably exist in any affective-social mode regulating acceptance by conspecific groups. For boys, group acceptance tends to be based initially on respect and only later on affection. Gilligan used the imagery of the web and the pyramid to represent gender-dimorphic concepts about the ideal social organization. In her view, women are organized in a web of connectedness; men, in contrast, are organized in a pyramid of competitiveness. It seems to me that boys and men often have profound feelings of intimacy with other males. These feelings, however, tend to be processed by the male mental apparatus and are often experienced in a competitive, pyramidal mode rather than a weblike mode. Affection is conditioned upon respect because young boys idealize strength more than nurturance. Gilligan noted that even by age eleven, when issues of responsibility and conflict are discussed by boys the interpersonal matrix is depicted by aggressive imagery, whereas girls tend to focus on themes of caring relationships. Chapters 2–3 of this book emphasize the significance of rough-and-tumble activity in male development. Competency at rough-and-tumble interactions can be viewed from Gilligan's perspective as well. Since the organization of boys' interpersonal world is heavily focused on aggressivity and competitiveness, displaying adequate functioning within this mode tends to lead to acceptance. The experience of male–male bonding relationships, beginning prior to adolescence during the postoedipal phase, provides the foundation for the lifelong fascination of many men with exclusively male forms of social life such as teams, clubs, and military organizations. This experience organizes an important nonerotic aspect of male psychological life. Membership in the world of males appears to support the potentially fragile sense of masculine self-regard during the postoedipal years. This support is both needed and valued by many men afterward as well. It is this type of experience with other males that is frequently painfully distorted during the juvenile phase of childhood in homosexual males. This disturbance during postoedipal life can be described at the level of bonding behavior, at the level of psychoanalytic structural theory, and at the level of the psychology of the self. I believe that this postoedipal phenomenon is of central etiological significance with regard to the origins of predominant or exclusive homosexuality in males. Thus, the time frame during which sexual orientation in males may be influenced is not limited to the preoedipal or oedipal phases of childhood but includes the juvenile phase as well. This phase of life may have received less attention than it deserves because the misleading term latency has been used to describe it. The postoedipal, prepubertal phase is hardly a quiescent time, however. It is a phase of enormous activity surrounding the development of the masculine self and the fusion between lustful affect and the type of image-stimulus that determines erotic fantasy and therefore sexual orientation. (In this book, the terms latency age and juvenile age are used interchangeably. I have continued to use the word *latency*, i.e., latency age, to refer to the postoedipal-prepubertal time of life. Many analysts use this term so frequently that it has come to mean a particular time interval in common psychoanalytic parlance.)

16

Male Sexual Fantasy Differentiation

Reviewing cross-species and cross-cultural contributions to clarifying early developmental influences on human sexual orientation, Gadpaille (1980) observed:

> With the exception of core gender identity, optimal periods for the development of other increments of sexual identity and capacity for optimal function have not been widely investigated. I have presented elsewhere evidence in support of the hypothesis that the optimal period in [the] human for the acquisition of heterosexual readiness—that level of ego development at which one is prepared to follow the natural dictates of the sexual drive to act on heterosexual desire without undue anxiety, guilt, inhibition, displacement, or other dysfunctional emotional interference—occurs in childhood, some time between, or perhaps covering, the period from toddlerhood to the beginning of puberty. (p. 353)

My concepts differ in emphasis from Gadpaille's, although they are derived from much of the same developmental data. Rather than describing a phase from toddlerhood to puberty in terms of a "natural" tendency toward heterosexual readiness, I see the phase simply as critical for differentiation of sexual orientation. From the point of view of adaptation it makes sense that the pubescent person, charged with sexual feelings, should have a mental representation of the desired sexual object. I suggest above that in males sexual imagery usually becomes fixed in the prepubertal and pubertal developmental phases. This time interval is determined biologically, possibly as a consequence of prenatal and pubertal androgenization, but the gender of the erotic image is not (except possibly in rare subgroups, as discussed in chapter 2).

An additional perspective about the process of sexual fantasy differentiation is provided by borrowing a model from neurobiology. Neurobiologists distinguish between the organizational and activational effects of sex steroid hormones. The organizational effects influence the physical construction of the central nervous system. For example, male and female brains differ as a result of exposure to androgen at a critical period of prenatal life. This difference is thought to be associated with numerous sex differences in behavior. Activational effects of androgen, which occur postpubertally, influence the intensity and frequency of certain types of behavior. The forms of the behaviors, however, are determined not during the postpubertal activational phase but during the (more or less irreversible) prenatal organizational phase (McEwen 1983). I suggest that the unmasculine self-representation is analogous to a particular hormonal environment at a critical period of development. Once formed in this environment, homosexual fantasies are analogous to a physical structure in the central nervous system that has differentiated. Once differentiated, homosexual fantasies do not require the presence of disturbed gender role/identity to continue. The gender-disordered self-representation is not differentiated and in fact often appears to change during subsequent developmental phases.

This model extends the organizational-activational concept from physiology to psychology. According to the model, the period during which the sexual fantasy fully emerges into the mental apparatus is organizational. During this phase, the form of the sexual fantasy may be altered by numerous influences falling along a biopsychosocial spectrum, just as Freud envisaged. Psychodynamic influences are profound during this childhood phase, and the interval during which they exert their effects is in my view more protracted than some theorists have proposed. Many of the potentially influential mechanisms (negative oedipus complex, etc.) have been well described by psychoanalytic clinicians. On the other hand, the behavioral effects associated with puberty are best envisioned as activational. The final form of the homosexual fantasy is usually determined close to this time and it continues to exist in awareness because of processes qualitatively different from those involved in its initial organization. I thus suggest that the relationship between childhood psychological functioning and adult psychological functioning is discontinuous. The point of discontinuity is the point at which sexual fantasy differentiates.

This model dispenses with the idea that the differentiated homosexual fantasy in adults is motivated by unconscious anxiety. The proposed model is, however, close to traditional psychoanalytic models with regard to the influences that may lead to exclusively homosexual fantasy during the organizational phase. These models assume that a homosexual script may emerge in the permissive environment of a feminized or demasculinized self-concept. Both the homosexual fantasy and the enabling self-concept may originally serve defensive functions (identification with powerful mother, transformation of hate for a brother into love, and so on), and both may be symptomatic. The relationships between predisposition and conflict, however, are variable enough that this need not always be the case. Specifically, the model contains room for the idea of strong biological predisposition toward differentiated homosexual fantasy.

If this theory is accurate, then what is the basis for the dissociation between sexual fantasy and gender role identity that I hypothesize occurs in many boys during and after adolescence? As I see it, during adolescence and young adulthood the capacity for abstract reasoning and theorizing increases and the person's social world greatly expands. In addition, the meaning of the categories masculine and feminine change (Flavel & Markman 1980; Gilligan 1982; Kohlberg & Ullman 1974). Despite the existence of a homosexual script, self-labeling can change to accommodate a masculine label. According to this model, many boys become homosexual in a preadolescent environment in which they felt unmasculine and remain homosexual after they learn to view themselves as masculine. A large number of homosexual men thus seem to leave behind the childhood psychopathology associated with gender disturbance. In these individuals, superego and ego ultimately evolve normally despite childhood gender-self impairment. It is possible that, using Kohut's terminology (1971, 1977), key transmuting internalizations occur in these individuals, but later than normal and long after homoerotic fantasies have become diferentiated. With such internalization comes self-repair: the self is no longer perceived as damaged and self-esteem regulation is internalized and normalized. This assumes that many people accomplish without professional intervention what others can only accomplish through psychoanalysis. Childhood gender role/identity disturbances and diverse symptoms can occur in the backgrounds of men who do not manifest deviancy or clinically significant psychopathology as adults.

The concepts of deviant development and psychopathology during adulthood are often condensed in psychoanalytic clinical discussions. The theory I propose here takes issue with such condensation. In my view, a history of gender identity pathology during childhood should not be taken as evidence that differentiated homosexual fantasies in adults are motivated by unconscious irrational anxiety. It is also clear that a large group of men does not leave the psychopathology of early life behind. Gender identity disorders and/or various other symptoms sometimes persist. New symptoms and syndromes probably often start as a reaction to differentiated homosexual fantasies. Homophobia among idealized parents, teachers, and friends may be internalized by mechanisms of introjection and identification, leading to chronic depression and low self-esteem. This social-psychological dynamic is discussed in the chapter on masochistic character disorder. Not all individuals who experience this process become masochistic, however (despite being chronically depressed). This dynamic would not necessarily lead to different rates of depression in adults at opposite poles of the Kinsey scale. There are so many reasons for depression in adult life that group rates of depression may not reflect this mechanism.

Before proceding with the next part of the theoretical exposition, a brief summary is indicated.

There appears to be a relationship between homosexuality and childhood gender disturbance. Abundant research suggests that an unmasculine or feminized prepubertal self-image increases the likelihood of predominant or exclusive homosexual orientation. A masculine prepubertal self-image decreases the likelihood that an enduring link between sexual affect and same-gender sexual objects will be formed. A prepubertal unmasculine self-image is not the single cause of homosexuality, however, and it may also precede heterosexuality or bisexuality. Prepubertal self-evaluation as appropriately masculine depends to a large degree upon positive social experiences with other males— peers, older men, or both. These experiences are not unitary causes of masculine self-regard, however; they simply increase the probability of its emergence. They are best conceptualized as aspects of the environment conducive to a certain type of psychological growth. In many cultures, these positive social experiences often depend on a juvenile-age boy's manifesting some degree of competency at rough-and-tumble competitive activities. Such competency is not sufficient to develop masculine self-esteem, nor is its absence sufficient to develop a sense of unmasculinity. Its presence, however, increases the likelihood that a boy will be accepted by other boys and men.

Just as biology dictates the timing of gender identity differentiation during childhood, so it dictates when the imagery of erotic fantasy differentiates. Erotic fantasy differentiation, like gender identity differentiation, restricts future behavioral options. Sexual fantasy differentiation in males differs from gender identity differentiation in a number of respects, however. Whereas the core gender identity of normal children may be internalized largely as a result of social instruction, structuralized sexual fantasy, which usually emerges later in development, is not directly taught. It arises as a result of subliminal cognitive and physiological processes and symbolic processes that may be largely unconscious. Sexual fantasy differentiation occurs later in life than gender identity differentiation and, hypothetically, often depends on a basic judgment made about the self: the self assesses whether it is (adequately) masculine. This judgment is different than the earlier, more concrete judgment whether the self is male.

The notion of masculinity, more abstract than that of maleness, does not involve a process of psychological differentiation. Gender identity differentiates, and sexual fantasy differentiates, but the sense of masculinity does not differentiate. The sense of masculinity reflects continuous self-evaluation in terms of gender-valued ideals. In young children these ideals are conceptually concrete and relatively simple. In older boys they are conceptually abstract and much more elaborate. This in turn means that the contents of the ego ideal are subject to the influence of cognitive development and social experience. The contents of differentiated sexual fantasy, in contrast, are hypothesized not to be subject to the influence of cognitive development and social experience after differentiation has occurred.

For example, let us consider a gender-disturbed boy at two different periods of his life: the juvenile phase and late adolescence—early adulthood. During the juvenile phase this youngster believed that he was not adequately masculine because he lacked competency at and/or interest in male sex-typed activities that were valued by male peers and adults, including his father. As a result he was shunned and scapegoated by males. He may or may not have been accepted by females; if so, his friends and activities would have been girllike. In this psychological context, the boy probably, to his surprise, found himself experiencing erotic fantasies that were exclusively homosexual.

During adolescence, the boy's concepts about masculinity and femininity became much more complex. In addition, his interpersonal world greatly expanded. As a college senior, therefore, he has friends of both genders who value him and whom he values. These individuals do not sex-type rough-and-tumble activities as masculine, as did the boys he knew when he was younger. Perhaps when the young men who are now his friends were juvenile age, they were not harshly judgmental about stereotypical male behavior. Unfortunately, however, he did not know them as boys: the only males he knew had rigid values about what constituted masculine behavior. When young, the boy shared these values; he knew no better. As he grew older, however, the young man came to believe that activities and interests he previously felt were unmasculine are in fact quite masculine. His cognition became more abstract and his interpersonal world less constricted. As his concepts about masculinity changed, his sense of masculine self-regard also improved. Despite all these far-reaching changes in psychological functioning, however, his erotic fantasies never changed. His sexual orientation remained homosexual, as if it had differentiated like a physical structure.

TWO MODELS OF ADULT HOMOSEXUALITY: ARRESTED DEVELOPMENT VS. SEXUAL FANTASY DIFFERENTIATION

The predominant issue relevant to an understanding of sexual orientation and psychopathology is that of the potential for growth of the entire personality, despite the limits set by differentiated sexual fantasy. The theoretical perspective provided by differentiation theory as proposed above is different from that of classic psychoanalytic theory, which was succinctly put in a well-known statement by Karl Menninger: "From the standpoint of the psychiatrist, homosexuality constitutes evidence of immature sexuality and either arrested psychological development or regression. Whatever it be called by the public there is no question in the minds of psychiatrists regarding the abnormality of such behavior" (quoted in Bayer 1981, p. 39). The traditional psychoanalytic view is that homosexuality in adults occurs as a result of active mental processes that can be described psychodynamically. In homosexual men, these psychological developmental processes are said to be arrested, which means that heterosexuality can theoretically return if these processes are freed. Regression (i.e., to a fixation point) is believed to occur because of unconscious irrational anxiety. According to this model, if this anxiety diminishes through resolution of unconscious conflicts, then pathological regression also diminishes. This in turn leads to repression of the primitive-infantile fantasies that had previously been conscious.

According to this psychoanalytic model, homosexual fantasies are actively maintained in conscious mental life in the same way that all pathological symptoms and fantasies are. The meaning of homosexual fantasies in the adult can, according to this model, be understood in terms of their function. Much psychoanalytic literature is devoted to analysis of the function of homosexual fantasy and activity and this literature has been extensively reviewed (Fenichel 1945; Wiedeman 1962, 1974; Socarides 1978). The role of preoedipal cannibalistic oral-aggressive and anal-sadistic unconscious fantasies in homosexuality is stressed by a number of clinicians (Numberg 1938, Bibring 1940, Bergler 1959). Bychowski (1954) emphasized the association between homosexuality and ego weakness. Many analysts stress developmental and psychodynamic similarities between homosexuality and sexual perversions (Gillespie 1956, Miller 1956, Socarides 1978). The analytic literature describes homosexual fantasy and activity as defending against castration anxiety, separation anxiety, and dread of self-annihilation. Homosexuality is also hypothesized to defend against negative affects generally. As Socarides (1978) put it:

> Homosexuality is a living relic of the past testifying to the fact that there was once a conflict involving an especially developed component instinct in which complete victory was impossible for the ego and repression was only partially successful. The ego had to be content with the compromise of repressing the greater part of infantile libidinal strivings (primary identification with the mother; intense unneutralized aggression towards her; dread of separation; and fear of fusion) at the expense of sanctioning and taking into itself the smaller part. For example, the wish to penetrate the mother's body, or the wish to suck and incorporate and injure the mother's breast undergo repression. In these instances, a piece of the infantile strivings has entered the service of repression through displacement and substitution. Instead of the mother's body being penetrated, sucked, injured or incorporated, it is the male partner's body which undergoes this fate; instead of the mother's breast, it is the penis with which the patient interacts. Homosexuality thus becomes the choice of the lesser evil. (pp. 70–71)

Socarides' theory is not, I believe, valid for homosexual men in general; it is only (and only possibly) applicable to psychopathological subgroups. This is further illustrated in the quotation below. Here Socarides focuses on the relationship between the preoedipal developmental mechanisms outlined above and the function of homosexual fantasy and activity during adulthood.

> Two defense mechanisms, identification and substitution, play a crucial role. The homosexual makes an identification with the masculinity of his partner in the sexual act. In order to defend himself against the positive oedipus complex, that is, his love for his mother and hatred for his father and punitive aggressive destructive drives towards the body of his mother, the homosexual substitutes the partner's body and penis for the mother's breast. Homosexuals desperately need and seek a sexual contact whenever they feel weakened, frightened. depleted, guilty, ashamed, or in any way helpless or powerless. In the patients' words, they want their "shot" of masculinity. They then feel miraculously well and strengthened, thereby avoiding any tendency to disintegrative phenomena (they thereby enhance their self-representation). They instantly feel reintegrated upon achieving orgasm with a male partner. Their pain, fear, and weakness disappear for the time being and they feel well and whole again. (p. 71)

Here the function served by sexual contact for "homosexuals" is discussed without reference to the function served by sexual contact in general. Many heterosexual men, for example, also need and seek sexual contact whenever they feel weakened. In fact, subgroups of borderline and psychotic patients from all points on the Kinsey scale use sexualization pathologically, driven by a need to buttress the sense of self. Such mechanisms as identification and substitution, which Socarides attributes to homosexual men, probably occur predominantly in bisexual borderline men. (As pointed out in part 2, homosexual phenomena may be amplified for pathological reasons in subgroups of bisexual patients.) The functions of sexual fantasy and activity in men at higher levels of ego functioning are varied (Stoller 1979), but they include (in heterosexual, homosexual, and bisexual men) the expression of warmth and caring and sexual passion in the service of love.

The theory of sexual fantasy differentiation that I propose is different from that of Socarides and similar clinicians. I suggest that the psychological mechanisms by which sexual fantasy is maintained after differentiation are not active. Once fantasies differentiate as exclusively homosexual, they persist as a consequence of now passive structuralization, analogous to core gender identity differentiation. The model I propose further differs from a model of arrested development because my model does not suggest that in homosexual men vital parts of the total personality cease to develop in parallel with so-called arrested sexual development. In fact, a central feature of my model is that sexual fantasy differentiation is best understood as a phase of the differentiation process that begins prenatally. The rest of the personality, as it unfolds over time, is subject to different principles of organization. Personality "development" or "unfolding" is *not* integrated around heterosexuality in the sense that most psychoanalytic theories assume it to be.

In discussing the issue of homosexuality as psychopathology (chapter 12), I agree that homosexuality (including ego-dystonic homosexuality) should be dropped from the *Diagnostic and Statistical Manual*. At first glance this might seem inconsistent, since I emphasize the relationship between the onset of homosexuality and gender disturbance. The rationale for not considering exclusive homosexuality during adulthood as a form of psychopathology emerges from the model set forth above. If sexual fantasy differentiation is a phase-specific process, and the rest of the personality can continue to grow and develop no matter what the gender of the differentiated fantasies, then we can conceptualize a developmental track appropriately termed healthy for homosexual men. Beginning with the phase of sexual fantasy differentiation, there is good reason for using the same parameters to evaluate health and illness in all males, regardless of sexual orientation. Prior to differentiation, when homosexual phenomena are pathological (from a psychoanalytic perspective), they are best conceptualized as symptoms of an underlying disorder (usually gender identity disturbance) rather than as the primary manifestations of some type of "homosexual disorder." This view leaves room for the possibility that in a group so far insufficiently studied, homosexuality may appear "de novo," possibly for predominantly biological reasons and/or through psychological pathways that do not involve childhood pathology.

17

Sexual Fantasy, Ego, and Self

By the time Stoller formulated the concept of core gender identity (1968), the concepts of ego psychology had long been before the psychoanalytic community (Hartmann 1964) and it was widely recognized that drive theory had limitations, particularly in explaining the development of ego functions. Meanwhile, Kohut and his colleagues, working independently of Stoller, were formulating the basic concepts of psychoanalytic self psychology (Kohut 1971, 1977; Gedo & Goldberg 1973). Both ego psychology and self psychology provided perspectives about cognition and social behavior that could accommodate the new concept of CGI. Since gender identity acquisition was theorized to involve cognitive, perceptual, and social experience and behavior, and since it did not appear to be drive-related in an immediate, direct way, it seemed useful to many to conceptualize it in terms of ego and self.

Most psychoanalysts today would probably readily agree that basic psychoanalytic frameworks for understanding gender identity acquisition and self psychology have radically changed during the past two decades. This is probably not true of the determinants of erotic fantasy. Erotic fantasy appears so obviously to be drive-related that it seems almost inevitable that theories about it will be anchored in topographical and structural theory—which were originally constructed to help explain erotic behavior. In this chapter I argue that conflict theory is useful only in understanding specific, limited aspects of erotic fantasy. Other dimensions of erotic fantasy properly belong to a psychology of the self, not to a psychology of drives and conflict.

In chapter 1, four dimensions of sexual orientation are described: erotic fantasy, erotic activity with others, sense of identity, and social role. I emphasize there that the latter two psychological constructs involve cognitive-social behavior, not erotic experience and activity, and I suggest that one's sense of identity as gay or straight can be conceptualized in terms of Erikson's concept of ego identity. As described in clinical vignettes and in chapter 14 (on adolescence), the sense of identity evolves during adolescence and young adulthood.

Here I focus not on gay identity but rather on erotic fantasy during childhood and early adolescence. Juvenile or latency-age children have a sense of self-cohesion even though their identity as gay or straight has not yet coalesced.

SELF, GENDER SELF, AND SEXUAL GENDER SELF

Boys' self-concept is shaped by two major psychosexual differentiations. Core gender identity differentiation occurs in early childhood and shapes the self-concept in terms of gender. I hypothesize that a second psychosexual differentiation occurs in late childhood and early adolescence. This late-occurring differentiation, which has received relatively little psychoanalytic attention to date, shapes the self-concept in terms of erotic fantasy.

The differentiation of erotic fantasy divides childhood into two phases with regard to the experience of erotic imagery. The predifferentiation phase is characterized by great potential for conscious experience of a variety of erotic images. The types of imagery that are consciously experienced may be influenced by diverse factors, including neurotic conflict. Following the differentiation phase, however, the erotic image—heterosexual, homosexual, or bisexual—can best be conceptualized as a structural part of the core self-concept. After differentiation, the conscious presence of an exclusively homosexual erotic image no longer can be understood in terms of psychoanalytic theories of drive and conflict. Bisexuality is conceptualized differently (see chapter 18). These points are developed more completely below.

The Male Gender Self and the Female Gender Self

It is generally accepted that during early childhood, well before the oedipal phase, a sense of self-cohesion develops (Stern 1985). This includes, also in early childhood (probably during the second year of life), gender-self consolidation. From this perspective, a well-known remark of Kohut's must be qualified: "I suggest that we undertake the examination of the existence of a rudimentary self in earliest infancy from a perhaps surprising starting point, namely by stressing that the human environment reacts to even the smallest baby as if it had already formed such a self" (1977, p. 99). In fact, the reaction of the human environment to newborns is virtually always gender bound. Parents are not told by obstetricians, "Congratulations! It's a person!" They are told, "It's a boy" or "It's a girl." Following gender announcement, male and female infants embark upon different developmental pathways. After completion of the first postnatal differentiation phase, the sex differences in developmental pathways become even more pronounced

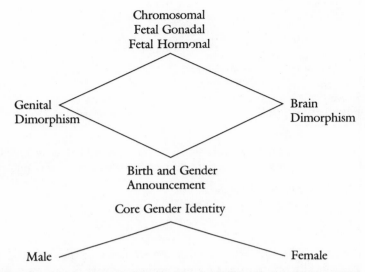

Fig. 17.1 Sequential components of gender identity differentiation (Money & Erhardt 1972, p. 3)

(Money & Ehrhardt 1972, Friedman, Richart & VandeWiele 1974). Where-as the prenatal differentiations were physiological, the differentiation of core gender identity can best be conceptualized as psychobiological. The critical timing of postnatal gender identity differentiation is biologically determined, although how this occurs is not yet known.

It has been insufficiently emphasized in psychoanalytic theory that males' and females' selves unfold along different lines. At least from the time of CGI differentiation, and possibly even earlier, it seems best to conceptualize two self theories: the theory of the unfolding male self and the theory of the unfolding female self.

The culmination of the *first* major phase of the unfolding of male and female selves is the differentiation of core gender identity. Money and Ehrhardt suggest that gender identity differentiation should be concep-tualized as an integral part of a differentiation sequence beginning prenatally (fig. 17.1).

The Male Sexual–Gender Self
I suggest that in males differentiation of erotic imagery as heterosexual or homosexual should be conceptualized as an additional part of the sequence diagrammed by Money and Ehrhardt. The terminal part of the sequence I propose is shown in figure 17.2. The preceding points may be summarized as follows: The cohesive nuclear self becomes in effect a gender self, either male or female, during the second year of life. This age has been described in psychoanalytic theory as preoedipal. I suggest that in boys the postoedipal

Core gender identity: Male (differentiates prior to age 3)

* Erotic fantasy differentiates exclusively heterosexual	* Erotic fantasy differentiates bisexual	* Erotic fantasy differentiates exclusively homosexual

*Time phase unknown but probably involves a large range between early oedipal years and early adolescence. The cutoff for differentiation may be close to puberty.

Fig. 17.2 Sexual fantasy differentiation

years are also critically important for the structure of the self. The affect of lust, biologically programmed to increase in intensity during late childhood, functions at that time as a new organizer of inner life (although sexual feelings do exist earlier). Male self-representation and consolidation are not complete until the conclusion of the late-occurring stage of erotic fantasy differentiation. Once lust and image are irreversibly linked, orienting erotic fantasy is best conceptualized as a self structure. Following completion of the differentiation phase, the male self is bounded and shaped both by gender and by limits on erotic options. In males, the gender self of early childhood is modified and becomes a sexual–gender self in late childhood. This is a normative phenomenon of self-definition. Just as almost all young boys are psychologically male, so most older boys belong to one of three categories: male with exclusively heterosexual erotic fantasy; male with exclusively homosexual erotic fantasy; or male with heterosexual and homosexual erotic fantasy.

THE HOMOSEXUAL FANTASY IMAGE AS A SYMPTOM DURING CHILDHOOD

I believe it remains conceptually useful for psychoanalysts to utilize a model of homoerotic fantasy image as a childhood symptom when considering lifelong, exclusive homosexual males. I must qualify this theory, however: unlike some theoreticians, I do not mean that the homoerotic image *must* be interpreted as a psychological symptom in every single case. I simply mean that the model of homoerotic fantasy image as a psychological symptom during childhood, prior to the differentiation phase, is frequently useful and probably may be helpfully applied to a great many individuals.

The term symptom is used here in a psychodynamic sense. According to traditional models, were it not for the existence of the symptom, the unpleasure generated by internal unconscious conflict would become conscious by overwhelming the ego defenses. The selected symptom, be it conversion reaction, phobia, or some other form of behavior, such as homoerotic image, theoretically leads to a sense of diminished unpleasure. In response to an internal signal of danger, the symptom also symbolizes a compromise between an unconscious wish and fear. The symptom functions to preserve psychological equilibrium but at a decreased adaptational level (Brenner 1973, 1976). In general, the mechanisms leading to symptom choice are not known. Psychoanalysts tend to rely on models of constitutional predisposition to help explain, for example, why one person with an obese gambler for a father becomes obese, but not a gambler, while another becomes a gambler but not obese. The rationale for the idea that the homoerotic image, in some subgroups, may be conceptualized as a symptom (e.g., similar to a conversion symptom) is empirical. Research has shown that childhood gender disturbance is often associated with individual and family psychopathology. It has also been demonstrated that childhood gender disturbance often precedes homosexuality (see parts 1–3). I speculate that as a general rule, a two-stage process leads to consciously perceived homoerotic imagery: (1) representation of the self in terms of imagery of gender disturbance, followed by (2) representation of the erotically desired others in terms of homosexual imagery. The *specific* reasons that (2) follows (1) are not known, any more than they were when it was hypothesized that maternal identification somehow caused homosexuality.

The differentiation theory outlined in this book posits that an exclusively homoerotic image may appear in consciousness during late childhood / early adolescence for reasons that are probably frequently psychopathological but need not necessarily be so. According to this theory, the psychodynamic *reason* that the homoerotic mental representation is conscious soon becomes irrelevant. No matter what its determinants, the homoerotic image, as a consequence of an innate biological clock, can become irreversibly and exclusively linked to lustful affect if it occurs in the conscious mind during late childhood. This idea of irreversibility is similar to that which applies to core gender identity. The irreversible nature of the connection between erotic image and lustful affect seems to be a general property of the male mind during late childhood / early adolescence. Although the contents of the mind during this phase may be influenced by pathological psychodynamic sequences, the process irreversibly linking the affect of lust with a visual image is normative in the same sense that the process of CGI differentiation is.

At this point I consider further the theory of sexual differentiation in terms of the concepts of ego and self. Hartmann (1964) defined the term ego as "a substructure of the personality defined by its functions" (p. 114). The functions that together constitute the ego include memory, perception, reality testing, the operation of the defenses and character traits, and the synthetic, integrating activities of the mind. Additional functions are described by Hartmann and others. Hartmann suggested that certain aspects of the ego are not derived from conflict between the drives and reality but rather are autonomous: "We may speak of an autonomous factor in Ego development in the same way as we consider the instinctual drives autonomous agents of development" (p. 119). The determinants of the primary structures of ego autonomy regulating memory, perception, and motility are thought to be partly biological and partly experiential. Phase-specific aspects of maturation influence these primary autonomous processes and in turn are influenced by psychobiological landmarks whose timing is independently determined.

> Concerning the development and the growth of the autonomous characteristics of the ego we may make the assumption that they take place as a result of experience (learning), but partly also of maturation—parallel to the assumption more familiar in analysis that processes of maturation intervene in the development of the sexual drives. . . .
>
> The problem of maturation has a physiological aspect. Speaking of this aspect we may refer to the growth of whatever we assume to be the physiological basis of those functions which looked at from the angle of psychology we call the ego; or we may refer to the growth of such apparatus which sooner or later come to be specifically used by the ego (e.g., the motor apparatus used in action). . . .
>
> We have to assume that differences in the timing or intensity of their growth enter the picture of ego development as a partly independent variable: e.g., the timing of the appearance of grasping, of walking, of the motor aspect of speech. . . .
>
> The presence of such factors in all aspects of the child's behavior make them also an essential element in the development of his self experience. (p. 121)

Hartmann also observed that structures originally deriving from conflict between drive and defense may undergo what he termed a change in function. They can then function in the service of the ego as "structures of secondary autonomy."

> What started in a situation of conflict may secondarily be part of the nonconflictual sphere. . . .
>
> . . . What developed as a defense against an instinctual drive may grow into a more or less independent and more or less structured function. . . .
>
> Because we know that the results of this development may be rather irreversible in most normal conditions, we may call such functions autonomous, though in a secondary way (in contradistinction to the primary autonomy of the ego I discussed before). (p. 123)

Hartmann's ideas have direct and obvious applicability to the theory of sexual object selection and differentiation discussed here. They are not sufficient, however, to describe the mental processes involved in the genesis *and perpetuation* of sexual fantasy. This requires consideration of the self as well as consideration of the ego as a mental agency. The term *self* in this book refers to the organization of the personality as a whole, in keeping with usage put forth by Kohut and members of his school. The term *ego* refers to a narrower segment of behavior than *self* (Gedo & Goldberg 1973).

Let us now direct our attention to the population of children in whom it is hypothesized that the motivation to experience exclusively homoerotic imagery (in the enabling environment of gender-disturbed self-representation) can best be understood in traditional psychoanalytic terms—that is, in whom the childhood homoerotic fantasy is a symptom. Hartmann's concept of primary and secondary autonomy can now be applied to this homosexual population, since the notion of psychosexual differentiation implies the concept of change of function. What once originated as a compromise formation in the context of intrapsychic conflict acquires autonomy as a consequence of having been, as it were, in the right mental place at the right time. The erotic image, which during one phase could be meaningfully conceptualized in terms of structural theory, now no longer can be.

I posit that following a critical phase, homoerotic imagery undergoes a change of function. This change is helpfully conceptualized as involving additional change in the mental agency in whose domain the differentiated fantasy belongs. After these changes occur, it makes the most sense to think of the erotic image as a core and autonomous structure of the self.

THE POSTDIFFERENTIATED HOMOEROTIC IMAGE: SELF PSYCHOLOGY VS. DRIVE-CONFLICT PSYCHOLOGY

In arguing that the effects of male erotic fantasy differentiation should be conceptualized in terms of self psychology, I extend the domain of self psychology beyond that proposed by Kohut and his colleagues. These theorists, however, have been incisive critics of the limitations of drive psychology. Kohut (1977) commented:

> The explanations of drive psychology of the structural model of the mind and of Ego psychology are satisfactory only insofar as the circumscribed area of the psychology (and especially of the psychopathology) of conflict is concerned. They deal with conceptual units too elemental to encompass the more complex psychic configurations we can recognize in health and disease as soon as our focus begins to encompass the participating self. (pp. 74–75)

In contrast with the view I propose of homoerotic imagery in the lifelong exclusively homosexual adult is the view that following differentiation the homoerotic image *is* best conceptualized as a symptom of unconscious irrational conflict. In this view, the homoerotic image is conceptualized in terms of drive-conflict theory. The two different perspectives are illustrated by Brenner's (1976) comments about conflict and symptom:

> A symptom "is a persistent or repeated evidence of a psychic conflict. . . .". . .

The fact that symptoms are persistent gives one a certain advantage in analyzing them. They present themselves as objects of study again and again and often over a long period of time. One can observe repeatedly the psychic context in which they reappear as well as the context that is associated with their recession or disappearance. . . .

There are forms of psychotherapy that focus exclusively on symptoms. By whatever different names they are called—conditioning, behavior modification, sex therapy—they have in common intentional neglect of the dynamics and history of the psychic conflicts of which symptoms are but one of the consequences. They focus only on the symptoms and they seek to cure symptoms—not to remove their cause. Analysis, by contrast, seeks to remove the cause of symptom formation, by enabling a patient to deal better with the conflicts that caused his symptoms in the first place, with the result that his symptoms disappear along with other improvements that take place in his mental life. (p. 144)

If one conceptualizes differentiated homoerotic imagery as a part of the structure of the self, one can properly psychoanalyze a homosexual person without expecting homosexual imagery to be replaced by heterosexual imagery. If, on the other hand, the homoerotic imagery is conceptualized as a symptom within the purview of conflict-drive theory, then one would expect psychoanalysis regularly to lead to radical and lasting change in sexual orientation. There is no adequate evidence that this is generally the case (Acosta 1975, Panel 1983).

The issue of change of sexual orientation, however, necessitates another qualification to the theory of erotic fantasy differentiation developed thus far. Although data are scant, the possibility cannot be ignored that a few individuals who appear to have differentiated as exclusively homosexual do in fact change their sexual orientation during adulthood. Often these people add heterosexual fantasy and activity to their behavioral repertoires. Although considerable movement toward the left side of the Kinsey scale occurs, some homosexual fantasy is usually retained.

For example, Pattison and Pattison (1980) studied eleven men who claimed to have changed their orientations from exclusive homosexuality to exclusive heterosexuality following profoundly meaningful religious experiences. Seven of these men continued to experience homosexual fantasies or impulses. Of the remaining four men, two "at some time" in their lives (prior to the change in sexual orientation) had considered themselves bisexual. Of the two remaining subjects, one was a twenty-one-year-old man who had identified himself as homosexual at age thirteen and had changed sexual orientation at age twenty, only one year prior to the study. Interestingly, he still retained some homosexual fantasies, although they were somewhat less intense than those of the seven men mentioned above. Thus, only one subject of the eleven in this study, a twenty-six-year-old unmarried man, actually reported complete change in erotic fantasy.

Other reports of change in sexual fantasy life exist (Bancroft 1974; Liss &

Welner 1973: Myerson & Lief 1976; Wellman 1956; West 1977). How is one to interpret the phenomenon of erotic fantasy/activity change in the light of the theory proposed in this book? Is the theory not weakened by such cases, even if they occur only rarely? I respond to this line of criticism as follows: the psychological theory put forth here is directed not at behavior as if it occurred in a vacuum but at human behavior, that is, the behavior of people. Most people seem to behave in conformance with the theory described in this and the preceding chapters. Some people, however, may not fit into this theory. If so, they should certainly be better understood by the psychoanalytic community than they are today. The reasons for apparent plasticity of erotic imagery in a relatively few men (irrespective of their Kinsey scale ratings) are not known. Perhaps there are interactions between the conscious experience of erotic imagery and the ability to be hypnotized or the capacity to experience other altered states of consciousness (Kroger & Fezler 1976). Individuals who seem to stand as exceptions to a general theory highlight the need for additional information and research. This is certainly true of the developmental theory put forth here.

Above, I focus on the concept of secondary autonomy. The model I propose, however, also leaves room for the possibility of direct, strong, constitutional predisposition toward homosexuality. Homoerotic imagery in such individuals can perhaps best be described in terms of the concept of primary autonomy. As previously noted, detailed description of individuals in whom the concept of primary autonomy could reasonably be applied remains to be provided. Many important questions about the psychodynamic aspects of male sexual orientation remain open. For example, the underlying biopsychosocial mechanisms leading to the relationship between self-representation and exclusive homoerotic fantasy are not clear. Psychodynamic explanations of the association between homosexuality and childhood gender disturbance have been offered by many psychoanalysts. Most of these theories were advanced even before the validity of the association between homosexuality and childhood gender disturbance was clearly established. A critical overview of the analytic and nonanalytic literature on the etiology of homosexuality suggests that, taken together, these psychodynamic theories are probably helpful in understanding aspects of childhood gender disturbance and homosexual object selection in subgroups of males. In other subgroups, however, the fundamental mechanisms responsible for the association between homosexuality and childhood gender disturbance must be considered obscure.

Psychodynamic theories have not adequately distinguished between erotic imagery and gender-valued self-representation. That is, the same sequences of psychodynamic mechanisms can be invoked to "explain" both homoerotic image and disturbed gender-self representation. The idea of pathological maternal identification illustrates this point. Global psychodynamic mechanisms must not be confused with specific biopsychosocial sequences that describe etiology. The same criticism applies to theories of psychodynamic aspects of male bisexuality as opposed to exclusive homosexuality. There is no psychodynamic theory in my view that adequately explains why some primarily homosexual males retain the capacity for some degree of heterosexual arousal while others do not. Similarly, it is unclear why some primarily heterosexual males have the capacity for some degree of homosexual arousal. Most psychoanalytic theoreticians have been interested primarily in the homosexual side of the homosexuality–heterosexuality spectrum. Many of these theorists underemphasized the fact that major questions concerning the developmental psychodynamics of heterosexuality in males are unanswered to date. When faced with the problem of clarifying the etiology of a specific behavior or set of behaviors, the contemporary psychoanalytic community still finds the concept of constitutional predisposition as useful as Freud did. It is now possible to acquire empirical information on specific biopsychosocial interactive sequences involving subjects with specific attributes. Psychoanalytically informed collaborative modern research may clarify many open questions in the sexual orientation field.

18

Hierarchy and
Sexual Orientation

The psychoanalytic concept of hierarchical organization of the mental apparatus must be critically reevaluated in light of modern ideas about gender and
sex. Rappaport (1960) succinctly reviewed the importance of the concept of
hierarchical organization in psychoanalytic theory:

> According to [the Jacksonian or neural integration hierarchy] model, the
> nervous system consists of a hierarchy of integrations in which the higher ones
> inhibit or control the lower, and damage to or suppression of the higher ones
> reinstates the function of the lower. When Freud abandoned his neurological
> anchorage . . . he ceased pursuing neuropsychological speculations and hypoth-
> esized hierarchically organized psychological systems patterned on Jackson's
> hierarchy of neural levels. . . . This is implied in one of the specifications
> of the reflex-arc model, namely, in the sequence of the Systems Unconscious,
> Preconscious, Conscious. . . . its utility is that it provides the means for systemat-
> ically coordinating those behavior phenomena which are not attended by volun-
> tary control and/or consciousness with those which are. Not only are the
> concepts of the Systems Unconscious, Preconscious, and Conscious (as well as
> those of the id, ego, and superego) organized according to this model, but Freud
> assumed that every advancement in psychic organization is accompanied by a
> new censorship . . . and his conception of the multiple layering of defenses with-
> in the ego also follows the same pattern. . . .
> . . . In Freud's theory, inhibition of lower levels by higher ones served as the
> model for the conceptualization of conflict. Thus inhibition became a dynamic
> event: the result of a clash of forces. To begin with . . . these forces were concep-
> tualized as the libidinal affects vs. the ego, the latter being the "ruling ideational
> mass" which serves reality, society, and morality. Later . . . this conception of
> conflict yielded to that of drives vs. censorship, the latter representing ego (self-

preservative) drives. . . . The final conception . . . was that of the interstructural conflict between the ego and the id, with the participation of the superego on one or both sides. . . . Thus, the Jacksonian model . . . served as the foundation for the concepts of unconscious conflict, inhibition, unconscious drive forces and counterforces, which led to the theory of symptoms, and ultimately to the theory of mental structure. (p. 23)

Core gender identity (CGI) is not a psychological construct that can be described in hierarchical terms. It is at the bottom of a hierarchy of cognitive organizational schemata, whose highest reaches contain abstract ideas about masculinity and femininity. Core gender identity is nonhierarchical when (as in the vast majority of human beings) it differentiates as male or female. In those rare instances when CGI does not differentiate, however (usually in hermaphrodites), the behaviors that appear to express gender identity at any given time are probably hierarchically organized.

Differentiation of erotic fantasy is much more complicated from the vantage point of the hierarchical model of the mind than is differentiation of CGI, because erotic fantasy involves more variability than gender differentiation does. Since almost everyone's gender differentiates as either male or female, a general principle about the nonreducibility of CGI can be applied to most people. A principle of nonreducibility of sexual fantasy, however, does not apply to most people. I advance a much more modest hypothesis: among most lifelong, exclusive homosexual men and most lifelong, exclusive heterosexual men, the differentiated erotic fantasy construct is irreducible, no matter what the influences in its original genesis. The principle of hierarchy no longer applies to it. It influences and shapes subsequent development in the same sense that CGI influenced and shaped previous development.

In discussing the concept of hierarchy Gedo and Goldberg (1973) observed, "in certain situations, regressions to more archaic modes of organization may occur, but functions that have attained autonomy from conflict may not participate in returns to more primitive positions" (p. 106). Gedo and Goldberg did not discuss homosexuality or heterosexuality in this context, but I think the above statement describes what happens to men with differentiated homosexual or heterosexual fantasies who experience severe psychopathology. The concept of regression to archaic modes of organization accurately describes the functioning of many psychological systems. The part of the self system consisting of differentiated sexual fantasy, however, is not subject to such regression.

TIM'S PSYCHOBIOGRAPHY RECONSIDERED

The case of Tim (presented in chapter 14) illustrates how the model proposed above might work. Tim's preadolescent development fits into traditionally accepted psychoanalytic models. His preadolescent intrafamilial relationships shared certain features with the disordered familial relationships often reported in the backgrounds of homosexual men (see chapter 5). Furthermore, because of poverty and social isolation, Tim's juvenile or latency age peer relationships were abnormal. These factors may have influenced sexual object selection prior to final differentiation. The mediating pathways could theoretically have been a negative oedipus complex, a prepubertal judgment (although not necessarily with pejorative connotations) that the self was unmasculine, and an intense longing for acceptable male companionship. Whatever the particular combination of biopsychosocial influences on sexual object selection, at some point in Tim's development the link between sexual affect and type of fantasized image appeared to be irreversibly forged. The exact age at which sexual imagery irreversibly differentiates is not known. However, given the fact that Tim experienced sexual imagery well prior to adolescence, it may be assumed that by mid- to late adolescence the imagery had differentiated as homosexual. Unfortunately for Tim, cultural abhorrence of homosexuality imposed particularly painful cognitive dissonances and adaptive strains on his efforts to create a sense of identity. Only in adulthood, many years after healthy heterosexual youngsters, was he able to achieve a notion of who he was in relation to others. Nonetheless, he ultimately accomplished this task.

BISEXUALITY AND UNCONSCIOUS HOMOSEXUALITY

The preceding discussion focused on life-long predominant or exclusive homosexuality. Consideration of bisexuality in its great diversity calls attention to additional issues.

The experience of many practitioners suggests that a functionalist approach is useful for understanding homosexual phenomena. Rather than dismissing such an approach in light of the preceding sections of this chapter, I want to advance the following hypothesis: in order for the postpubertal male to repress either homosexual or heterosexual fantasies, he must be meaningfully bisexual with respect to erotic imagery. By this I mean that erotic imagery is or has been consciously perceived to be directed toward both genders.

As noted in some of the clinical cases presented earlier, the imagery does not have to be bisexual at any specific moment in time in order for a man to be classified as bisexual. Many people capable of erotic arousal associated with imagery of both males and females may repress one component and experience themselves as heterosexual or homosexual at a given time. Care in taking the history will reveal, however, whether meaningful erotic arousal directed at the other gender was present in the past. Only in the group that has differentiated as bisexual in erotic fantasy can the orienting sexual imagery (that is, the consciously experienced erotic imagery that motivates sexual activity) be state-related. In men at opposite poles of the (lifelong) Kinsey spectrum, the gender of the object linked to the affect of lust is hypothesized not to be influenced by psychological state. The model for this type of categorization comes from the clinical situation and also from naturalistic sexual histories available to date (Gebhard 1972, 1974).

Psychoanalytic experience with retrospective distortion suggests that there are probably many patients whose initial sexual histories, as reported prior to extensive interviewing, transference regression, working through, and so on, change during the course of treatment. As a result of the psychoanalytic process of reconstruction, early experience may be recalled that is substantially different from that first reported. This clinical phenomenon illustrates that the two groups of exclusively heterosexual and homosexual men (those who can legitimately be placed at the poles of the Kinsey spectrum with regard to options available for lifetime erotic experience) are probably somewhat smaller than might be expected on the basis of initial presentation. Much need exists for data from the analytic community about change during analysis in current and remembered childhood erotic fantasy, and especially about the relationship between such change and actual erotic experience during childhood. Recognizing the sparseness of the database, I nonetheless suggest that late childhood and early adolescent differentiation of erotic imagery as heterosexual, homosexual, or bisexual limits the options available in the psychoanalytic situation. Sometimes during analysis a specific type of erotic imagery may appear to emerge into consciousness for the first time. I suspect that in these instances, lost memories will be recovered confirming that the supposedly novel fantasies were experienced during childhood. This conjecture remains to be validated by research data, however.

If one excludes from the general male population men who belong at either pole of the Kinsey spectrum for their entire sexual lives, one is left with a very large group of men. It is likely that these men, bisexual with respect to fantasy potential, most of whom consider themselves straight and some gay, account for a large percentage of the patients seen by analytic practitioners. I propose that if a man has had conscious access to bisexual erotic imagery, he may under certain circumstances repress or amplify either component, homosexual or heterosexual. These circumstances include unconscious irrational fears leading to sexualization as a defensive response (Coen 1981). Because of intrinsic features of cognition, including the psychobiological aspects of repression, I suggest that, postpubertally, orienting homosexual fantasy may be repressed only if heterosexual fantasy has already been experienced. Conversely, orienting heterosexual fantasy may be repressed only if homosexual fantasy has already been experienced. In cases of homosexuality vanishing after homosexual conflicts have been worked through, I suspect that the patients involved are actually bisexual. I cannot be sure about this, however, since detailed descriptive history of sexual fantasy is rarely included in the analytic literature. To date there is no generally accepted convention for documentation of sexual history.

UNCONSCIOUS HOMOSEXUALITY AND UNCONSCIOUS HETEROSEXUALITY

It is possible to define operationally the elusive concepts *unconscious homosexuality* and *unconscious heterosexuality* if these concepts are restricted to the bisexual population.

Unconscious homosexuality may be defined as fantasized motivation to experience homosexual activity that is unconscious because it is repressed. One infers the existence of unconscious homosexuality from critical analysis of all of the person's behavior; the inference is validated when the repressed homosexual fantasies emerge into consciousness. In some instances they amplify homosexual fantasies already present (thus the person moves to the right on the Kinsey spectrum). In other instances they appear in consciousness as if for the first time, previously experienced homosexual fantasies having been repressed. Overt homosexual fantasies motivate behavior in diverse ways depending on the patient's character structure: homosexual transference phenomena including homosexual love, admixtures of perverse or paraphiliac fantasies in a homosexual context, and acting out of the transference all may occur. Among people who are not in psychoanalysis or psychotherapy, conscious experience of homosexual fantasies may wax and wane naturalistically depending on life circumstances. With respect to psychopathology, the pathological functions of homosexual imagery, described by some analysts to characterize homosexuality itself, may motivate homosexual behavior in a subgroup of bisexual men. Consciously perceived homosexual imagery may be amplified in reaction to unconscious irrational anxiety involving preoedipal and/or oedipal conflicts. Evidence of gender disturbance sometimes, but not always, accompanies the homosexual component. (The pathological interactions between character structure and sexual imagery are discussed in part 2.)

I do not propose that amplification of homosexual imagery always indicates pathology. Pathological amplification appears common, however, and seems to account for many problems encountered routinely in clinical practice. Many people who experience amplification of the homosexual component of bisexual erotic imagery for nonpathological reasons never seek consultation with mental health professionals. Such amplification might occur in response to loving feelings for males, as a form of nonconstricting sexual expression, or as a liberating consequence of leaving noxious homophobic environments. Healthy amplification of homosexual imagery is probably common, just as pathological amplification of homosexual imagery is. In cases where a practitioner is required to judge the individual's balance between health and pathology, general clinical guidelines are applicable. The functions of the sexual fantasies are analyzed in the context of the patient's total adaptation.

Unconscious heterosexuality can be understood as similar to unconscious homosexuality. It may be defined as fantasized motivation to experience heterosexual activity that is unconscious because it is repressed. One infers the existence of unconscious heterosexuality from critical analysis of all of the person's behavior: the inference is validated when repressed heterosexual fantasies emerge into consciousness. In some instances they amplify heterosexual fantasies already present (thus moving a man to the left on the Kinsey scale); in other instances they appear in consciousness as if for the first time, since previously experienced heterosexual fantasies have been repressed. Overt heterosexual fantasies might motivate behavior in diverse ways depending on the patient's character structure: heterosexual transference phenomena, including heterosexual love, admixtures of perverse or paraphiliac fantasies in a heterosexual context, and acting out of the transference all may occur. Men who are not patients in psychoanalysis or psychotherapy may consciously experience heterosexual fantasy that waxes and wanes naturalistically depending on life circumstances. As outlined in part 2 of this book, heterosexual imagery is probably not used in the service of psychopathology as often as homosexual imagery is, but this phenomenon does sometimes occur.

The constructs of unconscious homosexuality and unconscious heterosexuality proposed here are radically different from those proposed by previous theoreticians. The primary difference is in the idea that the workings of the unconscious mind are bounded initially by gender differentiation and later by sexual fantasy differentiation. The same process of differentiation applies to homosexual and heterosexual boys. The content differs but the process does not. I hypothesize that following differentiation, most heterosexual men are not prone to unconscious homosexuality. There is no such construct in their unconscious minds. Similarly, following differentiation, most exclusively homosexual men are not prone to unconscious heterosexuality. The idea that boundaries are imposed on the working of the unconscious mind by the processes of gender and sexual fantasy differentiation in discrete subgroups of individuals abandons the model of a linear, optimally healthy development track. Unlike Rado and members of his school (1940, 1949), I suggest that the notion of a universal heterosexual motive, unconscious in homosexuals, does not fit the facts very well. In my view the concept of unconscious heterosexuality should be applied only to the bisexual population.

At this point it is helpful to elaborate on how erotic imagery in men might be repressed. All people probably have the capacity to repress the feeling of lust to some degree, although this capacity is probably dependent in part on psychoendocrine state. Functional hypoandrogenization decreases the capacity to experience lust, making repression easier, and functional hyperandrogenization (up to a point) increases the capacity, making repression more difficult. Men may experience focal decrease in sexual desire for a number of reasons, including unconscious irrational conflict. When decreased desire occurs for this reason, there are (at least) two ways of conceptualizing what has happened. A Kraeplinean nonpsychoanalyst might hypothesize that erotic desire has been extinguished, like the flame of a candle. A psychoanalyst would invoke the topographical model and hypothesize that the lust affect is still present in the mind but confined to the unconscious realm.

If lustful affect can be unconscious, does that not suggest that homosexuality can exist in the unconscious as well? If so, does this not contradict the notion proposed earlier that homoerotic fantasized imagery can be repressed only in bisexual individuals? I respond as follows: the gateway to consciousness does not admit "pure" lust, only the lust affect linked to visual imagery. The ways this imagery can be experienced consciously are limited as a result of the process of sexual fantasy differentiation that occurs in late childhood and early adolescence. Homosexual men can, of course, repress both the affective and imagistic components of a specific fantasy, just as heterosexual men can. For example, both homosexual and heterosexual men can lose desire for a specific partner because of unconscious conflict. Orienting erotic imagery, however, is not repressed. Inevitably, the homosexual man will experience lust again, and the lust affect will be linked to a homosexual fantasized image. The same applies to the heterosexual man. Thus limits are imposed on the possible conscious-preconscious experience of erotic fantasy by the differentiation of the sexual-gender self.

A clinical phenomenon described in chapter 11 (on paranoia) is relevant here. Ovesey (1955a, b; 1969) extensively discusses the tendency in some men whose conscious erotic experience is exclusively heterosexual to experience homosexual dreams or fantasies. These men's dreams or fantasies are never associated with erotic arousal. The self-representation imagery can be further altered by the defensive processes of some heterosexual patients, to emerge as obsessive ruminations and worries about "being" homosexual. Symptoms may take the form of auditory hallucinations, ideas of reference, or delusions in extremely ill patients. Should this type of clinical phenomenon be taken as evidence of unconscious homosexuality in men who are supposedly heterosexual but at a deep level not really so? I believe not. Throughout this book I stress the importance of the distinction between gender disorder and homosexuality. As noted in chapter 4, Freud frequently condensed the two categories of behavior, and subsequent analytic thinking has tended to equate passive-feminine with homosexual behavior. This unfortunate tendency ignores the distinction between gender-related and erotic experience and behavior. Keeping the distinction in mind, one notes that some men whose erotic fantasy is exclusively heterosexual represent the self in feminine or unmasculine gender-valued imagery. Clinically, this phenomenon is usually episodic and is associated with profound shame and loss of masculine self-regard. The episodes often occur in response to psychosexual stress, such as competitive defeat by a powerful male or failure to perform sexually. One patient, for example, was shamed by a powerful boss. "I felt like he whipped my ass," he said, "and I left our meeting with my tail between my legs." That night, the patient dreamed that he was gang-raped by hoodlums. He was further shamed by this dream because he had never experienced erotic arousal associated with homosexual imagery in waking life or in remembered dreams, and he had negative feelings about homosexuality.

One way of conceptualizing this phenomenon is to hypothesize that repressed homosexual conflicts and homosexual imagery emerged into consciousness as a consequence of regressive anxiety—the lust affect, however, remained repressed. A different way of looking at the phenomenon is to assume that the core conflict involved gender disturbance, not erotic experience. Homoerotic imagery was chosen to symbolize damage to the male (sexual-gender) self. This wound to the gender-valued self-representation was associated with damage to masculine self-esteem.

Ovesey described this theory of homosexual imagery in heterosexual men. Additionally, I suggest that exclusive heterosexuality may be understood as a differentiation, associated with loss of the capacity to experience meaningful homoerotic fantasy. I assume that because these men came through the sexual differentiation phase as exclusively heterosexual, no meaningful homoerotic fantasy option is available to them during adulthood. In these men, sexualization with homoerotic imagery cannot occur. In my view, the subgroup of men described by Ovesey suffer from gender/psychopathology more subtle than that described in *DSM-III-R*. Their gender disturbance is revealed primarily to psychotherapists and might best be called "atypical gender identity disorder."

These issues become even more complex in light of Ovesey's (1969) clinical observation that pseudohomosexual conflicts may motivate erotic as well as nonerotic homosexual imagery. This phenomenon is compatible with my developmental model. I suspect that it is restricted to the subgroup of males whose erotic fantasy differentiation during late childhood / early adolescence was bisexual. The homoerotic component of their bisexual complex can be amplified for a number of reasons, including pathological ones. Thus, when psychopathology-psychodynamics involves what Ovesey terms the pseudo-homosexual conflict, these men may amplify their homoerotic feelings.

The concept of hierarchy previously discussed with regard to exclusive homosexuality and heterosexuality is now reconsidered with regard to bisexuality. I hypothesize that the traditional hierarchical model *is* applicable to most men whose erotic fantasies differentiate as bisexual. The model described above suggests that the differentiation of sexual fantasy imposes boundaries and limits on mental functioning in categorical terms rather than along continuous dimensions.

I propose that sexual fantasy differentiates as a fundamental self structure in virtually all males. The gender self of preoedipal years becomes a sexual-gender self by adolescence. This progression occurs in a biologically determined, phase-specific sequence in males. A male's sexual-gender self is a precursor to sexual identity (identity as homosexual or gay, heterosexual or straight, or bisexual), which occurs in late adolescence or early adulthood.

In addition to its role in shaping self-representation and identity, sexual fantasy serves other adaptive and maladaptive functions, which tend to occur within the context of the three basic types of sexual fantasy self-structures: heterosexual, homosexual, and bisexual. Sexual experimentation, interest in pornography, and even most paraphilias are also limited and bounded in this way.

In bringing to a close this section on theory I emphasize that many key aspects of the mechanisms by which fantasized imagery is joined with lustful affect remain obscure. Research studies have elucidated some features of the context within which the linkage occurs in some subgroups of males, but the underlying mental and physiological mechanisms are not yet well understood. Description of ontogenetic unfolding of behavior helps correct misunderstandings but must not be construed as understanding of etiology.

19

Conclusion: Psychoanalysis, Science, and Homosexuality

The history of psychoanalytic thought about homosexuality reveals major problems pervading psychoanalysis today. Recently, formidable critics have suggested that psychoanalysis rests on an unstable foundation. It has not been scientifically validated, either as a system of psychology or as a method of treatment (Grunbaum 1984). Freud's efforts to understand symptoms and treat patients led to most of the central hypotheses of psychoanalysis. Subsequent advances in descriptive psychiatry, the neural sciences, physiology, psychopharmacology, clinical, developmental, and neuropsychology have invalidated some of these hypotheses and have posed serious problems for others.

Psychoanalysts' stance on homosexuality as a form of psychopathology has been of interest to contemporary academicians and the general public. Much material in this area was reviewed by Bayer (1981), who paid particular attention to the disagreements among psychoanalysts, psychiatrists, and gay activists over the American Psychiatric Association's decision to drop homosexuality (per se) from the diagnostic nomenclature.

A historical perspective about psychoanalytic models of psychopathology helps clarify the relationship between homosexuality and psychopathology. While theories that viewed homosexuality as psychopathology were being advanced by psychoanalysts such as Bergler (1959) and Socarides (1978), others were hypothesizing that diverse symptoms (even those of psychotic, psychosomatic, and affective disorders) resulted from anxiety produced by severe intrapsychic conflict (Arieti 1967). Hypotheses about psychodynamic mechanisms of influence on psychopathology have since been refined; they are now more modest, in keeping with increasingly sophisticated understanding of biopsychosocial interactions in health and disease. Knowledge of biological and social determinants of behavior has provided a new perspective on psychopathology, and many exclusively psychodynamic models of symptoms and syndromes have become outmoded. A number of older psychoanalytic assumptions about normal development have not stood up well. At present, for example, there is still no unified, integrated, cohesive body of psychoanalytic developmental theory generally valid for females (Bardwick 1971, Frieze et al. 1978).

Concepts about male homosexuality, of undeniable importance in their own right, are also an organic part of larger issues in the history of psychoanalytic ideas. Despite the centrality of homosexuality in psychoanalytic theory, assumptions about the etiology of homosexuality are only scantily supported by scientific evidence. In a voluminous literature on sexual orientation, one finds reports of relatively few scientific studies of the subject carried out by psychoanalysts. (The research reported by the Society of Medical Psychoanalysts, discussed in part 1, stands as a noteworthy exception to this general trend [Bieber et al. 1962].) Associated with the paucity of research studies is selective inattention to the distinctions between the case method and the scientific study method as ways of collecting, organizing, and interpreting data. This is a serious problem throughout psychoanalysis today.

For example, suppose that a psychoanalytic clinician-theoretician, using his private practice as a database, notices that almost all the homosexual men in his sample have unresolved preoedipal conflicts. He might reasonably infer that these men probably did not successfully negotiate the separation-individuation phase of early childhood. He might conclude that early childhood stress leads to obligatory, exclusive homosexuality and that stress occurring during the later oedipal phase leads to partial, nonobligatory homosexuality (i.e., bisexuality).

The scientific method of research is designed to provide safeguards against error: the clinical case method is not as effective in that regard. This psychoanalyst thus might come to his conclusion about homosexuality because he had access predominantly to homosexual patients with borderline levels of personality integration. His data might lead him to suggest that all homosexual men are borderline or that a similar developmental trauma occurs in each prehomosexual boy, leading to impaired separation and individuation. It is theoretically possible, however, that the dynamics noted by the analyst actually apply to all *borderline* individuals (including a subgroup of homosexuals) and are not specific for homosexuality at all.

This example does not simply focus on psychopathology and homosexuality but also illustrates that without agreed-upon methodological conventions, theories risk losing fit with reality (Panel 1983).

Whereas the scientific method is basically demonstrative, the clinical case method is primarily illustrative. At one time both approaches were actively used by the psychoanalytic community. Two major research projects were undertaken on human sexuality: the Benedek and Rubenstein study of the menstrual cycle (1939) and Bieber and colleagues' investigation of male homosexuality (1962). Psychoanalysts were heavily involved in research in many other areas as well. More recently, however, psychoanalysis has moved away from research toward clinical work and theory. This tendency has produced significant difficulties for psychoanalysis both as a system of psychology and as a form of therapy. Thus Edelson (1984) recently cited Rappaport, who observed that "much of the evidence for theory remains phenomenological and anecdotal even if its obviousness and bulk tend to lend it a semblance of objective validity" (p. 3). Edelson himself noted, "certainly some psychoanalysts have still felt free to indulge in the delusions that their heaps of clinical observations, case reports, vignettes and anecdotes do meet scientific requirements for empirical evidence" (p. 2).

Psychoanalysts have continually shown interest in the various meanings that people attribute to their experience and behavior. But behavioral models that primarily emphasize individual meanings risk providing an inadequate conceptual basis for therapy. A cardiologist who had to make treatment decisions using the type of database presently available to psychoanalysts treating patients with sexual orientation problems would understandably be anxious.

The weak scientific support for psychoanalytic assumptions is illustrated by the recent history of the relationship between psychiatry and psychoanalysis with regard to homosexuality. Homosexuality was dropped from *DSM-III* for scientific, not ideological, reasons. Psychoanalysts were held scientifically accountable for the claim made by many that homosexuality was pathological; the scientific database supporting their assertion was inadequate. Psychiatrists, on the other hand, possessed a number of well-designed investigations that raised serious questions about psychoanalytic assumptions that homosexuality per se is pathological (e.g., DHEW 1972; Saghir & Robins 1973). The situation was complicated by the fact that not all psychoanalysts believed homosexuality to be pathological. But those—Judd Marmor, for example—who took exception to the pathological model were not in the psychoanalytic mainstream: the orthodox psychoanalytic view of homosexuality was that it is pathological.

At the same time that psychiatrists were asking psychoanalysts to validate their claims scientifically, the gay community was also demanding accountability. Although the role of gay activists in this issue was much publicized, it did not in itself influence the *DSM-III* committee. Had there been a solid body of data contradicting the activists' claims, the American Psychiatric Association would have been obligated to retain the category homosexuality as a mental disorder. Had APA not removed homosexuality from its nomenclature, it would have had to explain why it chose to ignore extrapsychoanalytic scientific data and the opinions of some psychoanalysts in favor of one major psychoanalytic study (Bieber 1962) and the assertions of other select authorities.

Such a decision would have been incompatible with APA's position as a branch of medical science.

Whereas academic psychiatry has retained adherence to the scientific method, it often seems to have sacrificed a generally agreed upon integrative model of the mind. During the late 1940s and 1950s, the predominant psychiatric model of the mind was based on the psychoanalytic model. As the two fields lost touch, psychiatrists turned to progressively more reliable and valid methods of inquiry but often relinquished a general model of health and illness. Psychoanalysts meanwhile became preoccupied by models of the mind but often seemed to relinquish reliable and valid methods of inquiry. Patients could thus elect treatment by therapists, with reliable and valid methods of diagnosis and research but no integrative model of the mind, or psychoanalysts, with (more or less agreed upon) models of the mind but no reliable and valid methods of diagnosis or research. This has probably produced difficulties for many patients, including those with problems involving sexual orientation.

For example, naive reassurance of men with pathological homosexual symptoms is probably not uncommon among psychiatrists who adhere to the diagnostic methods of *DSM-III-R* without using a model of the mind to critically evaluate the whole patient. On the other hand, some psychoanalysts' overenthusiastic attempts to change patients' sexual orientations are probably often due to adherence to an outdated model of the mind. In *The Foundations of Psychoanalysis* (1984), Grunbaum advanced three conclusions about the validity of psychoanalytic theories:

1. Insofar as the evidence for the psychoanalytic corpus is now held to derive from the productions of patients in analysis, this warrant is remarkably weak.
2. In view of my account of the epistemic defects inherent in the psychoanalytic method, it would seem that the validation of Freud's cardinal hypotheses has to come, if at all, mainly from well designed extra-clinical studies, either epidemiologic or . . . experimental . . . but that appraisal is largely a task for the future.
3. Despite the poverty of the clinical credentials it may perhaps still turn out that Freud's brilliant theoretical imagination was actually quite serendipitous for psychopathology or the understanding of some subclass of slips. Yet, while psychoanalysis may thus be said to be scientifically alive, it is currently hardly well, at least insofar as its clinical foundations are concerned. Nor is there a favorable verdict from such experimental findings as we had occasion to canvass. (p. 278)

In considering how to improve the scientific foundations of psychoanalysis, many critics have pointed to the need for widespread clinical investigation (Panel 1983, Edelson 1984, Grunbaum 1984). But meaningful advances can be made on a less ambitious level as well. There are many aspects of human behavior, including sexual orientation, about which so little is known that a simple, prescientific, empirical approach could tell us a great deal. For example, a central question in the literature on psychodynamics and psychopathology in relation to sexual orientation involves the degree to which a man's Kinsey rating can change over time. This question bears on the issue of differentiation of sexual fantasy. No database of the entire population of boys and men in psychotherapy or psychoanalysis exists with which to answer these questions about Kinsey rating: What are the limits of lasting change in Kinsey number (in fantasy and/or activity)? What life events outside the therapeutic situation seem to be associated with change in Kinsey number? What are the transference dynamics apparently associated with such change? What are the developmental and familial characteristics of people who experience maximal change in Kinsey number compared to those who do not? What are the psychoneuroendocrine profiles, cognitive styles, neuropsychological characteristics, and sexual histories of the two groups?

Some of these questions can be addressed (at least in a preliminary way) by psychoanalytic practitioners; others require follow-up studies. The point of this example is that our ignorance about huge areas of behavior is so vast that the most elementary of empirical approaches can produce much needed information.

At present, research and therapy involving male sexual orientation is conducted within a social context that is often sexist and antihomosexual (Brown 1976, Frieze et al. 1978, Kleinberg 1980, Marotta 1981, Janssen-Jurreit 1982, Lewin 1984). From a research perspective, it is probably impossible to obtain a representative sample of men whose sexual fantasy and activity would be rated 4–5 or 6 on the Kinsey scale, because many such subjects will not volunteer for research studies despite assurances of confidentiality. It is likely that a large hidden population exists, investigation of which is difficult or impossible because of discrimination and prejudice. From a treatment perspective, irrational antihomosexual attitudes prevalent in contemporary culture often lead to painful emotional burdens for patients, their families, and their therapists, examples of which are illustrated in this book.

In order to help patients effectively no matter what their sexual orientation, analysts should reconstruct childhood histories as accurately as possible. These histories often reveal evidence of exposure to harshly sexist and homophobic peers and adults during the patients' early lives. Despite investigators' and psychoanalysts' humanitarian wishes, the interpersonal worlds of boys and men are often replete with sex-role stereotypes. Study is needed of the consequences and causes of such stereotypical thinking in both children and adults. I hope that such investigation and continuing study of prejudice in general will lead to progress in correcting antihomosexual attitudes and values. This is particularly needed at present in light of the AIDS epidemic (Altman 1987). Such studies would provide behavioral data needed for sound public health planning.

The issue of homosexuality may be viewed as a window that opens onto the vast area of normal and pathological human behavior. Given the extraordinary problems inherent in making sense of the complex interactions within and between multiple levels of behavioral organization, and notwithstanding the criticisms noted above, it is remarkable that psychoanalysis has been able to accomplish so much in such a short time. Many of the accepted facts about sexual orientation are attributable to insights originally contributed by psychoanalysts.

For example, the relationship between childhood gender identity disorder and homosexuality was presaged by the concept of maternal identification. Basic concepts of defense, symptom, unconscious motivation, irrational conflict, and the workings of the primary process seem vital and necessary for understanding human sexual behavior (Engel 1962, Reiser 1984). A historical perspective, however, suggests that the next phase of the growth of psychoanalysis must involve enthusiastic movement toward empiricism and integration of psychoanalytic views with those from other fields. This movement should enhance understanding of all areas of human behavior, including that of sexual orientation.

References

Readers unfamiliar with psychoanalytic terminology used in this book are referred to the following:

Moore, B. & Fine, B. D. 1968. *The Glossary of Psychoanalytic Terms and Concepts,* 2d ed. New York: International Universities Press. A new edition is in preparation.

American Psychiatric Association. 1987. Appendix C: Glossary of Technical Terms. *Diagnostic and Statistical Manual,* 3d ed., rev. (*DSM-III-R*). Washington, D.C.: Amer. Psychiat. Ass. Press, pp. 389–405.

Abraham, K. 1921. Contributions to the Theory of the Anal Character. Reprinted in *On Character and Libido Development.* New York: Basic Books, 1966, pp. 165–88.

Acosta, F. X. 1975. Etiology and Treatment of Homosexuality: A Review. *Arch. Sex. Behav.* 4(1):9–28.

Akhtar, S. 1984. The Syndrome of Identity Diffusion. *Amer. J. Psychiat.* 141(11): 1381–85.

Alexander, F. G. & Selesnick, S. T. 1966. *The History of Psychiatry.* New York: Harper & Row.

Altman, D. 1987. *AIDS in the Mind of America.* Garden City, N.Y.: Doubleday.

Apperson, L. B. & McAdoo, W. G., Jr. 1968. Parental Factors in the Childhood of Homosexuals. *J. Abnorm. Psychol.* 73:201–06.

Arieti, S. (Ed.) (1967). *American Handbook of Psychiatry,* 9th ed., vol. 2, pt. 2: The Psychoneuroses; pt. 3: The Functional Psychoses; pt. 5: Psychosomatic Medicine. New York: Basic Books.

Arlow, J. 1949. Anal Sensation and Feelings of Persecution. *Psychoan. Quart.* 18: 79–84.

Asch, S. S. 1985. The Masochistic Personality. In *Psychiatry,* vol. 1., ed. J. O. Cavenar and R. Michels. Philadelphia: Lippincott.

Bak, R. 1946. Masochism in Paranoia. *Psychoan. Quart.* 15:285–301.

Bakwin, H. D. 1968. Deviant Gender-Role Behavior in Children: Relation to Homosexuality. *Pediatrics* 41:620–29.

Bancroft, J. 1974. *Deviant Sexual Behavior: Modification and Assessment.* New York: Oxford University Press.

Bardwick, J. M. 1971. *Psychology of Women.* New York: Harper & Row.

Baum, M. J., Carroll, R. S., Erskine, M. S. & Tobet, S. A. 1985. Neuroendocrine Response to Estrogen and Sexual Orientation. *Science* 230:960–61.

Baumeyer, F. 1956. The Schreber Case. *Int. J. Psycho-anal.* 37:61–74.

Bayer, R. V. 1981. *Homosexuality and American Psychiatry: The Politics of Diagnosis.* New York: Basic Books.

Bell, A. P. & Weinberg, M. S. 1978. *Homosexualities: A Study of Diversity among Men and Women.* New York: Simon & Schuster.

Bell, A. P., Weinberg, M. S. & Hammersmith, S. K. 1981. *Sexual Preference: Its Development in Men and Women.* Bloomington: Indiana University Press.

Bene, E. 1965. On the Genesis of Male Homosexuality: An Attempt at Clarifying the Role of the Parents. *Brit. J. Psychiat.* 111:803–13.

Benedek, T. & Rubenstein, B. B. 1939. Correlations between Ovarian Activity and Psychodynamic Processes, pt. 1: The Ovulative Phase; pt. 2: The Menstrual Phase. *Psychosomatic Medicine* 1:245–70, 461–85. Also see T. Benedek, *Studies in Psychosomatic Medicine: Psychosexual Functions in Women.* New York: Ronald Press, 1952.

Bergler, E. 1944. Eight Prerequisites for Psychoanalytic Treatment of Homosexuality. *Psychoan. Rev.* 31:253–86.

———. 1951. *Counterfeit Sex.* New York: Gruen & Stratton.

———. 1952. *The Superego.* New York: Gruen & Stratton.

———. 1956. *Homosexuality: Disease or Way of Life?* New York: Hill & Wang.

———. 1959. *1,000 Homosexuals.* Patterson, N.J.: Pageant Books.

Berliner, G. 1958. The Role of Object Relations in Moral Masochism. *Psychoan. Quart.* 27:38.

Bibring, G. L. 1940. On an Oral Component in Masculine Inversion. *Int. Z. Psychoan.* 25:125–30.

Bieber, I., et al. 1962. *Homosexuality: A Psychoanalytic Study of Male Homosexuals.* New York: Basic Books.

Birk, L., Williams, G., Chasin, M. et al. 1973. Serum Testosterone Levels in Homosexual Men. *New Engl. J. Med.* 289:1236–38.

Blos, P. 1962. *On Adolescence: A Psychoanalytic Interpretation.* New York: Free Press.

Blum, H. 1980. Paranoid and Beating Fantasies: An Inquiry into the Psychoanalytic Theory of Paranoia. *J. Amer. Psychoan. Ass.* 28:331–61.

Bohlen, J. & Heston, C. C. 1986. Personal communication.

Boswell, J. 1980. *Christianity, Social Tolerance, and Homosexuality.* Chicago: University of Chicago Press.

Braatan, L. J. and Darling, C. D. (1965). Overt and Covert Homosexual Problems Among Male College Students. *Genetic Psychology* Monographs. 71:269–310.

Brenner, C. 1973. *An Elementary Textbook of Psychoanalysis,* rev. ed. New York: International Universities Press.

_____. 1976. *Psychoanalytic Technique and Psychic Conflict*. New York: International Universities Press.

Brodie, H. K. H., Gartrell, N., Doering, C. et al. 1974. Plasma Testosterone Levels in Heterosexual and Homosexual Men. *Amer. J. Psychiat.* 131(1):82–83.

Brown, D. G. 1963. Homosexuality and Family Dynamics. *Bull. Menninger Clin.* 27(5):227–32.

Brown, H. 1976. *Familiar Faces, Hidden Lives*. New York: Harcourt Brace Jovanovich.

Bychowski, I. G. 1954. The Structure of Homosexual Acting Out. *Psychoan. Quart.* 23:48–161.

Cameron, N. 1959. The Paranoid Pseudo-Community Revisited. *Amer. J. Soc.* 55:52.

_____. 1967. Paranoid Reaction. In *Comprehensive Textbook of Psychiatry*, ed. A. M. Freedman & H. I. Kaplan. Baltimore: Williams & Wilkens.

Carlson, G. & Cantwell, D. P. 1980. Unmasking Masked Depression in Children and Adolescents. *Amer. J. Psychiat.* 137:445–49.

Cass, V. C. 1984. Homosexual Identity Formation: Testing a Theoretical Model. *J. Sex Research* 20(2):143–67.

Churchill, W. 1967. *Homosexual Behavior among Males: A Cross-Cultural and Cross-Species Investigation*. New York: Hawthorne Books.

Clark, T. R. 1975. Homosexuality and Psychopathology in Nonpatient Males. *Amer. J. Psychoan.* 35:163–68.

Cleckly, H. 1964. *The Mask of Sanity*. St. Louis: C. V. Mosby.

Coates, S. & Person, E. S. 1985. Extreme Boyhood Femininity: Isolated Behavior or Pervasive Disorder? *J. Amer. Acad. Child Psychiat.* 24(6):702–09.

Coates, S. & Zucker, K. 1988. Gender Identity Disorder in Children. In *Clinical Assessment of Children: A Biopsychosocial Approach*. Ed. C. J. Kestenbaum & D. T. Williams. New York: New York University Press.

Coen, S. J. 1981. Sexualization as a Predominant Mode of Defense. *J. Amer. Psychoan. Ass.* 29(4):893–920.

Cooper, A. 1980. Masochism: Current Concepts. Panel chaired by A. Cooper. Reported by Fisher, *J. Amer. Psychoan.* 29:673–88.

_____. 1984. The Unusually Painful Analysis: A Group of Narcissistic-Masochistic Characters. In *Psychoanalysis: The Vital Issues*, vol. 2, ed. G. H. Pollock and J. E. Gedo. New York: International Universities Press, pp. 45–67.

_____. In press. The Narcissistic-Masochistic Character. In *Psychoanalytic and Psychotherapeutic Perspectives*, ed. R. Glick. Hillsdale, N.J.: Analytic Press.

Cooper, A. et al. 1964. The Masochistic Character: Panel Discussion. *Bull. Ass. Psychoan.* 3.

Dank, B. M. 1971. Coming Out in the Gay World. *Psychiatry* 34:180–97.

Deutsch, H. 1942. Some Forms of Emotional Disturbance and Their Relationships to Schizophrenia. *Psychoan. Quart.* 11:301–21.

DHEW (Dept. of Health, Education and Welfare). 1972. *NIMH Task Force on Homosexuality: Final Report and Background Papers*. Pub. no. (HSM) 72-9116. Washington, D.C.: GPO.

Diamond, M. 1982. Sexual Identity: Monozygotic Twins Reared in Discordant Sex Roles and a BBC Follow-up. *Arch. Sex. Behav.* 11:181–86.

Dörner, G., Gotz, F., Rohde, W. 1975. On the Evocability of a Positive Oestrogen

Feedback Action on LH Secretion in Female and Male Rats. *Endokrinologie* 66:369–72.

Dörner, G., Rohde, W. & Schnorr, D. 1975. Evocability of a Slight Positive Oestrogen Feedback Action on LH Secretion in Castrated and Oestrogen-Primed Men. *Endokrinologie* 66:373–76.

Dörner, G., Rohde, W., Stahl, F., Krell, L. & Masius, W. G. 1975. A Neuroendocrine Predisposition for Homosexuality in Men. *Arch. Sex. Behav.* 4:1–8.

Dörner. G. 1976. *Hormones and Brain Differentiation.* Amsterdam: Elsevier.

Dörner, G., Geir, T., Ahrens, L., Krell, L., Munx, G., Sieler, H., Kittner, E. & Muller, H. 1980. Prenatal Stress as Possible Aetiogenetic Factor of Homosexuality in Human Males. *Endokrinologie* 75:365–68.

Douglas, C. J., Kalman, C. M. & Kalman, T. P. 1985. Homophobia among Physicians and Nurses: An Empirical Study. *Hospital and Community Psychiat.* 36(12): 1309–11.

Durkheim, E. 1897. *Suicide,* ed. and trans. G. Simpson. New York: Free Press, 1951.

Easser, B. R. & Lesser, S. R. 1965. Hysterical Personality: A Reevaluation. *Psychoan. Quart.* 34:390–495.

Eckert, E. D., Bouchard, J., Bohlen, J. & Heston, L. 1986. Homosexuality in Monozygotic Twins Raised Apart. *Brit. J. Psychiat.* 148:421–25.

Edelson, M. 1984. *Hypothesis and Evidence in Psychoanalysis.* Chicago: University of Chicago Press.

Ehrhardt, A. A. & Meyer-Bahlburg, H. F. L. 1981. Effects of Prenatal Sex Hormones on Gender-Related Behavior. *Science* 211(20):1312–18.

Ehrhardt, A. A., Meyer-Bahlburg, H. F. L., Rosen, L. R., Feldman, J. F., Veridianon, P., Zimmerman, I. & McEwen, B. S., 1985. Sexual Orientation after Prenatal Exposure to Exogenous Estrogen. *Arch. Sex. Behav.* 14:157–77.

Ehrhardt, A. A., Epstein, R. & Money, J. 1968. Fetal Androgens and Female Gender Identity in the Early Treated Adrenogenital Syndrome. *Johns Hopkins Med. J.* 122:160–67.

Ehrhardt, A. A., Evers, K. & Money, J. 1968. Influence of Androgen and Some Aspects of Sexually Dimorphic Behavior in Women with the Late Treated Adrenogenital Syndrome. *Johns Hopkins Med. J.* 123:115–22.

Engel, G. 1962. *Psychological Development in Health and Disease.* Philadelphia: Saunders.

———. 1977. The Need for a New Medical Model: A Challenge for Biomedicine. *Science* 196:129.

Erikson, E. H. 1959. The Problem of Ego Identity. In *Identity and the Life Cycle.* Psychological Issues, vol. 1, 1. New York: International Universities Press, pp. 101–64.

———. 1968. *Identity, Youth and Crisis.* New York: Norton.

Evans, R. B. 1969. Childhood Parental Relationships of Homosexual Men. *J. Consulting Clin. Psychol.* 33:129–35.

Fairbairn, W. R. D. 1956. Considerations Arising out of the Schreber Case. *Brit. J. Med. Psychol.* 29:113–27.

Fast, I. 1984. *Gender Identity: A Differentiation Model.* Hillsdale, N.J.: Analytic Press.

Federn, P. 1952. Psychoanalysis of Psychoses. In *Ego Psychology and the Psychoses,* ed. E. Weiss. New York: Basic Books, pp. 117–65.

Fenichel, O. 1945. *The Psychoanalytic Theory of Neurosis*. New York: Norton.

Ferenczi, S. 1911. Stimulation of the Anal Erotogenic Zone as a Precipitating Factor in Paranoia. Repr. in *Final Contributions to the Methods and Problems of Psychoanalysis*. New York: Basic Books, 1955, pp. 295–98.

Fisher, S. 1973. *The Female Orgasm*. New York: Basic Books.

Flavell, J. H. & Markman, E. M. 1980. Cognitive Development. In *Handbook of Child Psychology*, vol. 3, ed. P. H. Mussen. New York: Wiley & Sons.

Flavin, D. K., Franklin, J. E. & Frances, R. J. 1986. The Acquired Immune Deficiency Syndrome (AIDS) and Suicidal Behavior in Alcohol-Dependent Homosexual Men. *Amer. J. Psychiat.* 143:1440–42.

Ford, C. S. & Beach, F. A. 1951. *Patterns of Sexual Behavior*. New York: Ace Books.

Freud, A. 1965. *Normality and Pathology in Childhood*. New York: International Universities Press.

Freud. S. 1905. *Three Essays on the Theory of Sexuality*. In *Standard Edition*, ed. and trans. J. Strachey (hereafter *SE*) 7:125–243. London: Hogarth, 1953.

———. 1908. Character and Anal Eroticism. *SE* 9:167–75. London: Hogarth, 1959.

———. 1909. *Notes upon a Case of Obsessional Neurosis*. *SE* 10:153–318. London: Hogarth, 1955.

———. 1911. Psychoanalytic Notes on an Autobiographical Account of a Case of Paranoia (Dementia Paranoides). *SE* 12:3–82. London: Hogarth, 1958.

———. 1914. On Narcissism. *SE* 14:67–102. London: Hogarth, 1957.

———. 1915. Instincts and Their Vicissitudes. *SE* 14:117–40. London: Hogarth, 1957.

———. 1917. On Transformations of Instinct as Exemplified in Anal Eroticism. *SE* 17:125–33. London: Hogarth, 1955.

———. 1917. Mourning and Melancholia. *SE* 14:237–43. London: Hogarth, 1957.

———. 1919. A Child Is Being Beaten. *SE* 17:177–204. London: Hogarth, 1961.

———. 1920. Beyond the Pleasure Principle. *SE* 18:3–68. London: Hogarth, 1955.

———. 1921. Circular Letter, with Otto Rank. In *Homosexual Behavior*, ed. J. Marmor. New York: Basic Books, 1980, p. 395.

———. 1922. Some Neurotic Mechanisms in Jealousy, Paranoia, and Homosexuality. *SE* 18:221–32. London: Hogarth, 1955.

———. 1924. The Economic Problem of Masochism. *SE* 19:157–79. London: Hogarth, 1961.

———. 1925. Some Psychical Consequences of the Anatomical Distinction between the Sexes. *SE* 243–58. London: Hogarth, 1961.

———. 1935. Letter to an American Mother. In R. Bayer, *Homosexuality and American Psychiatry*. New York: Basic Books, 1981, p. 27.

———. 1937. Analysis Terminable and Interminable. *SE* 23:209–53. London: Hogarth, 1964.

Friedman, R. C., Richart, R. M. & VandeWiele, R., eds. 1974. *Sex Differences in Behavior*. New York: Wiley & Sons.

Friedman, R. C., Wollesen, F. & Tendler, R. 1976. Psychological Development and Blood Levels of Sex Steroids in Male Identical Twins of Divergent Sexual Orientation. *J. Nerv. Ment. Dis.* 163(4):282–88.

Friedman, R. C., Green, R. & Spitzer, R. 1976. Reassessment of Homosexuality and Transsexualism. *Ann. Rev. Med.* 27:57–62. Palo Alto: Annual Reviews.

Friedman, R. C. & Stern, L. O. 1980a. Fathers, Sons, and Sexual Orientation: Replication of a Bieber Hypothesis. *Psychiat. Quart.* 52(3):175–89.

―――. 1980b. Juvenile Aggressivity and Sissiness in Homosexual and Heterosexual Males. *J. Amer. Acad. Psychoan.* 8(3):427–40.

Friedman, R. C., ed. 1982. *Behavior and the Menstrual Cycle.* Basel, N.Y.: Marcel Dekker.

―――. 1983. Book Review: *Homosexuality* by Charles W. Socarides, M.D. *J. Amer. Psychoan. Ass.* 31:316–23.

Frieze, I. H., Parsons, J. E., Johnson, P. B. J., Ruble, D. N. & Zellman, G. C. 1978. *Women and Sex Roles: A Social Psychological Perspective.* New York: Norton.

Frosch, J. 1983. The Role of Unconscious Homosexuality in the Paranoid Constellation. In *The Psychotic Process.* New York: International Universities Press.

Gadpaille, W. J. 1980. Cross-Species and Cross-Cultural Contributions to Understanding Homosexual Activity. *Arch. Gen. Psychiat.* 37:349–56.

Galenson, E. & Roiphe, E. 1981. *Infantile Origins of Sexual Activity.* New York: International Universities Press.

Gebhard, P. H. 1972. Incidence of Overt Homosexuality in the U.S.A. and Western Europe. In DHEW (Dept. of Health, Education and Welfare) pub. no. (HSM) 72-9116, pp. 22–30. Washington D.C.: GPO.

―――. 1974. Situational Factors Affecting Human Sexual Behavior. In *Sex and Behavior,* ed. F. A. Beach. Huntington, N.Y.: Krieger, pp. 183–92.

Gedo, J. E. & Goldberg, A. 1973. *Models of the Mind: A Psychoanalytic Theory.* Chicago: University of Chicago Press.

Gershman, H. 1983. The Stress of Coming Out. *Amer. J. Psychoan.* 43(1):129–38.

Geshwind, N. & Behan, P. O. 1984. Laterality, Hormones and Immunity. In *Cerebral Dominance,* ed. N. Geshwind & A. M. Galaburda. Cambridge: Harvard University Press, pp. 211–24.

Gillespie, W. H. 1956. The Structure and Aetiology of Sexual Perversion. In *Perversions: Psychodynamics and Therapy,* ed. S. Lorand & M. Balint. New York: Random House.

Gilligan, C. 1982. *In a Different Voice.* Cambridge: Harvard University Press.

Gladue, B. A., Green, R. & Hellman, R. E. 1984. Neuroendocrine Response to Estrogen and Sexual Orientation. *Science* 225:1496–99.

Glass, S. J., Devel, H. J. & Wright, C. A. 1940. Sex Hormone Studies in Male Homosexuality. *Endocrinology* 26:590–94.

Glick, B. S. 1959. Homosexual Panic: Clinical and Theoretical Considerations. *J. Nerv. Ment. Dis.* 129(1):20–28.

Goffman, E. 1963. *Stigma.* Englewood Cliffs, N. J.: Prentice-Hall.

Gooren, L. 1986. The Neuroendocrine Response of Luteinizing Hormone to Estrogen Administration in Heterosexual, Homosexual and Transexual Subjects. *J. Clin. Endometab.* 63:583–88.

Grauer, D. 1955. Homosexuality and the Paranoid Psychosis as Related to the Concept of Narcissism. *Psychoan. Quart.* 24:516–26.

Green, R. 1985. Gender Identity in Childhood and Later Sexual Orientation: Follow-up of 78 Males. *Amer. J. Psychiat.* 142(3):339–441.

―――. 1987. *The "Sissy Boy Syndrome" and the Development of Homosexuality.* New Haven: Yale University Press.

Greenson, R. R. 1968. Disidentifying from Mother. *Int. J. Psychoan.* 49:370–74.

Grellert, E. A., Newcomb, M. D. & Bentler, P. M. 1982. Childhood Play Activities of Male and Female Homosexuals and Heterosexuals. *Arch. Sex. Behav.* 11:451–78.

Grunbaum, A. 1984. *The Foundations of Psychoanalysis: A Philosophical Critique.* Berkeley: University of California Press.

Habel, H. 1950. Zwillingsuntersuchungen an Homosexuellen. *Z. Sexualforschung* 1:161–80.

Harris, L. J. 1978. Sex Differences in Spatial Ability: Possible Environmental, Genetic and Neurologic Factors. In *Asymmetrical Function of the Brain,* ed. M. Kinsbourne. Cambridge: Cambridge University Press, pp. 405–522.

Harry, J. 1982. *Gay Children Grown Up: Gender Culture and Gender Deviance.* New York: Praeger.

———. 1983. Defeminization and Adult Psychological Well-Being among Male Homosexuals. *Arch. Sex. Behav.* 12(1):1–19.

Hartmann, H. 1950. Comments on the Psychoanalytic Theory of the Ego. In *Psychoan. Stud. Child* 5:74–96. New York: International Universities Press. Repr. in H. Hartmann, *Essays on Ego Psychology.* New York: International Universities Press, 1964.

———. 1964. *Essays on Ego Psychology.* New York: International Universities Press.

Heath, R. G. 1975. Brain Function and Behavior. *J. Nerv. Ment. Dis.* 160(3):159–75.

Henry, G. W. 1941. *Sex Variants: A Study of Homosexual Patterns.* New York: Hoeber. Abstr. in B. Zuger, A Neglected Source-book on Homosexuality. *Brit. J. Psychiat.* 133(1978):87–88.

Hetherington, E. M. 1983. Socialization, Personality and Social Development. In *Handbook of Child Psychology,* vol. 4, 4th ed., ed. P. H. Mussen. New York: Wiley & Sons.

Hier, D. B. 1979. Sex Differences in Hemispheric Specialization: Hypothesis for the Excess of Dyslexia in Boys. *Bull. Orton. Soc.* 29:74–83.

Hier, D. B. & Crowley, W. F. 1982. Spatial Ability in Androgen-Deficient Men. *New Engl. J. Med.* 306:202–05.

Hoenig, J. 1985. The Origin of Gender Identity. In *Gender Dysphoria: Development, Research, Management,* ed. B. W. Steiner. New York: Plenum Press, pp. 11–33.

Holeman, R. E. & Winokur, G. 1965. Effeminate Homosexuality: A Disease of Childhood. *Amer J. Orthopsychiat.* 35:48–56.

Hooker, E. 1956. The Adjustment of the Male Overt Homosexual. Paper read at meeting of the Amer. Psychol. Ass., Chicago, 30 August. Repr. in *The Problem of Homosexuality in Modern America,* ed. H. M. Ruitenbeck. New York: Dutton, 1963, pp. 141–61.

———. 1965. Male Homosexuals and Their Worlds. In *Sexual Inversion: The Multiple Roots of Homosexuality,* ed. J. Marmor, New York: Basic Books.

———. 1967. The Adjustment of the Male Overt Homosexual. *J. Psychol.* 31:18–30.

———. 1972. Homosexuality. In DHEW (Dept. of Health, Education and Welfare), *NIMH Task Force on Homosexuality: Final Report and Background Papers.* pub. no. (HSM)72-9116, pp. 11–22. Washington, D.C.: GPO.

Huston, A. C. 1983. Sex Typing. In *Handbook of Child Psychology,* vol. 4, 4th ed., ed. P. H. Mussen. New York: Wiley & Sons, pp. 387–469.

Hutchinson, G. E. 1959. A Speculative Consideration of Certain Possible Forms of Sexual Selection in Man. *Amer. Naturalist* 93:81–91.

Imperato-McGinley, J., Guerro, L., Gautier, T. & Peterson, R. E. 1974. Steroid 5a Reductase Deficiency in Man. *Science* 186:1213–15.

Imperato-McGinley, J., Peterson, R. E., Gautier, T. & Sturla, E. 1979a. Androgens and the Evolution of Male Gender Identity among Male Pseudohermaphrodites with 5a Reductase Deficiency. *New Engl. J. Med.* 300:1233–37.

Imperato-McGinley, J., Peterson, R. E., Stoller, R. & Goodwin, W. E. 1979b. Male Pseudohermaphroditism Secondary to 17b Hydroxysteroid Dehydrogenase Deficiency: Gender Role Change with Puberty. *J. Clin. Endocrinol. Metab.* 49:391–95.

Imperato-McGinley, J. I., Peterson, R. E., Gautier, T. & Sturla, E. 1981. The Impact of Androgens on the Evolution of Male Gender Identity. In *Pediatric Andrology,* ed. S. J. Kogan & E. S. Hafez. Hingham, Mass.: Kluwer. Repr. in *Sexuality: New Perspectives,* ed. Z. DeFries, R. C. Friedman & R. Corn. Westport, Conn.: Greenwood Press, pp. 125–40.

Insel, T. R., ed. 1984. *New Findings in Obsessive-Compulsive Disorder.* Washington, D.C.: Amer. Psychiat. Ass. Press.

Isay, R. 1985. On the Analytic Therapy of Homosexual Men. *Psychoan. Stud. Child* 40:235–55.

Janssen-Jurreit, M. 1982. *Sexism: The Male Monopoly on History and Thought.* New York: Farrar, Straus, Giroux.

Jonas, C. H. 1944. An Objective Approach to the Personality and Environment in Homosexuality. *Psychiat. Quart.* 184:626–41.

Kallman, F. J. 1953. *Heredity in Health and Mental Disorder.* New York: Norton.

Kass, F., MacKinnon, R. A. & Spitzer, R. L. 1986. Masochistic Personality: An Empirical Study. *Amer. J. Psychiat.* 143(2):216–18.

Kendler, H. 1947. S.F.: A Case of Homosexual Panic. *J. Abnorm. Soc. Psychol.* 42(1): 112–19.

Kenyon, F. E. 1974. *Homosexuality in the Female in Contemporary Psychiatry: Reviews from the British Journal of Hospital Medicine, 1966-1972,* ed. T. Silverstone & B. Barraclough. Kent: Headley Bros.

Kernberg, O. 1975. *Borderline Conditions and Pathological Narcissism.* New York: Jason Aronson.

———. 1976. *Object Relations Theory and Clinical Psychoanalysis.* New York: Jason Aronson.

———. 1984. *Severe Personality Disorders.* New Haven: Yale University Press.

———. 1985. Narcissistic Personality Disorder. In *Psychiatry,* vol. 1, ed. J. O. Cavenar & R. Michels. Philadelphia: Lippincott, pp. 1–12.

Kestenbaum, C. 1985. Putting It All Together: A Multidimensional Assessment of Psychotic Potential in Adolescence. In *Adolescent Psychiatry,* vol. 12, ed. S. C. Feinstein, M. Sugar, A. H. Esman, J. G. Looney & A. A. Schwarzberg. Chicago: University of Chicago Press, pp. 5–17.

Kinsey, A. C., Pomeroy, W. B. & Martin, C. E. 1948. *Sexual Behavior in the Human Male.* Philadelphia: Saunders.

Kinsey, A. C., Pomeroy, W. B., Martin, C. E. & Gebhard, P. H. 1953. *Sexual Behavior in the Human Female.* Philadelphia: Saunders.

Kirsh, J. A. & Rodman, J. E. 1977. The Natural History of Homosexuality. *Yale Scientific* (Winter):7–13.

Klaf, F. S. & Davis, C. A. 1960. Homosexuality and Paranoid Schizophrenia: A Survey of 150 Cases and Controls. *Amer. J. Psychiat.* 116:1070–75.

Klein, H. R. & Horowitz, W. A. 1949. Psychosexual Factors in the Paranoid Phenomena. *Amer. J. Psychiat.* 105:697–701.

Klein, M. 1932. *The Psychoanalysis of Children*. London: Hogarth.

Kleinberg, S. 1980. *Alienated Affections: Being Gay in America*. New York: St. Martin.

Klintworth, G. L. 1962. A Pair of Male Monozygotic Twins Discordant for Homosexuality. *J. Nerv. Ment. Dis.* 135:113–25.

Knight, R. 1940. The Relationship of Latent Homosexuality to the Mechanism of the Paranoid Delusion. *Bull. Menninger Clin.* 4:149–59.

Kohlberg, L. & Ullian, D. Z. 1974. Stages in the Development of Psychosexual Concepts and Attitudes. In *Sex Differences in Behavior*, ed. R. C. Friedman, R. M. Richart & R. L. VandeWiele. New York: Wiley.

Kohut, H. 1971. *The Analysis of the Self*. New York: International Universities Press.
———. 1977. *The Restoration of the Self*. New York: International Universities Press.

Kolata, G. 1983. Math Genius May Have Hormonal Basis. *Science* 222:1312.

Kolb, L. C., Rainer, J. D., Mesnikoff, A. et al. 1961. Divergent Sexual Development in Identical Twins. *Proceedings of the Third World Congress of Psychiatry*, vol. 1. Montreal: McGill University Press, pp. 530–34.

Kolodny, R. C., Masters, W. H., Hendryx, J. H. & Toro, G. 1971. Plasma Testosterone and Semen Analysis in Male Homosexuals. *New Engl. J. Med.* 285(21): 1170–74.

Krafft-Ebing, R. 1898. *Psychopathia Sexualis*. Repr. Brooklyn: Physicians & Surgeons, 1922.

Kreuz, L. E., Rose, R. M. & Jennings, J. R. 1972. Suppression of Plasma Testosterone Levels and Psychological Stress. *Arch. Gen. Psychiat.* 26:479–82.

Kroger, W. S. & Fezler, W. D. 1976. *Hypnosis and Behavior Modification*. Philadelphia: Lippincott, pp. 171–73.

Leavy, S. A. 1985. Male Homosexuality Reconsidered. In *Sexuality: New Perspectives*, ed. Z. DeFries, R. C. Friedman & R. Corn. Westport, Conn.: Greenwood Press, pp. 141–59.

Lewin, T. 1984. A New Push to Raise Women's Pay. *The New York Times*, 1 January 1984, sec. 3, p. 1.

Liss, J. L. & Welner, A. 1973. Change in Homosexual Orientation. *Amer. J. Psychother.* 27:102–04.

Loewenstein, R. M. 1957. A Contribution to the Psychoanalytic Theory of Masochism. *J. Amer. Psychol. Ass.* 5:197–234.

Loraine, J. A., Ismail, A. A. A., Adamopoulos, D. A. & Dove, G. A. 1970. Endocrine Function in the Male and Female Homosexual. *Brit. Med. J.* 4:406–08.

MacAlpine, I. & Hunter, R. A. 1953. The Schreber Case: A Contribution to Schizophrenia, Hypochondria and Psychosomatic Symptom Formation. *Psychoan. Quart.* 11:328–71.

Maccoby, E. E. & Jacklin, C. N. 1974. *The Psychology of Sex Differences*. Palo Alto: Stanford University Press.

MacCulloch, M. J. & Waddington, J. L. 1981. Neuroendocrine Mechanisms and the Aetiology of Male and Female Homosexuality. *Brit. J. Psychiat.* 139:341–45.

Mack, J. E. 1983. Self-Esteem and Its Development: An Overview. In *The Development and Sustaining of Self-Esteem in Childhood,* ed. J. E. Mack & S. L. Ablon. New York: International Universities Press.

MacKinnon, R. & Michels, R. 1971. The Obsessive Patient. In *The Psychiatric Interview in Clinical Practice.* Philadelphia: Saunders, pp. 89–110.

Manosevitz, M. 1970. Early Sexual Behavior in Adult Homosexual and Heterosexual Males. *J. Abnorm. Psychol.* 76(3):396–402.

Marmor, J. 1980. *Homosexual Behavior.* New York: Basic Books.

Marotta, T. 1981. *The Politics of Homosexuality.* Boston: Houghton Mifflin.

Martin, A. D. 1982. Learning to Hide: The Socialization of the Gay Adolescent. In *Adolescent Psychiatry,* vol. 10, ed. S. C. Feinstein, J. G. Looney, A. Z. Schwarzberg & A. D. Sorosky. Chicago: University of Chicago Press, pp. 52–66.

Masters, W. H. & Johnson, V. E. 1966. *Human Sexual Response.* Boston: Little, Brown.

Mavissakalian, M., Turner, S. S. & Michelson, L., eds. 1985. *Obsessive-Compulsive Disorder.* New York: Plenum Press.

McConaghy, N. & Blaszczynski, A. 1980. A Pair of Monozygotic Twins Discordant for Homosexuality: Sex Dimorphic Behavior and Penile Volume Responses. *Arch. Sex. Behav.* 9(2):123–31.

McEwen, B. S. 1983. Gonadal Steroid Influences on Brain Development and Sexual Differentiation. *Reproductive Physiology,* vol. 4. *International Review of Physiology,* vol. 27, ed. R. O. Greep. Baltimore: University Park Press, pp. 99–145.

Meissner, W. W. 1978. *The Paranoid Process.* New York: Aronson.

Meketon, B. W., Griffith, R. M., Taylor, U. H. & Wiedeman, J. J. 1962. Rorschach Homosexual Signs in Paranoid Schizophrenics. *J. Abnorm. Soc. Psychol.* 65(4): 280–84.

Mendelson, J. H. & Mello, N. R. 1974. Alcohol Aggression and Androgens. *Ass. Res. Nerv. Ment. Dis. Res. Publ.* 55:225–47.

Mendelson, J. H., Mendelson, J. E. & Patchu, I. 1975. Plasma Testosterone Levels in Heroin Addiction and during Methadone Maintenance. *J. Pharm. Exp. Ther.* 192:211–17.

Meyer-Bahlburg, H. F. L. 1982. Hormones and Psychosexual Differentiation: Implications for the Management of Intersexuality, Homosexuality and Transsexuality. *Clinics in Endocrinology and Metabolism* 3:681–700.

———. 1984a. Introduction to Special Issue on Gender Development: Social Influences and Prenatal Hormonal Effects. *Arch. Sex. Behav.* 13(5):391–93.

———. 1984b. Psychoendocrine Research on Sexual Orientation: Current Status and Future Options in Progress. *Brain Res.* 71:375–97.

Miller, P. R. 1958. The Effeminate Passive Obligatory Homosexual. *Arch. Neurol. Psychiat.* 80(5):612–18.

Miller, W. L. 1956. The Relation between Submission and Aggression in Male Homosexuality. In *Perversions, Psychodynamics and Therapy,* ed. S. Lorand & M. Balint. New York: Random House.

Mohr, J. W., Turner, R. E. & Jerry, M. B. 1964. *Pedophilia and Exhibitionism.* Toronto: University of Toronto Press.

Money, J. & Ehrhardt, A. A. 1972. *Man and Woman, Boy and Girl*. Baltimore: Johns Hopkins University Press.

Money, J. & Lewis, V. 1982. Homosexual/Heterosexual Status in Boys at Puberty: Idiopathic Adolescent Gynecomastia and Congenital Virilizing Adrenocorticism Compared. *Psychoneuroendocrinology* 7(4):339–46.

Money, J. & Russo, A. J. 1979. Homosexual Outcome of Discordant Gender Activity Role in Childhood: Longitudinal Follow-up. *J. Pediat. Psychol.* 4:29–49.

Money, J., Schwartz, M. & Lewis, V. G. 1984. Adult Erotosexual Status and Fetal Hormonal Masculinization and Demasculination: 46XX Congenital Virilizing Adrenal Hyperplasia and 46XY Androgen-Insensitivity Syndrome Compared. *Psychoneuroendocrinology* 9(4):405–15.

Moyer, K. E. 1974. Sex Differences in Aggression. In *Sex Differences in Behavior,* ed. R. C. Friedman, R. M. Richart & R. L. VandeWiele. New York: Wiley & Sons, pp. 335–73.

Myerson, A., Neustadt, R. & Rak, I. P. 1941. The Male Homosexual: Hormonal and Clinical Studies. *J. Nerv. Ment. Dis.* 93(2):209–12.

Myerson, P. & Lief, H. 1965. Psychotherapy of Homosexuals. In *Sexual Inversion,* ed. J. Marmor. New York: Basic Books.

Nichols, S. E. & Ostrow, D. G. 1984. *Psychiatric Implications of Acquired Immune Deficiency Syndrome*. Washington, D.C.: Amer. Psychiat. Ass. Press.

Niederland, W. 1968. Schreber and Flechsig. *J. Amer. Psychoan. Ass.* 16:740–48.

———. 1984. *The Schreber Case*. Hillsdale, N.J.: Analytic Press.

Numberg, H. 1938. Homosexuality, Magic and Aggression. *Int. J. Psychoan.* 19:1–16.

O'Connor, P. J. 1964. Aetiological Factors in Homosexuality as Seen in Royal Air Force Psychiatric Practise. *Brit. J. Psychiat.* 110:381–91.

Ovesey, L. 1954. The Homosexual Conflict: An Adaptational Analysis. *Psychiatry* 17(3):243–50.

———. 1955a. The Pseudohomosexual Anxiety. *Psychiatry* 18(1):17–25.

———. 1955b. Pseudohomosexuality, the Paranoid Mechanism and Paranoia: An Adaptational Revision of a Classical Freudian Theory. *Psychiatry* 19(4):341–51.

———. 1969. *Homosexuality and Pseudohomosexuality*. New York: Science House.

Ovesey, L. & Person, E. S. 1973. Gender Identity and Sexual Psychopathology in Men: A Psychodynamic Analysis of Homosexuality, Transsexualism and Transvestism. *J. Amer. Acad. Psychoan.* 1:53–72.

Panel. 1983. Toward a Further Understanding of Homosexual Men. Presented at the meeting of the Amer. Psychoan. Ass. New York, 18 December. Summary by R. C. Friedman in *J. Amer. Psychoan. Ass.* 34 (1986):193–206.

Parker, N. 1964. Homosexuality in Twins: A Report on Three Discordant Pairs. *Brit. J. Psychiat.* 110:489–95.

Pattison, E. M. & Pattison, M. L. 1980. "Ex-Gays": Religiously Mediated Change in Homosexuals. *Amer. J. Psychiat.* 137(12):1553–62.

Perloff, W. H. 1949. Role of the Hormones in Human Sexuality. *Psychosomatic Medicine* 11(3):133–39.

Person, E. & Ovesey, L. 1974a. The Transsexual Syndrome in Males, pt. 1: Primary Transsexualism. *Amer. J. Psychother.* 28:4–20.

———. 1974b. The Transsexual Syndrome in Males, pt. 2: Secondary Transsexualism. *Amer. J. Psychother.* 28:174–93.

———. 1974c. The Psychodynamics of Male Transsexualism. In *Sex Differences in Behavior,* ed. R. Friedman, R. Richart, and R. VandeWiele. New York: Wiley & Sons, pp. 315–25.

———. 1983. Psychoanalytic Theories of Gender Identity. *J. Amer. Acad. Psychoan.* 11:203–26.

———. 1984. Homosexual Cross Dressers. *J. Amer. Acad. Psychoan.* 12:167–86.

Pillard, R. C., Poumadere, J. & Carretta, R. A. 1982. A Family Study of Sexual Orientation. *Arch. Sex. Behav.* 11(6):511–20.

Pillard, R. C. & Weinrich, J. D. 1986. Evidence of Familial Nature of Male Homosexuality. *Arch. Gen. Psychiat.* 43:808–12.

———. Unpubl. MS. Male Homosexuality Runs in Families.

Planansky, K. & Johnston, R. 1962. The Incidence and Relationship of Homosexual and Paranoid Features in Schizophrenia. *J. Ment. Sci.: Brit. J. Psychiat.* 456:604–15.

Puig-Antich, J. 1980. Affective Disorders in Childhood: A Review and Perspective. *Psychiat. Clin. N. Amer.* 3:403–24.

Rado, S. 1940. A Critical Examination of the Theory of Bisexuality. *Psychosom. Med.* 2:459–67.

———. 1949. An Adaptational View of Sexual Behavior. In *Psychosexual Development in Health and Disease,* ed. P. Hoch & J. Zubin. New York: Grune & Stratton.

Rainer, J. D., Mesnikoff, A., Kolb, L. C. et al. 1960. Homosexuality and Heterosexuality in Identical Twins: Discussion by F. J. Kallman. *Psychosom. Med.* 22:251–59.

Rappaport, D. F. 1960. *The Structure of Psychoanalytic Theory.* Psychological Issues, Monogr. no. 6. New York: International Universities Press.

Rasmussen, S. A. & Tsuang, M. D. 1984. The Epidemiology of Obsessive-Compulsive Disorder. *J. Clin. Psychiat.* 45:450–57.

Reich, W. 1949. The Masochistic Character. In *Character Analysis.* New York: Noonday Press.

Reik, T. 1941. *Masochism in Modern Man.* New York: Farrar & Straus.

Reiser, M. 1984. *Mind, Brain and Body: Toward a Convergence of Psychoanalysis and Neurobiology.* New York: Basic Books.

Rhees, R. W. & Fleming, D. E. 1981. Effects of Malnutrition, Maternal Stress or ACTH Injections during Pregnancy on Sexual Behavior of Male Offspring. *Physiol. Behav.* 27:879–82.

Rose, R. 1985. Psychoendocrinology. In *Williams Textbook of Endocrinology,* 7th ed., ed. J. D. Wilson & D. W. Foster. Philadelphia: Saunders, pp. 653–82.

Rosenfeld, H. 1949. Remarks on the Relation of Male Homosexuality to Paranoia, Paranoid Anxiety, and Narcissism. *Int. J. Psychoan.* 30(1):36–47.

Rothstein, A. 1981. *The Narcissistic Pursuit of Perfection,* 2d rev. ed. New York: International Universities Press.

Ruse, M. 1981. Are There Gay Genes? Sociobiology and Homosexuality. *J. Homosexuality* 6(4):5–34.

Saghir, M. T. & Robins, E. 1973. *Male and Female Homosexuality: A Comprehensive Investigation.* Baltimore: Williams & Wilkins.

Salzman, C. 1960. Paranoid State Theory and Therapy. *Arch. Gen. Psychiat.* 1(6):679–93.

Salzman, L. 1980. *The Treatment of Obsessive Compulsive Personality*. New York: Jason Aronson.

Salzman, L. & Thaler, F. 1981. Obsessive Compulsive Disorders: A Review of the Literature. *Amer. J. Psychiat.* 138:286–96.

Sanders, J. 1934. Homosexueele Tweelingen Nederl Genesk. 78:3346–52. (From an abstract in English prepared by E. Slater.)

Sappenfield, B. R. 1965. A Proposed Heterosexual Theory of Delusions. *Psychol. Rep.* 16(1):84–86.

Shapiro, D. 1965. *Neurotic Styles*. New York: Basic Books.

———. 1981. Sadism and Masochism: Central Tendencies. In *Autonomy and Rigid Character*. New York: Basic Books.

Sherfey, M. I. 1966. The Evolution and Nature of Female Sexuality in Relation to Psychoanalytic Theory. *J. Amer. Psychoan. Ass.* 14:28–128.

Sherman, W. & Sherman, T. 1926. The Factor of Parental Attachment in Homosexuality. *Psychoan. Rev.* 13:32–37.

Siegelman, M. 1974. Parental Backgrounds of Male Homosexuals and Heterosexuals. *Arch. Sex. Behav.* 3(1):3–19.

———. 1981. Parental Backgrounds of Homosexual and Heterosexual Men: A Cross-National Replication. *Arch. Sex. Behav.* 10(6):505–12.

Snortum, J. R., Marshall, J. E., Gillespie, J. F. et al. 1969. Family Dynamics and Homosexuality. *Psychol. Rep.* 24:763–70.

Socarides, C. W. 1974. Homosexuality and the Medical Model: A Psychoanalytic Reputation of the Claim to Normalcy. *Bull. Ass. Psychoan. Med.* 13(3):43–48.

———. 1978. *Homosexuality*. New York: Jason Aronson.

Starcke, A. 1920. The Reversal of the Libido: Sign in Delusions of Persecution. *Int. J. Psychoan.* 1:231–34.

Starka, L., Sipova, I. & Huni, J. 1975. Plasma Testosterone in Male Transsexuals and Homosexuals. *J. Sex. Res.* 134(2):134–38.

Stepansky, P. E. 1977. *A History of Aggression in Freud*. Psychological Issues, vol. 10 (3), monogr. no. 39. New York: International Universities Press.

Stephan, W. G. 1973. Parental Relationships and Early Social Experiences of Activist Male Homosexuals and Male Heterosexuals. *J. Abnorm. Psychol.* 82:506–13.

Stern, D. N. 1985. *The Interpersonal World of the Infant*. New York: Basic Books.

Stoller, R. J. 1968. Sex and Gender. New York: Science House.

———. 1974. Symbiosis Anxiety and the Development of Masculinity. *Arch. Gen. Psychiat.* 30:164–72.

———. 1975. *Perversion: The Erotic Form of Hatred*. New York: Pantheon.

———. 1979. *Sexual Excitement: Dynamics of Erotic Life*. New York: Pantheon. Repr. Washington, D.C.: Amer. Psychiat. Press. 1986.

———. 1985. Gender Identity Disorders in Children and Adults. In *Comprehensive Textbook of Psychiatry*, vol. 1, 4th ed., ed. H. I. Kaplan & B. J. Sadock. Baltimore: Williams & Wilkins, pp. 1034–41.

Stone, M. H. 1980. *The Borderline Syndromes*. New York: McGraw-Hill.

Sullivan, H. S. 1953. *The Interpersonal Theory of Psychiatry*. New York: Norton.

———. 1956. *Clinical Studies in Psychiatry*. New York: Norton.

———. 1962. *Schizophrenia as a Human Process*. New York: Norton.

Sulloway, F. J. 1979. *Freud, Biologist of the Mind*. New York: Basic Books.

Terman, L. M. & Miles, C. C. 1936. *Sex and Personality.* New York: McGraw-Hill.

Thompson, N. L., Jr., Schwartz, D. M., McCandless, B. P. & Edwards, D. A. 1973. Parent–Child Relationships and Sexual Identity in Male and Female Homosexuals and Heterosexuals. *J. Consulting Clin. Psychol.* 41(1):120–27.

Troiden, R. R. 1979. Becoming Homosexual: A Model of Gay Identity Acquisition. *Psychiatry* 42:362–73.

Troiden, R. R. & Goode, E. 1980. Variables Related to the Acquisition of a Gay Identity. *J. Homosexuality* 5(4):383–92.

Van Den Aardweg, G. J. M. 1984. Parents of Homosexuals—Not Guilty? Interpretation of Childhood Psychological Data. *Amer. J. Psychother.* 38(2):181–89.

Van Ophvijsen, J. 1920. On the Origin of the Feeling of Persecution. *Int. J. Psychoanal.* 1:235–39.

Walters, O. S. 1955. A Methodological Critique of Freud's Schreber Analysis. *Psychoan. Rev.* 42(4):321–42.

Ward, I. L. 1972. Prenatal Stress Feminizes and Demasculinizes the Behavior of Males. *Science* 175:82–84.

———. 1984. The Prenatal Stress Syndrome: Current Status. *Psychoneuroendocrinology* 9(1):3–13.

Wellman, M. 1956. Overt Homosexuality with Spontaneous Remission. *Can. Med. Ass. J.* 75:273–79.

West, D. J. 1959. Parental Relationships in Male Homosexuality. *Int. J. Soc. Psychiat.* 5:85–97.

———. 1977. *Homosexuality Re-Examined,* rev. ed. London: Duckworth.

Westwood, G. 1952. *Society and the Homosexual.* New York: Dutton.

———. 1960. *A Minority: A Report on the Life of the Male Homosexual in Great Britain.* London: Longmans, Green.

Whitam, F. L. 1977. Childhood Indicators of Male Homosexuality. *Arch. Sex. Behav.* 6(2):89–96.

———. 1980. The Prehomosexual Male Child in Three Societies: The United States, Guatemala, and Brazil. *Arch. Sex. Behav.* 9:37–99.

Whitam, F. L. & Zent, M. 1984. A Cross-Cultural Assessment of Early Cross Gender Behavior and Familial Factors in Male Homosexuality. *Arch. Sex. Behav.* 13(5):427–41.

White, R. 1961. The Mother-Conflict in Schreber's Psychoses. *Int. J. Psycho-anal.* 42:55–73.

Wiedeman, C. H. 1962. Survey of Psychoanalytic Literature on Overt Male Homosexuality. *J. Amer. Psychoan. Ass.* 10:386–409.

———. 1974. Homosexuality: A Survey. *J. Amer. Psychoan. Ass.* 22:651–96.

Wilson, E. O. 1975. *Sociobiology: The New Synthesis.* Cambridge: Belknap.

———. 1978. *On Human Nature.* Cambridge: Harvard University Press.

Young, W. C., Guy, R. W. & Phoenix, C. H. 1965. Hormones and Sexual Behavior. In *Sex Research: New Developments,* ed. J. Money. New York: Holt, Rinehart & Winston.

Zuger, B. 1970. Gender Role Determination. *Psychosom. Med.* 32:449–67.

———. 1976. Monozygotic Twins Discordant for Homosexuality: Report of a Pair and Significance of the Phenomenon. *Compr. Psychiat.* 17:661–69.

———. 1984. Early Effeminate Behavior in Boys: Outcome and Significance for Homosexuality. *J. Nerv. Ment. Dis.* 172(2):90–97.

Index